A Sentimental Journey  culture of the World War II home front in Wilmington and Southeastern North Carolina. "The Defense Capital of the State," it became a mighty contributor to the war effort and the country's unique wartime boomtown, earning it the right to be proclaimed as "America's World War II City."

The area had all the armed forces stationed in large numbers, a shipyard producing 243 cargo vessels, the vital state port, industries at capacity, and German prisoner of war camps. Thousands left to fight; 191 New Hanover County boys died. Two high school graduates received the Medal of Honor. Strategically located, it endured constant civilian defense drills and restrictions, U-boats sinking ships offshore (one fired on a defense plant), and until 1944, the threat of attack.

The population nearly tripled. Demands for goods and services including housing, schools, food, and recreation overwhelmed. How officials managed the social, civic, juris-dictional, racial, and governmental complexities during the city's economic heyday—while handling huge construction projects, war workers, citizen stresses, black markets, crime wave, equal justice, and weekend hordes of soldiers—is portrayed through firsthand accounts and the daily newspapers. The author's vivid boyhood remembrances weave through and interpret the story.

A Sentimental Journey is the first book on the home front to cover the war's impact on a specific geographic area to this extent.

TO: Thomas Moore
Thank you for your
interest in North Carolina
WWII history
Best wishes,

A Sentimental Journey

[signature]
24 Oct. 2016

Other Books by Wilbur D. Jones, Jr.

Forget That You Have Been Hitler Soldiers: A Youth's Service to the Reich, with Hermann O. Pfrengle. White Mane, 2002.

Hawaii Goes to War: The Aftermath of Pearl Harbor, with Carroll Robbins Jones. White Mane, 2001.

Condemned to Live: A Panzer Artilleryman's Five-Front War, with Franz A. P. Frisch. White Mane, 2000.

Arming the Eagle: A History of U.S. Weapons Acquisition Since 1775. Department of Defense Systems Management College, and Government Printing Office, 1999.

Gyrene: The World War II United States Marine. White Mane, 1998.

Giants in the Cornfield: The 27th Indiana Infantry. White Mane, 1997.

From Packard to Perry: A Quarter Century of Service to the Defense Acquisition Community. Department of Defense Systems Management College, 1996.

Congressional Involvement and Relations: A Guide for Department of Defense Acquisition Managers, Four Editions. Department of Defense Systems Management College Press and Government Printing Office, 1986–1996.

Glossary: Defense Acquisition Acronyms and Terms, Two Editions. Department of Defense Systems Management College Press, 1987–1990.

Visit his website: *www.wilburjones.com*

A Sentimental Journey
Memoirs of a Wartime Boomtown

By
Wilbur D. Jones, Jr.

White Mane Books
Shippensburg, Pennsylvania

Copyright © 2002 by Wilbur D. Jones, Jr.

ALL RIGHTS RESERVED—No part of this book may be reproduced in any form without permission in writing from the publisher, except by a reviewer who wishes to quote brief passages in connection with a review.

This White Mane Books publication
was printed by
Beidel Printing House, Inc.
63 West Burd Street
Shippensburg, PA 17257-0708 USA

The acid-free paper used in this book meets the guidelines for permanence and durability of the Committee on Production Guidelines for Book Longevity of the Council on Library Resources.

For a complete list of available publications
please write
White Mane Books
Division of White Mane Publishing Company, Inc.
P.O. Box 708
Shippensburg, PA 17257-0708 USA

Library of Congress Cataloging-in-Publication Data

Jones, Wilbur D.
    A sentimental journey : memoirs of a wartime boomtown / by Wilbur D. Jones, Jr.
      p. cm.
    Includes bibliographical references and index.
    ISBN-13: 978-1-57249-325-4 ISBN-10: 1-57249-325-9 (alk. paper) --
    ISBN-13: 978-1-57249-318-6 ISBN-10: 1-57249-318-6 (pbk.)
    1. World War, 1939-1945--North Carolina--Wilmington. 2. United States--Social conditions--1933-1945. 3. Wilmington (N.C.)--Social conditions. 4. Wilmington (N.C.)--Biography. 5. Wilmington (N.C.)--History. 6. Wilmington (N.C.)--Ethnic relations. 7. African Americans--North Carolina--Wilmington. I. Title.

F264.W7 J66 2002
940.53'75626--dc21

2002028866

PRINTED IN THE UNITED STATES OF AMERICA

*These memoirs are dedicated to the
members of the New Hanover High School classes
of 1939, the class of my
sister, Elizabeth Jones Garniss,
who fought the first half of the war,
and 1943,
who fought the last half,*

*and to the 191 boys in uniform from New Hanover County
who did not live to see our victory.*

Contents

List of Illustrations viii
Preface xii
Prologue xviii
Acknowledgments xxvii

Chapters
  1 "Some of Those Boys Are Never Coming Back" 1
  2 War Comes to Forest Hills 22
  3 "Wilmington Was in Danger; The War Was at
      Our Doorsteps" 38
  4 The Shipyard and the "Defense Capital of the State" 55
  5 "The Invasion of Camp Davis" 70
  6 "The Guy Who Pushed Him in Already Rented It" 87
  7 "Our Generation Sure Got It in the Neck" 97
  8 "Crackpot Economists and Social Reformers" 111
  9 The *Afrika Korps* at Home in Wilmington 127
10 "Thieves Are Holding High Carnival" 143
11 "The Man of My Dreams" 162
12 "No, We Were Always Chaperoned" 179
13 "Needed in So Many Occupations" 196
14 "What Are We Fighting For?" 207
15 Four "Breathless Years" 221
16 "Heroisms Won by Wilmington's Men in Khaki" 238

Epilogue 256
Notes 261
Glossary 278
Bibliography 283
Index 294

Illustrations

Forest Hills School principal Katherine Von Glahn and teacher Emma K. Neuer, ca. 1944 xiv
I prepare to board World War II B-17G *Flying Fortress* "Aluminum Overcast" for flight around Wilmington, 1999 xvi
Wartime New Hanover High School in Wilmington xxii
My father, Wilbur D. Jones, and neighbor Herbert McClammy, mid-war xxiv
My sister, Viola Elizabeth Jones (Garniss), as an NHHS senior, 1939 xxiv
Army Lieutenant William McGee, who rented a room at our house in 1942–43, with me xxix
NHHS 1944 class yearbook dedicated to boys serving in armed forces 4
NHHS's Company D, Army Junior ROTC, parading south on Front Street in downtown Wilmington, 1942. Leading is Captain McCulloch B. "Mac" Wilson 6
Along 11th Street in "The Bottoms," Williston Industrial (High) School friends 6
Captured midget Japanese submarine visited Wilmington on May 4, 1944, on nationwide bond tour 9
Early 1943 war map of Southwest Pacific combat area 11
Ensign Joseph R. "Joe" Reaves and father and uncle, 1943 14
L. W. "Billy" Humphrey, Jr., and sister Elise Humphrey, 1945 17
Neighbors Charlie Mitchell and Patty Southerland outside NHHS, 1944 17
Neighbor army Lieutenant James G. Thornton, Jr., on wedding day with his father, James G. Thornton, 1944 24
Captain John Richard "Dick" Garrabrant interrogating captured German officer four days after landing on Utah Beach, 1944 25
Cartoon "Out Our Way" depicting kids at war with neighborhood Japanese enemy, 1945 27
Cartoon "Side Glances" depicting neighborhood boys and girls against the enemy, 1942 29

Illustrations ix

Grammar school buddies Ronald G. "Ronnie" Phelps, L. W. "Billy" Humphrey, Jr., and I visit Forest Hills School, 2000	31
Neighbor Lieutenant Commander Louis A. Hanson, Coast Guard Auxiliary commander, ca. 1944	33
Wartime postcard of Camp Davis, N.C., army anti-aircraft artillery base north of Wilmington	40
Pretty girls in jeep interrupting soldiers' duties on Wrightsville Beach, 1942	46
Mrs. Charles (Hannah) Block at Carolina Beach, late war	48
Soldier Clayton Smith, former shipyard worker, late war	56
First Liberty ship launched at Wilmington shipyard, SS *Zebulon B. Vance*, December 6, 1941	59
C-2 type hull SS *Sweepstakes* launched at shipyard, January 22, 1944	62
Shipyard apprentice Robert S. "Rob" Pollock outside apprentice dormitory, 1943	67
Army air forces B-24 *Liberator* pilot Lieutenant Colonel George S. Boylan on cover of *Liberty* magazine, April 17, 1943	69
Camp Davis army band in review, 1943	73
Camp Davis Lieutenant Justin Raphael, 1944	76
2-1/2 ton truck stuck at Camp Davis, aka "Camp Swampy" and "Camp Muddy," 1943	77
Wilmington airport prior to the war	79
Emerson Willard and brother Martin Willard, early war	81
Soldiers performing do-it-yourself show at Bluethenthal Field, mid-war	83
Popular "pin-up girl" actress Betty Grable visited Wilmington and Camp Davis, 1942	85
Negro Williston Industrial (High) School, ca. 1945	99
My sixth-grade class at Forest Hills School, 1945	104
Sergeant John J. Burney, Jr., in France, 1945	107
NHHS principal Thomas Tristam "T-Square" Hamilton, 1943	107
Army air forces Lieutenant Heyward C. Bellamy, 1944	108
Some of my wartime memorabilia collection	113
Otto Leeuwenburg dairy farm, late war	119
Cartoon "Side Glances" titled "I hope the rest of you children spent your summer as profitably as Wilbur!" 1942	122
German prisoners of war who worked daily on the dairy farm of Otto Leeuwenburg	129
William A. "Bill" and Aline Hufham Spencer, 1943	138
Former Wilmington German prisoner of war Bernhard Thiel, postwar	141
Wilmington's Cape Fear Hotel, wartime	147
Wilmington's Front Street, looking north, 1943	152

Newspaper advertisement for "Billroy's Comedians," 1942	159
Cartoon "A Selectee's Diary" titled "Went to Battery Dance," 1941–42	164
Marine First Lieutenant Robert A. "Bobby" Goldberg, Jr., with his F4U *Corsair* fighter, late war	169
Lieutenant Clifford C. "Cliff" Morris, Jr., and his B-17 *Flying Fortress* crewman, 1944	170
Camp Davis Sergeant Daniel R. Shinder and bride Frances Rabunsky, 1941	171
Katharine Meares Harriss and Jane Sprunt on North Front Street, 1943	174
Army Private George Burrell Byers, 1943	174
Local girls hanging out with army officers at Robert Calder cottage at Wrightsville Beach, 1942	176
My sister, Elizabeth Jones, and her husband-to-be, army officer candidate George H. Garniss, 1943	177
Cartoon "A Selectee's Diary" titled "Pay Day," 1941	180
Members of First Composite Anti-Aircraft Battery, Royal Artillery, with local girls, 1943	186
Wilmington Mayor Bruce B. Cameron's house at Wrightsville Beach burns to the ground, 1944	187
Boardwalk, amusement area, and lifeguards at Carolina Beach, 1945	190
Second and Orange Streets USO building in downtown Wilmington, 1943	192
Sergeant Jack F. Hart and actress Jinx Falkenburg in Burma, 1944	193
Mrs. Robert (Hattie) Hardwick and Mrs. Lewis (Mary Belle) Ormond of the Wilmington American Red Cross Motor Corps, mid-war	197
Kathleen Somersett of the Women's Army Auxiliary Corps, 1942	201
My mother, Viola M. Jones, a volunteer Red Cross Nurse's Aide, 1946	203
Williston Industrial graduate and army Private James Otis Sampson, Jr., 24th Infantry Regiment, late war	209
Shipyard workers Elias T. Gore and Ezekiel Williams, 1943	211
Army Private Willie Anthony Owens, 1944	218
My house at 102 Colonial Drive and Guilford Avenue in Forest Hills, 1943	222
George N. Norman in the Negro branch of the government employment service, late war	228
Belk-Williams department store advertisement, "Our Schoolboys Today!" 1943	230
Pilot Captain William G. "Billy" Broadfoot, Jr., 495th Fighter Squadron, in India, 1944	231

Addie Lee Gaylord in the Camp Davis telephone switchboard, 1941	231
Blanche Stanley and James Walker Memorial Hospital nurse classmates, 1943	234
Navy Specialist First Class Jesse Helms, Wilmington recruiter, 1942	241
Army Corporal Thurston Eugene "Gene" Edwards, 251st Field Artillery Battalion, in Germany, 1945	241
"Wilmington Welcomes Congressional Medal of Honor Winner," army Captain Charles P. Murray, Jr., 1945	247
Navy Pharmacist's Mate Second Class William David Halyburton, Jr., posthumous recipient of the Medal of Honor	252
Army aviation cadet Percy L. Heath, Tuskegee Airman, 1945	255
Cartoon "Out Our Way" titled "Why Mothers Get Gray," 1945	257

Preface

Since the mid-1990s, I knew for two reasons I had to write a book on the history of the Wilmington, North Carolina, area during World War II. I spent the first 21 years of my life here, including ages 7–11 during the war, and as an author and military historian knew of the historic significance of the area's war effort. This story had never been told, but had to be. As circumstances later proved, the privilege and responsibility became mine.

As the year 1996 approached when I would retire from the federal government after nearly 41 years of service to the Department of Defense, my wife Carroll and I decided to move to Wilmington. Reaching the decision was tough and the subject of many late-night discussions. We wondered if this former sleepy little town had matured adequately to suit most comforts we had been accustomed to, and simultaneously retained the charm, warmth, and relaxed lifestyle we also were seeking. We eliminated the two other possibilities, for personal reasons her home in Los Angeles where we had lived for most of the 1960s, and remaining in crowded, sometimes-frenetic Northern Virginia. Wilmington sold itself.

Whether I could "go home again" depended on making psychological adjustments to a different way of life. I believed I could. Wilmington was my roots, my foundation, my heritage, a place I always held fondly. I had a few relatives in the area and many classmates and lifelong friends, and my parents were buried there. Most of all, it contained a thousand memories, whose reliving deeply appealed to this nostalgic historian.

Over the years on visits I had driven through my boyhood neighborhood, past my house at 102 Colonial Drive, my Forest Hills grammar school, and the backyards and used-to-be woods and fields, the railroad tracks and creek, where we boys had played Marine and soldier growing up during wartime. (Without us, I often tell my gyrene veteran friends with tongue-in-cheek, they would not have won the Pacific War.) My school-days pals and I reminisced about the throngs coming and going at the train station, war bond stamp drives, army truck convoys monopolizing city streets, air raid blackout drills, German army prisoners encamped across from Williston

School, P-47s roaring overhead, new kids moving into town, no meat, ships torpedoed off the beaches, the horde of shipyard workers and GIs on Front Street on weekends, and long lines at the picture shows.

In 1995, after attending the V-J Day commemoration on Wilmington's Battleship North Carolina Memorial that ended the war's 50th Anniversary, the passion had engrossed me. I began embarking on a sentimental journey, a sentimental journey home, to write a wartime history of my community, my people, and my childhood.

In September 1997 we moved, accelerating this sentimental journey. The Lower Cape Fear Historical Society asked me to chair Wartime Wilmington Commemoration, 1999. From it emerged a 20-month, 125-event project recognizing Southeastern North Carolina's role in WWII and honoring those who served. The project received three history awards. Subsequently I started the follow-on World War II Wilmington Home Front Heritage Coalition to establish a WWII museum here. These related efforts have enhanced my book mission.

My journey home consisted of many stops and many reflections to gather my thoughts and chart my course. Here is one such stop:

> The bucket veneer wooden seat on the row's aisle fit me more snugly than in 1944, 55 years earlier. Then it was also easier to slouch down, avoiding the teachers' wary eyes, the leg room decidedly less limiting. With little coaxing, the scene flashed quickly and clearly while I sat in the Forest Hills School auditorium remembering my grammar school years. Oh, that dreadful morning when my sixth-grade teacher Miss Harriet McDonald startled me during a school stage performance with a heavy hand on the right shoulder and emphatically whispered, "Wilbur, you must report to Miss Von Glahn immediately."
>
> Heart pounding rapidly, somehow I walked the 50 feet to the principal's office as directed. To encounter Von Glahn—and I had a good idea what was coming—was tantamount to facing the enemy handcuffed under glaring white lights in some official basement headquarters in occupied Europe. We boys often maligned Katherine Von Glahn, of German descent, who had been teaching forever. We were convinced she and our fourth grade teacher, Mrs. Emma K. Neuer, another martinet, with their names surely must be agents for the Gestapo. At least that's the way we felt they treated us most of the time.*
>
> That day I had been bad, and soon the tall, husky, ancient disciplinarian ushered me out the school door toward home, suspended for the day, humiliated in front of my classmates, but dreading the worse to come. My parents would be beside themselves, and my rear end braced

---

* With enlightened maturity, students appreciate teachers more fully long after. This was my case with Von Glahn, Neuer, and McDonald. Strict, but fair, they knew how to instill knowledge and discipline. In memory I owe them much. Neuer's son John graduated from West Point in 1943, became an aviator, and visited our school. Our feelings toward her were somewhat ameliorated.

for a monumental spanking. Von Glahn's note to them was my sentence, but with time I might scramble a defense, of scant consolation. My father would not be home from work until after his Legion meeting that night, and my mother was putting in her usual volunteer Red Cross Nurse's Aide hours.

The way they "treated us," we boys at Forest Hills School felt convinced that our principal, Katherine Von Glahn, and fourth grade teacher, Emma K. Neuer, had to be agents of the Nazi Gestapo. Here Von Glahn, *center*, and Neuer, *right*, plot their next disciplinary actions against us, ca. 1944.

Provided by Forest Hills School

* * *

Books about the WWII American home front abound, but most are generic or universal subject-specific (i.e., national scrap drives, women in the workforce, etc.). *A Sentimental Journey* is geographical-area specific, a personal exploration of a community encased within a unique regional war effort—a subject historians have not undertaken to any extent.

This book fuses memoirs of varying perspectives: a city, a county, their natives, wartime visitors, husbands and children in uniform, and of course mine. It is also the memoir of the *Wilmington Star-News* and how its pages reported and interpreted the war. My remembrances, reactions, and conclusions link and interpret these perspectives. The book is also a snapshot study of the area's life and culture told in a series of vignettes and anecdotes, but is neither a chronological nor an all-inclusive history. Although my Wilmington background influences my contributions, impartiality and objectivity prevail. Most of my observations will please local readers, others will not, but all will inform. New Hanover County, the record shows, had both a decided upside and a downside.

Approximately 90 percent of my research is original source material from more than 220 personal interviews, wartime letters, author's surveys, news items collected from the microfilm records of virtually every daily *Morning Star* and *Sunday Star-News* from early December 1941 through December 1946, and the American Legion Post 10 wartime scrapbooks kept by my mother, Viola M. Jones. The interviews are with county residents living here during the war, transient wartime residents, classmates, and contemporary friends and neighbors. Highlighting the book are some 80 mostly unpublished photographs and other illustrations.

Some editorial notes are in order. (To reflect the record of the times, this book cannot be "politically correct" by today's definitions.)

- To be as historically accurate as possible, and add a "down home" flavor, when appropriate I wrote in certain vernacular of the day. Examples: I used the term Negro(es) for the current African American(s), or black(s), and Negress to indicate a female. When the alternative period word "colored" is used, it is usually being quoted from other sources. I used "girl" when applying to women past high-school age, which it did except for one's mother's age, and "boy" for all men in uniform in their country's service.
- To show proper respect of the time, when referring to adults I used the title I knew them by then as teachers, parents, officers, etc.: Miss, Mrs., Colonel, etc.
- For the names of females who were unmarried then I used their maiden names. That's how I knew them—and how others knew them—then, and in most cases even how they're referred to 60 years later by their classmates and friends. Example: in the text my female classmate Willie Stanford is by that name. Later she married classmate Louis Leiner. When cited in the notes, the full maiden-married names are used for women who subsequently married—and which are known to me, ergo: Willie Stanford Leiner. In the bibliography she is listed as Leiner, Willie Stanford (her current name). In the index she is listed under her maiden name (with known married name in parentheses): Stanford, Willie (Leiner). Okay, it may be a bit confusing, but you'll soon get the drift.
- The *Wilmington Star-News* did not use the titles "Mr.," "Mrs," or "Miss" in referring to Negro males and females, usually only their first and last names, married or not. The newspaper referred to white females by title, either by their husband's entire name or with their own first name: Mrs. H. M. Roland, or Perida Roland. Women are "Miss" unless identified as "Mrs."
- A glossary of terms and abbreviations is included. This should be helpful because of the many governmental agencies and wartime abbreviations mentioned.
- While WWII Negro remembrances and activities are adequately covered, my original intent was to report more details. Less information is available primarily because the Negro *Cape Fear/*

Wilmington Journal files were destroyed in a 1970s fire. Although I interviewed a number of present African Americans, my repeated efforts by advertising in the *Journal*, spreading the word, and trying to establish contacts with Williston Industrial alumni to collect more information, brought limited success. Why is beyond me. The *Star-News* coverage of Negro persons and events was limited, and photographs of Negroes did not appear. In the newspaper style of the day, Negroes were identified as such. If not, the person was assumed to be white. Wilmington had virtually no other minorities except for a few Americans of Chinese descent.
- New Hanover High School (NHHS) graduates of the classes of 1939 and 1943, to whom this book is dedicated, are identified if known.
- Wilmington's wartime army air base (airport) had several names. For simplicity and consistency I call it Bluethenthal Field, its locally accepted name, except where inappropriate.

Easily the most exciting event during my writing this book came on May 16, 1999, the day the WWII B-17G *Flying Fortress* "Aluminum Overcast" came to town during Wartime Wilmington Commemoration. Along

With camera strapped on, I prepare to board the "Aluminum Overcast," an Experimental Aircraft Association WWII B-17G *Flying Fortress,* for a flight during its visit to Wilmington in May 1999. Without a doubt, it was the thrill of my lifetime to relive my fantasy in the 8th Air Force out of England. A crewman and *Star-News* editor, John Meyer, *right,* accompany.

Author's collection

with the media, the crew of this vintage warbird of the Experimental Aircraft Association took me along on its first flight after landing at "Bluethenthal Field." It was an immense, irreplaceable lifetime thrill.

During takeoff and landing looking out the waist gun ports—sure—I could plainly see the red crosses on the trucks and tents, the olive drab jeeps and fuel trucks scurrying by, the British "WAAFs" in bluish-gray uniforms waving from the runway, the quonset huts, the multitude of wind socks, the headquarters building wearing the sign of an 8th Air Force Bomb Group somewhere in England. Once I made my way forward to the Plexiglas nose cone at the bombardier's seat, feeling suspended in air, as "Overcast" headed out over Carolina Beach into the Atlantic Ocean. There it was, the sensation—my God, we were flying over the White Cliffs of Dover into the Channel. To France? Holland? Germany? We came back, no flak holes, all four engines turning, but not without my singing out loud "Coming in on a Wing and a Prayer." A crewman looked at me and smiled. Surely he understood. I will never forget the experience.

Sometimes I wonder if I was born 10 years too late.

Wilmington, N.C.
September 2002

Wilbur D. Jones, Jr.

Prologue

In mid-December 1941, when Camp Davis at Holly Ridge was one year old, Wilmington took stock.

> During the 365 days...a teeming military center has arisen from virgin pine lands 30 miles from here, another even larger military camp [New River Marine Base] has been started a little farther away, a gigantic shipbuilding industry has found its home here, the nation has entered the greatest war in the world's history, and a few other things have happened....[also] a chemical plant supplying materials vital to the manufacture of aviation gasoline, a big air base being built, one of the largest gasoline storage facilities in the south, two navy supply bases, and some others....Wilmington's population has nearly tripled, its purchasing power has outstripped every other city in North Carolina except one, and its income has jumped to several times its former figure....In less than a year, Wilmington has grown faster and progressed farther than it would have in the next 50 years under normal circumstances.[1]

Southeastern North Carolina, with its population, economic, social, and cultural hub in Wilmington in New Hanover County, was a mighty contributor to the United States' war effort in World War II. For numerous reasons it was perhaps the country's most unique wartime boomtown. Each military service was stationed here, the shipyard was a massive producer of cargo vessels, the port was a key shipping point for vital war materials, numerous other defense industries produced at capacity, and the area dispatched its sons and daughters by the thousands to fight the enemy. One hundred and ninety-one boys from New Hanover County did not return.

The county more than doubled from its pre-war population of 43,000 with the heavy influx of military personnel and war workers and their families. Quiet Wilmington, only 50 years earlier the state's largest city, crept along for decades afflicted by geographical isolation, suddenly found itself by location an exploding national center of military life and defense production at the edge of the Atlantic conflict.

In the sum of all aspects, the magnitude of the area's diverse activities and its complete absorption by the impact were unequaled by any American city. How it attempted to manage the accompanying social, civic, jurisdictional, and governmental complexities in relation to its economic boom is a compelling subject for closer study by more than just historians. *A Sentimental Journey,* therefore, has vast national appeal to any reader interested in WWII, particularly its effects on the home front, and American cultural history.

With several exceptions the area was totally unprepared for such an onslaught of people, activities, and responsibilities which began in early 1941. Immediately after the Japanese attack on Pearl Harbor, Hawaii, on December 7, which forced the nation into war, the area's defense requirements began to multiply. Infrastructure and support services were pushed past the limits in many instances, and almost burst with ever-increasing demands for basic goods and services. These demands included housing (perhaps the most serious problem); food products and eating establishments; clothing, gasoline, tires and other strictly rationed items; school classrooms; social services; public transportation; and entertainment facilities.

The community constantly struggled to operate within frequently changing edicts from capitals in Washington and Raleigh, and its own internal pressures to serve the war effort, administer to its citizens, manage its huge construction projects, cope with civic stress and the racial chasm, combat the black market and a substantial increase in crimes, and apply equal justice. Elected and public leadership was generally adequate, particularly from city officials, and if inexperienced with managing a crisis of this proportion, valiantly tried adjusting through trial-and-error, usually with success.

Meanwhile, the populace was generally patriotic and took pride in its war role, made forward strides, enjoyed a temporary increase in stature (an airy haughtiness diminished a subliminal chip-on-the-shoulder), and projected optimism in planning for the unknown post-war future.

The self-appointed "voice of conscience" was the *Wilmington Star-News,* whose daily editions exhorted women to volunteer for aircraft recognition and hospital work, men to buy more bonds, common sense from the Office of Price Administration (rationing), housewives to save their cooking fats, and jaywalking downtown to cease.* But "the conscience" essentially passed on the rising tide of murders, prostitution, robberies, accidents, and petty crimes—as accustomed readily identifying those committed by Negroes (perhaps 75 percent of its news items about Negroes were negative)—and any particular hue and cry against criminals.

---

* No doubt, the journalistic-patriot publisher R. B. Page cast the daily newspaper squarely in the war effort. "Our chief aim—to aid in every way the prosecution of the war to complete victory." [*Wilmington Morning Star,* January 7, 1943]

Its strategic coastal location and war effort required Wilmington to mount a massive civilian defense program. Washington and local military officials bombarded the populace with fears of possible enemy attacks by sea and air, issuing through 1943 a drumbeat awareness of proper preparations. German U-boats ravaged offshore during that time, sinking ships close off our coast which belched their debris upon favorite bathing spots. London's heroic defiance became a bit of a watchword. Home front efforts included airplane spotters; Inland Waterway patrols; air raid wardens, drills, lighting dimouts, and total blackouts; no bathing suits at the beach after dark; auxiliary police and firemen; rolling bandages for area military hospitals—a hundred ways for the people to get involved. Some civilian defense jobs were kept manned, others were not. Most were subject to the availability of caring citizens. Occasionally positions were short but none were in jeopardy. I heard of conscientious people who worked at several such volunteer jobs or in civic service, and many others who lifted no finger.

Even as the casualty lists grew,[*] social life proceeded as usual at the country club and beach clubs, as did school activities, sports events (some high school games were canceled), and big band appearances at night clubs, except when gasoline shortages prohibited "pleasure driving." Wrightsville Beach's Lumina pavilion, the area's premiere nightlife attraction, flourished from patronage by soldiers and their girls. Romance ruled. Everyone of an age fell in love, if only for a moment. Multitudes of area girls became engaged to or married visiting GIs.[†] For many teenage girls and young "spinsters," the war admittedly was the most exciting time of their life.

The major activities in the area's war effort included:
- North Carolina Shipbuilding Company (Wilmington)—built 243 Liberty, C-2, and AKA-type vessels for the navy, Maritime Commission, and private lines; the largest employer in the state with a peak of 23,000 in 1943, on eastern side of Cape Fear River
- Camp Davis, Holly Ridge (Pender and Onslow Counties)—army coast artillery and anti-aircraft artillery training base; a peak of some 50,000 trained there; one hour north by vehicle[‡]

---

[*] Perhaps every block had at least one or two boys in uniform. What is now downtown historic Wilmington had a Gold Star mother on nearly every block. In my neighborhood, it seemed like a boy from every other home joined the service; most were officers, many of them fighter and bomber pilots. Their exploits and visits home created quite a stir for us school boys who sought to emulate them. My heroes to this day, not all came home alive, including at least three from right down the street.

[†] In 1943 my sister met an army officer candidate from Camp Davis at our home (like many locals, we rented out a room to soldiers and invited them for Sunday meals), became engaged, and married him in 1946 after his service in India. So typical. The love story is in chapter 11.

[‡] All highways out of Wilmington were narrow and two lanes. Travel time depended on vehicle volume and weather.

- Fort Fisher, Kure's Beach* (New Hanover County)—army antiaircraft artillery advanced training base; one hour south
- Camp Lejeune, Jacksonville (Onslow County)—Marine Corps training base, the largest on the East Coast; one and one-half hours north
- Bluethenthal Field Army Air Base (Wilmington)—army air forces P-40 and P-47 fighter training field, and B-24 anti-submarine patrol base
- Fort Caswell Naval Station, Fort Caswell (Brunswick County)—navy inshore-warfare patrol (anti-submarine) base; two hours southeast on Cape Fear River
- Coast Guard and Coast Guard Auxiliary patrol and rescue bases at Wrightsville Beach (New Hanover County), one-half hour east, and Wilmington
- Port of Wilmington, on the Cape Fear River—shipped lend-lease materials to Europe and other war materials, and imported petroleum, 18 miles upstream from ocean
- Atlantic Coast Line Railroad headquarters (Wilmington)—a workhorse in moving troops, equipment, material, and passengers
- Ethyl-Dow Chemical Company, Kure's Beach (New Hanover County)—only East Coast plant manufacturing ethylene bromide high-octane additive for military aviation gasoline, one hour south†
- Other war industries around Wilmington included small ship and craft repair facilities, truck farms, fertilizer plants, clothing manufacturers, pulpwood producers, floating drydocks construction, and more
- Three prisoner of war camps (Wilmington)—in 1945 held a peak of some 550 German *Afrika Korps* soldiers captured in North Africa, who worked on farms and dairies and in other local industries, and were subject to constant community fascination

The combat deeds of Wilmington area men are legion. Hundreds were decorated for valor and service. Overseas duty molded and hardened those who would return to lead Wilmington's eventual post-war transformation. *A Sentimental Journey* engages the reader with some of these deeds and experiences.

- Two Medal of Honor recipients graduated from Wilmington's New Hanover High School, the only high school I know of claiming

---

* After the war the name became just Kure Beach.
† Whether a German U-boat actually fired on the Ethyl-Dow plant on the night of July 24–25, 1943, has been debated locally ever since. Some old-timers say it happened, others say it's a myth. Interesting new information is presented in chapter 4. A mystery still? You decide.

that distinction for WWII. They were army Lieutenant Charles P. Murray, Jr. ('38), awarded for valor in France in December 1944, and navy corpsman William D. Halyburton, Jr. ('43), awarded posthumously for valor on Okinawa in May 1945.
- Three Wilmingtonians were decorated heroes at the Battle of Midway. Two were rightful, the other not. For sinking the Japanese carrier *Kaga*, USS *Enterprise* (CV-6) carrier pilots Carl David Peiffer (NHHS '34) and Clarence Earle Dickinson, Jr. (NHHS '32) received the Navy Cross, Peiffer posthumously. Army air forces B-17 formation leader Brooke E. Allen (NHHS '29) received the Distinguished Service Cross (the army equivalent to the foregoing navy's highest award), but his bombs hit no targets. Dickinson also received a Navy Cross for sinking a submarine four days after Pearl Harbor, and three Navy Crosses all told.
- New Hanover County's 191 dead and missing in action during service in the armed forces and merchant marine were augmented in numbers by another 57 dead who had a direct connection to the county.* Local boys died on battlefields in Tunisia, Italy, France, Belgium, Luxembourg, and Germany, and Cape Gloucester,

Wartime New Hanover High School in Wilmington. Other than additions and recent renovations, it is basically the same building.

Provided by Patty Southerland Seitter

---

* The connections included prior residency, schooling, or employment, or having families living here during the war.

Saipan, Peleliu, New Guinea, the Philippines, and in the skies above and waters around them, or in other situations related to their service. Three sailors were killed during the attack on Pearl Harbor, one while fighting on the USS *Arizona* (BB-39). Two Negro sailors were among those killed during the huge 1944 ammunition depot explosion at Port Chicago, California. Two families lost two sons each, one losing both within several weeks after the Normandy D-Day invasion. Like Peiffer, two NHHS graduate fighter pilots—Robert A. "Bobby" Goldberg, Jr. and James B. "Jim" Lynch II—who were KIA were from leading families, extremely popular, heads of their classes, and considered bound for unlimited success.
- Local men fought on other storied battlegrounds including Normandy, the Bulge, Colmar Pocket, Arnhem Bridge, Siegfried Line, Burma, Sicily, Coral Sea, Guadalcanal, and Iwo Jima. They served in ships and submarines, bombers, tanks, and field hospitals, as well as in the infantry, artillery, and support services.
- One family sent six sons into the nation's service, and several sent four into the armed forces. All survived.

* * *

Wilmington, of course, was the South. So were my Forest Hills neighborhood and my roots. I was born in Wilmington's James Walker Memorial Hospital on July 9, 1934, to Wilbur David and Viola Murrell Jones. I graduated from Forest Hills School in '47 (skipping the first grade, I was forever the youngest by a year in all my classes), NHHS in '51, and the University of North Carolina in '55.

My father, born in 1892 and raised in a large family of tenant farmers on the border of poor Onslow and Jones Counties, served in the navy during World War I as a hospital corpsman with the Marines in the Caribbean. In 44 years with Carolina Savings and Loan Association here, he advanced his eighth-grade education into becoming its chief executive. My mother, born in Wilmington in 1903, was also educated through eight grades. Her divorced mother, Hattie Murrell, kept the downtown women's public restroom to support her three children, while my mother took care of a younger brother. Mother never had a paid job outside the home but excelled in volunteer and civic work during and after the war. Sweethearts during WWI when she was only 14, my parents married here in 1921. He died here in 1967, she in 1973. Both are buried in Wilmington's Oakdale Cemetery.

My sister, Viola Elizabeth "Lib" Jones Garniss, born here in 1922, an Agnes Scott College alumna and former social worker and bank employee, has lived in the Seattle, Washington, area for some 30 years.

My father, Wilbur D. Jones, with neighbor Herbert McClammy in our backyard, mid-war.

Author's collection

My sister, Viola Elizabeth Jones (Garniss), as a New Hanover High senior. *The Hanoverian* (NHHS), 1939.

Author's collection

(While working on this book I have been continually reminded of my parents, where they came from, what they made of themselves, and what they raised me to become. These reflections caused consideration of what tremendous strains and stresses community leaders and parents were under during the war. Somehow, my parents maintained their work, volunteer, personal, and family lives in rational balance. How, I will never know, because I was a natural boy getting into natural mischief.)

War dominated but did not totally preoccupy my life or my friends' lives, including playtime. Proper growing-up came first. Our parents saw to it that we learned, thought, and did the right things as necessary groundwork for a full, productive, and virtuous life. For their examples and inspirations, I am always indebted. My generation, those born in the Great Depression—or roughly between the years 1932–40—are sometimes called the "forgotten generation." Our childhood was radically blurred during the most fearsome conflict the world has seen. Now mostly retired, by default we are the bridge generation between those who won WWII and their offspring, the Baby Boomers, whose indelible traits have been protest against traditions and authority their parents had built during and after returning from the war.

Interpreting for and mediating the two generations might be my generation's unwelcome task, and not an easy one. The task also includes passing along history to those who follow. Some of the proven tenets and values that got us through the war crises now might be considered outmoded. But they are applicable here because they speak of those characteristics that were the cornerstone of my generation's upbringing, the strength and fabric gained from the denials and deprivations to which we adjusted, the core of which was WWII. Hopefully these characteristics have found their way subtly into the pages of this book.

I further beg the reader understand the difficulties in comparing current city and county governments with those of wartime Wilmington. Various similarities in responsibilities exist, such as those of the Board of Education, but in those days the city dominated political, economic, civic, and social activities primarily because it was the population and resource center. Draw a box. The county jurisdiction (extremely hard to realize now) roughly began at 17th Street to the east, Greenfield Lake to the south, Hilton Park to the north, and the Cape Fear River to the west. My county was basically rural farming country with few modern roads, in some places lacked electricity and running water, and was isolated to a large extent from urban intercourse. "Going downtown" from the beaches or sounds or Castle Hayne was a *real big deal*, because only handfuls of retail, dining, and entertainment establishments such as mom-and-pop grocery stores, fish houses, and filling stations existed outside the box. County law enforcement and fire protection were less in numbers and unpredictable. Cases where the city fire trucks literally stopped at the city limits while fires burned nearby in the county were not unusual.

At least all county residents had city mailing addresses, but county residents (like today) paid no city taxes. Several "suburbs" like the Oleander and Forest Hills developments contained many of the area's leading citizens, and living outside the limits was never a deterrent to broad participation in community activities or the war effort. To folks like my parents, the jurisdictions were one and the same.

In the time line of history for the Wilmington area, WWII will always appear as an abruptly peaking and then equally descending bell curve. But for our purpose here, it witnessed the rise and fall of America's unique wartime boomtown.

Acknowledgments

Writing this book was possible only because of the hundreds of present or former Wilmington-area residents who remembered World War II here, and provided me with tons of interesting material: interviews, surveys, letters, photographs, and other original documents. For this tremendous enthusiasm, support, cooperation, and participation, I am forever grateful. Folks supported my effort and the value of this project because they wished to record and preserve a major period in our local history.

I sincerely appreciated the hundreds who answered my requests for material, particularly those members of the New Hanover High School classes of 1939 (my sister's), 1943, and 1951 (mine). Many referred me to additional sources. I respect those Wilmingtonians who shared their painful remembrances of personal or family tragedies when loved ones in uniform died. No matter of time or circumstance has removed those memories, only dimmed them slightly. Each of the persons who contributed to this project is mentioned in the bibliography.

Aside from the more than 220 personal interviews, the most detailed research was the six months it took me to read virtually every microfilm copy of the *Wilmington Morning Star* and *Sunday Star-News* from December 1941 through December 1946. For their exceptional assistance in this aspect, I thank director of reference Jerry Parnell and his capable staff of the William Madison Randall Library, University of North Carolina at Wilmington. Special thanks go to Beverly Tetterton of the New Hanover County Public Library for helping me get started, her periodic reference assistance, and continuing support.

In exploring the German POW story and the life of area African Americans, I thank Margaret Sampson Rogers for use of her memory, files, and referrals. Linda Pearce and the late George Norman and the late Bill Childs were also helpful here. Vince Lindenschmidt loaned me a copy of the 1945 local telephone directory which proved valuable in checking names, addresses, and the like. Harold Fussell reminisced with me at the Hugh

MacRae Park Memorial to WWII dead. David Stallman gave me material on Camp Davis. WWII combat infantryman John Burney was perhaps my most enthusiastic supporter, believed in my goals (including proper local recognition for Medal of Honor recipients Billy Halyburton and Charles Murray), remembered my parents fondly, and became a dear friend renewed as if I had not lived away from Wilmington for all these years.

Several people gave me a customized tour of historic areas key to my research. Herman Alberti of Holly Ridge took me on a guided tour of old Camp Davis in his four-wheel-drive vehicle (absolute requirement). Philip Jones guided me through the old shipyard, now the North Carolina State Port. Wilmington International Airport officials E. L. Mathews, Jr., and Julie Wilsey gave me a runway view of Bluethenthal Field's WWII infrastructure.

Two lifelong friends and grammar and high school classmates, Bill Humphrey and Ronnie Phelps, not only provided bits of information and joined me for a walking tour of our old Forest Hills neighborhood, but kept encouraging me.

Certainly my heavy involvement with Wartime Wilmington Commemoration, 1999, a project originated by the Lower Cape Fear Historical Society, helped immensely to generate interest in this "companion" work. I thank Cathy Myerow and the Society board for their encouragement. Two prominent local historians, Dr. Chris Fonvielle, of the history department at UNCW, and Dr. Everard H. Smith reviewed my draft manuscript and made significant recommendations leading to an improved product. Chris, whose family business history links directly back to mine (our fathers were in business together), offered frequent counsel and boosting. Ev's guidance, research, and writing on wartime Wilmington, particularly on the USOs, was exceptionally helpful and allowed me to concentrate on other specifics.

My family agreed I should take on this effort, and strongly encouraged and motivated me through it, perhaps a little influenced by my extra-strong hint this book—my 15th—would be my last. *(Will it? Now I don't think so. The follow-on manuscript to this book, "Volume 2" with more local-interest details, names, vignettes, and photographs, is drafted and awaiting publication arrangements.)* My wife, Carroll, my best and most serious editorial critic on whose judgment and sharp eyes I rely heavily, believed this project's link to my roots was not only historically necessary, but good for my peace of mind after returning to my hometown to live. As usual, she was right again.

The army lieutenant is William McGee, a Camp Davis anti-aircraft artillery officer who rented a room in our house during 1942–43. We called him just "McGee." The kid with the popcorn is me.

Author's collection

Chapter 1
"Some of Those Boys Are Never Coming Back"

On the cool Sunday afternoon of December 7, 1941, I stayed inside to play alone in the sun parlor. Here on the largest radio set in the house, we could get only a few stations. I tuned to our local WMFD and half-heartedly listened to the Redskins professional football game from Washington. I heard something that sounded important about the Japanese bombing the U.S. military base at Pearl Harbor in Hawaii. The news statement had cut into the broadcast, and later the game announcer remarked hearing how high-ranking government persons were being paged on the public address system to go to this place or that. At age seven and a-half, and a third grader, I knew much of the world was at war, but of course failed to grasp the significance. I continued to play until my parents summoned me for serious talks. My sister was away at college, and they would try to reach her by phone.

Gurney J. "Jack" Hufham was a newspaper route boy for the *Wilmington Star-News*.[1] On the afternoon of December 7, he was playing football at Robert Strange Park with friends. Stedman Dick, in charge of the carriers, knew where to find them and rounded them up with the news. He needed them to deliver the extra editions about ready to roll off the presses. They jumped on their bicycles, filled up the baskets with papers, and took to the streets. "*Extra! Extra! Japs Bomb Pearl Harbor!*"

Soon out of papers, Jack had to return to the plant at Front and Chestnut Streets for more. The next day when war was declared he also sold extras and stood on corners and walked up and down 5th and 6th, and Chestnut and Princess. The papers were quickly gone. "Didn't see much reaction. They just grabbed the papers and ran. I'll never forget that, selling those papers" on December 7 and 8. The paper cost a customer five cents, with half that going to the carrier. The eighth was Hufham's biggest cash day ever.

Norman Davis was hanging out with Sanford Doxey at Jarman's Drug Store that day with his dad's 1941 Plymouth. Hearing the news, Norm jumped into the car and rode to the *Star-News*, got a load of extras, and sped to the Hillcrest housing project whose Negro residents were primarily Camp Davis noncommissioned officers. "We went through there hollering 'extra' and they came running to their doors."[2]

(As soon as possible, the government began bringing home heroes to push the war effort. Wilmington Lieutenant Clarence Earle Dickinson, Jr., recipient of three Navy Crosses, in July 1942 told the Wilmington Rotary Club "that the war can be won or lost at home." A New Hanover High and Naval Academy graduate, Dickinson sank a Japanese submarine four days after Pearl Harbor,* and helped sink the carrier *Kaga* at Midway. A little over a month later he was here. "'We must remember this is going to be a long war, at least three years. It's not just a matter of men going to Camp Davis and Fort Bragg. The sooner we realize that this is war and that some of those boys are never coming back, the more progress we can make. No matter how eager and ready we on the battlefield are to go, we can do nothing without the tools of war....It's up to the people back home to stick behind us.'"[3])

(The next day on American Heroes Day, his hometown honored him and other local men. "Wilmington is proud of its brave, gallant sons who follow the Stars and Stripes to the fighting fronts of every continent. It is men like Moore, Dickinson, Allen, Peiffer,† [and others] who keep the tradition noble that where Wilmington boys go the enemy shall know the justice of our cause—the resolute reality of our mission."[4])

"I'll never forget on Pearl Harbor day we had a hell of a hard time finding it," recalled Victor G. Taylor. He tried unsuccessfully to until learning the next day it was in Hawaii. "And Guadalcanal—that was like on another planet. Unconsciously, it was a very good geography lesson."[5] Taylor's geographical bewilderment was shared by countless Wilmingtonians who asked each other, scratched their heads, or pulled out an atlas. To people five or six and older living then, where they were, what they were doing, and how they found out is indelible in their memory.‡

---

* Dickinson, piloting an SBD-3 Douglas *Dauntless* dive bomber from Scouting (Squadron) Six off the carrier USS *Enterprise* (CV-6), on December 10 sank the damaged and surfaced submarine *I-170*, the first enemy ship sunk after Pearl Harbor.

† Navy Radioman Second Class Clyde Carson Moore (killed in action at Pearl Harbor), Dickinson, army air forces Lieutenant Colonel Brooke E. Allen (Midway), navy Ensign Carl David Peiffer (KIA at Midway).

‡ The Liston W. Humphrey family was in New York for the Macy's Thanksgiving parade. On the way home they stopped in Washington the weekend before Pearl Harbor. While Billy played with squirrels around the White House, he saw the Japanese delegation entering for negotiations. Eloise had seen Japanese ships loading up with metals and was worried they would "shoot it back at us. Everyone felt the Japs were just crazy to do what they did—start a war with us." [Interview with Eloise and L. W. "Bill" Humphrey, Jr., September 7, 1998]

The radio spread the word. Joe Johnson listened to it on the family Philco. Ann Williams' parents left her at home alone to go to the movies. "I was terrified in hearing about it on the radio. When they got home I was all right."[6] John Mintz was riding around in Southport with friends when WMFD interrupted the broadcast. He had never heard an interruption before for a breaking news story. The children of Sam and Mary Emma Gresham were listening to Santa Claus on the air when the news hit that family. Like my parents with me, "I had a lot of explaining to do to the kids," she said.[7] Peggy Moore was with best friend Susanne Hogue driving down Market Street with a Camp Davis West Point graduate in his convertible. Susanne was dating the officer, and Peggy local boy Jimmy Metts. They heard on the car radio that we were at war. The soldier shouted "hooray!" and off they went to the country club to sit at the bar listening to the war news.[8]

Citizens caught short by events reacted either dumbfounded, quizzical, emotional, or deflated. Some might have been ecstatic. Leonard Gleason Allen (NHHS '43) was playing basketball at the home of baby doctor George Johnson with friend George, Jr., and several others. Mrs. Johnson emerged from the house with word. The boys decided to go on home. His gang figured they might have to serve depending on how long it lasted. University of North Carolina student William "Bill" Schwartz (NHHS '39) was with a date at the theater in Chapel Hill. They left the movie by about 3:30, walked down Franklin Street, and heard the news at the Tau Epsilon Phi House. "Everybody was asking the question, where is Pearl Harbor?" He then phoned his parents that he was going to join the navy V-7 program, finish school, and become an officer. He did, and at Okinawa in 1945, his destroyer escort was sunk by kamikazes.[9]

Gibbs Holmes skipped church at St. James Episcopal that day to go flying with Horace Pearsall, Jr., to see the Liberty ship SS *Zebulon B. Vance* launched here the day before. William Nathan "Bill" Kingoff had just learned of his grandfather Alex's death. "My grandmother [Nellie Kosch] had said we'd be in the war before the end of the year, and she was right." At school the next day, students heard a Philco radio on stage playing Roosevelt's speech to Congress requesting a declaration of war. Bill summed up everyone's surprise and shock. "I thought it was like cops and robbers; it was just a game and would soon be over. We had focused on Germany, not Japan."[10] Oh how lives quickly changed. "We must all do our part," Addie Lee Gaylord's father told his family,[11] a sentiment repeated in countless households.

The day is indelible. Laura Roe Fonvielle was playing croquet at Eliza Symmes' home at 22 Mimosa Place. "Somebody's mother came outside and told us we were at war. Even that didn't make an impact on me. Where was

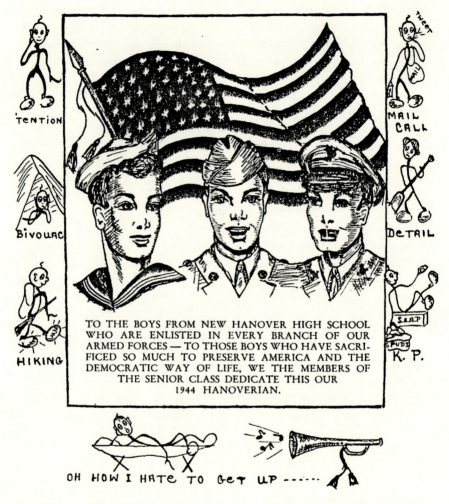

New Hanover High School's 1944 yearbook was dedicated to its boys serving in the armed forces.

The Hanoverian (NHHS), 1944

Pearl Harbor?" Now "I ride by there every day. I think about it all the time."[12]

(Sixty years later, the subject of Pearl Harbor and America's entry into the war assumed a new, more profound meaning for me. At my publisher's request, my wife Carroll Robbins Jones and I coauthored the book *Hawaii Goes to War: The Aftermath of Pearl Harbor*. The book is a history with photographs of the first six months of the Pacific War and civil life on Oahu, wrapped around Carroll's remembrances as a girl witnessing the attack and remaining there for nine months. Her father was assigned to the destroyer USS *Shaw* [DD-373] that blew up, and was soon to ship out on combat duty until badly wounded in 1945. Her mother was a professional photographer who was quickly credentialed by Associated Press, the army, and navy to shoot aftermath photos. Convincing Carroll to tell her story, and publish her mother's photos, had been a 41-year effort.)* It was released in May 2001 at the same time as the blockbuster movie *Pearl Harbor*.

Before the smoke had cleared around the naval base, Hickam Field, Schofield Barracks, and other installations on Oahu, Wilmington had paid a price thousands of miles away. Three local sons were killed in action during the attack, and others heavily consumed in the fighting.

* * *

The Following Days

Students tuned to President Roosevelt's December 8 radio broadcast in my Forest Hills and other grammar schools. I remember trying to rationalize what was going on so far away in context with only what we could see immediately in our lives—parents, family, friends, and school. We were confused, but I cannot say that in the beginning my friends and I gave it much thought, and surely failed in its long-term meaning. None of this was anywhere near our small world. If any one factor helped explain some of this to us, it was made known to us by Wilmingtonians that the link to the earlier World War I hardships (albeit brief) still lingered. And what could possibly surpass that?

Students at the white NHHS and Negro Williston Industrial (High) School looked at it differently. Immediately boys showed concern, pondering the war's length and depth on their own college and working futures. They gave it more time as days passed. "The war didn't really do much at the high school level," said 1942 NHHS graduate McCulloch B. "Mac" Wilson. "We were aware the war was going on, and by the time we graduated we were even more aware." The theme of courage in the Legion Stadium graduation ceremony was spelled out by seniors sitting in chairs. "We pretty well knew where we were going—it was only a matter of time." Wilson had three years of ROTC (Reserve Officers Training Corps), and he was from an army family. "Patriotism was something we just accepted, didn't think about. It was second nature to us in that generation."[13]

Cornelia Haggins' Williston classmates were not affected by the war until their junior year in 1944. Then the boys realized what probably lay ahead. Shortages didn't bother her family. "Momma used to work for the Allens [Ernest and Vivian], cooked, did everything for them. When she

---

* Wilbur D. Jones, Jr., and Carroll Robbins Jones, *Hawaii Goes to War: The Aftermath of Pearl Harbor* (Shippensburg, Pa.: White Mane Publishing Co., 2001).

Company D, Army Junior ROTC unit, New Hanover High School, parading south down North Front Street in Wilmington, 1942. Leading is Captain McCulloch B. "Mac" Wilson, Jr., later an infantryman with the 69th Division in France. The guidon is Robert Ferguson. Lieutenants are, *left to right*, George Saffo, Charles H. Boney, and James Blanie Wilson.
Provided by McCulloch Wilson

Along South 11th Street, one of numerous unpaved city streets in "The Bottoms," Williston Industrial (High) School friends Loyd William, *left*, and Richard Purdy pose with sisters Mary, *left*, and Cornelia "Nealie" Haggins, 1945.
Provided by Cornelia Haggins Campbell

bought for them, she bought for us. We ate the same thing they ate. We ate good meat."[14]

Wilmington was transformed from a quiet but bustling peacetime city to one dedicated to an all-out war policy Monday night [the 8th]. On the surface, there was little noticeable effect or change in the city's routine life. But beneath the surface, machinery was quietly set in motion for the protection of this entire section and plans were mapped for coping with any situation or emergency which may arise....The declaration of war was received here calmly. No fanfare or demonstration greeted the action. A resigned view that 'it had to come' seemed to be the consensus opinion....[15]

* * *

What Would We Children Think?

"Children's War Questions Need Honest Answers," announced a January 1943 newspaper article by columnist Ruth Millett.* "Will daddy have to go to war?" Temptation was to give the first answer and shield the child, but one child psychologist said that is wrong. "they should be given honest, straightforward answers to questions about the war. 'War will take its death toll of American families, and children will deepen and mature when they stand side by side with others who must face it....'" Don't put them off or give false security.[16]

One way or another we kids picked up on that message, but I'm not too sure how well my mother explained it to me. Her tendency was to shield me from bad things and much of what I absorbed was from sources outside the home (a World War II child's version of a "drugstore cowboy"). My father, a navy WWI veteran, was too old for service; so that portion of Millett's advice didn't apply to me or my friends, most of whose fathers were in similar situations. How it applied to the community around me finally started keeping me awake at nights. Maybe I didn't read Millett until more than 55 years later, but perhaps my parents did. What they taught me certainly reflected her judgments and patriotism, even though she hardly invented those principles. Her columns urged participation in the war effort, the war offering parents "'a wonderful opportunity for teaching them [children] cooperation and responsibility'" by adult actions.[17] And, she added, "'the war is forcing "kids" to grow up fast.'"[18] It certainly did.

---

* Ruth Millett's frequent syndicated columns in the *Star-News* society pages were both a moral voice and "how-to-cope" advice. She "was the Ann Landers of the 40s and 50s. In my opinion she should have received a medal for her war efforts....There is no way to measure how much her column kept up morale and inspired women to 'make do,' keep up family spirits with absent husbands, stretch their limits to work outside their homes and keep writing cheerful letters to their military relatives." Well said, by Doris Dickens Wilson, a Women's Auxiliary Army Corps member who served in the Wilmington filter center in 1942–43. [Doris Dickens Wilson World War II Memoir, 1996. New Hanover County Public Library]

I believe she was right. "'One of the biggest jobs the United States will face when the war is ended,'" a senior state official prophesied here in 1943, "'is to restore in youth its shaken faith in the nation's fundamental institutions....Wilmington cannot engage in a better enterprise than the salvaging of this "lost generation"....'"[19] Here again, we were salvaged well. As NHHS classmate Roddy Cameron stated, parents "must have done a good job of sheltering the children from the trauma of war."[20]

Children were not the only ones who may have felt sheltered. For student Evelyn Volk (NHHS '43), the war had little impact except getting letters from her fiancé Clifford C. "Cliff" Morris, Jr. and brother Ralph (NHHS '39), both bomber pilots in Italy. "I really don't remember hard times because my parents were taking care of me. I don't know that I had much social life." She worked as a hospital Nurse's Aide and her mother at the filter center.[21]

* * *

War on Front Street

Eventually trophies of war made their way here. "A Jap naval officer, 4'3" tall, in charge of the two-man suicide submarine now on exhibit at Front and Market Streets for the benefit of Bundles for America, would be surprised to learn that his ship was captured before he could fire either of his torpedoes has been shown to over 10 million Americans as a war relic."[22] Taken on December 8, 1941, it had traveled over 40,000 miles to 1,400 cities in 44 states. I remember this midget sub. For a donation to some war fund we could touch it and climb around. We boys were more the size of the crew. This was so exciting.

The city occasionally hosted displays and demonstrations of our army's equipment, vehicles, weapons and the like, in connection with a holiday or war bond drive. The area outside the downtown post office was another favorite exhibit area. Probably I was there for them all. I remember seeing, feeling, and crawling over and through all sorts of rolling stock from jeeps to tanks, and 50-caliber machine guns to 105mm howitzers, and tents to sand-bagged emplacements. The very idea of standing next to and talking to a real live American soldier in battle uniform was a dream come true. Boy, did it add realism to the next day's war games in Forest Hills! I can still smell the oily-steel of 2½-ton trucks, feel the rough canvas cots on my rear, and sense the smooth, brown, polished wood stock of the M1 Garand rifles they *actually let us hold.* When visiting these exhibits, the rest of the world stopped. If even luckier, my father had left me there with loose instructions to walk the couple of blocks to his office in time to head home for supper.

As the war grew longer, I paid more attention to the stories it created, expanding to include *Colliers, Time, The Saturday Evening Post,* and especially *Life,* if only to thumb through. I postponed bathroom visits

This captured midget Japanese submarine, beached off Oahu following an aborted attack on Pearl Harbor on December 7, 1941, visited Wilmington on May 4, 1944, on a nationwide war bond tour. It is exhibited in the 100 block of Market Street at the corner of Front Street. The corner Trust Building next to the bow and Tom's Drug Co. across Front are still in business. The sub traveled some 40,000 miles to 1,400 cities. We boys enjoyed the thrill of seeing and touching it.

Courtesy of Cape Fear Museum

and remained in my seat to watch the movie news reels. I stayed with newscasters H. V. Kaltenborn, Elmer Davis, Walter Winchell, and network broadcasts when they came on, and remember the scratchy voices of foreign correspondents like Edward R. Murrow doing the unbelievable task of reporting directly from a battlefield, or an invasion beach. *You could hear the guns and explosions.* Learning about the men in uniform, their equipment, and the weapons that kept them alive fascinated me. A student of military sorts, I collected, drew sketches, clipped pictures and articles, all the while acting out. I learned how they lived, and I fought off imagining how they might have suffered and died, a gruesome thought that plagued both my sleep and reverie.

How they died, and when, where and how many, first frightened us, then revolted us, and later simply numbed us as the figures rose and circumstances of combat worsened (if that was possible). For example, one of our earliest shocks was casualties suffered at the Tarawa Pacific atoll in November 1943. "It was a real sick day when the Marines went into Tarawa," a Wilmingtonian remembered. "The first reports back from there were really terrible. Don't believe folks were ready for that."[23] Motion pictures of the scene at Tarawa, later an Academy-Award winning film, were particularly appalling. The commentators started talking about "lessons learned in the bloodiest fight in all the Marine Corps' proud history."[24] When we played our war game, we tried to orchestrate its action without necessarily its carnage. We obviously were oblivious to realism, but we improvised.

The second anniversary of Pearl Harbor "Finds the Allies Ready for Blows at Axis," the newspaper read, reviewing significant progress. "Since Pearl Harbor, more than 126,000 names have gone on to the casualty lists of the armed forces, about 27,000 dead....Three things predominate among the reasons why the tide of battle turned in our favor—production, naval and merchant ship building, and strategic planning. Munitions factories in this country are now pouring out...6-1/2 times the rate in pre-Pearl Harbor days. The navy now has more than 800 combatant ships." The army now had well over seven million men.[25]

We followed the war news and tracked every development through Esso oil company and *Star-News* war maps and written accounts. The early months were mostly bad. Even when the tides turned in favor of the Allies in 1943 and 1944, we were drawn to the casualty figures and hoped not to find a local boy reported dead, missing, or a prisoner of war. My mother, who kept the wartime scrapbooks on our boys for the Legion post, scanned sources for this information. By January 1944, we knew details of captured American forces in the Philippines' 1942 Bataan Death March,* "'a horror story

---

* I was sure a soldier from the Brookwood neighborhood died in that march, but I have never been able to determine his name.

NEW WAR ACTION SPOTLIGHTS THE SOUTHWEST PACIFIC

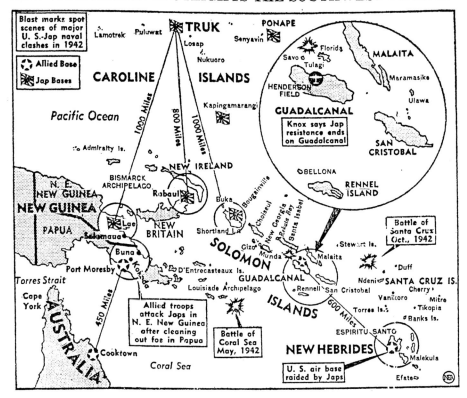

We boys closely followed the war news, reading and listening to all we had time for and could digest. This early 1943 newspaper map of the combat area in the Southwest Pacific was the type that helped us keep our bearings and plan our neighborhood campaigns.
Wilmington Sunday Star-News, February 7, 1943

scarcely paralleled in the annals of modern war.'"[26] "War bond sales should be vitally stimulated by the harrowing reports of Japan's persecution of our POWs," said neighbor James G. Thornton, county drive chairman. "No sacrifice that we can make at home can even approximate the dreadful privations our soldiers have suffered in Japanese prison camps." School children had treasure hunts seeking bond pledges and conversion of war stamps books to bonds, and so far two thousand pledges had been obtained.[27]

* * *

Running out of Steam

Midway through the war, although we were obviously unaware of that point, Wilmingtonians were running out of steam. Not only shipyard employment, but other war industries and efforts appeared to have peaked momentarily. The initial surge of personal enthusiasm and patriotism had expired, and what was left now was a long, deep breath and weighing again of all commitments for the long haul. Conditions and mentalities changed once people realized *we were no longer going to lose the war*. What would carry us through to the end, besides being buoyed by victories, was purely loyalty and devotion as never before. And that other Americans, perhaps even the boys next door, would have to be killed in the process. Therefore, we should get it over with as quickly as humanly possible.

The news at the Anzio beachhead in Italy in March 1944 was depressing, halting the drive on Rome. Allied forces were stuck and taking heavy hits. It helped to understand their plight by local visual association. "Draw a line 10 inches long, on a scale of one inch to the mile," a source advised. "This approximates the distance from Wilmington to Wrightsville Beach. Using this line as a diameter, extend lines at each end for five inches at right angles, then connect the tips of these by additional lines. The rectangle thus completed will contain 100 square miles—the size of the Anzio beachhead....Allies are fighting a glorious battle there....But it is obvious that the Anzio action must be forced through to a successful issue...."[28]

The president's death on April 12, 1945, shocked Wilmington and posed questions on the course of the war. Virginia Harriss was standing beside St. James Church when she heard newsboys hollering "Extra, Extra, President Roosevelt Dead!" She ran home to her mother crying.[29] Wilmington police and MPs called at the Princess Street officers club the night he died and "requested" that music and dancing cease. Club operator Mary Maple immediately stopped the dancing. Some citizens had complained about the club and "wanted to know 'if it was true that there was a dance at the officers club while other men in the armed services were grieving the death of Mr. Roosevelt.'"[30] Merchants agreed to Mayor W. Ronald Lane's request that all business activities be halted from 4–5 p.m., and that businesses open on the day of burial be closed for 30 minutes at 10 a.m. "Telephones in the editorial rooms of the *Wilmington Evening Post* rang continuously after the first word was received of the President's demise."[31]

Morale in Wilmington began high and remained high. Apparent signs of dissension were missing, and the few protests and objections were directed primarily at federal bureaucrats and agencies, most notably the Office of Price Administration and the rationing programs. Patriotism as a goal and shibboleth was universal, but noticeably in reality was not, no matter how odd that may seem. For every newspaper advertisement playing on an American's patriotic heartstrings, or imploring increased involvement in the war effort through financial or volunteer support, there were as many incidents of slackers and shirks, black marketeers, and criminal acts.

Some leading citizens with vision and the best of intentions went to lengths to promote total involvement that included taking care of business interests and national interests simultaneously. If they made money, it was in some respects a credit to their entrepreneurial instincts and risk-taking investment skills as well as the order of supply and demand. But first Wilmington had to handle the fundamental symbol. Can you imagine? It took more than 10 months after Pearl Harbor before officials hoisted an American flag over City Hall, and it had to be borrowed from Greenfield Park. Local stores had run out of flags, and for a long time people were unable to buy them. "No greater injustice could be done than to think Wilmington lacking in patriotism," an observer aptly wrote.[32]

* * *

The Early Volunteers

No one would doubt the patriotism of those who served, most assuredly the early-war volunteers. Joseph R. "Joe" Reaves was among many of the NHHS '38 class who volunteered. "Patriotism was No. 1. We had to go in there to do our share. I was very happy, pleased and thankful that my health was such that I could get into the navy to fly. Camaraderie was wonderful."[33] To James M. "Jim" Lee, "there was never any question of our going" after NHHS graduation in 1944. "The government rallied everybody. I can't think of anybody who didn't want to go. Being in ROTC gave me a love of the military and helped me choose my career. Gave me a broadened sense of what was happening."* But he heard some Wilmington men used soap on their body to raise blood pressure, claimed flat feet, read the eye chart wrong, and all of a sudden couldn't hear.[34] I found out the same thing.

The newspaper singled out certain leading young citizens for recognition. "Wilmington's young men are living up to the city's best military tradition." Draft quotas by January 1942 were more than filled. Army Lieutenant Bruce B. Cameron, Jr., a 1938 Virginia Military Institute graduate, had entered his father's business immediately. But in February 1941 he volunteered for active duty and helped build Camp Davis, and later was sent to Fort Bliss, Texas, as a general's aide.[35] Cameron also recalled "a lot of people went to work at the shipyard to keep from getting drafted. They had a lot of young men [who stayed] out of the army. You didn't feel too good about" their not serving. "I was disappointed to have to get out.† I had been with them [my battalion] from the start."[36]

---

* Lee entered the army that year and graduated from West Point in 1949. He fought in the Korean and Vietnam Wars and was promoted to lieutenant general, one of two Wilmington WWII veterans who achieved that rank after the war. The other is George S. Boylan of the air force. In March 1944, the army promoted Wilmingtonian Raymond A. Wheeler to lieutenant general.

† Cameron was summoned stateside from New Guinea after the death of his father, Mayor Bruce B. Cameron, in 1944, and discharged. His younger brother Daniel D. "Dan" Cameron, who fought from Normandy deep into Germany, remained in Europe.

Ensign Joseph R. "Joe" Reaves with his father Joseph W. Reaves, *left*, owner of Reaves & Watters Grocery downtown, and grandfather Charles W. "Uncle Charlie" Watters, before heading for navy flight training, 1943.
Provided by Joe Reaves

Richard C. "Dick" Andrews wanted to serve, and at age 15 almost got away with it. "I wasn't one of the best students in high school" and was sent to Fishburne Academy in 1942. He and two other under-age friends decided to join the navy. "They got their parents' permission. I had my guardian's signature on onion skin paper and transferred it to the application. The recruiter at the post office contacted my guardian by phone, and he knew nothing about it. I just knew we had it made. The other guys entered the navy, and I caught a little hell for doing it." They both came back.[37]

* * *

The Victory Signal

As early as August 1944, local authorities began planning publicly for a victory signal to sound when the war in Europe ended, and for closing stores and offices. As more territory was liberated, plans accelerated. When Paris fell, Franco-Americans living here were jubilant. Olga Sears was "so happy for my countrymen." Mrs. D. S. Howes lived in France before coming to this country 24 years ago and knew Paris well. "I am so glad that the French people did it....I know they are glad to get rid of the Boche." The two women married Wilmington soldiers in France after WWI.[38]

By the end of March 1945, Wilmington had completed its victory day plans primarily "directed toward a day of prayer and thankfulness rather than celebration." Alcoholic beverage control stores would close immediately.[39] By late April, false reports of victory in Europe stunned the city. "For one hour and 45 minutes last night, Wilmingtonians were delirious, extremely happy and overawed with the news that Germany had surrendered unconditionally." But at 9:45 p.m. came an announcement that the statement was false. They were certain it was true or would be very shortly. "Two Marine lieutenants from Camp Lejeune who together had seen 49 months of service in the South Pacific said: 'Great news. Not over yet. Two down and one to go'....'That leaves just one more island to take [Japan].'"[40]

At last. May 2. "Hitler Dead, Per Nazi Radio. Adm. Karl Doenitz to Command the German Nation."[41] May 8. "German Surrender Reported; Reds Take Last German Bastion." The Associated Press disclosed exclusively Monday, May 7, that Germany had surrendered completely and unconditionally.[42] "Wilmingtonians accepted quietly and matter-of-factly yesterday the news of Germany's unconditional surrender." Immediately following newspaper and radio announcements, Sheriff C. David Jones ordered firemen in charge of sounding the siren system to stand by for the official announcement of V-E Day from President Harry S Truman. Having come this far, strangely the populace conceded V-E Day was not really here until Truman's announcement. Stores and government offices took an immediate holiday.[43] Truman's proclamation came May 8, and offered Japan chance to surrender unconditionally "before it is too late."[44]

The local V-E Day celebration was milder than in 1918, an observer noted. Peace in Europe was

> an occasion for meditation and serious thanksgiving, rather than demonstration. While autos raced through downtown with horns blasting and paper was torn up and thrown from windows as a substitute for confetti and in direct violation of the appeal to save paper as an essential war material, the fuss was soon over and even the school children, freed from their studies, quickly scattered. By shortly after noon the streets...had assumed their customary appearance on Sunday. With general business suspended there was little traffic....The war is but half won. A stubborn, vicious, bestial enemy remains to be conquered....[45]

The war effort had to be resumed without letup, including the accustomed propaganda. "The ferocity of war against the Japs and the intense struggle to wrest each small island from Nipponese hands is shown in the new army, navy and Marine Corps official film, 'Fury in the Pacific.'" Shown at the Bailey, Carolina, Royal, Manor, and Bijou theaters during April 11–23, it featured action on Peleliu, Anguar, and Iwo Jima.[46] I went to see it, as I had about all the others.*

The stubborn enemy succumbed four months later when a "Single Bomb Equal to Power of 2000 Big Forts Crashed with Annihilating Forces on Jap Army Base on Hiroshima Monday."[47] On August 15, "Japanese Quit, Pres. Truman Releases Word of Surrender at 7 p.m. (EWT)."† The news reached here shortly before sunset. All Wilmington "houses of business"

---

* Since 1995 it has been my professional pleasure to help honor our veterans by returning with them to the Pacific battlefields of Iwo Jima twice, Okinawa, Saipan, Tinian, and Peleliu.
† The formal surrender treaty signing took place on the battleship USS *Missouri* (BB-63) in Tokyo Bay on September 2. Then the war was considered officially over. The term V-J Day is given to

were immediately closed "in observance of the end of World War II." Soon thousands of citizens jammed Front Street and thousands of autos filed past horns blasting, crowds gathered at the post office and sang patriotic songs. "There was no description of Wilmington's celebration of the defeat of Japan last night, save that of utter jubilation....The tears flowed freely and unshamely [sic]."[48]

Where were you, where was I? On V-E Day we had been let out of school, and I spent the day at home listening to the radio and racing around my block. On V-J Day, because it was night, my parents and I stayed home. The radio again was our ear to the world. Far into the night, my family offered prayers and expressions of thanks, deliverance, and hopes for the future. We prayed for the quick and safe return of my sister Lib's fiancé, army Lieutenant George H. Garniss, stationed in India. We got through to a few people when our party line wasn't tied up. The next day my friends and I played, and I went back to drawing more pictures of Jap airplanes going down in flames. Seemed like it just had not ended.

* * *

The Impact of Wartime

The war impacted Wilmingtonians according to the extent of their personal and emotional involvement in it. Although each person gave up something, and some sustained more physical sacrifices than others, few were deprived of material possessions or sustenance for life. Those who lost loved ones bore a special scar, which some carry to this day. People tended to view the war as an individual first than as a group, a community, and a nation. Considering the plight of Europe and Asia, we recognized our blessings and our divine good fortune. Individual and family lives needed reconstruction, and few, even those with vision, cared to foresee the future of atomic energy and the Cold War.

A number of women I interviewed felt the accelerated social life and interaction touched them the most. "Instead of just meeting people around the corner, we met a wide variety of people from all over," Sally Josey said. "I had a small college debt and was working hard to pay it off." Her distant cousin died in the Bataan Death March, but no one in her close group was lost.[49] For young women who lived here, one reminisced the war years as "the best time of our lives. I was able to detach myself. It didn't bother me at all."[50] Manette Allen Dixon (NHHS '39) "was thankful I had no brother who had to go in, but so blessed to have such a good life, good parents, was

---

both that day and to August 14 (U.S. time) when Japan actually capitulated. To me the 14th is more significant, a date undoubtedly shared by the 10 million in uniform. More so, my next-door neighbors had a daughter born on the 14th. My mother asked them to name her Viola Jones Humphrey, after herself to commemorate V-J Day. They chose to name her Elise.

Colonial Drive next-door neighbor L. W. "Billy" Humphrey, Jr., proudly holds his brand-new sister, Elise, in his front yard. She was born on August 14, 1945, V-J Day, the day the war ended. My mother, Viola Jones, tried hard with tongue-in-cheek to get the Humphreys to name the girl for her ("VJ").

Provided by Elise Humphrey Coble

My neighbors Charlie Mitchell and Patty Southerland cavort outside New Hanover High School, 1944. Charlie entered the navy. Adolescent me had a huge crush on Patty. To this day, I can see why I did, and why she was so popular.

Provided by Patty Southerland Seitter

very fortunate. We didn't have to worry about having anybody over there." She was making good money at the shipyard. "I just bought clothes and had a good time."[51] "At least we weren't getting bombed," Patty Southerland reminisced. "We were in the lucky part of the war. It was the best time of my life. We were entertained thoroughly, simple and naive entertainment, and thought it was just great." So many of the boys left high school to enter the service. "We were obligated to write to them and keep them happy. Everybody I knew came back, those who were close to me."[52]

Whose heart was most fervently tugged by the war, a mother's, a wife's, a sister's? "You can't make plans for the future. You lived for the day, you lived hard for the day," wartime newlyweds Lieutenant Claude and Mary Daughtry said. "We will never forget the summer of '42," when they met at Wrightsville Beach while he was training at Camp Davis and courted and partied.[53] He didn't go overseas until 1945. Home folks naturally were concerned with their boys overseas. My neighbor Lucretia Thornton's family "didn't realize it was such a terrible thing. We got all excited. I wasn't even thinking about my brothers, that they would be serving. I was just 12 years old." She well remembers her father, "kind and passionate, so admirable of him" to turn over home to service people temporarily while they were awaiting quarters, in their Forest Hills home as well as their beach house.[54] Her brother, The Citadel graduate and tank officer James G. "Jimmy" Thornton, Jr., was KIA in Germany on September 14, 1944.

Rationing and shortages caused my classmate Evelyn Bergen's family "only minor inconveniences, certainly nothing serious. Our life was perfectly pleasant except for the worry and anxiety about loved ones. Everyone just pitched in and cooperated in every way possible....We all felt a very strong sense of patriotism and dedication to our country and our armed forces." Her Belgian mother, Christine DeBusscher, had married her father, Charles, a native Wilmingtonian, in 1930 in Belgium.[55]

> Without a doubt, my mother suffered the most in our family during the war. When the Germans invaded Belgium, my uncle Jacques DeBusscher, a doctor in the Belgian army, was taken prisoner and sent to Germany to work in a hospital. My grandparents fled by car and were refugees, finally finding shelter with a farmer in France. But as the Germans occupied France, they were very quickly sent home to Belgium. Some time after that, all contact with them was lost for two years and my mother did not know if they were dead or alive. Finally after the war ended, a cousin over there got word to Christine through the Red Cross that her parents and brother were all right.

R. E. Corbett noted the obvious for many folks: "We had been through the Great Depression. So when the war came along we didn't feel deprived. We hadn't had anything anyway."[56] John Debnam's family "had to make certain sacrifices, not that they were great hardships."⁵⁷ To backyard neighbor Tabitha Hutaff McEachern, "A lot of people suffered a lot, but they suffered for things they could do without."⁵⁸ Her son George Hutaff McEachern added, "People who grew up during the war had a feeling of cohesiveness and working together that you don't see anymore."⁵⁹

Obtaining a job writing sports for the *Star-News* while in high school had the biggest impact on William F. "Bill" McIlwain, more than being drafted into the Marines after graduation in 1944. Otherwise, "You took things for granted—that's how it was."⁶⁰ Betty Henderson felt the beginning of many women in the workforce was the war's largest impact. Lots of women came from all over the area, some to work with their husbands. "I was just doing a job and not philosophizing about it. Coming from Agnes Scott [College], I thought women could do just about anything."⁶¹

The huge influx of workers and military personnel and families greatly impacted anyone living locally. "The war not only changed the economic situation in Wilmington, it also changed people's feelings with all those people coming in here," Betty Buck stated. Her brother Bob had six teachers in the first and second grades who were wives of servicemen and very transitory.⁶² The Gibbs Holmes family's Harbor Island home "was pretty well worn out after all the army people had lived there." For Gibbs, "the fact that we had to move to town" made a lasting impression on her.⁶³

Some folks, either oblivious, or preoccupied, or too young or innocent, escaped from the war altogether. "We didn't talk to each other about it," Jocelyn Peck said. "I felt I was forced to date a lot of strange people. We were not too impacted, went merrily along."⁶⁴ Laura Roe wasn't affected too much by the war. Her boyfriend Walter Lee McCormick called her at Hollins College to say he was about to ship out. "I didn't really miss him, never thought about him getting killed. I think more about it now rather than when I was living through it [the war]. I was right there in the midst of it but was not really aware of what was going on."⁶⁵

Willie Stanford "didn't pay much attention to the devastation of World War II." No one in her immediate family went into service and she knew no one who did or who was killed. Her grocery-store owner father was deferred. "We just fed the people. To this day I don't save coupons. During war we sat there and licked and pasted stamps into ration books."⁶⁶ Ann Williams believed that "when you're 10–11 years old you don't know what you're missing. It was a way of life when you had the air raids. I never had a threatening feeling. It was not constantly on my mind. I'm sure the war was very alive in the minds of my parents, but they never conveyed this to me. I don't know consequently what we did for the war effort, except that we had a house full of people. Someone would ring the doorbell and we would invite them in." The man she later married, Joseph H. "Joe" Johnson, Jr., added, "I can't remember how it altered my life as a boy."⁶⁷ The war had "very little" impact on high-schooler Raymond Holland, whose father owned the MacMillan Buick-Pontiac dealership. "The shortages we had didn't really affect anyone at my age. We hardly knew it," but "You certainly learned a lot about history."⁶⁸

Only the passing of time would draw some into the war's web. My sister, Elizabeth, "hadn't actually heard Roosevelt's announcement as I was...visiting shut-ins in the downtown area of Atlanta....The full impact of this news was an accumulative one, because at first my daily schedule was not altered, but as classmates started speaking of their fathers and older brothers who were resuming or entering the military service, changes in our personal lives were becoming apparent."⁶⁹ After the war started, hers were minimal. "The summer of '42 was spent conducting Bible schools in remote areas of western North Carolina....It wasn't until I returned home in the summer of '43 that I grasped the extent of the changes that had taken place...."⁷⁰

There were those who for astoundingly selfish reasons didn't want to let go of the war. Mary Cameron Dixon was riding the bus down Front Street in 1944. She heard a shipyard worker say he wished the war would go on and on because he never had it so good. An old woman got up and beat him over the head with an umbrella for saying it. But the driver stopped the bus and pulled her off. Mary felt the wrong person had been ejected.⁷¹

Fortunately our little world had many others like Mrs. Charles (Hannah) Block, a volunteer dedicated to the war effort in numerous nonroutine ways. She served as the Carolina Beach head lifeguard, official hostess and chaperone at the 2nd and Orange USO and Woodrow Wilson Hut, organizer of girl hostesses for dance trips to local bases, piano player during shipyard rallies, you name it. "My thoughts were that wherever I was needed, there I would be. In those days we lived for other people."⁷²

Sometimes without realizing any rationale or intent, I just blocked out the war and tried to live what otherwise could have been a normal life. I could not go far. Late in the war when the movie newsreels began showing the horrendous liberated concentration camps and their ovens and gas chambers and stacks of dead, I frequently wrestled with sleepless hours of visions and crying and with a pounding heart, and kept a light on all night or crawled into mother's bed. These revelations were embedded as surreal until I visited Dachau in 1959.

Wilmingtonians at Pearl Harbor

On December 7, 1941, at least 20 Wilmington area men in the armed forces—15 navy, three army air forces, and two army—were known to be on duty at, or operating out of, Pearl Harbor. Three were killed in action on board ships. At least six civilians were living or working there. Those who died were:

- Battleship USS *Arizona* (BB-39) Signalman First Class Harvey Howard Horrell, of 914 North 4th Street, previously reported as missing in action, was killed in action. His mother Maggie J. Horrell "was in tears last night as she spoke matters pertaining to her dead son. 'He enlisted in the navy at the age of 18 and almost since the time he received his preliminary training at Norfolk, Virginia, he has been stationed at places far distant from Wilmington.' For that reason, she said, she had not seen him for about 12 years." He was unmarried but had two brothers.[73]
- Boatswains Mate Herbert Franklin "Bert" Melton, son of Mr. and Mrs. George Melton of Masonboro Sound, "died at his post aboard a U.S. vessel [USS *Oklahoma* (BB-37)]," according to a message his mother received. Melton, 25 (his birthday was December 7), graduated from New Hanover High School in 1936 and entered the navy that year. His wife and young son lived in Long Beach, California. He had two brothers and five sisters in North Carolina.[74]
- Destroyer USS *Shaw* (DD-373) Radioman Second Class Clyde Carson Moore, 23, an NHHS graduate, had served in the navy since 1939. His wife Maie Waters Moore of 215 Dawson Street survived him. Moore, "the second New Hanover County man known to have been killed while fighting for his country, died instantaneously in an explosion aboard his ship, a destroyer." His brothers Robert and Ralph, both serving on ships in the Pacific, wrote letters home about it. His parents were Mr. and Mrs. J. R. Moore of Castle Hayne, "who are believed to have the distinction of having had more sons in the United States Navy than any other family in North Carolina." Six sons had enlisted in navy. Two served in the 1920s. Ralph E. and Robert H. were serving in the Pacific at the time, and another brother Jack was stationed elsewhere. Moore, one of 128 aboard *Shaw* who died, was buried in the St. Louis, Missouri, National Cemetery in August 1949. None of the bodies in that group was identified, and they were interred together. His wife remarried.[75]

Chapter 2
War Comes to Forest Hills

A speedy bike ride would get you to the Solomon Islands or Central Pacific within three minutes from anywhere in my neighborhood. Such dispatch was important when warriors were gathering to execute the day's plan of attack against the hated Japanese enemy. Plans formulated by quick, short phone calls (in allegiance to wartime phone usage restrictions), or agreements ending the previous day, were necessary for picking sides to play war.

In my wartime-Wilmington childhood, the boundaries of one's world were most likely the neighborhood. On Saturdays mine expanded into teeming downtown by bus, and on Sundays to church, the outskirts, or beaches by the family Pontiac when gasoline was saved. Except for an occasional sightseeing excursion to a nearby military base, or a rare visit to Daddy's relations in Onslow County, communications with the outside came from the daily newspaper, WMFD or any radio station we could raise, *Movietone News* at the theaters, and *Life* and other serious magazines.

Stretching my immediate neighborhood of Forest Hills depended upon the power of my Iver-Johnson bicycle or Chuck Taylor sneakers, whether it was raining or shining, and no-nonsense instructions from my mother. One element sure to curtail distant week-day adventures from the base territory was the need to return home to listen to the afternoon serials of Hop Harrigan, Terry and the Pirates, and the Lone Ranger, or do it at a friend's house.

For nine months of the year, my grammar school was a hub of my neighborhood activity. Attempts to involve us children in the home front war effort originated there, including collecting scrap material, war bond and stamp drives, civilian defense training and air raid drills. On top of this came education and indoctrination in nationalism, morale, sacrifice, and support for our fighting forces, subtle at times perhaps. We school children naturally fell in line, for they were the types of community involvement employed in Wilmington 25 years before in the Great War, but now greatly expanded.

Without the benefit of Little League baseball, select soccer, or similar adult-regimented sports programs, organized activities for us kids were limited to church, scouting, and the YMCA downtown. Otherwise we were on our own, which on the whole we preferred. In this regard I later realized that the experience I gained was the foundation of future organizational and teamwork skills—whether from playing ball or soldier.*

We school boys had friends who were girls, and sometimes played games with them. But the very imagined ferocity of combat, as brought vividly to our doorsteps, appealed only to boys' approaching adolescence, patriotism, and sense of duty-to-come in a male-first society. Consequently, the majority of our play related to the war, a pastime to which girls predictably did not subscribe. Besides headlining the news, war was apparent in our material possessions (or lack of) as well as our psyche.

Admittedly, exposure to the government's incessant propaganda influenced our way of thinking and responding, but who was to say that the news sources were anything but reporting world events accurately within security precautions. My youthful rationale, of course, was to believe them. Thus I paid attention, and before I knew it, the war itself had become the principal factor in my life outside of family. Even school, for the most part. I studied the war, discussed it, and wished to participate in it at my level in most waking hours. I'm sure its fascination helped steer me into careers in the navy and national defense, and the love and preservation of history. I firmly believe I was destined to be an author and historian. Through my writing ability I would be able to pay tribute to World War II America and its generation for what they—we—did for our country and to maintain our freedom. Exposure also came obliquely. For example, war games, war toys, and war books and magazines proliferated from early 1942-on. We boys bought, collected, used, swapped, and saved them. They became my generation's pop culture.†

---

* My sister accurately described me decades later as "then of the Comic Book and Lone Ranger Generation." "He was usually in his Marine outfit as he would for hours engage in our backyard in landings and battles on a South Pacific island. Even in those days he knew the names....Little did we know that his interest in the Marines would later culminate in his taking a trip back to Iwo Jima while researching his book *Gyrene*." [WWII Memoir of Elizabeth Jones Garniss, February 2, 1999]

† Hold on, please. My interest in and study of military history does not cast me as a jingoist, warmonger, or Prussian mercenary. The attraction of WWII history is that it actually was a "good war" in terms of goals and objectives. Our national sovereignty was at grave risk, and we had no alternative but to work together to defeat our adversaries. As a boy I witnessed and later studied the massive combination of patriotism and all-out national effort necessary to win, the circumstances of which we will never see again. My home town's deep involvement in the war effort was before me daily.

Believe it or not, my empathetic family rewards my love and involvement in WWII history at Christmas and birthdays. In recent years I have received "grown-up war toys" including the Battle of Midway computer game, a smashing Corgi metal B-17 nicknamed (truthfully) "Sentimental Journey," and GI Joe depicting the Wheeler Field pilot at Pearl Harbor and in the movie. This really is a fun profession.

Furthermore, we watched our neighbor fathers and sons go away to war. It seemed like every other home in Forest Hills had a man in the armed forces. They thrilled us boys, and we feigned scoffing off the notion of anyone getting killed, and wrestled with uncomfortable night visions trying to block it out. No, not to someone we knew. We admired our boys and to a degree immaturely envied their opportunity. When they visited at home, we rushed to see them in uniform, hear their experiences, and hopefully be handed insignia and equipment items or battlefield souvenirs.

Sadly not all returned alive. So near, yet we grieved remotely from afar, unable adequately to express youthful sympathy to stricken parents or siblings, particularly since many of our local dead were buried on foreign soil or never found. Six men from within a couple of blocks of my house died in the service of our nation, three in combat. Except for the faded memories of a gradually diminishing number of relatives and friends, they are hardly remembered.*

Major William Albert Brown, Jr., U.S. Army glider pilot, killed in action on March 24, 1945, in Germany; family lived at 2305 Market Street.

Captain James Goodlet Thornton, Jr., U.S. Army tank leader, KIA on September 14, 1944, in Germany; parents and sisters lived at 208 Forest Hills Drive.

Captain Ralph Waldo Soverel, Jr., U.S. Army Air Forces, killed March 28, 1943, in California plane crash; parents lived at 239 Brookwood Avenue.

Second Lieutenant LeRoy C. Robertson, Jr., U.S. Army, died in Surinam on May 17, 1943; parents lived in Forest Hills.

Warrant Officer Harry L. Hundley, U.S. Marine Corps infantry officer, KIA on June 22, 1944, on Saipan; father lived at 133 Forest Hills Drive.

Neighbor army Lieutenant James Goodlet Thornton, Jr., on his wedding day, with his father, James G. Thornton, prominent banker and civic- and war-effort leader. July 20, 1943. Thornton was KIA in Germany on September 14, 1944.

Provided by Frances Thornton Reynolds

---

* Not all the names of New Hanover County men who died, including one from my neighborhood, are included on American Legion Post 10's beautiful memorial monument in Hugh MacRae Park of only 149. I have updated the list from exhaustive research.

Ensign Herman John Gerdes, Jr., U.S. Navy, submarine USS *Robalo* (SS-273), failed to return from mission near Philippines in August 1944; parents lived at 114 Keaton Avenue.

My parents knew the families of these boys. Thornton's sister Lucretia was my Forest Hills schoolmate. Ironically, a Thornton-Soverel connection existed at the Wilmington Savings & Trust Company. Ralph Soverel was a senior bank officer there, and James G. Thornton, a pillar in the war effort, was its president. The Soverels were members of my church. Brown was the brother of my high school classmate Olive Jean Brown.

Three more brave neighborhood men gave their lives. Army infantry Captain John Richard "Dick" Garrabrant, a Wilmington native, was KIA near Montebourg, France, four days after he landed at Normandy on D-Day. His brother Bill, a schoolmate, family and widow lived in Oleander. Army Sergeant George H. Walker, Jr., died in a plane crash on May 13, 1942. His family lived in Colonial Village. Army infantry Private Herman E. Tyson, the

This photograph of Captain John Richard "Dick" Garrabrant, *center*, of the 8th Infantry Regiment, 4th Division, interrogating a captured German officer four days after landing on Utah Beach on D-Day, June 6, 1944, appeared in the *New York Times*. His sister Betty Garrabrant Cantwell saw it in the newspaper and requested a copy. The same day he was KIA leading an assault on the enemy near Montebourg, France, for which he was awarded posthumously the Distinguished Service Cross.

Provided by his daughter, Margey Garrabrant

brother of classmate Norman E. Tyson, who lived on nearby Gibson Avenue, was KIA on February 4, 1944, in Italy.

Irreverently perhaps, we boys died a thousand deaths in the Solomons and Central Pacific but would survive to fight again and help win the war. We must have believed these enthusiastic patriotic expressions would enhance local morale and be transmitted some way to the boys overseas, another way of contributing to the war effort. We took the play to heart and let our imaginations run wild. To achieve victory, somebody had to be the hero and somebody had to die. More Japs and Germans died or were captured than Americans, of course.

We sweltered in the jungle heat of Guadalcanal, especially after the book *Guadalcanal Diary,* released in early 1943, became our reference manual.* We went out and found or constructed pretended replicas of the seawall at Tarawa, the caves of Peleliu, and the ridges of Okinawa. When we periodically shifted our war theater to Europe, fields, backyards, and the creek became French and German farms, villages, and countryside. Unscripted, while acting out the raging battle underway on Iwo Jima, for instance, we knew the outcome simply had to end with victory. Willing victory was another way we helped.

We chose our heroes from magazine pages, newsreels, and features in *War Comics.* I well remember being a lucky part of the victorious gun crew of "Machine Gun Smitty," who saved the Marines in the Battle of the Tenaru River on "the Canal" in '42 by killing hundreds of Japs in their futile charge. He was Sergeant Al Schmid, blinded during the action, recipient of the Navy Cross—everybody wanted to be him. That sandbagged-foxholes defensive position, with wooden machine gun, was probably the best we ever built.

Facsimiles or substitutes had to do—usually without unavailable metal—for whatever equipment we required, and still it had to be as authentic as possible. The sweatier and grimier you got, the more authentic. Risking mother's wrath was acceptable; go home filthy enough and she would get used to your being a warrior. So what? You had to bathe anyway.

To be a warrior, if you had equipment, a weapon, and were motivated, and could get to any site on your own, *you were one.* To be excluded you would need to make most of us real mad. The more players, the better the frontal charges and the broader the field of play. No one volunteered being the enemy. The younger boys often were so designated, and occasionally that meant me, but somebody had to be. We might take turns. The uniforms didn't change regardless. We participated decked out in either school or play clothes and toy weapons and whatever cast-off military gear we had

---

* Richard Tregaskis, *Guadalcanal Diary* (New York: Random House, 1943). A best-seller, it made a huge impression on me. I proudly display my edition from the first printing. I can still feel and smell the cool, loose sandy dirt which clung but had to be brushed off before entering the house.

Our efforts to fight with the Marines in every island battle paid off: we cleared the Japanese out of (lily-white) Forest Hills right away. I often told my Marine friends while writing the book *Gyrene: The World War II United States Marine*, they could not have won the Pacific War without us.

Wilmington Morning Star, January 10, 1945
Out Our Way reprinted by permission of
Newspaper Enterprise Association, Inc.

collected or was loaned: helmet liners, cartridge belts, packs, pre-war metal weapons, caps, canteens, leggings, and more, whatever had come our way from Wilmington servicemen.* We wore old sneakers or school shoes (they were rationed, two pairs per year), which really made our mothers angry. You just had to know who was on your side and who wasn't. We also had to keep track of supper time and who had to leave early, and make room for any latecomers.

We had only a few rules, like counting to 100 before you could get up and resume play after pronounced "dead" (scout's honor—no fudging here),

---

* Each boy also wore these items to school or around town. In February 1943, the War Department banned civilians from wearing insignia and uniforms and imposed severe fines and imprisonment as deterrents. Camp Davis authorities cited the "principal buyers [in post exchanges and stores] being numerous young soldiers who have passed them around to members of the fair sex as tokens of affection." [*Wilmington Morning Star*, February 24, 1943] Of course this didn't mean us, and no one I knew got into trouble.

but hand-to-hand exchanges on the parapets might get testy. Spats, including who-shot-who-first, were usually settled with big talk, shoving, and intimidation, or by older boys, with fists only as a last resort. Usually the louder voice prevailed, sometimes mediation, but eventually somebody's rights and ego were restored and we proceeded. Games could last indefinitely, interrupted only by darkness, parental directives, or the weather. But rarely boredom. Depending on school, homework, or family plans, we tried to set schedules, but some of our most-fun times were spontaneous. Gangs of players were not always required. Two boys together could manufacture all sorts of fantasies which could switch from the woods to backyard dirt piles with little soldiers and toy tanks and planes, or carry over into indoor games on rainy days. Each of these activities I enjoyed, and when alone could easily entertain myself by acting out or sketching the war news.

Sometimes kids from "outside" adjacent neighborhoods, mainly the blue-collar Delgado-Spofford Mills bigger boys to the west, or older, tougher Mercer Avenue-East Wilmington crowds we avoided, would venture into our neighborhood. They might bully us, tamper with our earthworks for spite, or force their way into our games. Heck, as long as they wanted to fight Japs that was all right with me, but I was afraid of them.

Our main area of play as Marines and soldiers in Forest Hills was the woods and fields east of Colonial Drive, south of Market Street, and between Colonial and Mercer Avenue. After the war my father's Moore-Fonvielle Realty Company opened a major upscale suburban residential development there called Beaumont, and within a few years almost all traces of our battlegrounds succumbed to progress.*

The favorite spot there was the thick woods behind the Colonial Drive house of classmate Margaret Thomason's family, just a few yards from Burnt Mill Creek, our neighborhood waterway. The Thomasons kept a sizable stable of horses surrounded by broad maples, stately oaks, tall pines, and brushy undergrowth, enriched by the Wilmington region's typically dominant soil pattern of gray sand and loose black dirt. Digging all sizes of foxholes and trenches was easy, and old feed and seed sacks and empty paper concrete bags could be filled and placed as sandbags where we dug, supplemented by hacked-up fallen trees. Miniature fortresses sprang up with some historically incorrect semblance of World War I France, untypical

---

* During summers while a student at the University of North Carolina in the early-mid 50s, I worked for the company as a construction laborer, observing the passing of these physical links to childhood. There could have been one exception, perhaps. Dr. Chris E. Fonvielle, whose father, uncles, and grandfather had been in that business together with my father, told me when he was young and moved into a West Renovah Circle house in the 60s he remembers seeing what appeared to be the remains of one of our forts in his backyard. As the Wilmington area's leading Civil War historian, he just might know.

War comes to Forest Hills through this characteristic cartoon: "Don't ask me why there are so many boys in the neighborhood, but there's no manpower shortage in this army, so we don't need any female snipers."

Wilmington Morning Star, October 16, 1942
Side Glances reprinted by permission of Newspaper Enterprise Association, Inc.

of the Pacific's nature of fighting. We might also throw together lean-tos or once in a while pitch a small tent if someone brought their father's, occasionally for the convenience of a neighborhood girl or two serving (until no longer needed) as "nurses" or "Red Cross canteen workers."

In 1999 I interviewed Wilmington native and WWII army officer Henry Von Oesen at his residence on West Renovah Circle in Beaumont, smack in the middle of that gloried old battlefield. While waiting at the door I peered around both sides of his house toward the old Thomason place, and up into some familiar hardwoods I probably climbed. On shaking hands again after decades, I remarked, "Henry, did you know your house is standing on Guadalcanal? And Tarawa and Iwo Jima, too?"

Living on the Atlantic coast, our natural enemy was Germany and the Nazis. Intuitively we boys were drawn more closely to the Pacific War being fought by many Marines who had trained at nearby Camp Lejeune, than the all-army North African and European affairs. To me there was something extra special about the Marine esprit de corps and brotherhood, an enduring magic it was my fortune to highlight in the successful book *Gyrene*, a project of tribute and admiration I began on a grant from the Marine Corps.*

This is not to say we didn't fight the Germans. We did, from the Sahara Desert and Tobruk through Normandy and across the Rhine. Wilmington perched on the periphery of that war. Their U-boats prowled off our coast well into 1943, leaving their evidence on our beaches. Our strategic position in the war effort made us a likely target IF an attack ever came, a threat pounded into us by the authorities. In 1944 the army began interning here hundreds of their defeated *Afrika Korps* troops from Rommel's Tunisian campaign, and we citizens were allowed to drive by their stockade and gawk or stop and get out and gawk. No Japanese prisoners encamped in Wilmington, but the idea of seeing German soldiers in the flesh had the double effect of making us more determined than ever to defeat them, and also humanizing them. But the ground offensive against Japan began earlier in the war, in August 1942, than it did against Germany in French Northwest Africa, November 1942, and grabbed our interest first.

The Beaumont battlefield area was one of several. Backyards, side yards, and alleys in some portions of the extended neighborhood became permanent or impromptu invaded islands. This scenario risked provoking the ire of fathers whose lawns, Victory and flower gardens, storage bins, and garages might come under fire or fit into a trench pattern. In my backyard behind the garage and alongside Billy Humphrey's next-door property line, he and I built a comfortable two-man dugout with sandbags and scrap lumber (and kept secret stuff hidden there, like special codes and toy trucks).

Occasionally we played soldiers around the Atlantic Coast Line Railroad freight tracks that sliced north-south through Forest Hills a block from the school. Frequently traveled then with petroleum products, military cargo, and shipbuilding materials headed to and from the shipyard and state port, the tracks challenged those who would dodge the trains or cavort along the beds. Placing coins on the tracks for flattening was one

---

* Wilbur D. Jones, Jr., *Gyrene: The World War II United States Marine* (Shippensburg, Pa.: White Mane, 1998).

Buddies since early grammar-school days, Ronald G. "Ronnie" Phelps, L. W. "Billy" Humphrey, Jr., and I at the front entrance to Forest Hills School, 53 years after graduating. See the 1945 class picture at the same spot.

Author's collection

thing, but, looking back, racing the engine over the trestle was downright dangerous and foolish.*

Our Forest Hills regulars were quite a crew with varied ages and sizes, and differing levels of athletic or war-fighting ability. The core I will never forget: Billy Humphrey, Bobby Copeland, George Autry, Herbert McClammy, Q. B. Snipes, Graham Burkheimer, Glenn Avery, and Bobby McCumber.† Billy and I didn't always play war. We were Cub Scouts for a while. Once on a den hike my hatchet slipped and I whacked a big chunk out of my right ankle (still blessed with a scar). In the summer of 1945 we went to Camp Sequoyah in the North Carolina mountains. Before accepting us, camp officials actually visited in our homes. Our fathers drove us to Raleigh, an all-day trip, where I spent my first night away from home. Then we boarded a train for Asheville. I distinctly remember two ugly experiences from that week. I got scared to death on our overnight camping trip when the counselors began telling ghost stories and had to be escorted back to the main camp and put to bed, spoiling the overnight of a counselor who had to remain. I embarrassed myself. The other was the extremely uncomfortable train ride to Wilmington. Without air conditioning, the cars had only windows for ventilation, which seemingly sucked in all the smoke and cinders from the coal-burning engine. The train was overflowing with military personnel, and part of the way I sat on my suitcases. We thought we would never get home.

We often welcomed boys from the Brookwood area, our immediate westward extended neighbors adjacent to Forest Hills Drive. Our groups sometimes exchanged battle sites or gathered on neutral ground along the creek at the school. Sometimes our group would fight theirs. When we laid down our arms, we mingled for other pastimes and retired to someone's house for water. Their ringleaders included Harold Laing, Jackie Black, Kenneth Murphy, Herman Postma, D. C. North, Fowler Low, and Billy West. "It was the bad boys street," remembered Cecelia Black, someone's sister.[1]

The corner vacant lot opposite my house where Colonial Drive and Guilford Avenue intersected was used by across-the-street neighbor Dick

---

* On May 17, 2000, lifelong pals Billy Humphrey, Ronnie Phelps, and I spent hours walking these tracks, the creek, and the old Forest Hills neighborhood. It's amazing how much smaller and shorter the trestle is now. Only a couple of trains use this route daily, but the tracks and bed look awfully familiar. We had been there before many times. Ronnie was raised on a dirt road off Wrightsville and Mercer. He recalled walking to school and turning on to Forest Hills Drive. "I stopped when I got to this point. I knew there was something different about this neighborhood" with its large homes and wealth. Not his lifestyle, but we kids whose parents bought there thought nothing of it. [Interview with Ronald G. "Ronnie" Phelps, May 17, 2000]

† At least four of these are dead, and since moving here going to funerals of older family friends or childhood friends is a monthly expected way of life. Several old buddies I see occasionally, but Billy and Ronnie remain the ones with whom I have had the closest contact.

Hanson and friends for playing war. Several years older than my crowd, they built caves and fortifications and hung rope swings in the pines, but failed to approach the Beaumont camps in artistic effort or realism. Being early teenagers, their attention must have been elsewhere much of the time, and few battles of consequence took place at that corner. It was their playground, mostly to be avoided by us younger soldiers.

Such a field of action so close to my bedroom window was, however, accentuated by the fact that I was surrounded by immediate neighbors who entered the service. Next to the vacant lot, homeowner Cornelius Morse's son Neil, Jr., was an army captain in the Pacific. Dick's father, Lieutenant Commander Louis A. Hanson, from 1942-on supervised the Sixth Naval District Coast Guard Auxiliary out of Charleston, South Carolina. The older son Private Louis A. Hanson, Jr., entered the army in July 1944 from New Hanover High School. Next door to them and directly across from me, Lieutenant (Junior Grade) George L. Mitchell, Jr., was on a navy tank landing ship in the Southwest and Central Pacific for 16 months in the campaigns for Saipan, Tinian, Emirau, and the Green Islands. His younger navy brother Charlie reached the Pacific when the war ended. A few doors down, Bobby McCumber's father served as an army officer, and because the family lived in

Lieutenant Commander Louis A. Hanson, *right*, U.S. Coast Guard Reserve, Sixth Naval District Commander of the Coast Guard Auxiliary. My across-the-street neighbor, he volunteered for active duty and left his lucrative chemicals business, ca. 1944.

Provided by Richard "Dick" Hanson

a garage apartment deep on their property, Colonel James McCumber turned his front yard over to us and other neighbors for prosperous Victory gardens. From behind me on Guilford, Lieutenant (Junior Grade) James B. Lounsbury served as an obstetrician-gynecologist at the Norfolk, Virginia, naval hospital, leaving two daughters, Bobbie and Jean, as younger playmates.

Homes throughout the neighborhood sent their men without hesitation. One particular cluster of homes on the other street was heavily impacted, as neighbor Victor G. Taylor stated. "If you come down Forest Hills Drive—Dr. Charles Graham was a navy doctor, Jim Frank Hackler in the army air forces, Billy Broadfoot in the air force, Bryan Broadfoot in the merchant marine, the two Thornton boys—there was not a block in the city of Wilmington that did not have someone in the service."[2] His statement only begins to report the impact of my immediate neighborhood's devotion to duty. You talk about role models. We had plenty of them. Within a few doors of each other, the following boys shipped out: Joe Block, Billy, Winston, and Bryan Broadfoot, Jim Hackler, Harry Hundley, John Loughlin, Lester Preston, Walker Taylor III, James Walbach, and Jimmy and Bill Thornton. By 1945, many of the men living around me had gone. Fathers who did not serve were either considered too old, like mine, physically unqualified, or for essential war work or other reasons were not called.

My extended Forest Hills neighborhood reached from Market Street (U.S. Highway 17 to Camp Davis and Camp Lejeune) one block away on the north into Oleander on the south, a long two-thirds of a mile. East-west it included Mercer Avenue to Brookwood. The one criterion was that all the kids went to Forest Hills School. Forest Hills and Colonial Drives begin parallel southward from Market with Colonial on the east, and cross like an "x" at Burnt Mill Creek a few yards from the school. After the "x" they separate again and continue southward to Wrightsville Avenue for about one-quarter of a mile.

Another popular battlefield playground was the hill, cliffs, and woods behind the houses of Peter Browne Ruffin, Louie E. Woodbury, Jr., and E. B. Bugg on the eastern side of Forest Hills Drive near Wrightsville Avenue. The area casually sloped down to the railroad tracks and Mercer. My classmate Louie Woodbury III remembered "there were always war games back there."[3] This spot was a convenient midway meeting point for Forest Hills and Oleander kids who sometimes mixed to meet the enemy. Prime participants at the cliffs site included friends from the area of Colonial Village, also part of the extended neighborhood. This small development off Mercer built right before the war housed numerous schoolmates. Many of their parents had moved to Wilmington for war work. Led by Joe Johnson, Ronnie Phelps, and Rex Bennett, they were one of the most homogenous groups in our school. Gentry Lewis, Scooter Hobbs, and other more congenial Delgado-Spofford Mills boys who attended Washington Catlett School often visited there for war games. Barefooted boys from unpaved Mercer barged in, led by Clarence and Marion Ennett, Lonnie Jones, and John Henry Jenness. "They were street-wise and pretty tough at times. They lived a different lifestyle than you folks in Forest Hills."[4] But they went to our school.

The Oleander section contained the subdivisions Glen Arden, Magnolia Place, Country Club Pines, and Oleander. Like Forest Hills, Oleander homes were part of the Wilmington "suburbs" and owned by "well-off" families visible in the business, professional, and civic worlds and high in social circles. None of our extended neighborhood was within the city limits. We lived in New Hanover County, had a Wilmington post office address, our fathers paid less taxes, and we managed with slightly fewer services and conveniences than the city folks. Fortunately the buses ran pretty much on time out our way. Not until November 1945 did voters approve extending the city into our area, and it took effect in January 1946.*

Popular Oleander battle sites included Park Avenue which dissected the section, with its recently dormant trolley tracks running from downtown eastward to Wrightsville Beach, and along Oleander Drive, a state highway leading to the beach and the largest county road. George Rountree III and his friends Tommy Thompson, Gene Robinson, and Louie Woodbury built forts in the wooded area where Independence Boulevard is now. Pretending passing cars were enemy tanks, they shot rubber bands at them from homemade wooden guns. When they were short a player or two, they would call us Forest Hills boys. A trip to these sites was worth it for another reason. We could surreptitiously attempt to smoke the dry "Indian cigars" which grew only on certain trees in the medians of Park and Live Oak Parkway—vainly trying not to gag in front of peers.

Our successful efforts to win the Pacific War left no lasting neighborhood scars, even though our war games continued sporadically over the next couple of years until petering out. The hundreds of military truck convoys that came through town that captivated us, many using the narrow but main Market Street thoroughfare, left mostly tire marks. (My old streets have been paved at least once since, but a few unpatched missing slabs now reveal the pavement we played on.)† No P-47 *Thunderbolt* from nearby Bluethenthal Army Air Base crashed in our vicinity, although 21 army aircraft did in the Wilmington area during training or patrol flights, killing

---

* This question of extending the city limits was one of the most interestingly debated non-war issues and took years to conclude.

† By May 1944, 75,240 army vehicles and 175,672 soldiers had been safely convoyed over county streets. Vehicles included tanks, trucks mounted with guns, jeeps, and high explosives. The largest was 300 trucks and 5,400 soldiers. Police escorted numerous generals and other high-ranking military officials about. No serious military accidents occurred. Convoys avoided the heavy traffic around shipyard peak rush hours. [*Wilmington Morning Star*, May 3, 1944]

two-thirds of the pilots. Yard foxholes eventually filled in, and temporary structures went to the woodpile or trash can. In a city of only Negroes and whites and a handful of Chinese Americans, by default we boys must have done our job: our neighborhood was devoid of any Japanese for the duration.

Sometime after the war was over, our gang realized we had to find new important things to do. Soon those things became, in no particular order, girls, school sports teams, and jumping into New Hanover High. After I finished the eighth grade in 1947, my mother and I had jammed my war mementoes and collectibles—books, magazines, comics, newspapers, drawings, photographs, pieces of uniforms and equipment, toy soldiers, ships, and planes, everything I owned—into boxes, closets, and the basement. In ensuing years as I traveled the world after finishing the University of North Carolina, living in Italy, Southern California, Northern Virginia, and then back in Wilmington, I re-packed all the boxes and they tagged along. Not a pack rat by any means, but practical and very nostalgic, not only were the memorabilia deeply meaningful for periodic browsing, but I clung to the hope that eventually they would be historically useful.

Once I became an author and historian, the pleasure this memorabilia has brought me is impossible to measure. They are a direct, concrete link to the halcyon days of my childhood and reminders of Wilmington's wartime contributions. I frequently thank Mother for having the foresight to help me save them. I occasionally use them as "show and tell" in my countless lectures to school kids and adults, encouraging handling, reminiscing, and fantasies.

In 1999, during the height of the Wartime Wilmington Commemoration, the William Madison Randall Library of the University of North Carolina at Wilmington sponsored a wonderful 14-week exhibit of my war artifacts in their lobby labeled "Boyhood Memories of Wartime Wilmington." The satisfaction I received from the historical and educational value of the exhibit, with recognition and appreciation from old friends and new, students and faculty, native townspeople and newcomers, was extremely gratifying. Once our campaign to establish a WWII museum in Wilmington is achieved, they will have a permanent new home to educate and be enjoyed way into the future.

A Ninth Birthday Present[5]

July 9, 1943

From: "Daddy Boy"
To: Son
Subject: Souvenir World War #1

    I congratulate you on your Ninth Birthday Anniversary and in memory of World War #1, I present to you this pistol as a gift with the understanding that you are not to use it in any shape, way, or form until you become eighteen years of age.

    I am very happy indeed to have a little son like you to give this old relic to. It was captured in the country around Santiago, D.R. (West Indies). This pistol was taken from a bandit as many others were and turned over to the American Marines. It is my desire that you keep this pistol in memory of your Dad's service in World War #1.

With lots of love and best wishes, I am,
Your loving "Daddy,"
/s/ WDJones

(The pistol was a Smith & Wesson revolver model ca. 1914. My father was a navy Hospitalman Apprentice First Class serving with the 6th Marines in the Caribbean. I never played with the pistol, and kept it safely put away until donating it and the letter to Wilmington's Cape Fear Museum in 1999.)

Chapter 3

"Wilmington Was in Danger; The War Was at Our Doorsteps"

Once gooey black oil washed up on our beaches, we learned, it either congealed into a sticky mass near the shore line or sank into the sand. Either way, bathers and beachcombers avoided the residue and swore at the inconvenience, at Wrightsville Beach especially. The oily messes that periodically appeared in 1942 and 1943 are the most vivid memories I have of the American ships that were sent to the bottom, or were severely damaged, by German U-boats somewhere within range. Maybe some of the mess was German, we wondered. Shipboard debris such as wood, clothing, and other floatable objects sometimes rested along the stained water's edge, until plucked as souvenirs or removed by the Coast Guardsmen or soldiers stationed nearby. My friends and I attempted to make light of the polluted areas by foot-racing incoming oily, foamy waves, or seeing who could collect the oddest bits of flotsam.

On July 19, 1942,

"for the first time in its history of more than 200 years, Wilmington was plunged into a real air raid alarm and blackout at 3:49 a.m." The army said "suspicious activity along the coast near Wilmington caused the sounding of an air raid alert, and officials declared 'it was no practice alarm'....Cries of 'douse that light,' 'pull that car over,' and many other orders could be heard in the already darkened streets....Guards were more than doubled around the post office...their submachine guns presented a formidable appearance to the average citizen....For one hour and three minutes, the entire city was lost on the face of the earth, as even the tiniest cigarette gleam was extinguished."[1]

The newspaper then sternly commented, "It was the real thing. Wilmington was in danger. In a very definite way, the war was at our doorsteps."[2]

From the day after the United States entered the war, all Wilmingtonians suddenly became aware of our vulnerability and how close the war could come to our shore. Authorities exhorted us continuously for more than three years to prepare for any emergency. At times all I knew about this was what I tried to understand from the newspaper, or heard from my parents or randomly in school, unless I stumbled into evidence—like on the beach. Eight- and nine-year olds were hardly well read, and "facts" exchanged in school talk could be suspect. (Our teachers taught to a standard plan, interjecting current events, patriotism, and supporting the war effort.) My father, however, whose business was at 2nd and Princess Streets, circulated downtown daily and picked up inklings of what was happening, like why armed soldiers were stationed around the post office at Front and Chestnut. "Be prepared," an observer implored. "We know that Wilmington is such a target as the Nazis must covet because of its oil terminals and its shipyard....We are urged to remember Pearl Harbor."[3]

* * *

From Surprise to Mobilization[*]

Monday, December 8, 1941. The morning paper headlines soberly announced: "Wilmington Area Placed on Alert Against Sabotage." "War Stirs City; All Flay Japs." And the afternoon paper:[4] "Home Guard Ordered in Readiness." "County Defense Councils Asked to Meet." "Coast Guard Ordered to 'Be Alert' Here." "No Japs Believed Living in this Area."[†] At this point in the brand new war, and for months to come, the public subsisted on a mixture of facts, rumors, innuendo, distortions, imagination, and hysteria for information on local defense conditions. Reeling to gather our senses, it was your pick at the time which one you believed or doubted. But surely everyone sensed immediate emergencies.

"This war is no longer something we read about—it's real," warned the army captain in charge of the local air raid information center, days after Pearl Harbor. "We are playing the game for keeps."[5] But first, because the army had been assigned security responsibilities for the region, things had to be done the army way. "As a highly strategic area, Wilmington necessarily has been placed on an 'alert' basis," one opinion began. "Military guards have been set at industries and other points which are essential to

---

* The state civilian defense director criticized the Wilmington area after the mid-July 1942 alert which began this chapter. It "was handled so poorly that 'we should consider ourselves fortunate that we escaped catastrophe.'" Delays came in sounding alarms and accomplishing the blackout. That the Wilmington "civilian defense forces broke down during the early Sunday morning alert was immediate and condemnatory." Mayor Hargrove Bellamy retorted: the statement was "unjustified...[and] not conducive to building up confidence in those responsible...." [*Wilmington Morning Star*, July 21, 1942]

† On December 13, 95 foreign-born local citizens voluntarily registered with authorities "to prevent embarrassment of such civilians here in case an investigation is ordered by the government." [*Wilmington Sunday Star-News*, December 14, 1941] By February 1943, all alien or foreign-born youths over 14 were required to register with the Immigration Service. More than 200 lived here.

Chapter Three

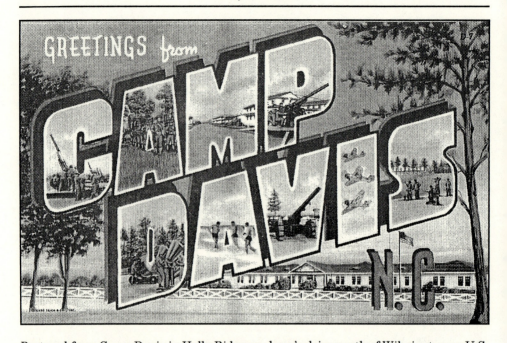

Postcard from Camp Davis in Holly Ridge, an hour's drive north of Wilmington on U.S. 17, a major army anti-aircraft and coast artillery training center. An advanced training base at Fort Fisher and a firing range on Topsail Island were camp extensions. Built in early 1941, the camp had a significant immediate and ongoing impact on the life and culture of Southeastern North Carolina until it closed in 1945.

Provided by Richard Witherspoon

defense and to the safety of our community. The guards are performing as much a war duty as if they were in combat with an enemy. Their orders are strict and it may be accepted as a definite fact that they will be obeyed to the letter....In wartime every person in the vicinity of any area under guard is suspect. This is said, not to alarm, but to safeguard the people of Wilmington....When they say halt, halt."[6]

It didn't take long. An army guard near a military area opened fire on three civilian motorists "who approached his post and ignored his command to stop." The gunfire caused them to stop immediately and no one was hurt. Guards "have been instructed to take similar action when their commands to 'halt and be recognized' are not heeded."[7] They were also placed at five major county bridges and other key points to prevent sabotage or damage (which never came).

People were drastically concerned. From where and what direction would we be hit? "In thinking of Wilmington's defense one's mind involuntarily turns to the east," rationalized one major voice. "The ocean is there. It would seem that attack would come from there. But an equally vulnerable point, particularly for sabotage, is to the west, directly across the river. The defense council has had it under study for weeks." Maps were prepared "revealing every building, every wooden space, every pathway and road, every area that needs clearing, for a distance of five miles—two in New Hanover County and three in Brunswick County. The topographical picture thus drawn shows what lighting is required...and how the whole area can be patrolled for the protection of the shipyard, oil terminals and other harbor properties."[8]

For the civilian populace, feeling immensely helpless, civilian defense—the means by which the public prepared to defend themselves—became the one sure and patriotic way to *do something*. The all-volunteer New Hanover County Defense Council, the initial coordinator of local civilian defense efforts, fortuitously had begun planning months ahead. So by December 13, more than 300 citizens from 10 to 65 years of age had registered with the Council as volunteers. "Among those who have already registered are Spanish American and World War veterans, bookkeepers, clerks, railroad conductors, high school and grammar school pupils, office workers, housewives, and industrial workers."[9] By the end of the year, 250 "prominent citizens" attended a conference for organizing county air raid systems. The Council conducted "manifold civilian defense activities here" coordinating all county defense activities not directed by the army. By January 1942, approximately 2,000 had signed on.[10]

Choose one. Volunteer opportunities included service as air raid wardens, messengers, nurses aides, medical corps, rescue squad, emergency food and housing corps, decontamination corps, staff corps, fire watchers, aircraft spotters, auxiliary policemen and firemen, bomb squad, demolition and clearance crews, road repair crew, and in recreation and child care. By January 1943, the number of volunteers under the Defense Council began to peak: 5,295 in the Civilian Defense Corps; 948 in the Aircraft Warning Service; and 1,576 in the Citizen Service Corps, a total of 7,819. Of the county's estimated population at the time, this represented approximately better than one in ten.

At the war's first anniversary, the Office of Civilian Defense, headed by Sheriff C. David Jones, had 4,000 workers; the shipyard had 18,000 employees; the governments had erected 2,595 wartime housing units; and the city experienced four blackouts, one of which was an official army alert. Medical personnel had staffed three casualty stations and a blood bank. "'As a working unit, the OCD actually functions. It has had organized practices, and thru tests it has determined that the entire system can be assembled and put into action in 5 minutes time.'"[11]

* * *

Blackouts and Air Raids

On the night of December 16, 1941, Wilmington was one of the initial East Coast cities to experience a full-dress rehearsal of a wartime enemy air attack. The simulated air raid took place earlier in the afternoon, and the practice blackout from 9–9:30 p.m. "If a military policeman stops you during either...don't question, but obey him implicitly," officials said. "It was far from being a perfect blackout," but it was "very successful" and "Wilmington has reason to be proud of itself...." Some downtown businesses received broken windows, but police could not say whether it was citizens' overzealousness to extinguishing lights or for robbery.[12]

The first of numerous blackouts, air raids, and other alerts ahead, at first they thrilled adults and children alike. Everyone wanted to follow instructions correctly. During drills, people rushed to windows to pull down the shades and turn off lights near windows, lest your street's air raid warden, out on the prowl, knocked sternly on your door. (Ours was a Mr. Schwartz, a neighbor who took his job seriously.) No lights were supposed to shine through, but blackout shades and curtains were difficult to find, and sheets or blankets had to suffice. During hot weather, you suffered a bit until the all-clear signal. If we knew the drill was coming, I hurried to finish my homework and the family its meal while there was light. Sometimes fighter planes zoomed overhead performing their role in the practice bomber-intercept drama. A central switch somewhere doused street lights. Cars were not allowed to move. Drivers caught when the siren sounded were confined to the car with lights off. When Diane Snakenburg's warden father had to respond to a drill she was terrified, not of the drill but over her father's going out into the unknown dark.

A kind of curfew fell. We kids couldn't play outside or visit each other either, and were forced to the radio for contact with the world. Telephone calls were prohibited. Sometimes my bedtime would come before the blackout was lifted. I lay there wondering what was going on, and whether we would ever be invaded. Months after the fear of imminent attack subsided, those haunting apparitions of concentration camp atrocities kept me awake. I remember them now.*

Because preliminary plans and systems had been drawn before the war, the area's air raid warning system was reasonably well organized. The focus quickly shifted to a dire need for aircraft spotters and fire watchers and wardens. "Only a volunteer force...knowing what to do and how to do

---

* These types of drills were limited to coastal cities most likely, so the defense planners believed, to be attacked by enemy air or surface forces. Folks raised inland in North Carolina or in West Virginia or Colorado faced none of this, and cannot imagine what it was like to be caught up in these types of military maneuvers or have the fear of war brought directly into your street. We certainly felt more sympathy and compassion for Londoners and Muscovites.

it, could save the city...from a holocaust."[13] Finally, in early May 1942 the first block and street wardens to complete required training received their soon-recognizable logo "CD" (civilian defense) arm band insignia, and warden staff and chiefs of the city's 10 zones also received the first government-issued steel "CD" helmets. City air raid warden M'Kean Maffitt asked businesses and civic and professional clubs to cooperate on air raid protection for downtown. "'It's the biggest job that Wilmington has ever been faced with. My shoulders are not big enough to carry it out.'"[14] The Council began surveying city buildings for those with possible air raid shelters, and designated some.

With army assistance the Council promulgated mundane rules from the federal Office of Civilian Defense on how to behave during an enemy air raid. In retrospect rather obvious, they were new to all and not taken lightly. "If bombs start to fall near you, lie down. You will feel the blast least that way, escape fragments and splinters. The safest place is under a good stout table....A mattress under a table combines comfort with safety." Acting smart was one matter, but sacrificing it all was a little too much to ask of us. So take a mattress. "Should your house be hit, keep cool....Just keeping cool hurts the enemy more than anything else you can do."[15] Oh yeah, only if it's somebody else's house maybe. To young kids, this was not amusing talk, but we practiced it at home and at school. In class, I suppose because it was ridiculous to seek meaningless shelter under tables and desks, we scrambled into the basement cafeteria. We welcomed the drills as opportunities to play grab-ass.

Short-notice blackouts and air raid drills held randomly were scrupulously monitored and evaluated. Authorities ordered residents to "obey faithfully blackout instructions...and has reprimanded persons who failed to comply...."[16] After the mid-July 1942 alert, a local army official stated, "the public must learn that when the air raid alert sounds without warning, it is most definitely the 'real thing' and not a practice drill."[17]

Authorities exposed the population to any number of eventualities through demonstrations, exhibits, and training. The Army Chemical Warfare Service and other agencies presented traveling exhibitions. Aircraft spotter observation posts sprung up throughout the county. Built and maintained by citizens, the volunteer spotters searched the skies with binoculars day and night and reported any sightings to the army's information and filter center downtown.

By summer 1942, the Southern Bell Telephone Company urged subscribers to keep the phone lines open during emergencies. "The usual reaction of the American public is to do just what they are told not to do, but in this case I hope it will not happen that way. In an emergency such as an air raid, every telephone will have a vital part to play in the protection of the public. It will be impossible for fast efficient service to be rendered if the lines are cluttered with many inconsequential calls."[18] Much to the annoyance of frequent telephone users, not long afterwards the phone company implored—almost dictated—users to restrict the number and length of calls to keep lines, particular party lines, open at all times.

Air raid and blackout drills and alerts continued into 1944, but not until participating in a statewide blackout in September 1942—nearly 10 months after the war started—were officials confident the system would function properly under emergency conditions.* Warnings kept coming. "Enemy May Attempt Raids on United States During Coming Months," a July 1943 statement from Washington said. Look out for bombing attacks "to cripple forthcoming Allied offensives by creating a public clamor for withdrawal of air strength from the battle zones to the home front. 'The war is approaching a vigorous summer, and anything can happen.'"[19]

One had to wonder where and how the newspaper got information on which to base its assumptions. Were its pretenses to offer fear, vigilance, overprotectiveness, or pure speculation? "...It would be folly of the most tragic sort to discount the army's position that in war anything can happen....A bombing attack is within the realm of possibility. Any failure to be prepared for it would be tremendously costly....Unjustified optimism is overshadowing the need for greater defense effort on the home front."[20]

The final army-ordered blackout drill was on February 8, 1944, "to remind us that there is still a war and also to give defense forces a bit of practice....While there is no longer reason to believe...[in] an invasion, it's quite possible that he may send his subs to shell the shores and planes to bomb coastal cities." The drill was "'very thorough; it was as complete as any I have observed in Wilmington,'" an army official stated.[21] Finally our community had it together.

Blackouts were over, but how much longer would the paper continue to play its call to arms? One answer was, as long as the government furnished it with propaganda. For example, on New Year's Eve 1944, the local civilian defense office issued instructions for conduct in case of robot or rocket bomb attacks, based on the German V-2 rockets then showering England. Previous instructions assumed naively the Germans would give advance warnings of attack. "'The public should realize the danger and be constantly on the alert, particularly in the coastal areas.'"[22] The next day, however, "no cause for alarm. It is NOT an announcement that Wilmington will be raided. It is simply a precautionary step....Therefore, don't be

---

* The test was "'about as perfect as humanly possible,'" and some 3,500 city civilian defense workers took part. [*Wilmington Morning Star*, September 30, 1942]

alarmed."²³ After three years of scares, drills, false alarms, and mental and physical preparations and letdowns, who knew how much more the adults had left to get excited about? But the odds were the constant rubber band stress-stretch-and-retract factor might be required clear through until victory. We kids thought it was all but over by New Year's.

* * *

U-boats

Until early summer 1942, in spite of the persistent U-boat activity offshore, authorities were slow to promulgate and enforce regulations limiting lighting near the coast "to prevent [passing] ships from being silhouetted against the light and thus rendered 'sitting ducks' for the Nazis."²⁴ The luminescence of the mass of lights from Wilmington, the beach communities, and nearby military camps was feared as potentially aiding the enemy. This fear factor impacted preparations for air raid drills, blackouts, and dimouts. From 1941–44, Wilmington's famous Hilton Park Christmas tree, 75 feet tall with 2,500 lights and first lit in 1929—the "world's largest" living Christmas tree, was darkened.* "Known the nation over through post cards and magazine articles, [it] will be blacked out....The tree made a too-conspicuous landmark from the air and because the electricity required would serve a better purpose in national defense industries."²⁵

Finally, the army ordered dimouts along the coastal areas, prohibiting citizens within 20 miles of the shore from showing outside lights, and requiring vehicle owners to blacken the top half of their headlights.† All vehicles operating in a zone five miles from the ocean had to use only parking lights and travel under 15 mph. The first violator of the new dimout regulations in June 1942 was found guilty of reckless operation for driving 75 on Wrightsville Beach at night and fined $30 and costs or 20 days labor on the county roads. Boat lights were limited to running lights. Beach roads remained open to drivers at any time until mid-July when U.S. Highways 74 and 76 were closed "because of evidence recent submarine sinkings along the coast 'were assisted by lights from motor vehicles.'"²⁶

In December 1942 the army placed all of New Hanover County under regulations extending the dimout to an average of 25 miles from the coast. "Wilmington will become a darkened city when the new rules...are finally carried out. 'It will work a hardship on many to comply...for blackout shades

---

* Citizens enjoyed an enormous sense of relief when the 2,500 lights went on again in 1945, a firm reminder that the war was behind us. At Christmas 2001, the venerable old tree, standing for more than 200 years and a bit tired from hurricane poundings and age, was turned on for the 77th season.

† Wartime residents remember painting car headlights black and have their own special story of some exciting experience or mishap. The Forest Hills streetlights were among those with blackened tops.

are practically unavailable.'"[27] Upper portions of the city's "white way" street lights were painted black, illuminated outdoor signs were extinguished, and cars had to drive with low beams already blacked out. Enforcement was unequal.[28]

Regulations were extremely hard to police, and there would be more violations and penalties. Public indifference to the simple chore of opaquing headlights was unfathomable. Eighteen months into the war, an editorial chided car owners about "how poorly Wilmingtonians have complied with the army regulation." Approximately half the local cars had not complied. "There is no reasonable excuse for this...no cost to owners...firemen at any station will apply the black paint free to all applicants....It is too bad that this indifference should have persisted so stubbornly that the city authorities have had to instruct police to make arrests for violations....The army has said this must be done...."[29] One month later approximately one hundred motorists had been arrested. But the problem of luminescence was never fully controlled.

The army was everywhere. While defending Wrightsville and Carolina Beaches against possible German attacks, the soldiers allowed pretty girls to interrupt their duties. At Wrightsville, *left to right*, Laura Roe, Catherine Russell, Margaret Parks, and Elizabeth Roe took over, 1942.

Provided by Catherine Russell Stribling

In the army's coastal boundaries and restricted zones, items "absolutely forbidden" to be in the possession of civilians and military personnel not on duty included bombs, explosives, radio transmitting sets, codes or ciphers, drawings, maps of military installations, and pictures. No one could use a camera, binoculars, field glasses, or similar instruments.[30] On the extreme, both Wrightsville and Carolina Beaches banned shorts and bathing suits on the beach after dark, an "emergency measure and for the safety of inhabitants of the resorts and of the Allied nations."[31] The rationale: you could be a spy from a German U-boat who just swam ashore. At Carolina Beach the boardwalk area including to seaward was generally open. Not only were photographs restricted, but also making sketches or paintings of objects within the zone. Only duty army personnel were allowed between sunset and sunrise, and residents were subject to challenge by sentries. Restrictions were later lifted.

Harold Laing remembered Wrightsville machine gun emplacements, horse patrols, and private boats circling in an area where a ship had gone down. Jim Fountain saw German torpedoes along Carolina Beach and heard guns roaring at Fort Fisher. Once some one hundred people stood around the next morning after one that missed its target had landed. Pearl Winner recalled "it was nothing to pick up shells [bullets] on the beach and see oil spills. You would have to walk out a way waist deep to be able to swim to avoid the oil globs which had sunk."[32]

People had no way of knowing if these types of defense measures were successful. Authorities issued little if anything for public consumption about sightings, attacks, and sinkings. But area residents had every reason to believe American losses were being taken and sailors killed. Numbers recorded that the subs were "menacing our coastal waters with impunity, causing tremendous tanker losses and overrunning the hospital and medical facilities...."[33] By my eighth birthday in 1942, 347 Allied and neutral ships had gone down in the Atlantic since Pearl Harbor.

Myths persist about German spies and saboteurs being landed at Wrightsville and Carolina Beaches in boats, German newspapers being left in Wilmington theaters, and spies in civilian clothes being captured with local theater ticket stubs in their pockets. How these myths were started is untraceable. Some old-timers believe them, some don't. Hannah Block, a deputy sheriff and Carolina Beach head lifeguard, saw two spies caught while coming in from the beach in rubber boats. "If you were on the beach you had to see the Liberty ships on fire. We were constantly on the lookout. We had soldiers with dogs on the beach, soldiers on horses on the beach."[34] (See Ralph Horton's remembrances in the accompanying sidebar on the U-boat firing on the Ethyl-Dow Chemical Company.)

Mrs. Charles (Hannah) Block, a civic leader in the war effort and head lifeguard at Carolina Beach, late war.
Provided by Block

Another account of evidence exists. Late one night in August 1943, Lieutenant Carlton H. Sprague was duty officer for his unit, the 558th Anti-Aircraft Artillery Automatic Weapons Battalion, stationed at Fort Fisher. His C Battery beach patrols captured four Germans wearing navy uniforms who came ashore in a beached small submarine south of Fort Fisher, and walked them to Sprague's command post. He accompanied the group back to the shore where he saw the submarine from about 100 to 150 yards away. The Germans spoke good English and caused no problems. "I felt the way this worked out these fellows had no intention to go back" or to carry out their mission. He believed "they were to sabotage the channel in the Cape Fear River, which would detain ship traffic. They wanted to be POWs." Army intelligence soon took away the Germans. He has no idea what happened to them or the sub. "We were busy" undergoing intensive training. "The next morning I had to be back on the firing range."[35]

Spies and saboteurs just didn't happen, according to Wilmington native Billy Sutton, a Coast Guardsman who patrolled the beaches. "If they had landed, they could not have evaded our patrols for long, and they would have had to get rid of their equipment."[36] He and other sentries apparently found nothing on the beaches to indicate Germans had been there.*

My recollections support the believers. Such intrusion was highly plausible; otherwise, shall we say, the newspaper would not have intermittently injected the probability of spies being among us. What did they know the rest of us didn't? They, too, got around town and asked questions and listened. The intrigue and debate will continue as long as anybody cares.

In April 1942 Navy Secretary Frank Knox grimly stated at the peak of German successes that the Battle of the Atlantic "has taken a turn for the

---

* Mounted Coast Guardsmen allegedly patrolled every inch of every beach between Wilmington and Florida. "They'll be hard-riding, quick-shooting horsemen, each trained to fight as a guerilla....They are...to put up a delaying fight which will enable civilians to evacuate the beaches and enable our armed forces to move in....Neither storms nor high tides can stop them." [*Wilmington Sunday Star-News*, December 6, 1942] This was Sutton and his mates.

But they were only a portion of the guard and patrol forces along area beaches. The army had a rifle company at Carolina Beach and numerous gun positions and sentries at Wrightsville. The navy operated patrol craft out of Fort Caswell in Brunswick County. The Coast Guard had major patrol craft bases at Wrightsville and Wilmington, and the civilian-manned Coast Guard Auxiliary operated in the rivers, creeks, inlets and Inland Waterway.

worse, with attacks by German U-boats on Allied shipping to England and Africa increasing." The Nazis were still producing their submarines.* By late 1942, German U-boats in the Western Atlantic were destroying U.S. and Allied and neutral merchantmen in alarming numbers. Discouraging news was made even bleaker: "Rough weather and longer hunting nights of winter tended to favor the underseas over patrol forces which guard our shipping."[37]

Two weeks later Knox persisted in warning East Coast residents of the possibility of enemy attacks as "nuisance action for us and a suicide operation for their fliers."[38] This was purely propaganda to keep coastal Americans on a war edge and deceive the enemy as to what our government really believed. Historians agree the tide and nature of the Battle of the Atlantic dramatically turned against the Germans in May 1943 both in numbers of Allied merchant ships lost and U-boats sunk. From then until victory, ship losses steadily decreased and U-boat losses steadily increased greater than their replacement boats and crews could be readied. Wilmington authorities may not and the people could not have realized it by then, but any air or land threat had long been removed. The enemy never did have the capability: no operational trans-Atlantic bombers, no aircraft carriers, and no amphibious invasion force. But we weren't supposed to know this—in case. And the undersea threat had largely disappeared from the Western Atlantic.

The U-boats remained a frequent topic of concern and conversation in our area until 1944. As a means of warfare and demon adversaries linked directly to the very ships we built here, they somehow struck a romantic chord as well as unseen terror, and captured the imagination, if not the front pages.†

The army suspended all dimout regulations affecting the Wilmington area on November 1, 1943, including the beaches with the exception of the B zones. Within those zones headlights had to be dimmed but not necessarily painted and large signs could be illuminated. "While Wilmington has not generally observed the dimout, except in these two aspects, the nearby beach resorts are expected to benefit from its abolishment." The downtown

---

* The historic operating area and merchant ship graveyard along the North Carolina coast called "Torpedo Junction" was centered in the Cape Hatteras area. Wilmington could be considered at its southern extension, but was not included within the literal definition of that area.

† "The U-boat arm grew from 57 boats at the beginning [of the war] to 1,170 boats; 863 were operational. Losses were 781, but at the end [German navy chief Admiral Karl] Doenitz still had 336. More than 39,000 men served in U-boats, and 32,000 found an ocean grave. 'It was the worst defeat of any branch of service in any war in history,' the [U.S.] Tenth Fleet historian noted." [Wilbur D. Jones, Jr., *Arming the Eagle: A History of U.S. Weapons Acquisition Since 1775* (Fort Belvoir, Va.: Department of Defense Systems Management College Press, 1999), 314]

"white way" could blaze again, and Legion Stadium lights could shine for football and baseball games. You can imagine the joy and utter relief. A major step in winning the war had been taken.* But it attached one caveat. "...It is urged that, in the coal crisis, all unnecessary lights remain extinguished as a conservation measure. This is entirely voluntary."[39] Until even *after* victory, Wilmington would always *find something* in short supply.

* * *

As the United States continued its battlefield successes into late 1944, other local civilian defense and military security functions began dismantling. The Coast Guard reduced greatly or deactivated many of their functions except for those protecting the port of Wilmington. Four days after V-E Day, on May 12, 1945, for the first time in three years, the regular local Saturday test of the air raid sirens was discontinued. (You had been able to set your clocks.) The county casualty station at my St. Andrews-Covenant Presbyterian, open throughout the war collecting blankets, splints, and other first-aid items, closed in June. On the 15th, the state Office of Civilian Defense discontinued its operation to coincide with the national office. A large painted marker sign for airmen on the roof of a tall downtown building with the word "WILMINGTON," local latitude and longitude, and arrow pointing to Bluethenthal Field, obliterated when the war began, was repainted.

If it was safe to fly a private plane into town, it must have been safe to go to the beach in a bathing suit with headlights on high, and without stepping into black oil.

---

* Police said it "would be easier to administer a 'stern reproof' with brighter lights while girls who work late at eating establishments, those girls who used to be called butter chips, when there was butter, expressed the thought that some of the 'Hi Babe!' atmosphere might be eliminated late at night. Wilmington looked splendid to one who had never seen it all lit up before—and it must have looked mighty fine to the home folks, too." [*Wilmington Morning Star*, November 2, 1943]

The *John D. Gill* Goes Down[40]

"The day of the sinking...was the day that World War II was brought home to Southport, and laid out on her front lawn. No hostile warships had operated off of the Cape Fear River since 1865...." The oil tanker SS *John D. Gill*, 523 feet long and 11,641 tons, "the largest and finest in the Atlantic Refining Company's fleet," was launched in November 1941. It carried a crew of 42 and a naval armed guard of seven.

On March 12, 1942, the loaded *Gill* was on her second voyage from Texas to her homeport of Philadelphia. "She was proceeding with extreme caution past Cape Fear, having been warned that submarines were in the vicinity." A torpedo from the German *U-158* struck at 10:00 p.m. amidships on the starboard side. "People in the Southport USO building on the grounds of Fort Johnston, looking out over Battery Island, could clearly see the flash and hear the explosion of the torpedo, and spot the later glow of fires of her burning oil. Coast Guardsmen in the building, today's Community Building, immediately raced for their boats to try for a rescue, ignoring their own risk and enemy action."

A life ring with a self-igniting carbide light tossed overboard ignited sea of oil and started the fires and magazine explosion. The burnt-out wreck sank about 9:00 the next morning. "The navy gun crew never had a chance to fight back against the submerged U-boat, and four of the seven died at their posts without being able to fire a shot." Rescuers saved 23 crewmen and recovered 16 bodies, including three armed guard, and rushed survivors to Southport's Dosher Hospital. "The victims were laid out in a row on the grass in front of the Garrison, Southport's front lawn." Bodies recovered were sent home for burial, but messman Catalino Tingzon was buried in Southport because the Japanese controlled his country, the Philippines. The *Gill* hero was quartermaster Edward F. Cheney, later presented Merchant Marine Distinguished Service Medal by President Franklin D. Roosevelt.

The *U-158* was bombed and sunk west of Bermuda on June 30, 1942 without survivors.

Etched in the memory of many Wilmington-area residents, the destruction and burning of the *Gill* so close to local beaches is the most prominent recollection of U-boat activity I encountered.

The Southport Historical Society, led by Susy Carson and Chris Suiter, erected a monument to the *Gill* and periodically hold observances there.

A U-Boat and the Ethyl-Dow Chemical Company

The Ethyl-Dow Chemical Company was one of the Wilmington area's most important war industries, its operations and products for security reasons largely unknown to local residents. Located at Kure's Beach south of Carolina Beach, Ethyl-Dow made an ingredient called ethylene (later "no-knock Ethyl") out of bromide in sea water for high-octane aviation gasoline which powered military aircraft. The plant was vital to the war effort. The plant closed by January 1946 and shifted its operations to its other such plant in Freeport, Texas.

To this day the plant remains the subject of one of the area's most enduring and tantalizing wartime tales. Depending on how Wilmingtonians look at it, the tale is either truth, myth, or rumor, or any combination.

Ralph T. Horton worked there in operations and administrative positions from 1937 until the plant closed in 1945.[41] "At that time we probably employed more people than the [Atlantic] Coast Line [Railroad] did, and at a higher rate of pay. We were frozen into the jobs there. We shipped many barrels of ethyl bromide to Russia...that was highly secretive. It was packaged in 55-gallon drums. Within this country it was shipped in bulk." (Horton, a longtime metals dealer, later served as chairman of the county commissioners.)

Horton described the process. To make ethylene, sea water was pumped over a tremendous slab area within a 150x300', 40'-high brick building. The slabs were wood mats. Water filtered through huge rotary tanks filled with sulphur which made a yellowish glow. CO_2 aided in the separation process. With acid added to the liquid, it entered a tank settling area that collected the bromide. From there it was pumped into the ethylene building where the several other chemicals were mixed into the liquid for the finished product, ethylene. "You could go out on the fourth floor of this building and throw it out the window and none would hit the ground. It would evaporate. It was highly flammable."

On several occasions, particularly during night shifts, Horton saw as many as three ships on fire to seaward at one time. "As soon as they crossed the bar [leaving the Cape Fear River] the submarines opened up on them." An early version of the PT (patrol-torpedo) boat patrolled Ethyl-Dow from the river mouth to the plant. The crew picked up several Germans from one of the U-boats. Coast Guard friend Linwood Roberts was on the crew of this craft, and later in the Normandy landing.

On the night of July 24-25, 1943, so the story goes, a German U-boat surfaced off the shore and fired its deck gun at the plant. Horton, on duty that night, was an eyewitness. "We were all blacked out on the ocean side. Their aim wasn't that good. The shells actually landed in Brunswick County. We heard the whistling sound. We were on the fourth floor of the bromide building and could see the shells exploding on the river at the water's edge." (The Federal Point peninsula of New Hanover County at that spot separating the ocean from the Cape Fear River to the west is less than one-half mile across.) With Horton then were Haywood Moore (the brother in law of Betty Henderson), the shift foreman; Dan Odom, one of the operators; and Billy High.

At the time the public knew only rumors about this event. The newspaper reported nothing until March 22, 1946.[42] "That a German submarine tried to shell the Ethyl-Dow plant at Kure's Beach during the war was given 'reasonable proof' yesterday by a letter to his father from A. B. Love, Jr. The attempt to shell the highly inflammable...[plant] took place on the morning of July 25, 1943, at 3 o'clock in the morning, it was learned." Love worked for Ethyl-Dow then, but moved to Ludington, Michigan. "He learned why the section was alerted for an air raid that day from a former army pilot, who is a Dow employee in Michigan. After the Nazi submarine had fired five rounds at the plant, all of them missing their mark by 'miles,' it was sunk the following day, according to Love's story."

"Love's account of the vain attempt to smash the local war industry was declared substantially true by [Lieutenant Commander] Louis Hanson, commander of the area Coast Guard Auxiliary at the time. The story came to light through accident. W. L. Tisdale, who Love knows, was in a barber shop in Michigan when he noticed a picture of a submarine on the wall of the shop, which is operated by a former army pilot. In conversation, they put two and two together, and concluded that the sub which the flier had helped sink the day after it is said to have shelled at the Kure Beach plant, would have some interest to Love, who Tisdale knew was from Wilmington. The letter states that on the morning of the attempted shelling, the sub spotted the plane, which had been ordered to guard the coast, and submerged before they could get to it. That was the sub picture which hangs in the barber shop in Michigan. Robert Cantwell, who was manager of the Dow Kure Beach plant, says the story is probably correct, because he remembers that a military plant guard told him that the alert was 'the real thing,' but refused to say what was wrong." (The highly respected Hanson was my across-the-street neighbor.) In October 1943 an army colonel admonished Ethyl-Dow employees, "'warning that the enemy will redouble his efforts to strike at the source of industrial production because the failure of its submarine campaign,'" and urged them to "'maintain stern vigilance against possible sabotage.'"[43]

That night at 3:00 a.m., an air raid siren awakenened sisters Catherine and Margaret Crowe, daughters of downtown First Presbyterian pastor Dr. William Crowe, Jr., in the manse next door. Shipyard lights went out, "which they never did in a practice raid, we knew this was the real thing," recalled Catherine. But nothing happened, at least then. Among their regular Sunday dinner guests were two officers from a British "sub chaser" operating in and out of Wilmington. The Sunday after the event at dinner the men startled the family. On the night of the 24th they were patrolling off Wrightsville Beach "when their ship suddenly had to <u>reverse</u> direction in order not to hit a German sub....It had thrown them against the opposite wall...below deck. They had been totally flabbergasted by the incident."[44]

The father of Frances Jordan (NHHS '43), Luther J. Jordan, was the volunteer head of civilian defense at Carolina Beach. He was responsible for seeing that someone was at city hall on the night of July 24, 1943, to answer the emergency phone, "should there be a message from headquarters in Washington." Her mother, Lula K. Jordan, was also a volunteer there. "One night my father was called to the city hall for an emergency. During the evening we could hear cars and people talking on 4th Ave near our house. With the constant mandatory blackout, we couldn't <u>see</u> anything going on. After the war he told us that was the night a German submarine had fired on the Ethyl-Dow Chemical plant, but overshot and the shell(s) landed in the Cape Fear River. Some of my classmates and others at the beach were part of the Civil Air Patrol and volunteered taking turns looking for enemy submarines or planes. They used a platform something like a lifeguard stand that was located on the beach between Carolina Beach and Kure Beach."[45]

George Burrell Byers (NHHS '43) lived in Sunset Park approximately seven blocks from the shipyard. The night of the alleged attack the lights went off at the yard and "it got real dark, dead silence, you could hear the crickets." Ethyl-Dow cut off their lights. He went inside. "All of a sudden one of the fighters from Bluethenthal Field went roaring over headed for the [Carolina] beach. I knew something wasn't right. That place just wasn't supposed to stop." He heard of the attack later by hearsay.[46]

Here you have two apparently substantive accounts *for* the shelling, and two more supporting it. While most Wilmingtonians I spoke with claim it is true, some still wonder about it and a few have told me they doubt it. The most vocal argument *against* the shelling having occurred is from David W. Carnell, who moved here sometime after the war and is obsessed with disproving the story.[47] "'...The plant was not shelled and there was no attack. The director of a Coast Guard museum at Virginia Beach [Virginia] told me that these myths exist all along the East Coast. No attack on the U.S. by German submarines in WWII has ever been confirmed....In the course of my research on the Ethyl-Dow bromine [sic] plant that led to the establishment of a historical marker at the site, I was most helped by extensive correspondence with Monroe Shigley, who was assistant plant manager at its startup and later plant manager, and, at the time of the submarine incident, manager of the plants at Kure Beach and in [Freeport] Texas. The incident occurred July 25, 1943. Mr. [Shigley] told me a surfaced sub was sighted, but dived before its identity was established or any action taken against it....The moon rose at 11:51 p.m. and was about one day past third quarter....[The] shutdown at the bromine plant because of the sub sighting came about 1 p.m....After the plant restarted about 3 a.m., sub chasers were visible working over the area where the sub had been sighted. These ships were likely from a convoy offshore....'"

Carnell's further research, including reference books on U-boat operations, reinforced his position that there was no shore bombardment activity against the U.S. Atlantic coast. "The escort activity...observed on the night the plant shut down was most likely the result of a false sonar contact," an occurrence with which he was familiar.[48] He contends the Germans no longer had subs operating in the area, and if so, he found no after-action reports about the firing. His blanket statement is suspect. My study of the Battle of the Atlantic has shown that while the tide definitely turned against the German U-boats in May 1943, it was still very likely boats were operating in the Gulf Stream shipping lanes. And, a sunken submarine would not return to port with or radio in any after-action reports.

Star-News writer Ben Steelman, a thorough researcher, in February 2001 wrote on the subject. "'Unless and until some rusty German shells turn up in a Brunswick County bog, however, the mystery seems likely to remain a mystery.'"[49] Still, I heard the rumors then and have heard them ever since the war. Did it occur? Yes, I believe so. Now who would like to join me to search for the shells?

Chapter 4
The Shipyard and the "Defense Capital of the State"

On late afternoons I occasionally went with my parents when they picked up Lib from work at the shipyard's main gate. Our black Pontiac became surrounded in the swarm of buses, taxis, bicycles, and more black cars that jockeyed for space. A mass of people spilled from the yard on foot, jamming the narrow roadways. I wondered how she could ever find us. As we waited I dared not get out, but was fascinated by the scene. Across from the gate on the east side of Burnett Boulevard were numerous little temporary wooden storefronts, sidewalk salesmen, blinking lights, neon drink-my-beer signs, and dingy people milling around smoking cigarettes and hailing passers-by. As months passed, I pictured this block-long strip as being out of a Hollywood movie set.

The shipyard was not part of my world. Unlike some of my friends, I don't remember going inside to a launching. For security reasons it was difficult to obtain entry, even when celebrities were here for big war bond rallies. So, my recollections of it are views from outside the chain-link fences. The shipyard's domain, on the other hand, reached far into town. It was the super magnet of the area's war effort, and its workers were everywhere, leaving their dollars, their sweat, their local color, and their trash. No one could miss noting that.

As numerous Wilmingtonians have said about those years, no matter how much impact Camp Davis, Camp Lejeune, Bluethenthal Army Air Base, and the other military activities collectively had on the area, the shipyard spearheaded the economic boom. Nothing touched it for sheer volume of opportunities and challenges. By late 1944, the North Carolina Shipbuilding Company led the state's business firms in war production. "The yard, together with the several military establishments in Southeastern North Carolina, has given Wilmington the title of Defense Capital of the State."[1]

The title was earned, proudly relished, but severely paid for in terms of social, jurisdictional, and cultural upheavals.

While the shipyard was the principal employer, two other major businesses with long links to the local economy were also substantial contributors to the area's role as the defense capital. They were the Atlantic Coast Line Railroad, headquartered locally, and the Port of Wilmington, North Carolina's largest. Their activities are also summarized herein.

Life at the North Carolina Shipbuilding Company from its opening on February 3, 1941, to closing on October 9, 1946, is the story of its people, its record, and its products. But first, back to the main gate. Read how Clayton Smith, a yard worker until called into the army in September 1944, helps describe the setting:[2]

Clayton Smith was a shipyard worker until drafted into the army in September 1944.

Provided by Smith

On either side of the road front of the employee entrance to the shipyard were several, for want of a better description, food stands. Such stands appeared to have been hastily erected and, were by and large, strictly "mom and pop" stores. A few of the more elaborate ones may have had a blaring juke box, which never seem to cease their ear-splitting din. Shift workers patronized these stands to provide their lunches and cigarettes, etc. I recall quite vividly one day I purchased a sandwich consisting of fried liver and onions among other items for the later lunch break....In unwrapping the sandwich, it was found to be crawling (quite literally) with maggots. Obviously, the local health department's control over these establishments was extremely lax or non-existent.

Prior to a shift change, it was the usual practice for those arriving at work to assemble in front of the clock-in gates some minutes before the whistle blew. It was not unusual to see one or two peddlers hawking their wares. I recall one individual standing on a small wooden box in order to be heard and seen. His specialty was "snake oil" which he promised would cure any and all ills. Regardless. One day I...inquired as to the potion's medicinal ingredients. He replied, rather annoyed, "hell, I don't know. I just sell the stuff."

The immediate area in front of the employee entrance gates also served as space for buses to load and discharge passengers. The distance from the shipways to the buses was about a city block, perhaps a bit more. When the whistle sounded ending the shift, everyone intending to ride those buses broke into a dead sprint in order to ensure themselves of a seat on the bus. Latecomers would be relegated to the "strap hangers'" section.*

Richard C. "Dick" Andrews lived in Sunset Park across from the yard. His introduction to enterprise was selling the *Raleigh News & Observer* at gate No. 2 located on the railroad track by the administration building, catching the shift changes. Selling about 75 per day, he netted $25-30 a week. Dick also tried peddling the papers at the shipyard dormitory right outside the yard. "It got so rough in there I finally had to give it up. They wouldn't pay you."[3] Herbert Fisher's father had a stand outside the main gate that "sold everything from soup to nuts, shotgun shells, nylon stockings, things you couldn't get elsewhere, but for a price. They'd [workers] spend it for anything—they were making more money than they had ever seen—whether it was a pack of gum or cigarettes."[4]

To many thousands of Southeastern North Carolina men and women, the shipyard was the biggest and best hope for finding work both before and during the war. Workers came from miles around, depleting farm labor as far out as Pender, Brunswick, Bladen, Duplin, and Columbus Counties, some commuting daily or weekly. Because it was war-essential defense work, male workers were deferred almost indefinitely. It helped solve any unemployment problems carried over from the Depression and paid well. In return, its demands were extremely high. Out in the yard, constructing ships was rough, dirty, and dangerous, shared by whites and Negroes. Some workers received benefits such as insurance and annual leave, others did not. Attempts to unionize lost, and employees served at the pleasure of management. Safety was poorly structured and haphazardly enforced, but improved over time. Injuries were frequent and deaths occurred on the job, not all reported publicly. Federal government officials highly praised the shipyard's production record and participation in war bond drives and community service, all well deserved.

The Newport News Shipbuilding & Drydock Company of Newport News, Virginia, one of the country's largest ship constructors, opened the NCSC as a satellite. Wilmington would have to handle merchant ship contracts Newport News with its huge volume of navy orders could not. In January 1941 it

---

* Fifty-five years later my adult suspicions were confirmed by conversations with numerous people about the "main gate crowd." Beer joints and cheap stores prevailed, and prostitutes plied their trade. Upstairs over several buildings provided consenting couples with a convenient access, if hardly private. Some natives believe a tattoo parlor was there. I am sorry the buildings were eventually torn down for nothing but a bare field, and that I found no photographs. What a dose of wartime Wilmington the structures could have added to a World War II cultural heritage trail.

"reluctantly agreed to develop a [competing] yard at Wilmington." The new yard's first Liberty ship contracts were signed the same month, and construction began in February on 60 acres of swampland alongside the eastern bank of the Cape Fear River in the vicinity of the city's World War I shipyard. "The parent company transferred some of its own personnel to the new yard, these ranging from management to apprentices, but many of the new executives appointed had no shipbuilding knowledge." Some skilled labor was recruited locally, but the yard was under great pressure to train and place inexperienced persons on the job.[5]

* * *

Shipbuilding as an Art

No doubt, the technicalities and processes of shipbuilding were exceptionally well managed from the front office to the yard and shops. By October 1942, the NCSC had become the state's largest industry, employing approximately 15,000, replacing R. J. Reynolds Tobacco Company. Among the 10 yards building Libertys it ranked fifth largest nationally, and second on the East Coast. Workers of more than 50 trades toiled in the shops, yards, and offices, operating on a seven-day schedule of three shifts around the clock. Christmas was the only day off until mid-1944 when the yard closed Sundays in the July-August heat.

On December 6, 1941, when the first Liberty, the SS *Zebulon B. Vance*, was launched, the payroll was 3,500. By February 1943, the average construction time from keel-laying to launching was 32.3 days, launching to delivery 11.2 days, for a total of 43.5, nationally the third best. (*Vance* had taken 280 days.)*

In May 1943 the [Senator Harry S] Truman Investigating Committee named the NCSC and Henry J. Kaiser's Oregon shipyard as the two most efficient Liberty builders. "Our yard is the lowest in the country in dollar cost and second in manhours per ship."[6] By the third year, the 100th ship

---

* At least seven distinguishable former shipyard buildings remain on the present site of the North Carolina State Port, and most are still in use. The old mold loft, or Building No. 5, with its five peaks, is the most prominent. Building C1 has three bays with a rusty WWII roof, two have new roofs, some have WWII machinery and equipment still inside. (Inside the mold loft building, with a little imagination you can hear and feel the shouts of supervisors, the rumble of trucks and passing railroad cars, and the clamor of cranes, forklifts, steel, and hundreds of men in motion fast at work turning out the next hulls.)

Ship Shed No. 2 (long grey metal building) is now Wheeling Steel Company. The Heavy Equipment Shop still stands. Shipways were replaced years ago with concrete docks for container and break bulk ships to offload and for storage. Building 022 and the Foremen's Building (now the Seamen's Center) are from WWII, complete with original asbestos siding. The apprentice dormitory on Burnett Boulevard is now the Marine Corps Reserve Center. Sixteen miles of railroad tracks are still in use, many upgraded in carrying capacity from WWII but using the same beds. The "war room" near the main gate is used for meetings and in May 1999 temporarily became the Port Authority's shipyard museum during Wartime Wilmington Commemoration.

The Liberty ship SS *Zebulon B. Vance* was the first hull launched at the North Carolina Shipbuilding Company, December 6, 1941, sliding into the Cape Fear River. Photograph taken by Wilmington aviation pioneer James C. "Skinny" Pennington, later a ferry pilot flying "The Hump" into China. Provided by Pennington

had been built in 30 days. By mid-war the yard shifted production from Libertys and basic C-2 hulls to navy AKA attack-cargo vessels. On D-Day in 1944, the yard launched its first, the USS *Torrance* (AKA-76). "...These ships will carry the attack. The order gives the yard a greater part in helping knock out the Japanese and Germans and achieve final victory."[7]

An accurate counting, even an educated estimation, of the total number of persons who worked at the NCSC during its five and one-half years of existence is difficult. From a peak of 21-25,000 in mid-1943, depending on the sources, a guesstimate is that at least twice that many punched a clock at one time or another. The yard deservedly boasted of its obvious economic impact. The greater part of its payroll was spent in Wilmington but numerous other Southeastern North Carolina counties "also feel its favorable effects in their trade channels." Approximately 23 percent of employees resided more than 25 miles from the city and about 6 percent live at nearby beaches.[8] The *Morning Star* boasted: "Wilmington has reason to be proud of its shipbuilding industry, both for its eminently successful products and its contribution to the economic welfare of the area. The city has made its contribution to the bridge of ships by which alone the flow of materials and men could be transported to battlefields....It devolves upon the city, its leadership and the entire citizenship, to exert its best united effort to see that the yard is kept open as long as a cargo ship is required for war transportation and...for the reviving of world commerce."[9]

Employment manager Richard L. "Dick" Burnett's truest test came as employment peaked. "Despite rumors prevalent here that the NCSC will lay off 'thousands of men in the next few weeks, the company is anticipating no such move.'" Burnett needed to reassure his people. Still the company had to release a few hundred men temporarily because there was nothing for them to do while the yard transitioned its manufacturing processes from Liberty to C-2 vessels. In six weeks we probably will be hiring "more men than ever."[10] But the number of workers continued to slide even after C-2 production gained steam.

The payroll was down to approximately 15,000 in February 1944. This sent several signals. Improvements in manufacturing and an uncertainty over future business had to be factors, but the principal reasons were a manpower shortage, and competition from other yards for what pool there was. Burnett stated the company is "shorthanded," and needs to add "a considerable number of additional workers, but is having great difficulty finding them."[11] So many men had been called into the armed forces and skilled replacements were not available. Tightened government employment relocation regulations deterred workers from moving from one war-essential position to another. Many were frozen to their present jobs, like it or not. In September 1944 sufficient contracts for the next 12 months were assured "because of the peacetime value of the vessels being built here, there is little or no likelihood of any cancellations...."[12] During 1944, the NCSC led the nation by delivering 60 C-2 hulls, the "Victory ship" improvements over the Libertys.

One of Their Own

"To the workers of the North Carolina Shipbuilding Company," wrote the Maritime Commission chairman in 1943 in the *Shipbuilder*:[13]

> Your own Liberty ship, the SS *Virginia Dare*, carrying a war cargo, met and repelled a series of air and submarine attacks and brought down seven enemy bombers. For eight blazing days she fought off high and low flying bombers, dive bombers and other planes making low frontal attacks in suicidal fury....As a result of the gun crew's marksmanship and your sturdy workmanship, your vessel was able to deliver her cargo....*Virginia Dare* should now be a name of special pride to all of you at the NCSC. Keep up your good work.

The *Dare*, along with NCSC-built SS *William Moultrie*, the newspaper continued, downed 15 German planes and repelled U-boat attacks during battles lasting several days. "...Surprisingly few North Carolina ships have been lost.* We like to think that the high quality we strive to build into them means that they answer the demand of their masters in such a capable manner that they are better able to avoid danger and, when they meet it, to escape disaster."[14] But for one, it was her "gallant end," the *Shipbuilder* sadly declared in May 1945. "She died fighting, with 15 members of her crew going down with her as heroes." Such was the fate of hull number 40, the SS *Henry Bacon*, which sank from a German aircraft attack off Norway. She had carried 7,500 tons of war cargo to Murmansk, Russia, and was heading home with 19 Norwegian refugees aboard. They survived, but the captain went down with the ship.[15]

* * *

An Uncertain Future

As early as November 1942, while heading toward maximum production, long-range forecasts on the yard's viability began. At a launching here, Governor J. Melville Broughton was the first official to predict that "because of the efficiency in production of the shipyard it will continue to operate as a permanent establishment after the war."[16] At the time it was maintaining a "ship-a-week" record, and for 1942 sent 53 Libertys down the ways. As the yard donated a $25,000 gift to the city "earmarked for a special reserve post-war contingency fund," an NCSC official stated, "I want to make it clear that the NCSC intends to remain here forever." Even though

---

* Twenty-eight ships built by the NCSC were lost: 23 Libertys sunk by enemy action and four scuttled to form the Normandy invasion breakwater. One C-2 was lost, a navy ammunition ship which exploded in the Pacific.

"contingency fund" had a certain suspicious ring, the newspaper immediately carried the baton. "This sets to rest rumors that the yard would close when peace comes."[17]

In June 1944, a Maritime Commission official prophesied, "It would not take great intelligence to deduct from these developments a more eloquent prediction of the future of this plant than any I could make."[18] Thus, optimism for the future abounded. It was inconceivable that the government, or Newport News, would shut down this extremely important facility.

Philip "Phil" Dresser had "said goodbye to my many shipyard coworkers when I joined the navy in 1944. The navy's starting pay was lower than the shipyard's wage and the navy did not pay overtime pay, but I was soon earning bonus pay for sea duty in the South Pacific." Discharged in 1946 after more than two years, he returned to Wilmington to work in the yard. "While 'downsizing,' [it] was still open with a few contracts to build state of the art cargo-passenger ships for commercial lines." He visited the waterfront and former coworkers, including the tool room where he had worked.

The C-2 type hull SS *Sweepstakes* heads down the shipway at the North Carolina Shipbuilding Company on January 22, 1944.

Provided by Robert H. Butler

A fellow worker greeted him effusively with, "Phil, you're looking good. Haven't seen you in a couple of weeks—have you been out sick with a cold?" He had "sailed halfway around the world and back, survived war at sea in the Pacific including a nightly threat of kamikaze attacks, survived typhoons in...a fairly small vessel, and returned to my home...in one piece. I quickly learned that my image was fading fast, first as an essential wartime shipyard worker and then as a salty sailor returned from the U.S. Navy and victory at sea. The war was over and it was time to get on with life as a civilian."[19]

Shipyard management was in accord. All 243 ships had been delivered, and it was time to close the door. "Time has flown so fast since the shipyard began its opperations five years ago and so much has happened in the world that it is difficult of realization," reported president Roger Williams. "We have accomplished our task and may forget the hardships and headaches in connection with it and enjoy the feeling it has been a job well done."[20]

Soon after the war the Maritime Commission decided to lay up surplus merchant ships along the Brunswick River's long-abandoned rice fields in Brunswick County across from Wilmington. It had the NCSC prepare a basin for a potential of five hundred ships and a floating drydock.* "The contemplated storage basin will be welcome, not only because moored ships are more attractive than marsh grass but also because the project means employment for many workers during dredging operations, but skeleton maintenance crews besides, and requires a drydock which will not only service laid-up ships but the cargo carriers that will be coming into the port as Wilmington commerce increases."[21]

The parent eventually saw to its offspring's demise. "At the end of WWII Wilmingtonians hoped to ease the transition to a peacetime economy by establishing a drydock facility in the port and by creating a state ports authority to promote shipping, similar propositions after WWI," a local historian reported. "Both Newport News and Todd Shipbuilding in Charleston opposed the potential competition from Wilmington, and the plan was doomed."[22] Wilmington began witnessing what no one dared dream during the wartime heyday. What happened to the pledges and predictions that the same good times would go on and on? The area's once economic backbone was rusting in idleness, facing a slow dissolution ever painful to locals who had been led to believe otherwise.

* * *

---

* Approximately one hundred ships were moored there in a reserve fleet status for several decades. Some were activated for the Korean War, others for Vietnam. By 1980 they were all gone, either sold, given away, or scrapped. To Wilmingtonians, seeing the ships was a reminder of the wartime boom and the war effort, days receding further and further into the past. Camp Davis had been since demolished, but the yard area had become the major state port. A kind of regeneration had occurred.

The Atlantic Coast Line Railroad

Until the shipyard opened, Wilmington was truly a "one-horse town." Everyone worked for the Coast Line. You grew up here, you worked there. It became your life's pursuit, like youths going into the Kentucky coal mines, a career in accounts receivable or freight audits. Not that it was bad. Working for the railroad was steady and comfortable, and as you slowly climbed your way up the corporate ladder you could afford Brookwood, then Forest Hills, then perhaps Oleander.

When war came, the choice of an expanding ACL or the shipyard opened up vast employment opportunities at decent pay. Headquartered at the north end of Front Street, the line was a major participant in national defense, even if overshadowed by the shipyard's immensity. I later found that many wartime residents somewhat overlooked in retrospect the railroad's round-the-clock activity, as if its pre-war preeminence had been usurped temporarily by the new shipyard. But the ACL was the principal means of transportation for military and civilian personnel, cargo, and war materials entering and departing Wilmington. It served the South Atlantic states on 5,100 miles of track with many connections to other systems. Three separate lines radiated from Wilmington tying in with the main track which ran from Richmond, Virginia, to Jacksonville, Florida. A fourth line ran to New Bern.[23]

The ACL's ability to deliver under increasing demands was due in large part to the management skills and tenacity of one man, Champion McDowell Davis. The career of "Champ" Davis ranged from messenger boy in 1893 to being named ACL president in October 1942 as the road headed toward its peak of war service.

Davis was a taskmaster. Lewis F. Ormond was the Coast Line's vice president of accounts until retiring in 1959.[24] "He was on the road a lot," his widow, Mary Belle Ormond, recalled. "He was Champ Davis' right arm in many respects. He was the only man who didn't pay any attention to Mr. Davis' orders. He was the only man who didn't go down to the Coast Line on Sunday. He told Davis, 'I go to church on Sunday.' Life was pretty hectic for all of them [the vice presidents]."

After the war's first year, revenues leaped to $115 million over 1941's $48 million. The ACL had drawn "a larger traffic surge than most other American railroads...[a] disproportionate gain in ACL's business: (1) the cessation of coastal water transport, and (2) the tremendous expansion of military and business activity in its territory." The line carried nearly nine million military and civilian passengers in 1944, as compared to fewer than two million in 1940. Most traveled longer distances than before, many of the civilians because of gasoline and tire rationing. Freight hauling of phosphate and construction rock, fertilizers, sugar, and petroleum were shipped in unprecedented quantities. The total of all freight increased from 18.8 million tons in 1940 to nearly 40 million in 1943. "It seemed as though they would run the wheels off their equipment."[25]

The shift to diesel from coal began too late in the war to help, and the "backbone" remained its five hundred steam engines.* Locomotive power and freight cars (the road had only 23,500 by 1945) were in short supply. Repairing and rebuilding became a necessity.[26] Federal and local officials begged citizens to limit train travel substantially "To Help Shorten the War...Travel Sparingly." The ACL implored, "There is an important and intimate reason why you are requested NOT to travel, unless it is absolutely necessary. For every day the war is prolonged increases the chances that someone close to you will become a casualty. And every way by which you can help *Shorten the War* increases his prospects of coming back to you!...Save all the Pullman and coach space you can for the men and women in the services, for people engaged in war work...."[27]

Nevertheless, seemingly at will, Wilmingtonians substituted travel by train for automobiles. National railroads "are already taxed to the near limit of their facilities, [and] the coming winter will witness a peak in railroad activity," a senior ACL executive stated. "The continued movement of troops and war supplies, the increase expected in passenger travel, and the extra load of hauling the tremendous wheat crop and the potato crop will contribute to the burden....This in spite of the fact that additional equipment is impossible to obtain....Every available locomotive and car has been drafted for war work, and many old units have been re-serviced for use."[28]

One of the city's largest wartime civilian construction jobs, the principal Coast Line headquarters, opened on January 24, 1945, with an open house.† The new Building D at Front and Red Cross, designed to harmonize with the A, B, and C buildings "will afford much needed relief from the present congestion in the general offices...."[29] The flood of people passing through the ACL station continued throughout the war, and the Travelers Aid and other local volunteer organizations did everything possible to ease their burden. For example, the Red Cross fed some three hundred servicemen on Christmas Day 1944 from its station canteen.[30]

---

* Davis had prepared for the summer 1943 nationwide coal mine strike by accumulating stockpiles of coal along the road's five thousand miles of track prior to the president's ordering miners back to work.

† The D building is one of three remaining structures from the days when the ACL's headquarters dominated the north end of downtown. Currently housing the Wilmington Police Department, the out-dated and unsuitable building's future is unclear once the department relocates, but possible demolition looms. The other two structures next to the river form the small Coast Line Convention Center, Wilmington Railroad Museum, and offices.

Often my parents took me to the depot at Front and Red Cross to pick up my sister from college or to watch the round-the-clock tempo of comings-and-goings. Wartime locomotives and train stations left indelible sensations—the odors of "burnt" steel, mountains of coal, dripping oil, and stale-sweet spilled soft drinks; silver wafting smoke, and hot hissing steam; the clamor of steel-wheeled baggage carts hustled by red-capped Negro porters; the clanging of bells; raspy departure announcements; the military uniforms slouched over rock-solid wooden waiting room benches; and men and women embracing in welcome or goodbye.

Another smaller line, the Seaboard Air Line Railroad, called the city home. The Seaboard covered a large South Atlantic territory but had only one connection into Wilmington from its main north-south route, a branch from Hamlet. Its tracks did connect with the ACL's. The SAL depot had far less traffic, but when meeting someone inbound, you had to make sure you were going to the right station.*

* * *

The Port of Wilmington

The state's leading port before the war, until the government designated Wilmington in 1943 to ship lend-lease cargoes and other war materials around the globe, it had experienced a downturn in activity. Port facilities ran along the Cape Fear River from the shipyard north through the downtown waterfront to the Northeast River bridge. Much activity took place around the petroleum terminal piers and storage tanks, a major East Coast petroleum depot. (Some piers and tanks are still in use.)

Considerable efforts for lend-lease authorization had floundered since 1941, and by April 1943, customs revenues were dropping consistently. In spite of the continued inflow of oil into the sizeable petroleum terminals, the reason was the "lack of imports, a reflection on war conditions."[31] "...There is reason to hope that Wilmington may at last share with Charleston [South Carolina] and Norfolk [Virginia] in lend-lease shipments....The Cape Fear River is taking no part in lend-lease commerce, despite the fact that the ships are here, the channel is deep enough for laden Victory ships and port terminals are adequate for a great victory of goods being sent across the ocean."[32] Governor Broughton lobbied hard on the city's behalf, and forecast a rosy future for the postwar port.

After lend-lease exports to Great Britain and the Soviet Union increased, so did other import and export activity. During 1944, the port

---

* The Wilmington Railroad Museum for Wartime Wilmington Commemoration, 1999, created an exhibit of a rural ACL train depot of the war years which remained for some time.

In 1960 both railroads merged and the headquarters moved to Jacksonville, Florida. With it went jobs, population, the economy, and tax revenues. Wilmington saw this as the end of the world.

handled 108,459 tons of war shipping on 16 ship sailings and joined other Atlantic Coast ports in establishing a tonnage record. Wilmington established its own all-time record for exports at $84 million in goods. Practically all commerce in 1944 was lend-lease supplies for Europe, and also war supplies for American armies. Imports declined considerably, however, from wartime retardation of trade and was only $16 million. Exports and imports from and to Wilmington exceeded those of Charleston, the port's main rival.[33] In July the port shipped 12 carloads of pre-fabricated houses to Britain, the first such shipment through Wilmington.

For the three-year period up to July 1945, 36 ships took on 213,000 tons of lend-lease cargo and war material resulting in the greatest payrolls from this activity than any similar period. "The vicissitudes of war have seen new commodities coming into the port for distribution," including coffee, cocoa beans, spices, tea, tin ore, nitrate of soda, and flour.[34] A thriving port stimulated the area's economic growth, a condition that helped get the city through post-war blues created when other wartime commerce evaporated.

* * *

The End of the Line

By August 1946, shipyard employment had drained to about two thousand, anticipating the expiration of work on the Grace Line's SS *Santa Isabel*, its 243rd and final hull. On October 9, the NCSC turned over possession of the $21 million facility to the Maritime Commission. Only 150 employees remained. Formal transfer was made 14 hours and one minute after the company delivered the *Santa Isabel*, more than five years and a half years following the first keel laying. In November, the Commission began offering for sale surplus equipment and commodities from stripped Libertys, "a salvage dealers' picnic."[35] Buzzards circled overhead. In December, "with a skeleton office force engaged in clearing up final details," the NCSC prepared to moved back to Newport

Shipyard apprentice Robert S. "Rob" Pollock, *right*, on the doorstep of the yard apprentice dormitory outside the main gate on Burnett Boulevard, 1943. Pollock later served in the merchant marine. The building, one of numerous shipyard buildings still used in the North Carolina State Port area, is the Marine Corps Reserve Center.

Provided by Pollock

News by year's end.[36] Then all was quiet. The shipyard had vanished. Railroad business and port traffic dipped significantly. It was like the bottom had dropped out. How long would this last? people asked. Was prosperity over?

Floating Drydocks

In April 1944, the first of two floating concrete drydocks for the navy was launched at a small construction facility near the Hilton bridge on the Northeast Cape Fear River. The 389x84' self-contained craft USS *ARDC-1* was the largest drydock ever completed entirely of concrete, and was capable of being towed anywhere. It took almost five months to build and then underwent outfitting here. The skipper came from two and one-half years of commanding naval vessels in the Pacific. "'Drydocks are a new type of duty for me, but I'll learn, I hope.'"[37]

The SS *Zebulon B. Vance* and Pearl Harbor

Launching of the *Vance*, the first keel laid and named for the state's Civil War governor, was long anticipated and widely celebrated as the start of a whole new dimension to Wilmington's economic life and contribution to national preparations for war. It dominated the news for days prior to the event. Headlines in the regular home edition of the *Wilmington Sunday Star-News* of December 7, 1941, proclaimed it, and advertisers gushed over it. Within hours, however, alert editors rushed an extra edition on to the city streets. The *Vance* was swept from the front page. The Japanese had bombed Pearl Harbor.

An army air forces B-17 bomber had flown over the ceremony, "its camouflaged fuselage glistening in the sun, zoomed across the ship as it lay on the ways." The pilot was Wilmington native Lieutenant George S. Boylan, Jr.,[38] soon a decorated combat veteran who was one of three Wilmingtonians with WWII service eventually achieving the career rank of lieutenant general. The *Vance* ended the war as an army hospital ship, the SS *John Meany*. "After many tens of thousands of miles of service as a freighter," the War Department converted her in November 1943.[39]

Army air forces Lieutenant Colonel George S. Boylan, a B-24 *Liberator* anti-submarine warfare pilot, on the cover of *Liberty* magazine of April 17, 1943. Boylan was one of three Wilmington WWII veterans who achieved the rank of three-star lieutenant general before retiring. The others were James Madison Lee, NHHS, '44, and Raymond A. Wheeler of the army. Boylan and Lee still live here.

Provided by Boylan

Chapter 5
"The Invasion of Camp Davis"

Surely we local folks must have thought for a long time that no one was left to guard Camp Davis just to look at our streets, theaters, restaurants and bars, USO buildings, churches, and bus and train stations. It seemed like all the soldiers were in Wilmington on weekends, elbow-to-elbow everywhere. Those awfully long lines for Front Street cafes and the movies, which conditioned us to aim for an early Saturday matinee. The noise, the laughter, the shouts, the wolf whistles, the broken bottles, the fights, the MPs, and the girls. What if we really had to go to war, I mean, what if the Germans were landing at Carolina Beach and the army needed them right away? Would Wilmington be in peril?

Generously mixed with the mass of shipyard and other war industry workers, Marines, airmen, and sailors, along with—not to omit us local citizens who believed we had a right to be there—the soldiers thought Wilmington was a resource to indulge. On a weekend it was one congested madhouse.

Townspeople might have been able to handle just the civilian onslaught, but the additional surge of personnel from nearby armed forces bases from 1942–44 was enormous. Consequently, on nights and especially from Friday evening through Sunday afternoon, as much as possible my family avoided downtown. There the newcomers, transients, and one-nighters tended to congregate. Some Wilmington natives claimed the county's weekend population, including the beaches, doubled under the heavy load. Public facilities were at or exceeded capacity, and ways of doing things moved slowly even after becoming accustomed to the extra demands. Troop and equipment truck convoys of all lengths often monopolized county and city roads from U.S. Highway 17 and Market Street to the shipyard, Fort Fisher, and Bluethenthal Army Air Base. You were led to believe we were literally bursting at the county line seams. Or were we sinking? Or both?

In and around Wilmington, no uniform stood out like army khaki. Most originated in Camp Davis. We didn't blame them for wanting to get away from Holly Ridge, their little nothing, pipsqueak intersection on Highway 17 an hour's bus ride north of Wilmington. (No one from *here* ever went *up there* except to pass through, like my family did on a rare visit with Daddy's relatives in poor Onslow County.) With all the trouble the Davis soldiers might cause, they brought a couple of much-appreciated commodities: cash, and bodies to socialize with our local girls. Wilmington harvested its share of each, and bent over backwards to absorb the soldiers temporarily—perhaps for no more than an evening—with hospitality and open doors. Mothers with sons away in the service cooked many a meal for strangers who might never reappear.

"'Holly Ridge as a whole did not seem to mind the invasion of Camp Davis,'" said native Darrel Ottaway, who ran the Camp Davis Restaurant for many years until it closed in the late 1990s. "'The soldiers were friendly. We liked it. It was exciting. One time they invited the entire little community to come eat. After the troops were fed, we walked through the chow line.'" The PX sold the kids candy, at a shortage everywhere else.[1]

What was Camp Davis and why was it there? Davis was the army's coast artillery and anti-aircraft artillery (AAA) training center, and until the Marine Corps' New River-Camp Lejeune geared up toward its maximum in 1943-44, Southeastern North Carolina's largest military installation.* In early 1941 the army sought a spot on a railroad (this one went into Wilmington) and isolated for its firing exercises into the ocean nearby. Not only isolated, Davis was laid out in the desolate Holly Shelter in rural Pender and Onslow Counties, a pocosin area of swamps, pines, marshes, ditches, thick brush, snakes and other attendant varmints, and on marginal farm land without even bare commercial value. Some say the reason was political influence, but for the life of me I cannot believe Pender or Onslow Counties had that much pull. But someone worked magic. Coincidentally, Onslow landed New River at about the same time. Some also questioned the Navy Department's senses for choosing *that site* for the Marines for similar reasons. Washington surely wasn't looking for another Great White Way or Hollywood to divert our boys.

---

* Lejeune opened as New River Marine Barracks in 1941 and was named Camp Lejeune Marine Corps Base in late 1942. Other smaller army stations in the Wilmington area included an Air Service Command communications repair unit on Castle Hayne Road, the Fourth Corps Area Quartermaster Depot on Nutt Street, MP offices at City Hall and South 8th, a prisoner of war side office co-located on South 8th, a Temporary Harbor Defense office at Carolina Beach, the Transportation Corps on Brunswick Street, and recruiting stations in the post office.

Navy offices included offices for Naval Intelligence, the Assistant Industrial Manager, disbursing, and recruiting in the post office, the Port Director in the Customs House (now Alton Lennon Federal Building), and a receiving station at Maffitt Village. The Coast Guard also had a Life Boat station at Fort Caswell, a Commissary Supply Depot and the Quarterboat "General Frederick Hodgson" at the foot of Princess, a Marine Inspectors office in the Murchison Building, and the Captain of the Port office in the Customs House.

The camp's "good-neighbor" relationship and civic participation with Wilmington thrived through mutual co-existence and dependency. Although the news the camp generated once it swung into operation was that of a continuing, steady hum of operation generating dollars for all its headaches, for area natives the biggest news out of Davis was its beginning and end. More than halfway between Wilmington and Lejeune in Jacksonville, Davis opened for business in April 1941. Its quick construction created economic excitement overnight. Its ultimate closing, on the other hand, was an agonizingly slow bleeding of on-and-off uncertainty on the local economy, a deathbed from the fall of 1944 for the next four years when it shut down without a whimper.*

Of all the area's military services, the army's presence was most prominent. The Marine Corps, with its large contingent at Lejeune, an hour and a half north of Wilmington also on Highway 17, was a distant second.

* * *

Holly Ridge and Camp Davis,
aka "Camp Swampy," and "Swamp Davis," and "Camp Muddy"

A fatality with Camp Davis' demise was the meteoric boomtown of Holly Ridge. The origin, life span, death, and ultimate epitaph of Camp Davis and the North Carolina Shipbuilding Company struck extremely familiar chords.† But the smallest of dots on a road map, Holly Ridge "exploded in gold-rush growth from 28 in 1940 to 110,000 at peak in 1943." (In 1980 it had 486).[2]

"Holly Ridge, prior to last December [1940], was just a store or two, a couple of filling stations, and half a dozen homes," *The State* magazine outlined in May 1941. "Then came the announcement that a huge new AAA [anti-aircraft artillery] base was to be located there....Men came from great distances, including Wilmington, seeking work. Any number of them camped in tents, waiting to be put on the payroll. And when they finally succeeded, they traveled back and forth daily from their homes. Large numbers made

---

* On November 4, 1998, Herman Alberti packed my friend Bill Humphrey and me into his old Jeep Wagoneer for a driving tour of as much as we could see, as far as we could go. Formerly the town mayor and now a realtor who lives on Highway 17 across from the old main post, Alberti was an informative guide and an accommodating, pleasurable host. He had worked at the camp post office during the war. The half-day tour was an excursion Bill and I had hoped to do for many years. I could not have written this book without it.

† Holly Ridge "has no intentions of returning to its former status of a sleepy, roadside hamlet after Camp Davis closes. Realizing that if it is to receive any help, such assistance must first come from its own citizens, a group of residents have...begun plans for a sweater and hosiery plant" that would employ 200-400. It "is setting an example that may well be followed by many other communities...that have reached new heights but now face deflation of their prosperity as the result of approaching peace." [*Wilmington Morning Star*, August 16, 1944] Intentions were not converted into action.

The Camp Davis band in review, 1943. Only a handful of wartime structures exist.
Provided by R. C. "Bob" Cantwell III

the trip on trucks where benches had been placed on each side and a canvas cover installed overhead. Stoves were put in during the cold weather so occupants could keep warm. On trips home after men had received their weekly pay, those same trucks were the scenes of some of the most exciting crap games you can imagine."[3]

Loney Alberti was a telephone operator next door to the post office. "'Local families benefitted from the construction by crowding together in their homes to make room for the boarders. Bulldozers and construction work almost turned the town into a mammoth pig pen. The camp was so wet and muddy that soldiers would carry the women workers in their arms to the buildings where they were employed'....The town's concentration of men and money drew bootleggers and prostitutes, according to reports."[4]

"Our dad (Pop Jones) owned and ran the Peoples Cafe," recalled Charles Jones and Stanley E. Smith, Sr.

> It started as a small hardware [store]....They were hurting for carpenters and all you had to have was a hammer, square and saw to get a job. Later, according to need, he changed it to a cafe. Food became hard to get so he then changed it to a beer joint. He had three young girls working there. All the shops and joints tried to have good-looking young girls to attract GIs to their place. We were about 11–13 years old...and worked in

the joint selling beer. We sold more beer in those years than one could drink in a lifetime, often 100 cases a night. MPs would hang out at Dad's place. As kids we were king. We were accepted and allowed anywhere without a pass. We could play at Farnsworth Hall and buy candy at the service club....Story has it that mosquitoes at Swamp Hollow [in back of the camp] were so bad that they would say, "Shall we eat him here or take him back with us? No, the big ones might take him away from us."[5]

The post became "the focal point of all army activities on the 320 mile Carolina coastline...Seeking isolation from interference to insure uninterrupted training...[the] massive silence is now broken by the din of ack-ack, while the shores near Sears Landing echo the cannonade of larger calibers.* Nor is this the first time that the noise of war has broken the peace of these lowlands, still haunted by the memories of Indians and pirates, slavers and Spanish marauders, Regulators and Tax masters, Green and Cornwallis, and climaxed by the greatest naval bombardment in the world's history at Fort Fisher....Camp Davis has touched the lives of many thousands in this war."[6]

A 1944 Virginia Tech graduate, Joe Cross arrived in Wilmington as a private en route to Camp Davis for officers candidate school.[7] "The army's best transportation awaited us, semi-trailer buses that only a soldier could love. What we expected ain't important. What we got was Holly Ridge, N.C." On Highway 17's eastern side, "the business district was complete with a small general store...a filling station and 'cracker box' U.S. post office." A grand entry tour into camp followed. "Beyond the equipment viewed, there was little to capture the imagination."

Automatic weapon firing was held at Topsail Island Beach because shells fell harmlessly into the water. The beach accommodated gun batteries and fire control directors, radio-controlled drones, and towed targets behind planes were used. One target was a model target radio-controlled plane known as a OQ28A, with twin counterrotating propellers. Sometimes the drones fell toward those firing, causing them to scramble. The searchlights for night tracking exercises could illuminate a target at 10,000 feet. After their 90-day training was completed, the candidates were driven into Wilmington to a downtown hotel where tailors from Rogers-Peet Company, military clothiers, measured them for uniforms. The new second lieutenants received them two weeks later.

"We didn't have time to spend our money because the stores closed at 3 p.m.," remembered Muriel Williamson.[8] She worked at Davis six and

---

* The famous Camp Davis swamps the soldiers wrote home about had more to do with the low-lying land and inadequate rainwater drainage than ecological inheritance. On day one it might be called Camp Swampy, the next day Camp Muddy.

one-half days a week from 7:30 a.m. to 5:30 p.m. Like most Wilmingtonians at the post, she depended on others for transportation. She daily walked to a pickup point to board a free army bus at 3rd and Princess Streets. The ride to work "seemed like forever." The highway was only two narrow lanes, but there was little traffic except mainly military vehicles. Most coworkers in the quartermaster's office were women or army enlisted men. "That's where I learned to smoke." Because she did not have access to the distant cafeteria, and with 30 minutes' time to eat, most of the time she packed her own lunch. Occasionally she and friends ate at a Holly Ridge restaurant. She transferred from Davis to Bluethenthal in 1945.

One significant first occurred at Davis. It was "here at Camp Davis," the official monograph boasted, "that the pioneer steps were taken in developing patriotic and courageous young women pilots to tow target planes, thus freeing male...fliers for combat duty. The WASPs (Women's Airforce Service Pilots) were officially introduced to the world here at Camp Davis and convinced a large gallery of visiting newspaper correspondents that they are a valuable adjunct to the military forces."[9] At least one WASP flyer lost her life towing a target in a 1943 crash when gunners accidentally hit her plane.

My father took me into Camp Davis a couple of times to look around, and the army wife renting at the Humphreys next door drove Billy Humphrey and me occasionally. Once in 1944 the visit had to do with my sister's sweetheart who was stationed there. Carved into my memory is a scene in Holly Ridge where masses of troops were boarding a train to be shipped out somewhere. When I drive through the area today I can visualize row after row of double-decked wooden buildings, bustling company streets, olive-drab vehicles grinding everywhere, and a tawdry lineup of bars, restaurants, and storefronts that beckoned along the highway.

* * *

In February 1944 there began a strung-out series of fits and starts to close the camp or keep it open. As the requirements for AAA personnel and new officers waned with the war's outcome in sight, the army sought to consolidate its training facilities. Officer candidates were immediately funneled into the infantry or other branches.

This happened to Justin Raphael. He arrived at Camp Davis in 1943 via an OCS-prep course at Fort Eustis, Virginia. On receiving commissions as second lieutenants, most of his class shipped out, but he remained to train with the 576th Automatic Weapons unit, a half-tracked vehicle with mounted 50-caliber machine guns. When he returned from leave on New Year's Day 1944, he had orders transferring him to the infantry at Fort Benning, Georgia. "Retreads" were sent to infantry; he went to the officers'

Chapter Five

Lieutenant Justin Raphael, a frequent visitor to Wilmington, 1944. Later fought in the Philippines as an infantry officer. After the war he settled here and married a local girl, Shirley Berger.
Provided by Raphael

basic course. After training troops in Texas for nearly a year, his major came by one day with big news: "'I'm sorry, Raphael. I've got your shipping orders.' I jumped for joy—I was going to get into the war." Dispatched to the Philippines, he landed at Lingayen Gulf in April 1945. One night in the field he put on a pair of striped pajamas for bed—"everybody laughed, it brought up morale." He fought in big Battle of Ipo Dam in June 1945. But he "never did cotton to the C.O."[10]

In September 1944 the army left Davis, of enormous consequence to the folks in Southeastern North Carolina who saw years of spending—"a rich source of revenue"—departing for other points. A caretaker force remained. Over the next couple of years the army air forces and the Marine Corps were temporary tenants. Efforts by local politicians trekking to Washington failed to keep the camp open permanently, and on February 17, 1946, it was deactivated. "At the highest pitch of the training program, large sites in the Fort Fisher and Sears Landing areas echoed to the staccato barking and deep grunts of the AA guns." Now they were all gone.[11]

Davis was not to die. The following month, the navy took custody to begin a two-year rocket-testing program called "Operation Bumblebee." Then after seven and one-half years, Camp Davis rested in peace, but totally void of prosperity. Once in a while over the years, a periodical has run a memory-lane piece on Camp Davis, which mainly only the area old-timers remember even in name. When you travel through the town of Holly Ridge you will make no more than one stop, at the traffic signal intersection with east-west Highway 50. A pole metal state historical marker to the camp is nearby, but it is so brief and incomplete and does no justice to what transpired there. I stop for a look ever so often, hoping to read something new, but the sign never changes. Such is always a nostalgic, empty moment.*

---

* During Wartime Wilmington Commemoration, 1999, the earnest historian and preservationist Cliff Tyndall, whose group interprets Camp Davis history, set up a weekend mini-camp at the intersection. It drew well over one thousand visitors, some of whom took tours of what is

Two and one-half ton truck stuck at Camp Davis, aka "Camp Swampy" and "Camp Muddy," after 1943 snowfall.

Provided by Daniel D. "Dan" Cameron

After the post's abandonment, wrote David A. Stallman, the only historian who has studied Camp Davis in detail, "most leased properties were returned to the original owners. The buildings and structures were auctioned off and salvage companies purchased many of them. A few structures are still being used today. The old fire station and a few barracks are now apartments, the bacon plant [now a packing company] is built around a Camp Davis cold storage and a few local houses have sections from the water treatment building."[12] Some remnants of structures still stand, including columns of Farnsworth Hall where Betty Grable, Dick Powell, and other celebrities entertained, Secretary of War Henry L. Stimson spoke, and heavyweight champion Joe Louis boxed.

Patches of enough battered, overgrown, thinly paved, and all-but-impassable streets remain to give an idea of the camp's interlocking grid. But a real stretch of the imagination is necessary for the observer to gauge a

---

left. Through acquisition of World War II vehicles, equipment, uniforms, and accessories, Tyndall's unit has succeeded in going to lengths to recreate Davis and WWII army life.

In 2000, Evelyn Bradshaw, curator of the Historical Society of Topsail Island's Missiles and More Museum, thanks to the Ottaway family, retrieved a number of photographs and mementoes from the closed Camp Davis Restaurant, once a main administrative building. The museum has a sizeable Camp Davis and WASP collection and is worth a visit.

picture of 1943. Holly Ridge itself of course shrunk drastically, but has expanded into some of the campgrounds near the highway. Several storefronts still stand on the intersection's east side. Most of the camp to the north, including the old air field, is now Camp Lejeune property and used for exercises. The whir of a few Marine Corps helicopters and vehicles is hardly reminiscent of days gone by. If you know how to get to the locals, particularly Herman Alberti, you might be able to see for yourself and turn on your mind and camera. And then there's Betty's Smokehouse on the highway for lunch, maybe the best home-cooked $4.95 meal in Southeastern North Carolina.

* * *

Bluethenthal Army Air Base

The local army-controlled airport underwent several name changes during the war, but eventually was known primarily as Bluethenthal Army Air Base. This was a hybrid of its predecessors: Bluethenthal Field, Wilmington Army Airport, Wilmington Army Air Base, and Bluethenthal Field Army Air Base. Its mission, however, remained consistent as first an anti-submarine warfare and air intercept patrol station, and subsequently a fighter aircraft training base for the balance of the war. Its location in the northern county near Castle Hayne was less than two miles from the city limits. The field was named for aviator Arthur Bluethenthal, the first Wilmingtonian to die during World War I, and was dedicated in 1928.*

The growth of Bluethenthal Field was wrapped in much more government censorship, with less public discussion and awareness, than the construction of the shipyard and Camp Davis. It started months later, even though the army immediately took over the airport the day after Pearl Harbor. By September 1942, expansion of the land, housing, and support facilities was in full swing. Although no details were available, reports were the airport "is considerably larger than it was a year ago." The road leading from Highway 17 at the Winter Park junction north to the airport had been closed, and another portion from Wrightsboro southeast toward the airport was relocated so civilian traffic could bypass the field.[13]

"Good news, even when it's censored to the hilt, is always welcome," opined the *Morning Star* in October. "Wilmingtonians may well be happy to learn that construction of army air forces installations here, at an estimated cost of more than two million dollars, has been approved by the War

---

* On April 24, 2001, Airport Authority officials gave me a tour of the WWII portions of the field. Much of the runway, tarmac, and hard-stand areas in use today were built during the war, and a hangar or two. Of particular interest is the firing range where P-47s bore-sighted their wing machine guns. The pit's steel and wood facade still contains hundreds of pock-marked bullet holes, and even an unexploded 37mm shell. Too bad the public doesn't have access.

Wilmington's airport prior to the war and the hangar of Pennington's Flying Service. The army took over the airport on December 8, 1941, and immediately converted it into the large Bluethenthal Field Army Air Base for anti-submarine B-24s and fighters. It was a major training field for P-47s who deployed to Europe. Some 21 army aircraft crashed in the area killing at least two-thirds of their pilots.
Provided by Anna Feenstra Pennington (NHHS '39)

Department....It is reasonable to assume that when the war is over and the army has left these parts the airmen will have given New Hanover County one of the best fields in this section of the nation."[14] The next day the army released more page-one news announcing plans for a $2 million expansion "to meet the increasing demand of air defense activity in North Carolina's tidewater area...." The amount included $400,000 for runways with the remainder for the military program. The Army Corps of Engineers handled the contracts for construction by civilian firms.[15]

Bombers were already flying out of the airport, and now the public had at least some idea of what was underway. The army's visible perimeter security operation was a deterrent to anyone driving or walking in the area for a closer look inside the fences. Until very late in the war, at the August 1, 1945, air force birthday open house, I probably entered a couple of times with my mother whose Nurse's Aide duties sometimes assigned her to the base dispensary. I remember the awesome picture teeming with military aircraft—especially the P-47 *Thunderbolts* we saw and heard overhead throughout the county—coming, going, and sitting still. Today every time I hear or see a propeller-driven aircraft passing by, instinctively I look up and see a WWII P-47, as if nothing is supposed to change.

The evolution of assigned aircraft supported the base's missions. Lockheed *Lightning* P-38 fighter aircraft attached to the First Air Force

Interceptor Command arrived first, on December 8, 1941, to begin coastal air patrol. Later they were replaced by B-17 *Flying Fortresses*, B-24 *Liberators*, and B-26 *Marauders* of the Bomber Command for Atlantic ASW patrol, and P-40 *Warhawk* fighters. As the U-boat threat abated by mid-1943, the air force was training *Thunderbolt* pilots. The fighters began arriving in August. The airport was also home for support squadrons including one that towed targets for Camp Davis AAA training. The P-47s are the ones locals remember seeing and hearing the most, and learning about their crashes and pilot deaths. While Camp Davis and Fort Fisher khaki was omnipresent on the ground, these roaring aircraft constantly kept the sky painted air force olive drab and silver.

The Bluethenthal Deaths

More newsworthy than any other items out of the army airfield were the public disclosures of area aircraft crashes and resultant deaths. By my count at least 21 planes crashed and 14 pilots died. There were probably more. We read about them in the paper, heard it on the street, and some of my friends witnessed a few of the aftermaths.

Many of the fatal accidents as reported included common threads. Most crashes involved P-47s from Bluethenthal, and 1944 was a very bad year for them. Pilots tended to be 20–21 years old, brand- or fairly new lieutenants, single, and from up north. They were all white. Nearly all were on combat training missions, and causes ranged from engine trouble to pilot error to midair collisions. A number of crashes occurred in or near populated areas, including at the Maffitt Village war housing project, in the Negro community of Love Grove, in Winter Park, near Wrightsville Beach, and near the airport. Several deaths occurred in Brunswick County. Three with fatalities occurred in the vicinity of Camp Davis. On August 1, 1944, two crashes happened at about the same time 50 miles apart, killing both pilots.

On September 29, 1944, two pilots were killed instantly in the same accident. From Bluethenthal, two P-47s collided in midair while on a combat training mission one mile north of Carolina Beach, plunging to the ground and exploding several hundred yards apart. The cause was undetermined, but the collision took place in a sudden severe rain squall. One plane exploded on the east side of Carolina Beach Road into Wilmington resulting in a hole in the ground the side of a small house. On the other side of the highway, a few hundred feet south of the Inland Waterway bridge, the other plane left a hole the size of the average garage. Small fragments were scattered over the countryside. In Wilmington the air base fire engine racing to the scene collided with a Tide Water Power Company bus at 4th and Nun Streets, sending six Negro passengers to Community Hospital.

An ambulance dispatched to that crash scene collided with a passenger car at 4th and Orange. There were no injuries and the ambulance proceeded. Dead: Captain Leo G. Bernatti, Brooklyn, New York, and Second Lieutenant Theodore F. Patti, Bridgeport, Connecticut. Bernatti had served 10 months in Africa prior to duty at BAAB, held the Distinguished Flying Cross and Air Medal with 10 oak leaf clusters, and the Presidential Unit Citation. Patti was a trainee. No property at the scene suffered damage.[16]

By the grace of God, these crashes caused no ground injuries or significant property damage. Several of the pilots had wives living in Wilmington. Some accidents are long remembered. William N. "Bill" Kingoff and friends walked from the North 17th Street neighborhood across the railroad tracks to Bluethenthal to watch the planes. Once they reached a P-47 crash site between south end of runway and Princess Place, in a real swampy area, right after the crash. "You could hear the drone of the planes all day long." His home was about two miles from the end of runway.[17]

The army often maneuvered in the fields of the Swart family in Castle Hayne near the airport. Helen Swart remembered "the girls 9, 10, 11 years old thought those boys [soldiers] were so good looking." The Swart boys got into their tents and messed around with their equipment. The large family lived in Bluethenthal's flight path. There were "so many airplanes in the sky like migrating birds," said Helen. "They rattled the dishes in the houses" when they flew overhead. "It was frightening." One of their farm workers saw a P-47 go down in a nearby field. Bob Swart said the worker "jumped three fences to go get him out of there [safely]." One plane dropped a target nearby.[18] When Emerson Willard was home on navy leave, he watched Bluethenthal planes bombing and strafing Masonboro Island across the Inland Waterway. One crashed on the island's beach. He called the airfield and then rowed his skiff over to the scene. One man died and the other survived.[19]

Emerson Willard (NHHS '39), *left*, and brother Martin Willard, early war.
Provided by Glenn and Miles Higgins

The crash story with the longest tail (or, tale) came to light in March 20, 2000, after lying dormant for 56 years. On February 25, 1944, a *Thunderbolt* was "thought to have crashed north of

Southport....The P-47 lost in the thick ground fog covering the area was piloted by Second Lieutenant Arthur E. Sepanen of Trenary, Michigan, who has been living with his bride of three weeks at 619 Market Street."* Several days later officials "flatly denied...that the piece of an airplane dashboard washed up on the northern extension of Carolina Beach," found by a local resident, was a part of the P-47 searched for since the disappearance. A companion said Sepanen flew into thick ground fog and it was not clear whether he fell into the swamp or ocean.[20] Two March 2000 newspaper items reported that substantial wreckage believed to be from a WWII P-47 had washed up on the beach at Ocean Isle just south of Southport.[21] Was this Sepanen's machine? I think so. I am still hearing from people who saw aircraft wreckage in Brunswick County's Green Swamp.

Wilmingtonians saw plenty of low-flying fighter planes over neighborhoods, some buzzing and dipping their wings. Was there a local connection? Carolyn Holland and friends "were at the age where they were dating all those cute boys from Bluethenthal Field," recalled Virginia Harriss. One pilot named Russ sometimes buzzed the Holland cottage at 314 South Lumina Avenue on Wrightsville Beach, waggling his wings. "My mother didn't like that at all," stated Carolyn's brother Raymond Holland. She dated Russ, but as Virginia said, the parents were more "scared to death about him because they knew nothing about him."[22] The Bluethenthal pilot son of the Borden Avenue A. R. Hardwicks buzzed their house to let his mother know he was coming home. Sometimes the shenanigans caught up. Flight Officer Leroy W. Saunders received a general court-martial for violating "Army Air Forces regulations prohibiting acrobatic flying at low altitude." Investigation found he had flown a P-47 "in the vicinity of the Wilmington municipal golf course." Proceedings were not to be made public until reviewed by higher authorities.[23] (But rarely was there a follow-up public item.)

Nearby soldiers died elsewhere as well as out of Bluethenthal. Andrews Mortuary in Wilmington contracted with Camp Davis to dispose of bodies resulting from training and other deaths there. "A lot of these guys couldn't take it," recalled Richard C. "Dick" Andrews. "The suicide rate at Davis was pretty high." The funeral home removed the bodies in their panel trucks and shipped the remains home. He often went along. "It's something the army wouldn't want to talk about but it was certainly true." Suicides were usually with a pistol. Davis had only a temporary morgue. He considered this kind of work as his contribution to the war effort.[24]

---

* Three Wilmington Negroes were killed, and 23 white Bluethenthal soldiers, members of a search party sent to find this plane, were injured when a civilian car bearing the Negroes struck two trucks of the army convoy eight miles south of Wilmington on Highway 17 at 11:45 p.m. on the 25th. [*Wilmington Sunday Star-News*, February 27, 1944]

Soldiers performing in do-it-yourself show at Bluethenthal Field, mid-war.
Provided by Hannah Block

Unlike Camp Davis, Bluethenthal had a future when the war ended. Since late 1941, the army had invested heavily in enlarging and improving the field's runways, lighting, buildings, radio equipment, and other infrastructure. Expenditures continued well into 1945.[*] Although numbers and operations were trimmed back, the base continued its training mission until being ordered inactive on September 30, 1945. Local plans to inaugurate airline service began. Wilmington's aviation life was taking a giant step forward, most uncharacteristic of other attempts to convert the wartime boomtown into a new definition of postwar normalcy.

* * *

Fort Fisher

The hallowed last bastion of the Confederacy,[†] at the extreme tip of New Hanover County, served as a "detached" (some would say isolated) advanced training and firing site for Camp Davis' AAA school.[‡] Troops

---

[*] "Already regarded by Air Corps [sic] officials as one of the best airfields in the nation for training cadets in advanced flying techniques, Bluethenthal Field will shortly be equipped with...a radio beam unit to guide pilots direct to the field." [*Wilmington Morning Star*, June 19, 1945] "Bluethenthal Field is now one of the largest fields in the country....[It] is capable of handling the largest land planes now in flight and has been host to the Boeing B-29...." [Representative J. Bayard Clark quoted in *Wilmington Morning Star*, November 20, 1945]

[†] Fort Fisher fell in January 1865, opening the Union army to the capture of Wilmington, the last Confederate port to fall.

[‡] An army company of the 104th Infantry was posted at Carolina Beach for much of the war guarding the county's southern beaches.

were shuffled in and out frequently, and its principal advantage besides being on bathing beaches was its closer proximity to downtown Wilmington. How detached were they? Not long after Pearl Harbor, the "lonesome soldiers" of the 156th Infantry put out a call for phonograph records. "Someone gave them a nice record player, but they have no records."[25] These types of requests continued. In February 1943, 29 local groups contributed furniture to the Battery C day room. Eventually Carolina Beach, several miles north, got a USO club. Matters improved, but not necessarily the girls. This resort attracted those from the "country." The best-looking and classiest ones always went to the 2nd and Orange Club or to Wrightsville Beach. To each his own. To Robert Doetsch, "when I was at Carolina Beach I didn't care about coming into Wilmington." Beach bars were so crowded every night that people were three to four deep and shoulder to shoulder getting a drink.[26]

Private Adrian Lawson had been assigned to the Camp Davis band.[27] "The band didn't know we were coming, didn't need us and didn't know what to do with us. They took the easy way out and transferred us to the nearest army base which was Fort Fisher" for duty with the 481st AAA Automatic Weapons Battalion. He was given a 50-caliber water-cooled machine gun. "I had never seen one so it was all new to me....All the streets were made of sand, streetlights were of the 'black-out' type and all the vehicles drove at night with just 'cat eyes,' no headlights. The barracks were small one-story huts with shutters and blackout curtains which had to be drawn at night. We went on several field problems...and dug in the 40mm and 50-cal. guns and simulated firing." In early June 1943 "there was an alert that a German U-boat had been sighted off the coast. The 40mm and 50-cal. guns were lined up on the beach and started firing across the water. It looked like the 4th of July with all the tracers ricocheting off the water. I was never sure if there had been an actual sighting or if it was just another field problem. We never heard anything more about it. Didn't get to Wilmington very often."

What's "Your Comparison of Fisher to Davis?" the *Camp Davis AA Barrage* newspaper asked resident troops. The answers: "Fisher without a doubt. Things are much more compact here with everything at hand....The ocean back here affords us 'Philly' guys with as much enjoyment as does Atlantic City." Also, "Here at Fisher it is much cooler because of the nearness of the Atlantic Ocean and the many trees that block the blazing sun....The transportation to Wilmington is much better." More, "Buses run more often and are less crowded. Carolina Beach is a swell resort. Why don't the guys at Davis come here as our guests for the weekend?" And, "We have the advantage at Fisher because of the social life at Carolina Beach. It is a miniature Coney Island with a boardwalk and carnival get-up."[28]

So, there you had it, Carolina Beach vis-à-vis Holly Ridge. Depended upon where the boys were from, maybe. But in spite of many gyrenes from

Lejeune and Cherry Point flooding Wilmington, who chose to avoid prospects of limited action and marginal girls in Jacksonville, Kinston, New Bern, and Morehead City, and the vastly outnumbered white hats from visiting ships and home-ported patrol craft, Wilmington was definitely an army town. No doubt, a khaki town.

Postscript

Camp Davis was one of the chief experimental stations for developing radar, "the secret 'seeing-eye' device." In the spring of 1942, "for the first time in history, an AA gun was aimed and fired entirely by radar and allied mechanical means." Experiments started there a few months after Pearl Harbor, "and the site became one of the most closely guarded spots in the country."[29] And Fort Fisher was the site of advanced development of the extremely successful anti-tank rocket gun, the bazooka.

Betty Grable

"*Betty Grable Arrives in Wilmington, Appears at Camp Davis Tonight—* Vivacious Betty Grable, Hollywood's blond bombshell with the make-you-wanta-woo personality," made five appearances with the USO show "Hollywood Follies" for a war bond rally. She arrived at the Wilmington train station with her show entourage on August 27, 1942, and then proceeded to Davis. She ate "army chow" in the mess hall with the soldiers, performed, and also performed the following day.[30] The *Sunday Star-News'* "Camp Davis Volley Fire" column reported that "Miss Grable was kept busy signing autographs in Service Club No. 1 later that evening. Every soldier's Aunt Esmerelda, Uncle Quagmire, and Niece Eneecksie must have been mailed plenty of handwritten samples."[31] Holly Ridge

Popular "pin-up girl" actress Betty Grable, *center*, visited Wilmington and Camp Davis in August 1942 to entertain the soldiers.

Provided by Patty Southerland Seitter

resident Herman Alberti caught her show in Farnsworth Hall, the largest and central auditorium.

Grable encountered New Hanover High School boy Richard B. "Dick" Jones that night at the club. At age 14 he worked there as soda jerk, taking the elongated camp bus from Wilmington to work. He made her a banana split. "She took about two bites of it—she wasn't about to harm her figure. I kept the dish for years after."[32]

20,000 for Football, 5,000 for Joe Louis

Camp Davis 24, Wake Forest 20—Camp Davis, N.C., September 25, 1943. "A last-minute fumble, covered by All-American Johnny Mellus of Camp Davis, cost Wake Forest College its first defeat of the season" before 20,000 soldiers, the largest attendance ever recorded at this army camp for any type of event. By contrast, only 7,415 spectators watched Duke's 61-0 win over Richmond at Durham.[33]

The *AA Barrage* newspaper, Camp Davis, January 22, 1944—"Joe Louis Here. Boxing, always a strong attraction for AA soldiers stationed here, broke all existing attendance records...when fully 5,000 Farnsworth Hall fans jammed every bleacher and ringside seat, occupied all available floor space, and actually clutched over-hanging rafters to witness an all-star ring show brought to them by world heavyweight champion Sergeant Joe Louis and his cross-country exhibition company."[34]

Chapter 6
"The Guy Who Pushed Him in Already Rented It"

While my sister was away at college for the first 18 months of the war, my parents joined the multitudes of Wilmingtonians renting rooms to servicemen and war workers. Until June 1943, a Camp Davis army officer made his temporary home in Lib's room and had some run of our two-story, three-bedroom, two-and-a-half-bath, Colonial-style house including meals. Other GIs shared our home. One moved out to get married. The one who stayed the longest was Lieutenant William McGee. When Lib visited on weekends and holidays from Agnes Scott, she returned to her room next to mine, and I slept with a parent while "McGee" took my bed. Once she graduated, she came home to work at the shipyard, and "McGee" got orders for overseas. What I remember the most about him is the military souvenirs he brought me, a couple of which I have today. I'm sorry I can't recall where he later served, but Mother corresponded with him for several years after the war. Then contact with him disappeared.[1]

If a story about the critical housing shortage in wartime Wilmington needs to be placed in the record, then this one might say it all. In varying forms it came from multiple sources; so we can assume it had a ring of truth. Early in the war a swimmer drowned at Greenfield Lake. On the shore, a man watched the floundering man recede beneath the waters. Before he disappeared the man ashore yelled out to him asking him where he was living. He got the answer, left the scene, and went to the drowning man's landlord. He wanted the room. "You're too late. The guy who pushed him in already rented it."[2] Yes, finding a place to live was that difficult, perhaps the single most severe problem on the area home front.

Housing was most acute in 1942 because of the influx of servicemen and war workers, and temporary defense housing projects took time and money to construct. People had to stay somewhere in the meantime. City and county residents simply were unprepared to host so many transients. No one had the experience, but together we were forced to adjust quickly.

By June, many shipyard workers had quit their jobs because suitable homes for their families were lacking.

Defense Housing Chairman Henry R. Emory reported, "'The labor problem is one of the foremost problems that the shipbuilding company has to meet....[It] cannot produce ships on schedule without the cooperation of citizens....Every householder and property owner here can do an immense service to the war effort by helping to provide shelter....'" He asked for registration of all available rooms, apartments, and houses. "'Hardly a single dwelling is on file at the Home Registration Office....Wilmington is already desperately overcrowded, and there are many families who cannot find living quarters. Four or five thousand more persons will likely be added to the payrolls of the shipyard alone in the next 60 to 90 days....Our citizens are going to have to make room for the newcomers. It is urged that they do so as a patriotic gesture. It is one of the best ways the public...can help the war effort.'"[3] This must have been one of the most influential statements of the war locally, because it worked.

* * *

The Need

No plea, none, was repeated as often and in so many ways by so many voices as that for rooms. Here on one hand you had the federal and local governments working hard spending lots of money together to build shelters for people whose lives were uprooted to support the war effort, and striving to keep them filled. For the surge period this temporary-permanent housing solution worked. On the other you had most Wilmingtonians—but not all—from Forest Hills to Dry Pond, doing their best to comply by turning their homes into transient hotels, and opening their privacy to yesterday's strangers. Rationing, U-boats, air-raid drills, and jam-packed movie theaters—so what. To tolerate such discomforts and fears amounted to little compared to enduring the invasion of one's home and being "put out." Southern hospitality only went so far. Almost everyone I spoke with felt that way. What did spur homeowners to act was a lofty sense of patriotism and a desire to do something with *instant impact* for the war effort. That overrode most trepidations, and the assumption that everybody else was doing the same thing in a small town where who-was, and who-wasn't, circulated quickly. It didn't take long to get over the initial uneasiness and get on with it.

In spite of this generally positive response, the area simply was unable to match every need with available shelter. The city in November 1942 established a War Housing Center, headed for the duration by insurance executive Louie E. Woodbury, Jr., to work as an arm of the Housing Authority of the City of Wilmington (HACOW) as the agent for the

National Housing Authority. His job was either to find or make rooms or to "convert buildings into dwelling units." The emphasis was on quartering servicemen and war workers. Momentarily forgotten was the housing need for new teachers to handle the exploding numbers of students.

Authorities literally paid owners to chop up a number of large properties into multiple residences. By year's end, some 280 apartments for essential immigrant war workers and others had been converted. Shipyard worker H. G. Bryant cut up his house in the 300 block of South 3rd into five apartments and had no trouble renting them.[4] Mary Cameron Dixon's family at the four-bedroom 6 Church Street house felt patriotic but would not "turn every inch of your home into housing." Her mother instead took in one boarder in one room.[5]

A finished carriage house was far superior to the 50 or so condemned structures some people found as housing. "'If the building code were enforced these people would be thrown on the streets with no place to go,'" Woodbury predicted.[6] Within days the city began condemning sub-par dwellings. Mayor Bruce B. Cameron promised an "aggressive policy toward elimination of the undesirable homes." What can't be done during the war will be finished post-war.[7] Realtors such as Foster-Hill sold the "Victory Home" to help solve the problem, and built some 80 of these five-room dwellings in the eastern section of the city just off Princess Street Road.[8] Woodbury praised county beach cottage owners "for their patriotism in deciding to remain in town this summer so that their beach property could continue to be occupied by army and war worker families."[9]

From June 1943 to June 1944, the housing center placed five thousand people in apartments in a period when employment had declined. Patriotic owners improvised to accommodate those in need. "We were just swamped at our house," said Addie Lee Gaylord, and couldn't rent a room to her High Point friend Doris Tienken who had come to work at Camp Davis. So, they put a cot out on the screened porch and she slept outside all summer.[10]

R. E. Corbett's mother, Gladys Corbett, converted three rooms in their Winter Park home into bedrooms for officers and wives and provided them meals. The arrangement compressed R. E. and his brother and sister into one room.[11] While son John J. Burney, Jr., was in the army, his mother, Effie Burney, rented two of their three rooms. Brother Louis slept on the living room couch. The first couple rented to was from Oregon. She thought she was going to the deep South and brought nothing but summer clothes. Mrs. Burney fed the renters from her Victory garden, sold poppies for the American Legion Auxiliary, and worked in civilian defense. She did her part for the war effort while her circuit-riding husband, Judge John J. Burney, was frequently away.

At the end of 1943, civic pride and room availability peaked. Wilmington landlords had offered 28,191 places for rent, the large majority in homes, apartments, and housekeeping rooms. The WHC had serviced 77 percent of newcomers who applied in 1943, but finding housing in 1944 figured to be more difficult because of the declining number of vacancies. A new shelter crisis ensued. "One indication that the invasion of Europe is rapidly approaching is to be found in the increasing number of Wilmington visitors. This may sound paradoxical, particularly as the movement of troops is away from and not toward the city....Wives, parents and other relatives, learning that their menfolk in uniform are soon to be moved out, make all haste to visit them near their quarters."[12]

People tried to find shelter on their own without government agency assistance. The newspaper "want ads" were full daily with prospective renters, and rarely from anyone offering. Classified ad, 1942: "Homely nondrinking family desire to rent near bus line; references."[13] In 1943, "Refined considerate lady desires permanent room and bath preferably near 2nd and Orange Streets."[14] And, the rarity, "Rooms, Colored Section—720 Ann. Shown by appointment only. Write Box TGM, *Star-News*."[15] Or private agencies acted on their behalf. "Need Rooms" became a familiar request. "Rooms for married couples and young women are being sought by the USO Women's Club."[16] There actually was the problem of finding places for women in a system geared toward men. In early February 1943, the Housing Center asked residents to "open their houses to young couples and single girls." Over one hundred such were on waiting lists, a "really serious" condition. Teachers, predominantly young women, had to share rooms. "...Many persons are hesitant about renting rooms to couples and girls because they felt that they may prove undesirable."[17] No one could say why.

By October 1943, "with all respect for the splendid work of the USO home for women at 3rd and Grace" and the Catholic USO center, Wilmington still required "a working women's hotel where some of the hundreds of girls and young women...may have a home-like environment at reasonable prices....Without their services many a business firm would be unable to continue...."[18] The situation for women never really improved. I knew no families who allowed female boarders, and I wonder now if mine would have if facing the choice.

Temporary shelter for one-nighters or other short-term visitors without advance arrangements was altogether another story. Area USOs and Travelers Aid case workers assumed the burden and literally scrambled on weekends. These transients found sleeping accommodations in many private homes for weekends, and church basements and meeting rooms were crammed with cots for soldiers on Saturday nights.

My Church of the Covenant Presbyterian (after a June 1944 merger it became St. Andrews-Covenant) was a key location in 1942–43. My father chaired the Defense Service Committee of church officers who oversaw the program. From December 12, 1942, through May 22, 1943, "we have furnished sleeping accommodations to 1,053 men of all branches of the service," his report read. "States represented 45 and the District of Columbia. [Most] taken care of have been OCS men from Camp Davis," and officers and enlisted men from camps all over eastern North Carolina.* An average of 43-plus per week used the facilities. "On several occasions men traveling through here carrying troops to distant points have found sleeping quarters here." Donations paid for laundry and janitor services, averaging $6.89 per week.[19]

From its outset, Camp Davis had a direct interest in housing availability for its civilians and military personnel and exercised due influence. Local people felt obligated to assist the army, and a few saw an opportunity for excessive financial gain. General Frederick H. Smith chided local real estate firms when he suspected some landlords of deception or evasion, and was determined "'to secure the indictment of any whose activities are in conflict with the laws for the control of rents.'"[20] Davis officials maintained cordial working relationships with Wilmington and New Hanover County government officials and civic leaders, who went to lengths to cooperate in all matters including housing availability and rent controls. But officer and enlisted wives "were at the mercy of unscrupulous property owners," according to local historian Everard H. Smith. "In April 1943, a scandal erupted when it was revealed that some of the most prominent citizens of Wilmington were renting their beach cottages to army wives for the fall and winter months [in unheated and non-winterized houses], then evicting them for personal occupancy during the summer." The OPA became aware and intervened. The women stayed.[21]

In June 1943 an acute housing shortage developed within Davis' commuting distance. "Military personnel transferred to this post are advised that families should not be brought to this vicinity until adequate quarters are first obtained."[22] Seemingly always unsettled, in July 1944 the cry for

---

* In August 2000, while sorting out the church's voluminous old records and files for further disposition, I found the committee's ledger, which included names and hometowns of visiting weekend servicemen. The signature of George H. Garniss, Camp Davis officer candidate, jumped off the pages at me. He is my brother-in-law. I telephoned him at their home in Issaquah, Washington, and asked where he was on the Saturday nights of September 11 and 18, 1943. Surprised by the question, he replied probably at my house courting my sister. When I told him where he had spent the night, oh yes, he remembered sleeping at the church. Fortunately for him, Daddy was not on duty there those nights. Daddy did not cotton to Yankees (George was from New Jersey) and did everything within reason, it seemed, to discourage Lib from getting serious with him. Mother, *even more* a Southerner, took the opposite approach. See chapter 11 for more on this story.

permanent housing sounded again: "Take Them In...another acute stage." As Davis began shutting down, soldiers continued to arrive in the area believing family housing was available only to find otherwise. It appears that no matter what processes were tried, local authorities were never able to grasp fully a mechanism for balancing housing supply and demand. The situation eased only after Davis closed in October and shipbuilding tapered off by year's end.

Only by February 1945 did local officials get a semblance of control, with nearly 20,000 residential units being registered (most in occupancy) on top of public housing. With Davis' reactivation in the spring, the newspaper urged landlords not to hold back units.* "Remember, housing can be hoarded just like any other commodity vital to the war effort."[23] The pendulum briefly swung back, but soon any housing requirements from Davis dried up again.

* * *

Kenneth Murphy's Brookwood family kept many soldiers in their home, and "all seemed to come from Detroit."[24] Young women, wives of shipyard workers and soldiers, went door to door looking for rooms to rent. "It became your duty to rent out any spare room you had. My mother rented out my [navy] brother Marvin's room and I slept in my sister's room. When she went off to college Mother rented hers. They got a cot and put it in the dining room for me to sleep on. I did not get my room back until after the war was over. [Families] would be there about 12 weeks....We had only one bath, so that was always a challenge to get in and out of the bathroom before someone else needed [it]."

Marine George J. Green was stationed at Camp Lejeune from July-October 1943.[25] "In mid-July my fiancée came to Wilmington from Chicago and we planned to wed. We were very fortunate to secure a small room on the main street of Wilmington lined with stately houses and trees" with the Bacon family. "For our honeymoon we secured another accommodation with a small kitchen but unfortunately spent the whole night killing bed bugs, and I assure you there were a lot of them. The Bacons felt sorry for us and insisted on us moving back with them." After training all day Green hitchhiked to Wilmington. He arose at 2:30 a.m., walked to the White milk

---

* Federal and local authorities deemed any local property owner with space to rent as a landlord, thereby subject to OPA rent ceilings and other restrictions, including immediate registration of availability of space. To a degree, landlords were unable to take advantage of the wartime boom. Tenants had recourse to housing officials and the OPA with complaints of all types, including rents charged. Authorities ordered landlords to decrease rents or make accommodating adjustments to their properties. As long as a renter paid, he could not be removed unless violating a substantial tenancy obligation. In June 1945 the Wilmington Real Estate Board sought a rental increase, pointing out that since 1942 national family income had risen 44 percent but rentals were unchanged. It soon became moot.

company, and made a deal with the truck driver who was to deliver milk to the tent camp. "After loading the truck I drove first to the rifle range and then on to tent camp while the truck driver slept. The only license I had was to drive a Marine vehicle. When I got to tent camp I took a quart of milk and hit the sack. At 7:30 the guys would awaken me and they would bring cereal and fruit from the mess hall."

After their honeymoon in September 1942, Lieutenant Claude and Mary Daughtry returned to live at Wrightsville Beach.[26] Before the wedding he had gone door to door looking for a vacancy and advertised in the *Star-News* offering a reward. His phone "rang off the wall—people mistakenly thought I was offering an apartment." Finally he found out a sergeant was moving from a one-bedroom completely furnished apartment (at $65 per month) on the oceanfront. Daughtry maintained contact, kept a file folder with leads, and was ready to move in immediately.

Few owners rented to both single men and women at the same time. Dorothy Ames "Dotty" Harriss' mother did, to young out-of-town girls working in Wilmington, and army lieutenants who slept in the back. "It was like a house party there."[27] At the time couples had to show a marriage license to get a room together. Once a couple came to the door of Elizabeth Bell's (NHHS '39) house asking for a room, saying they were married. Her mother told them they had no room, and the couple turned away. "After they left, Mother turned to Father and said, 'I don't believe they were married.'"[28]

At one time in 1941 four Camp Davis officers lived at Catherine Solomon's house in Forest Hills. Her mother, Louise Solomon, operated a USO information center and helped get soldiers rooms.[29] High school student James M. "Jim" Lee had a "hero worship" of the P-47 pilot who with his wife rented a room from his mother at 10th and Market.[30] "There was always something going on at our house," Caroline Newbold remembered fondly. Even with six children, the family rented rooms to soldiers and shipyard workers, people "from every walk of life." Sister Jessie Newbold (NHHS '39) later wrote a wartime memoir, "Ma Rents Rooms."[31]

Millard J. "Jim" Fountain's father, M. J. Fountain, Sr., rented a bedroom to shipyard workers and built a spare rental room. One tenant was Gene McWathy, who later helped build Disney World. Pearl Winner's Carolina Beach home was called "the Mickey Mouse house" with all its shipyard worker renters.[32] W. Eugene "Gene" Edwards remembered Wilmington as crowded and congested, with boarding houses renting beds for 24 hours for workers on three shifts, changing the sheets between sleepers. People commuted into the city to work, "tried to stay all week, go home on weekends."[33] This widespread three-shift routine was called "hot bunking" or "hot bedding."

* * *

The Projects

Three days after the nation entered the war, the executive director of the HACOW ordered guards placed on all five defense housing projects to "'guard against a possible sabotage,'" pointing out that both the shipyard and Camp Davis "'could be seriously affected if...the water supply for the projects became contaminated.'" He also made plans for air raid shelters.[34] His job got tougher from there.

As 1941 opened, our local Housing Authority, the state's first, operated two public housing projects for low income families, both completed in 1940. They were the Charles T. Nesbitt Courts for 216 white families on South Front Street, and the New Brooklyn Homes for 246 Negro families on North 5th,* both referred to as "slum clearance projects."[35] Dr. W. Houston Moore served as the HACOW chairman, and Henry R. Emory as executive director. At the time of Pearl Harbor, Wilmington had 1,737 public "war housing" units in the Nesbitt and Brooklyn complexes and in four defense housing projects: Greenfield Terrace (defense workers), Lake Forest (noncommissioned officers), Hillcrest (Negro NCOs), and Hillcrest extension (Negro defense workers). From then until the end of 1943, 3,762 more units were added.

War housing projects had to be approved by the National Housing Authority in Washington. Construction overlapped, but with the exception of Hillcrest they were all in the same general area of South Wilmington. Through a "declaration of taking, the Federal Government condemned and acquired title to land and paid the owners. The HACOW acted as the federal agent in arranging purchase of these sites and for the construction. Incrementally done, the work kept contractors humming throughout 1942, the height of the building boom. In the case of Maffitt Village, in June 1942 the government acquired some 123 acres near the southern end of the shipyard, and deposited a check for $15,609.56 to pay for the approximately 50 parcels.[36]

In the Wilmington area's largest nonmilitary wartime construction program, the federal government and local authorities from 1941–43 expended $16 million to provide temporary low-rent public shelter for area servicemen and workers at the shipyard and in other war industries and their families. "Public Housing Reaches Great Proportions During War" summarized a December 1945 headline. The story claimed that between May 1, 1940, and November 1943, Wilmington added more people to its population in one year (1942) than it had added in the two hundred previous years, and

---

* In January 1943 the name was changed to honor Dr. Robert R. Taylor, a Wilmington native, "an outstanding Negro educator." Until his death the previous month, Taylor was vice principal of Tuskegee Institute and an associate of the late Booker T. Washington. [*Wilmington Sunday Star-News*, January 10, 1943]

that the city's population rose from eighth to third in the state.³⁷ Overall, the Housing Authority built 5,495 units at an average cost of $2,893.

"In quick succession, war housing projects sprang up" in Lake Forest, Hillcrest, and Maffitt Village.* Units included masonry dwellings for two or four families, prefabricated de-mountable houses for shipyard workers, temporary dormitories, and furnished war apartments made of gypsum board construction. Maffitt Village was designed to be temporary in cost, construction, and livability. Its average unit cost was $2,566, including land, grading, utilities, and overhead. Rents ranged from $20 for a one-bedroom apartment to $34 for three bedrooms. Earl Page's family moved "upscale" to Vance Street in June 1942. "These were wooden houses, coal stoves for heating, kerosene stoves for cooking, but everything a little bit larger than [where we previously lived] at Fort Fisher. Dad [jokingly] summarized the living style by noting that we lost about a house once a week due to kerosene stove explosions...."³⁸

By August 1942, the seventh project was underway on 115 acres on the Carolina Beach Road within a mile of the shipyard for something new called "duration dormitories," so named "because of the speed with which it can be constructed with a minimum of critical materials...." And, the dormitories "can be removed after the need for it ceases to exist to avoid postwar ghost towns."³⁹ By December, the dormitory construction was completed and the Maffitt project's first 800 units were occupied. By July 1943, renters occupied 4,265 war housing units. With completion of the expanded Maffitt project, 6,029 families or individuals were living in government housing here. For the 5,037 war housing units it managed in 1944, the HACOW reported profits of $727,257, down from the year's budgeted amount by $87,096. This was due primarily to Maffitt Village vacancies as shipyard employment dropped. The federal government owned all such units and collected all profits after expenses.⁴⁰

As 1946 dawned, the area obviously required much less public housing, and the Housing Authority took steps to consolidate its wartime gains for the city's future. "'That there are still slums in Wilmington cannot be denied. Neither can it be denied that, with the heightening of the tempo of port activity plus the establishing of new industries, Wilmington is about to embark upon an era of expansion which will fully justify the name given the port in 1732. The name was "New Town."'"⁴¹ Such optimism lasted only so long. By early fall, officials had removed the excess structures from Maffitt Village, "once a haven for war workers seeking an abode in Wilmington...."⁴²

---

* The masonry Hillcrest project was for Negro noncommissioned officers and war workers and their families. Maffitt Village was named for Captain John Newland Maffitt, a local Confederate blockade runner hero in the Civil War. Intended for wartime residences, many units in Maffitt Village, Hillcrest, Nesbitt Courts, and Lake Forest are still occupied as either subsidized housing, public housing projects, or private dwellings. Masonry homes in Lake Forest are in the latter category. The units are prominent reminders of the war effort.

The Rolands' Garden House[43]

On a Sunday morning in October 1942, Mr. and Mrs. H. M. Roland stopped their Lincoln to pick up two Camp Lejeune Marines who were leaving St. Mary Catholic Church. Mrs. Roland, Perida, invited them to lunch "if you have the time." One of the Marines was Brooklyn, New York, Private Vince Norako. He "charmed her with his Brooklyn accent" and said, "Ma'am, we've got until 6 o'clock tomorrow morning." They went to the Rolands' Brookwood home and spent the afternoon.

The day worked out, and more weekend visits naturally followed, particularly from five original enlisted men "regulars." Mrs. Roland remembered, "Feeding those Marines—'sons'—was a problem. Sunday dinner routine escalated into the whole weekend." The family cook was Negro Annie Barden. Said Norako, "She loved to cook for us and of course we made her feel good."

One Saturday Norako helped the Salvation Army's captain count money and got a bunk in the big hall. "When I woke up on Sunday morning, I found there were a lot of strange people all around me." He told Mrs. Roland about this, and she then let him sleep in the garden house. The Rolands' Marines began sleeping in the garden house. Mr. Roland "was one of the best real men I've ever known. I improvised a plan. If we knew we were coming in for a weekend, one of us boned up on sports, one on business, etc. We took turns answering his questions. [County school superintendent] Mr. Roland thought we were all smart young men." Daughter Dorothy, then working in the Pentagon in Washington, said "these boys looked after [her younger] sister Mary and the boys who were trying to court her."

Perida told Vince that Dorothy liked chocolates.[44] He noticed her photograph on top of the piano. "Who is that lovely lady?" So, he bought 80 cents worth of Hershey bars at the PX and sent them to Dorothy "from your big brother in the Marine Corps." She knew "approximately" who he was—her mother had written her about the visits. One Saturday night Vince hitchhiked to Wilmington. His ride left him at the 3rd and Market YMCA in the rain. Mr. Roland drove over to pick him up, and he jumped into the back seat. Dorothy was in front. "Hello sister; hello brother," they exchanged. Vince fought on Okinawa. The two were married at Fort Myer, Virginia, in October 1945.

Over the years the Rolands tried to keep contact with the 22 boys and did with five. At their 60th wedding anniversary in November 1980, the five gathered to help celebrate, describing what Southern hospitality had meant to them over 35 years before. "The Rolands experienced normal parental concern as each of the boys went overseas and parental gratitude as each returned," Vince wrote. "They did their part to connect Lejeune to Wilmington during the war."

Chapter 7
"Our Generation Sure Got It in the Neck"

If one memory stands out above all in my wartime school days, it is those frequent instances when my head wandered from its second-story classroom to the Pacific jungles or the North African desert. While staring from my desk out the open window through the tall pines, I never let my lack of artistic capabilities deter the need to draw what I saw—hurriedly sketched battle scenes. B-17s dropping bombs, Sherman tanks firing cannons, Focke-Wulf 190s falling from the sky, Japs taking bullets, and Marines assembled in formation. The images were clear to me but never to my teachers. This very act of artwork, of course, helped the war effort. The Allies will prevail!

On my sentimental journey I discovered the desks and windows still in place, but updated. The worn, dark-stained wooden floor creaks even more. The hinged wall windows facing the hallway remain, with coats of paint the only difference. (I could never understand why they were there, except for increased air circulation since we had no air conditioning, but we did have heat.) The blackboards—not modern whiteboards—are used now as bulletin boards. Like remembrances of the good old days, some things never wear out. I still have so many of these sketches I now wonder why my teachers didn't confiscate more of them. Surely they tolerated. How could I have been that clever to disguise my work? It was the war effort. *

During a 1998 visit to the school, my first in decades, a cursory search of the boys' upstairs restroom revealed no "WJ" initials I confidently scratched into the walls for all-time. Coats of paint are like vanishing cream. The plumbing had been modernized at least once. The school remains a "relic-in-progress," highly functional and successful educational grounds amidst a sea of nostalgia.

---

* In January 2002, responding to the increased patriotism following the September 2001 terrorists attacks, my Wilmington Rotary Club in a project I put together donated some four hundred American flags to county public schools to fill each classroom needing them. Our symbolic presentation was a ceremony on the steps of Forest Hills, the oldest county elementary school in continued use. My old school. Where else?

On June 9, 1945, to the theme "America Singing" presenting the spirit of America in song from early times to the present, 222 seniors graduated from New Hanover High School in ceremonies at Legion Stadium. A number were missing. "In this fourth wartime commencement, many of the students are graduating under unusual circumstances," for nine boys had entered the armed forces during the school year and received their diplomas in absentia. John Weddell Harriss, then in the service, was home on leave and on the platform in uniform to receive his diploma. Two boys had completed credits after entering the service, and three seniors finished credits in summer school and were already in the military. One was Doris Iretta Hayes, then in nursing school.[1]

For many Wilmington-area students, high school days, traditionally the most unforgettable, enjoyable, and carefree times of their lives, were derailed or wrecked by wartime obligations. Read it from columnist Ruth Millett in May 1943:[2]

> High Schoolers Should Have Fun While They Can; Old Before Their Time—The high school kids had been worried for weeks over whether they would have a prom, the social high spot of the year....Finally the principal overrode the protest of a group of parents that a junior-senior dance wouldn't be patriotic and gave the go ahead sign....Most of the boys at the dance would soon be in uniform and the girls looked forward to jobs, or nurses' training, or college, streamlined to three years, with most of the fun cut out....After all, they are just kids and yet the boys are facing military service and the girls are having a pretty insecure time of it themselves. Why can't parents see that youngsters ought to have some fun—and that if possible they should still be able to count on the important highlights of their lives?
>
> As one 17-year old puts it: "Our generation sure got it in the neck. Just when we were old enough for drivers' licenses—there wasn't any gas or tires for us. Just when we were ready to start dating—they started telling us it wasn't patriotic to have dances in wartime. And just when we were thinking of pairing off and 'going steady' the boys started being drafted"....Many of them are already assuming adult responsibilities....Many a 15-year old girl now does the family cooking and looks after a couple of younger children while her mother and dad both work in defense plants.

* * *

Rapidly Changing Times

When the war started, New Hanover County had 23 public grammar (elementary) schools, nine inside the city limits. "According to the 1939 federal census, [the county] had a lower percentage of illiteracy than any other county in North Carolina except one." The 1941 enrollment was white 7,192, and Negro 3,574, with 2,392 students in the white high school, New

Hanover, and 731 in the Negro Williston Industrial (High) School. Other schools included two parochial schools of 227 students, one private school offering grammar and high school work, three business colleges, and one private law school. The public school term was 180 days.[3] A week after Pearl Harbor the county Board of Education committed to building nine new schools "to meet the needs of a vastly expanded enrollment."[4]

The workload was only beginning. From then on, the board together with the county government and federal funding assistance worked diligently to provide for the area's educational needs. Achieving that goal was attributable to strong community involvement and the exhaustive professional efforts of two public officials in particular, Board of Education Chairman Dr. John T. Hoggard, and Superintendent of Education H. M. Roland.

The schools first reached maximum capacity by early 1942, swollen by Camp Davis and shipyard worker dependents. School officials saw "no material changes in enrollment as the result of troop movements since the beginning of the war since very few of the army officers and men leaving the county are taking their families with them."[5] Some remained for the duration, others left in between to be replaced by incoming families. The cycle tapered off only after Camp Davis closed in late 1944. More pupils meant a requirement for more teachers. The absence of men in uniform necessitated replacing any men with more women instructors.

"Dear Williston," the Negro high school named Williston Industrial School, at the corner of 10th and Ann Streets, ca. 1945. Principal F. J. Rogers kept an effective rein on academics and student life of the "Tigers," and was active in the war effort. The building is now Gregory Elementary School.

Provided by Cornelia Haggins Campbell

The school board rushed through a major new construction program in 1942. The two-story modern brick Chestnut Street School opened in January 1943, designed to hold 800 students in grades 1–8 in 22 classrooms with a gymnasium, cafeteria, and library. Many of its new students transferred from Isaac Bear, which was then used as an annex for NHHS after 31 years as a grammar school.[6] Lake Forest and Sunset Park Schools opened at the beginning of the 1942–43 scholastic year, Lake Forest serving the housing project area's 1,059 homes, and Sunset Park that section's population.

The board authorized additions to three government-financed edifices including Winter Park and the Negro schools Williston Primary and Peabody. Williston, which serviced pupils south of Market Street, received a $40,000, two-story wing and auditorium to seat 800, and six new classrooms and a cafeteria. Peabody, for students north of Market, added four classrooms. "No pupil will be denied admission because of insufficient rooms or teachers," the newspaper forecasted. "No one...who has no understanding of construction problems under war conditions, can realize just what has been accomplished in the short time available...."[7] Buses transported children to schools, but those who lived less than two miles from their school were required to walk.

Approximately 350 teachers began school on September 11, 1942, to service an initial registration of 11,256. Pupils continued to pour in and by resumption of classes after Christmas the total was 12,900, and a month later, 13,241. Where did we put them? Well, 2,614 jammed into the high schools, and 1,357 into my third grade. The county soon ranked third in the state in enrollment. Carolina Beach School, designed for 280, had 510. By using space not intended for classrooms, new Sunset Park handled 579 instead of 480. The old Tileston School was teaching 1,252 in a building designed for 950. New Hanover High had approximately the same number as the previous year, 1,900, attributed to so many youths in the armed forces or working in war industries. It jumped up to the top of state high schools in enrollment and held that position for two years.

If not shortages in teachers and classrooms, then inevitably schools fell victim to the 1943 area food shortages. After one of his numerous trips to Washington seeking aid, Superintendent Roland said many more children depended on schools for lunches because of point rationing "'and the fact that more of their parents are working in defense jobs and have no time to prepare lunches.'"[8] My mother packed a sandwich for my lunch in one of those classic tin lunch boxes, later of wood when it wore out. That way I could eat outside. Occasionally I ate in the school cafeteria in the basement, also our air raid shelter, like on rainy days.

Roland's round-the-clock leadership continued through the summer of 1943. He obtained federal funding for continuing the county's forward-looking day care program* "by means of which young children are provided with food, rest, and recreation in supervised centers while their parents work in war industries."[9] He signed four hundred teachers and opened a new Negro primary school in Maffitt Village, and instituted "changes in courses of study and progress in old established courses better to fit the oncoming generation for the tasks ahead in the post-war world."[10] His high school "classes in defense work have accomplished the phenomenal."

Students registered in January 1944 were 9,988 white and 4,102 Negro. Teachers in congested areas carried a pupil overload of approximately 20 percent. One of the great difficulties "has been to accommodate the transient children of defense workers. In one school building...[were] pupils who had attended school the previous year in California." The teaching staff was from 36 states, impossible to envision three years earlier. "It has been necessary to adjust the viewpoints of both new pupils and teachers to the North Carolina courses of study, and at the same time see that no time is lost or progress delayed."[11] My class was fortunate to have local teachers of long standing, Mrs. Emma K. Neuer, Miss Miriam McEachern, and Miss Harriett McDonald, indelible names as years pass.

"The 'most normal' school year (which ended June 8) since Pearl Harbor" is how Roland described the situation in April 1945. Enrollment figures continued fluctuating. About 600–700 dropped out during the session, most losses to the armed forces, but approximately 500 new students entered with the temporary reactivation of Camp Davis.[12] The final year of the war found 14,544 registered, with the average attendance up 400 over the same time in 1944. An August report stated that 15,600 students had been enrolled that year.

Students must have been coming and going so quickly during the war that the paperwork was never able to conclude consistently. But the impact—and imposition—was unfinished. Before pronouncing "well done" to the Board of Education, handling the 1945–46 year loomed. Enrollment had dropped by January 1, 1946, but not to the extent anticipated by transient departures since the war's end. Many people formerly employed at the shipyard found jobs here and kept their Wilmington residences. It seemed like the school overflowed past my seventh grade year of 1946. I barely remember anybody who transferred out during the war, only a few who joined us.

* * *

---

* By July 1944, the Board of Education was managing eight nursery schools, funded by the Lanham Act. "'...One of the primary aims of the nursery schools is to foster these [desirable citizen] attitudes, habits and skills,'" said supervisor Ida B. Kellum. [Kellum quoted in *Wilmington Sunday Star-News*, July 30, 1944]

Roland was one of the prime movers in the passage H.R. 874, federal government aid to impacted school areas, that grew out of the wartime school problems. For one of the schools, Lake Forest, "There was some plan in someone's mind it could be used as a hospital" in case of emergency. Nurses used the downstairs area for clinics during the war. [Interview with Heyward C. Bellamy, March 31, 1999]

Forest Hills School

My school opened in 1926, 10 years before my parents built at 102 Colonial Drive, and when the area was a "distant" suburb two miles east of downtown Wilmington.* In August 1942 the school's boundary expanded. Increased numbers forced the construction of an entire new second story, "greatly enhancing the beauty as well as the usefulness of the building," built at a cost of $50,000 and funded by the Federal Works Agency. It was ready when we returned to classes after Labor Day in September 1942. This gave us six new classrooms (grades 5–8), a music room, and a larger library on the new floor. The basement cafeteria was completely renovated and a new kitchen built.[13] As for the influx of new kids, Harold Laing summed it up. "They seemed like foreigners."[14] Among our teachers for 1942–43 were three neighbors. It seemed like they kept an eye on us from all points in and out of class, which, of course, might have influenced our behavior.

We school kids frequently were called on to support the war effort, from buying war bonds and stamps to collecting scrap metal and Saturdays on neighborhood projects. One I recall distinctly was the 1944 Russian War Relief Drive. "We wish to acknowledge gratefully your contribution to Russian War Relief, Inc.," the letter read. "This receipt expresses our sincere appreciation and helps to conserve all possible funds to aid the Russian people." The letter's logo was a "'V' for Victory" imposed on the Soviet red star. Our gift, used clothing and many other items in 31 cartons weighing 825 pounds.[15] We really scratched through our closets for these donations and felt very close to someone far away in devastated Europe who might actually wear our unneeded clothes. We gathered what was overlooked in April 1945 in a major surplus drive of the United National Clothing Collection for War Relief, again run by the PTA. Our school was a collection point.

The keenest memory of school days belongs to Ronald G. "Ronnie" Phelps.[16] For the annual Christmas pageant, the glee club practiced for weeks. About Bryant Hare, one of the wise men: "He played better football than he did singing as a king. His family had all those jewels we wore, made him look good." Butterfly lover Mrs. Moody collected, mounted, and brought them in boxes into her classroom. Air raid drills: "Every student if they could afford a blanket brought one to school. We kept them there to lie on." About cafeteria food: "They did the best they could with wartime rationing." He was not aware of any poverty or free lunches. Our traffic

---

* In the 1960s the school added a new cafeteria building, paved driveway, and new sign, but otherwise there is very little difference in the way it looked during wartime. The rich deep red brick is as solid as ever. The gleaming white wooden columns at the front door stand welcoming students and visitors, and the tall, solid pines still beckon the breezes as they did when I stared out the open window through them, formulating my next piece of war art.

patrol boys reported the Mercer Avenue boys who walked to school down the railroad tracks and trestle, a forbidden route. Was the patrol asking for trouble from the tough guys? Some kids were bused in from war-housing Maffitt Village. We held war bond competitions between grammar schools and between classes at Forest Hills. Betty Bugg's father, E. B. Bugg, helped us. "Our class won more often than not because she would buy a $25 bond her father paid for."

Our class liked seventh grade teacher Miss Caroline Newbold, but because she was young and we were threshold teenagers, we gave her nothing but trouble.[17] Robert F. "Bobby" Cameron recalled, "She was such a nice person; we drove her crazy. She let us get away with everything."[18] Miss Newbold said, "Discipline was a problem when I went to Forest Hills," where she taught math and social studies. "I just didn't enjoy teaching at that time." Without an education degree, "I was sort of an emergency teacher. Miss [Principal Katherine] Von Glahn would come in and lay down the law and you children felt that she was the law, not Miss Newbold. You kids drove me out of teaching."*

She remembered doctor's son "little Billy" Dosher the most. "He was cute, but he was mischievous"† and Phelps was "a mischief maker." She fondly recalled Bryant Hare, Emily Carney, Margie and Ann Penton, and Artie Perry. They were ahead of us (and better behaved?). She taught at our school for two years and then quit for something more rewarding and less stressful. So my father hired her in 1946 to work at the Moore-Fonvielle Realty Company, where she would soon meet her future husband, Jimmy Swails, whose law office was in the same 2nd and Princess building.

The entire school always looked forward to the annual Christmas pageant not only because it meant Santa was near but because everybody except the youngest kids had some role. Of course Mary and Joseph and the leading roles belonged to 8th graders. Included in the 1943 cast of characters, with the program's request "Please do not applaud," were Joseph H. "Joe" Johnson, Jr., Norman Tyson, and me. Somehow we 5th graders snuck in there. I don't remember having much of a voice, but I did enjoy singing to myself college fight songs, *Mairzy Doats,* and other "Hit Parade" tunes.[19] Everybody walked to school. Cecelia and brother Jackie Black remembered the narrow bridge over Burnt Mill Creek on Forest Hills Drive, "a scary place with all the trees around the bridge," particularly on the way home, as Cecelia recalled.[20] Kids practiced air raids with their heads tucked between their legs and crunched over. The boys played on the opposite side of the playground from the girls, more by choice than rule.

---

* As she said that, she stared sternly at me during our interview as if still harboring something. For days I wondered: ill will, or relief?

† In the accompanying 1945 class photo taken at the school entrance, Dosher is the kid seated in the middle of the first row, hands up making a face at the camera. That's the way I remember him clearest.

It seemed like our school had continuous stage productions to occupy us and raise a few dollars for a worthy cause. I remember the 1945 8th-grade minstrel called "Dixie Roundup," applauded by the *Star-News* for being "exceptionally well directed and staged, with a talented cast presenting its many colorful acts in fine style....Entertainment at both presentations was far above

My fifth-grade class at Forest Hills School, 1945, front entrance. I am sitting on the left end of the third row with lower arms crossed. Next to me standing, in his brother Kenneth's white navy submariner's uniform, with hat, is Ronald G. "Ronnie" Phelps. At opposite end of the row, with left side obscured, in white T-shirt is L. W. "Billy" Humphrey. Both are lifelong friends. We three can still name every one of these kids.

Provided by Ronnie Phelps

the standard offered in schools of this age group...." Bryant Hare was interlocutor. The end men were Bill Garrabrant, Howard Penton, and Jack Sloan. Miss Von Glahn exhibited her extra talents as director, assisted by our music teacher, Miss Bischoff. Funds raised helped to buy a new movie screen in memory of Mrs. Mitchell, who died in 1945 after teaching there since the school's opening.[21]

* * *

Class of 1943, New Hanover High School

As the May 1943 graduation plans proceeded, an observer cast a somber note. "...Usually a time for rejoicing, this year will be a period of deep concern both for those who receive diplomas and for parents. Whereas in peacetime seniors look forward gleefully to vacation and relaxation of rigid discipline, and the making of plans to continue their education or finding jobs in the fall, now they must prepare to take their places in a nation at war and determine what they shall do to help in the victory."[22]

> "The most important thing that happened was the United States' declaration of war on Japan. We all gathered in the auditorium, the whole school, to hear the President's speech. After it was over they played the 'Star Spangled Banner,' and most of the girls had tears streaming down their faces and didn't even care. We boys just tried to look grim and important because we knew we'd fight some day. A few days later NHHS declared war on the Axis. Then almost before we knew it, it was June and time for school to close."—Class History[23]

When President Franklin D. Roosevelt appeared before Congress, the entire NHHS student body assembled to hear his speech. John J. Burney, Jr., an ROTC member, recalled where he was sitting. When a "big chill and snow" hit one winter, he asked his major, "are we gonna march today?" The reply, "They're fighting in Russia, aren't they?" With Lieutenant Eugene Laycock as the ROTC band leader, units "marched all over the place."[24] At 210 pounds, John, along with fellow football lineman and classmate Dewey Hobbs, appeared together in a newspaper photograph as the state's "two biggest tackles." Dewey played at Wake Forest and entered the ministry. Platoon sergeant John fought with the 254th Infantry, 63rd Infantry Division from France to Germany, and was wounded two times.* He later earned undergraduate and law degrees from Wake Forest.

> "Evelyn Volk is quite sad these days. Just ask her why, and she'll tell you Julian Everett's the answer. He's in the army" ... "Daisies to Billy Halyburton for his fight against 'evil' in NHHS" ... "Jimmy Hughes,

---

* Of the 23 varsity football players listed in the newspaper roster in September 1942, all seniors and juniors (21) served in the armed forces in WWII except Hobbs (heart murmur). Two died: soldiers James Arthur "Jimmy" Coughenour, the team's fastest man, was KIA, and John J. "Johnny" Goins of disease. The two freshmen served in the Korean War. [*Wilmington Morning Star*, September 11, 1942; Interview with John J. Burney, Jr., June 23, 2000]

aviation ordnance man, former NHHS student, visited school last week and talked about the sinking of the carrier *Wasp* [his ship]." He was badly injured, spent several weeks in a San Diego, California, hospital, is now on leave in Wilmington. He joined the navy in September 1941 ... The Wildcats edged Fayetteville 7–6 for their first conference football victory in five years. "The game was rough and tough, a survival of the fittest."—*The Wildcat*, November 25, 1942[25]

Many of the boys served in the ROTC unit, valuable experience to most. But to Mitchell "Mitch" Saleeby, ROTC "didn't stand me in good stead with the Marine Corps. You don't want to show you know anything. You want to be dumb and let them teach you." The ROTC used 1903 Springfields for drilling but once the war started wooden rifles replaced them. A member of the school's final boxing team, machine-gunner Mitch received the Bronze Star for valor on Iwo Jima.[26]

The ROTC rifle team's firing range was in two connecting classrooms on the school's first floor. "Nobody seemed to mind the gunfire," remembered Haskell Rhett. After he had been sworn into the navy, like many others he hung around the high school. Principal Thomas T. ("T-Square") Hamilton told him to get his file of misconduct out of the file drawer and tear it up, "'because you are going into the service and you're starting clean.' I thought that was a nice gesture on his part." Mr. Hamilton "didn't put up with any crap. We respected the teachers."[27]

North Carolina "war colleges" altered their curricula "to give men a taste of college before going off to war." Leonard Gleason Allen was one of the seniors who went off to the University of North Carolina to study and then return for graduation. Douglas Jewell, Sanford Doxey, and Bobby Taylor also went to Chapel Hill, and John Codington to North Carolina State. The only requisite was passing a test. Compulsory courses included Carolina Volunteer Training Corps and basic military training. An ROTC platoon commander, Gleason was put in charge of the seniors. They all received credits applied to high school graduation with the class.[28]

> High School ROTC Unit is Awarded Signal Honor—As result of "especially high standards of military training and soldierly discipline" maintained in the NHHS ROTC unit, the school was named "honor high school of the [army's] Fourth Service Command."[29]—*Morning Star*, April 29, 1943

Haskell lived next to Airlie Gardens on Bradley Creek and attended Bradley Creek School.[30] "When I went into the service it was one story; when I came back it was two stories." During afternoons following classes at NHHS, he either went downtown to a movie, came home, or went to his grandparents' house on South 4th Street, the W. D. MacMillan, Jr., family. Henry MacMillan, Jr., and Haskell's mother were first cousins. "I was a little bitty guy. John Burney and those boys he ran with were the big ones."

Sergeant John J. Burney, Jr., (NHHS '43) in France, 1945. Serving with the 254th Infantry Regiment, 63rd Division, he received two Purple Hearts for combat wounds. He frequently travels to France and Germany to see old comrades and enemies, now friends.

Provided by Burney

New Hanover High School principal, Thomas Tristam "T-Square" Hamilton. Feared by most students as a disciplinarian, he looked the other way in "rearranging" some student records to facilitate their entering the armed forces. By the time I reached NHHS in 1947, his previous reputation held fast and the latter was but a legend.

The Hanoverian (NHHS), 1943

As a student "I was bright and very lazy, just barely [put out] enough." Miss Rebecca Russ earned an appropriate nickname, "Taboo," because when she corrected students she said it was "taboo." He admired Miss Levine. "I was afraid of that lady. She taught me more math than anybody before or since. I was afraid not to learn it. She was from Beaufort and knew my father. It was a deadly combination for me."

During war bond drives, Emma Worth Mitchell, my across-the-street neighbor, remembered "we'd come prepared to buy stamps." If not playing sports students were encouraged to go to the gym during home room for exercise. Emma walked the mile and a half to school. Neighbor Ellis White took his car to school because he needed it for work. She hoped he would come by to pick her up. Emma entered Salem College in the fall, and caught the bus back and forth there, an eight-hour trip via Greensboro. "It stopped at every crossroad." She sent her belongings to Salem in a big steamer trunk via the Railway Express Agency, the best way to ship in those days.[31]

Mary Cameron Dixon's family lived at 6 Church Street.[32] She and her husband, classmate Heyward C. Bellamy, live there now.* Their class graduated 336 from a huge influx of students, and never had less than 30 per classroom. This was representative at an approximately 33 percent growth in county student population. "We used any room we could get, Isaac Bear building, some of Trinity Church, the old vocational building. The crowd increased in a hurry," Heyward remembered. "We'd get a crackerjack math teacher whose husband was at Camp Davis, would teach for a short time and then leave. The turnover was great." Teachers were well trained even though they turned over. "We were fortunate to have them." Mary remembered crowded classes with every seat taken, "but we were used to it. During the war you'd teach everywhere; every single room was occupied. You might have four classes operating in the auditorium."

Army air forces Lieutenant Heyward C. Bellamy (NHHS '43) in flight training, 1944.

Provided by Bellamy

---

* The Bellamys, high school sweethearts, were married in 1947 following his discharge as an army air forces officer. They both taught for years at NHHS (she was my Spanish teacher), and from 1968–81, Heyward served as superintendent of schools for New Hanover County, and was keynote speaker at my Class of '51 reunion in 2001.

School teachers distributed rationing stamps on nights and Saturdays as their community duty. Miss Levine was one. She issued ration stamps to Heyward that started a "love affair" between her and the family. She told him his father was a "fine example of a southern gentleman." Mary added, "Heyward was her A+ student." Motivated toward the army, ROTC member Heyward asked Dr. H. A. Codington, a World War I battlefield surgeon, for "an army physical." "Heyward, you are in the army now. You passed the physical." He left for active duty halfway through his senior year.

> Junior-Senior Prom is Held at School Gym—Dorothy Sutherland and Heatwole Thomas were crowned Mr. and Mrs. New Hanover High. Walter Barnes and Orchestra, composed entirely of high school students, played. Couples "danced to both 'sweet and hot music.'"—*Morning Star*, May 7, 1943[33]

On Friday night, June 5, "after promising 'to help American boys turn on the light of freedom for the oppressed peoples of the world,'" their high school years were over. They promised "to accept the hardships in all those areas that would guarantee continuance of...freedom'....The youths stated simply they were willing to join their fellows in the task 'without doubting the responsibility of the job fallen on their shoulders....'"[34]

Now it was their turn.*

* * *

"For the first time in four years...New Hanover County children will go to school without war," this August 1945 editorial aptly reflected.[35]

> For despite the fact that the war was fought far from our shores school children, from the youngest to high school seniors, were subject to its influence and suffered grave emotional reactions while it lasted. So many had fathers or brothers or uncles in the Armed Forces, so many felt their first deep sorrow on learning that loved ones would never come home, it would be inane to claim that because the battles were far away the children were unaffected by the holocaust....Violent death in combat will no longer engage children's hearts and imaginations as in the past....We have not done so well with the world of today. It will devolve upon them to do better with the world of tomorrow. Their success will depend upon the way they are prepared for the job.

The schools had done well as instructor, informer, preparer, and shield. I am incapable of rendering enough retrospective praise and thanks for the dedicated service of John T. Hoggard, H. M. Roland, J. W. Grise, T. T. Hamilton, F. J. Rogers, Katherine Von Glahn, William Blount, and the rest in New Hanover County education who strived hard for us, and succeeded. From my generation, all I can only offer is immense appreciation. They would be proud of what we have accomplished.

---

* At least five from the class of '43 lost their lives: KIA, navy, William David "Billy" Halyburton, Jr. (serving with the Marine Corps, posthumously awarded the Medal of Honor), Olin Hughes White, and Oscar Rockwell Jones; and Coughenour and Goins.

"Remember Pearl Harbor"[36]

"Remember Pearl Harbor!" the December 18, 1941, New Hanover High School's editorial shouted. "America is at war! Not just the government, not just the army and navy, but every individual American citizen, young and old, is at war with Hitler and his little yellow friends....High school students have as much at stake in this struggle as their parents or anyone else. This is our war; this is everybody's war. Not many of us in high school will be able to fight at the front in the army or navy; but each of us has a duty, a task to perform in the service of his country." At president Lehman Green's request, the student body voted unanimously for a declaration of war between NHHS and the governments of Germany and Japan.

In a special assembly, the principal, as new to this as anyone else, told students what to do during an air raid alarm. "We cannot say that the disasters which have so often come to thousands in other parts of the world will not happen here. Above all, keep cool. Don't lose your head. Do not treat air raid alarms lightly. Think twice before you do anything," and refrain from talking.

Chapter 8
"Crackpot Economists and Social Reformers"

I vaguely remember times when I might not have had enough of one thing or another, but that was likely more through "want" than "need." For myself and kids I knew, born and raised in the Depression, desires were tempered by circumstances beyond our control and limits were defined by what was at hand. Certainly I was not "deprived" and neither were my friends, to my knowledge. At times we "did without," when the kitchen contained no meat or sugar or butter, or driving was curtailed. Consequently, through my parents' savvy and resourcefulness, and favors from the local grocers, we managed. Everyone else was in the same boat. My patriotic parents invoked "sacrifices" for the war effort and "giving" to our boys overseas. If there were sacrifices, the adults bore them more than the children who were constantly reminded of our many blessings.

Conditions remembered the most by the hundreds of Wilmington wartime residents I asked pinpointed overwhelmingly: shortages and the "ration situation." (Next came air raid drills and blackouts, and housing problems.) Generated by shortages of numerous items needed for the war machinery, rationing undoubtedly was the most serious and persistent nuisance to be endured—one equally faced regardless of residency status, economic or social standing, or race. If anyone had an edge, it was through a bit of "influence" or "persuasiveness."

Rationing, perhaps the most poorly planned and managed federal government program to mobilize the population and prosecute the war effort, was also the most abused by those it was trying to help. Run by the federal Office of Price Administration and its local offices, and the affiliated New Hanover County War Price & Rationing Board, the program provided regulations, guidance, monitoring, tips, and enforcement—and constant carping—and with it needless bureaucracy and bungling.*

---

* Unpaid executives and a mix of volunteers and paid staff manned these offices and other civilian defense agencies. Your next-door neighbor might run the draft, health, or ration board. Did

It seemed as though the various levels of government authorities dealing in rationing and attendant price controls were constantly in a tug-of-war among themselves and the citizens over rule-setting, awareness, and compliance. Overall the public responded positively in supporting these restrictive and lifestyle-changing edicts, and with belt tightening certainly enough alternatives existed to stave off destitution.

Could rationing have been better planned and more efficiently operated, with wider benefits? The answers may partly lie here in a statement about the OPA and other involved federal agencies delivered by Wilmington Rotary Club President W. Eugene "Gene" Edwards in 1943: "In my opinion authorities should throw out all the crackpot economists and social reformers and put practical men with practical experience in charge to formulate plans for the food industry." With his father he ran the downtown W. M. Edwards & Son wholesale grocery and feed business on Dock Street, and supplied corner stores and the Colonial Stores and A&P chains. He knew something about the shortages.[1]

The people had been duly alerted. "Sacrifice, Conservation," the editorial began on December 19, 1941. "Individuals must reduce their consumer demand by at least one-third. This means that many so-called 'necessities' must be reclassified as a luxury and given up," citing gasoline usage. "To be fully cooperative, women will abandon much of their cosmetic glory and men go back to shaving with ordinary soap."[2] Alas. Soap, too, would join the scarcity list. "It seems there's going to be a lot of dirty faces in Wilmington before long."[3] Grime only enhanced one's warrior appearance and self-image, and never slowed me down.

* * *

The Rationing Program

Rationing nationwide began in January 1942. Reactionary and haphazard, it was the classic government emergency program hurriedly imposed (as if American involvement in the war were not looming). Rules frequently misled or were inconsistent. The local board valiantly tried to interpret, provide adequate notice, and police the programs, but often were confused by Washington and Raleigh who might not have known any better either.

Ration coupon and points books for gasoline and foodstuffs in particular became as tradeable as dollars. Ann Williams' family was typical. "You never asked about the price of hamburger. It was always how many points it was, whether I had enough ration points for it. It was not that we had a lot of money, but we were always worried if we had enough points."[4]

---

this aid your causes? Whether they dispensed favoritism remains unresolved. The only proof were illegalities that hit the newspaper or plain old rumors.

Two of the first products rationed were sugar and coffee. "It's back to school for millions of America's grownups this week, for a fourth R—a ration book which will be needed for buying sugar...probably until after the war," a May 1942 item stated.[5]

Wilmington received its first real taste of war rationing as thousands of housewives flocked to the county schools for War Ration Book #1. Proving the old adage the housewife is the head of the family... the overwhelming numbers were women.

Each person was allowed a half-pound of sugar per week. Its scarcity affected ingredients for everything from homemade cakes to chewing gum and manufactured confections. Tabitha Hutaff McEachern's family was the local Coca-Cola bottler, a business deeply impacted. Supplies, production, and deliveries were curtailed. "They could sell everything they could put in a bottle." People came to the 10th and Princess plant to pick up drinks and also to fill jugs with the free fresh water well spigot next door, my mother included. The other well spigot was at Greenfield Lake.[6] Its distinctive, slightly metallic taste was hardly a rival for Coke.

"Coffee has enlisted for Victory!" shouted the A&P Food Stores local advertisement. "You can still enjoy coffee, don't waste it," adding tips for making a "better cup."[7] The beverage became a "cup-a-day." "Looks as though stopping in a drug store for a cup of coffee is fast becoming a thing of the past....It'll be tough if you're one of those who like to snag an occasional between-the-meals cup of java."[8] Rae West recalled, "Nobody had coffee. If you got it, it was full of chickery."[9]

People seeing a line forming outside a store might jump in hoping to land something scarce, regardless of whether they normally consumed it, because it was available and might be sold or swapped. Owner Angus Olmstead of my neighborhood corner grocery, Broad Circle Food Store, tried to accommodate his regulars. He saved a

Some of my wartime memorabilia included ration books (Book Four shown here), wooden B-17 and submarine toys, comic books and other items a boy growing up during World War II would collect.
Author's collection

little meat for Mother and Fleers bubblegum for me, often dropping it off on his way home. But few could figure out how to beat the rationing of only two pairs of new shoes per person per year. This restriction was death to rambunctious and active school boys who wore them out just standing up during assembly!

Setting the pace, the newspaper fueled the opposition to the way OPA conducted business. In mid-1943 it opined, "The OPA has been in hot water from its start chiefly, we believe, because its orders have been not only voluminous but threatening....It has not seen fit to ask people to 'do this' because it was necessary in the interest of success in the war....The American people do not take kindly to dictation but are open to conviction. They will cooperate in restrictions, once they are shown the need."[10]

By November 1943, 79,194 county citizens of all ages had registered for War Ration Book #4, more than any previous registration: 56,462 whites and 22,732 Negroes. As with the civilian defense program, rationing and housing programs were segregated even in their training sessions. Increased availability of some foods, consumer items, and home appliances forecast for 1944 gave a rise to cheer. But newsprint paper became extremely scarce, forcing the *Star-News* to reduce its number of pages, refuse new subscriptions, or publish all advertising.*

As the war neared an end in 1945, the government came down again. To conserve electricity, the head of War Mobilization clamped a curfew on places of entertainment, "the action—most drastic of its kind during the war." But Wilmington owners thought their spots should stay open for defense workers.[11]

By December 1945, President Harry S Truman had lifted all major controls which "apparently opened the gates for an estimated $2 million construction boom in New Hanover County....Exclusive of home building, Wilmington is now in the midst of an unprecedented industrial building boom which...[should] give the community greatly increased employment."[12] At least that was the plan.

We on the home front got used to rationing and tolerated it as a "painless sacrifice" for the war effort and our boys in the front lines. When all was said and done, the *Morning Star* admitted in November 1946:

> Give credit to the members of local boards who gave their services in the difficult task of enforcing OPA decisions and interpreting as best they could the OPA contradictions, without compensation and most of the time with the echo of public complaint....It was an onerous duty

---

* "Despite this curtailment we are going to furnish as broad news coverage and as many features as we have been publishing....We are glad to do our bit in the war emergency, and solicit the patience and long continued friendship of our readers." [*Wilmington Sunday Star-News*, February 27, 1944]

they performed, often at heavy sacrifice to their business interests, and disruption of their domestic life. Whatever the attitude may be toward the OPA...the men and women who have constituted the local boards...deserve high praise.[13]

* * *

Gasoline

Seven months into the war the government decided to ration petroleum products, the lifeline of the war machine. On July 22, 1942, 11,133 county motorists, including many shipyard workers and 1,600 Camp Davis army personnel, began using their basic "A" coupon books, the lowest priority. "Yesterday many truck owners filled their gasoline tanks for the last time before they must begin to purchase it under the permanent program." Motorcycles and outboard motorboats also fell into that category. Some drivers obtained supplemental ration books, and traveling salesmen received an allowance of 470 miles per month under the "B" card.[14]

The intent was honorable and even enforceable, as the local War Price & Rationing Board chairman, O. H. Shoemaker, an "A" card holder, found out." If the county rationing chief has refused you extra gasoline for that vacation trip you've been wanting, don't think bad things about the fellow." It happened to him. The state regulator denied Shoemaker extra rations for a 1942 two-week vacation.[15] The A, B, or C windshield stickers became status symbols of sorts. Our Pontiac earned only an "A" because Daddy was expected to take the bus downtown to work, despite Mother's Nurse's Aide duties and their community involvement. A "C" sticker might tempt observers to think the owner was making the supreme contribution to the war effort, when that person actually operated the car for pooling riders to work at Davis or the shipyard, and the board deemed use of his vehicle more essential.

More than a year after Pearl Harbor, regulations were still settling in curbing use of civilian automobiles. Restrictions were clear, but the determining factor was the driver's conscience. Imagine that, a faculty beyond regulation. The loudest and toughest crackdown was on "pleasure driving." Its being banned altogether had been a matter of time. By January 1943, the issue had stirred up more hate and discontent toward the regulators than any item in the attempt to ration commodities needed for war. Much of the unhappiness was purely selfish, because drivers already had the wherewithal to take care of necessities. What was pleasure driving? It included going to amusement places such as parks, bowling alleys, and night clubs, touring or vacation travel, or making social calls. Yet, high schoolers continued to drive cars on double dates even though scrimping on gas. Were they siphoning (an outgrowth of rationing)? Necessary shopping trips were said to be vital, however, but quickly parking meter collections dropped dramatically when drivers stopped going downtown. And the merchants just howled.

Before people *fully understood* pleasure driving, statewide authorities—including local law enforcement—were out there cracking down on errant and "unpatriotic" motorists. OPA investigators "continued to stop motorists to ply them with inquiries as to whether their driving was essential....Drivers suspected of not being on necessary missions were referred to the...Rationing Board 'to show cause why their gasoline ration book should not be revoked'...."[16] Motorists spotted at oyster roasts and drive-ins, however, were not cited as violators. Whew! Those spots had always done a big business here. Within a few days authorities were touting a large decrease in pleasure driving, and the public's conservation awareness.

The *Star-News* was convinced OPA's handling of the gasoline distribution system was at fault and demanded an independent investigation. "Wilmington's experience with OPA meat investigations and other inquiries conducted by OPA agents has destroyed public confidence in the bureau."[17] Nothing came of this. In early 1943 OPA ordered an end to police enforcement of pleasure driving. From then on it depended on the "honor system." Conscience? A month later the local OPA bunch was at it again: "'Too much non-occupational driving,'" said Shoemaker, and "'too many gas books are expiring before they should....'"[18] This was mid-war, folks. The momentum to victory had not completely swung.

Talk about overregulation. The year 1943, especially January, saw it in heavy doses from the state OPA office. Such wisdom included a tip to shoppers: "'Get the goods at the nearest counter!...Just about everything the North Carolina housewife buys for herself for her home, except foodstuffs, comes under the inventory regulations.'"[19] With this kind of help, Wilmingtonians produced more at home (except gasoline).*

* * *

Foodstuffs

Sugar and coffee aside, all of a sudden, in December 1942, the area food supply dwindled.

> Two years ago [Wilmington] was a quiet little city, hoping for terminal facilities which would reestablish it as a primary Atlantic port and, by

---

* By 1945, it could be asked, had the upshot of three years of gas rationing also created road accidents? "Motorists had had to put up with shoddy gas during the war as in other things. It has been so low grade that carburetors required cleaning monthly....Drivers put up with it as a war necessity and all in all were glad to be able to drive their cars under any conditions, despite the added cost of operation...." [*Wilmington Sunday Star-News*, September 2, 1945] Pleasure driving now, anyone?

advancing its commerce, send the population up far in excess of the few hundred new residents it had acquired in the decade just past....In the face of this growth* the primary dispenser of foodstuffs and the authorities who regulate distribution thereof have done little or nothing to send into the area enough staple foods to keep up with the demand. How the people...can dodge actual hunger unless something is done quickly to replenish the dwindling supplies of food...is not easily seen.[20]

The federal government allocated food and other civilian consumables, rationed or not, *on the basis of the area's 1941 population*, rather than on its swollen numbers of people arriving to support the war effort. This gross miscalculation hampered distribution for much of the war, and drew the continuous disbelief and ire of local governments and the newspaper.

A vibrant county vegetable truck farming industry helped sustain local military and civilian needs throughout the emergency. Severe weather added to distribution problems in the 1943 growing seasons limited production and exacerbated the shortages, showing up in schools. "Many children are in want of nourishment because their parents and the cafeterias cannot obtain enough food for them....When they can't get it at school, their development and education suffer irreparable handicap."[21] My school cafeteria seemed to have enough.

People were warned not to hoard ("It is certain that everyone in the land will have an opportunity to buy all food necessary to sustain life and health"[22]); told how to dine out ("You can eat at restaurants within ration coupons...but the restaurants will serve only about half as much canned and other processed foods as they had last year"[23]); and told how to extract the maximum ("Don't pour ration points down the drain! Every drop of vegetable liquid can be used in gravies or soup stock"[24]).

Food rationing generated all sorts of this advice along with admonitions and pleas. No doubt rationing was required, but looking back I'm not convinced the people had adequate information needed to make their own judgments. While the press remained free and mostly open, the flow of source information to it, particularly from the governments, was filtered or prohibited. The end result also contained a mixture of propaganda, cheerleading, fear, and uncertainty.

To register for War Ration Book #2, consumers had to declare their pantry stocks of commercially processed foods at the time so that "no one persons or family will be allowed to have more than their fair share. This is the democratic way to make sure that everyone gets an even break."[25] Local

---

* "As nearly as can be reckoned without an actual count the city which contained but 33,407 souls two years ago, now had 90,000, and New Hanover County fully 120,000 against the 47,935 by the 1940 census." [*Wilmington Sunday Star-News*, December 13, 1942] Compare these numbers against ration books issued a year later, and with chapter 15.

grocers reported an immediate sale decrease of up to 50 percent in rationed items. Butter and margarine were now on the list. The latter raised eyebrows because it was taxed, and because it had to be made in one's own kitchen. "'...Any persons who color and serve oleomargarine or butter substitute to the public...[are] liable for tax as a manufacturer....'"[26] Wartime Wilmington residents remember all too well bringing home oleomargarine in a box, breaking open separate packets, and stirring a red/yellow food color into the lardy looking stuff to make their own product. It always tasted like you thought it would. I never understood why it wasn't sold already mixed. What a substitute.

Restaurants also ran into hard times, and some temporarily closed a couple of days a week because of a general food shortage or their lack of sufficient points with which to buy foodstuffs. This included the popular Crystal Restaurant, one of the city's largest. Proprietors claimed the OPA forced them to sell their vegetable dishes at a loss. The fact was Wilmingtonians were "being 'gouged' to the limit" in some establishments, and they in turn reported violators to the OPA.*

Area milk consumption skyrocketed but production leveled or dropped off depending on the availability of milk cows, farm hands, feed, and other factors. A number of dairies closed, and during the severest period only six were operating. Government officials and the newspaper provided conflicting information which confused and frightened the public. Its track of on-again, off-again availability dazzled like a maze, as producers periodically reported their problems, then issued consumers instructions. By December 1943, consumers heard they "should become gravely concerned about the present milk problem."[27] I loved milk and got plenty. It was all pasteurized whole milk, delivered to our back doorstep in glass bottles two or three times a week by the Echo Farm and Swart dairies. The cream on top Mother used for cooking, her tea, and Daddy's coffee.

Of all commodities, meat consistently was the most difficult to obtain on the open market. Local authorities in January 1943 instituted a "Share-the-Meat" educational campaign showing how to use substitutes to maintain balanced diets, and asking people to limit meat consumption. A few months later eating establishments instituted "meatless days" and offered nutritious facsimiles. My creative mother's skills persisted throughout the war while looking for other protein sources. In those days meat, fish, or other flesh at dinner and supper was perhaps more commonplace than now. Although a bit chubby, I probably ate a balanced diet prepared in the Southern style: high fat and high calorie content.

---

* Regulators got real picky. O. H. Shoemaker cited a restaurant that before the war cut pie into 6 slices and sold each for a dime. In 1944 it cut the same pie into 8 or 10 slices, in some cases 12, and sold them for a dime or 15 cents. OPA in 1942 ordered the Cape Fear Sandwich Shop to reduce the price of a bottle of beer from 25 to 11 cents.

New Hanover County dairies by 1944 were six, about half the number of 1941, in a day when storage and transportation of fresh dairy products were limited and milk consumption had skyrocketed. One large dairy continuing operations belonged to Otto Leeuwenburg on north Highway 17 (Market Street), late war.

Provided by son William C. "Bill" Leeuwenburg

Roberts Grocery, now a Wrightsville Beach landmark for decades, was across the street on Lumina Avenue from its present location.[28] Army wife Mary Daughtry got "in" with the butcher and agreed to trade liquor stamps for meat stamps. "He was a flaming alcoholic." She would enter the store and he would reach under the counter and give her a package. She never knew what was in there. Often this happened with other women in line.* "I didn't for any minute think I was doing anything wrong, but maybe I was." Husband Lieutenant Claude Daughtry had access to liquor at the Camp Davis officers club and didn't need his liquor stamps. If Mary wanted to drive into Wilmington on gas coupons "it couldn't be for frivolous purposes." She would put a chair in the back seat to say she was taking it for repair if she was stopped for driving alone.

The war a month from ending, the *Morning Star* again was driven. "'With no fresh meat cuts nine-tenths of the time and jowls, tails and cold cuts the remaining tenth, it would be interesting to know what the OPA considers an acute shortage.'" The writer asked for common sense from the

---

* Wrightsville grocery man C. S. Roberts was "found to be the first 'intentional' violator" by overcharging for meats. He received a six-month suspension. [*Wilmington Morning Star*, December 1, 1943] The Daughtrys escaped notice.

OPA.[29] Why start now? we wondered. We were ready to win the war. The local delegation to Washington to save Camp Davis learned that meat packers would deliver as much meat as they did 18 months before. At that time the area supply suddenly had been adequate. The mercurial "pressure" of supply and demand once more was relieved.

Eating Establishments

"Washington [D.C.] is talking about Wilmington," the 1943 article read, "since the publication April 30 in the *Washington Post* of a story entitled 'Problem in Wilmington Is to Get Something to Eat,' written by Agnes E. Meyer." The publisher's wife stated, "Wilmington makes Washington look like a land of milk and honey." She deplored the inadequate eating facilities here and denounced the sort of food obtainable. "The native population is no better off (than uptown eaters) because the butcher stores get supplies that look like a grim jest. The state of things is pathetic, if not indecent....I would not be a worker in Wilmington if you gave me the whole city." To this she jabbed, "The army wife is a more serious problem to Wilmington than in most other places." Otherwise, at least after her visit she praised the shipyard.[30]

Good that Mrs. Meyer didn't hang around, but she was near the mark. For the war's first two years the area did suffer from a lack of restaurants in number and quality. Attention to the condition started when none opened on Christmas 1941, and visiting Camp Davis soldiers were left without weekend meals. The situation was at its worst in 1943, when the number of bodies in town was its highest. The majority of white and Negro establishments were downtown and small, with counter stools and a couple of handfuls of tables. Restaurants couldn't seat or serve the multitudes of hungry downtown employees, war workers, armed forces personnel, and shoppers who descended upon them.* (Today's fast-food places did not exist.)

The ration board in April 1943 implored residents to eat at home if they could instead of crowding downtown facilities, especially on weekends, to save on ration points. "...Restaurant operators...are also on a rationed basis per individual served. 'It is unpatriotic to conserve your food points while those who cannot eat at home go with little food or none.'"[31] The request applied only to people who went into town to shop, attend moving picture shows, or negotiate other brief business. "We cannot issue extra gasoline ration privileges to any persons wanting to ride home to lunch in his car."[32]

The newspaper called eating at home making a "patriotic duty" out of a "bad situation."[33] Women shopping downtown were especially urged to go

---

* The army in November 1942 took over the Cape Fear Hotel coffee shop as a mess hall for three hundred personnel. It was the lone café in town capable of messing that many persons at a single meal.

home for lunch (see previous paragraph—confusing?), but a June survey indicated noon patronage had increased since the board's requests. Proprietors couldn't obtain enough food to take care of their "regulars." "'This is truly a serious situation...a desire to escape the drudgery of preparing a meal at home after shopping...[or] to save ration points....'"[34] My mother returned home when she had the car, or took a sandwich on her volunteer assignments. My father rarely came home and usually ate at the Crystal, Dixie Café, New York Café, H&W Cafeteria, or Futrelle's or Saunders' Drug Stores all within a couple of blocks from his office. The operators and waitresses knew him as a "regular," and he often lunched with friends or associates.*

The establishments further suffered in June 1945 when OPA reduced food supplies to most hotels and restaurants. Authorities urged everyone to cut the amount of food ordered and then "clean the plate" in deference to all those starving around the world.†

* * *

Moonshining and Alcoholic Beverage Controls

The war added impetus to the refinements of production and marketing of one of North Carolina's most renowned ancient arts, moonshining. Rationing included hard liquor and distilled spirits, and in many instances they were unobtainable legitimately because supply never matched demand. The under-market boomed. Hardly a week went by that authorities weren't destroying illegal whiskey stills and arresting bootleggers in our area. They said some of the stuff was downright decent, but since my parents were teetotalers, this kind of talk was way over my head.

After formal coupon rationing began in December 1942 (replacing the "bottle a day" plan), New Hanover County topped the list in state liquor sales in the 24 "wet" counties month after month throughout the war. Beer and wine were not regulated. By April 1943, ABC store profits, shared among county jurisdictions, had declined as much as one-half. In November, coupons were halved in value, the maximum amount set at two pints or one fifth or quart. The ABC board action was "in the interest of better

---

* Eating out was relatively cheap, even if portions shrunk and you weren't seeking Parisian ambience. For instance, the hole-in-the-wall G&J Café at 118 Market served a special lunch for 40 cents (if you could find a seat).

† Parents of my generation constantly directed children to eat everything placed before us for that reason. I can't begin to think of how many unfinished portions of liver, spinach, carrots, broccoli, and whatever else I didn't want I had to sit and stare at forever—being reminded each time about millions of children going without in India and China whom I didn't know at all. How my eating that mess would affect them I couldn't figure. My dog Jip could devour only so much of my "excesses." The only way I ever won was the time factor. Eventually Mother would leave. I was further confused when this regimen continued even after we won the war.

My wife, Carroll, and I tried a similar approach on our two sons, but stonewalling like their WWII father, they wore us down. Eventually we declared victory, too, and dropped it.

Chapter Eight

SIDE GLANCES

"I hope the rest of you children spent your summer as profitably as Wilbur!" the teacher is saying. "Now pay attention while he reads the essay he composed on why India is misunderstood." No kidding. This is the actual caption of this "Side Glances" cartoon. But, I hope I didn't look that nerdy.

Wilmington Morning Star, September 5, 1942
Side Glances reprinted by permission of Newspaper Enterprise Association, Inc.

distribution," and, the chairman stated, "no individual will get as much while more people will get whiskey."[35]

Important as liquor was to some, Washington "blasted prospects for an early resumption of whiskey making with the declaration it would be 'gambling with the war program.'"[36] The validity is difficult to comprehend, but the intent of pushing the war effort overrode any other logic. Was whiskey important to the soldiers' morale?* Tabitha Hutaff McEachern remembered that whenever a truck loaded with whiskey left Wilmington for the Wrightsville Beach ABC store, somebody in town phoned ahead and people lined up to get their share when it arrived.

Wholesale grocer W. Eugene "Gene" Edwards knew moonshining was big business.[37] The Negro Freeman family of Carolina Beach Road was well known for making it. "We sold plenty of sugar to people who made bootleg whiskey," Edwards said. Some of them "made good liquor" out of copper,

---

* By March, 16, 1944, 36,034 county people had purchased liquor ration books. The ABC store used that money to buy liquor to exchange for coupons. Presumably not all of the folks drank. Liquor coupons were a medium of exchange and barter for other commodities, aboveboard or not.

nongalvanized stills. "We had no idea what people would do with the sugar they bought from us; it was not within our restrictions." Bruce Freeman served in the Pacific islands, built a still, and made whiskey. Edwards claimed Freeman told him, "At the time I was the richest Negro on the island." Edwards never had a problem getting whiskey. No money changed hands. He simply left cartons of cigarettes on the counter as a favor to the store operators. It was "no problem to pay higher prices, because people were making all the money they could make anyway."

He was also aware that "some illegal activity was going on" in the food business. Some distributors and grocers sold above the price ceilings. "In order to get people supplies, I violated it at times." He would buy at ceiling, sell above, "could make a little profit." Cigarettes, liquor and sugar were important on the black market. "A lot of people got all they could and resold it."

* * *

The Black Market

Black marketeering hit the Wilmington area hard as soon as widespread rationing and price ceilings went into effect in 1942. The term meant selling any item above its regulated ceiling price, or any item for which ration points were not legally exchanged. The practice itself was illegal, but many persons broke the rules by transacting business either by willful design to gain a monetary or commodity advantage, or through ignorance or carelessness. Public officials and the newspaper continuously castigated both the practice and those who participated as either seller or buyer.

"Black market" applied to almost anything illegally obtained. Evidence in early 1943 uncovered a black market in transportation operating between Wilmington and Camp Davis wherein taxi drivers were hauling fares, some in private vehicles, thus violating the OPA limit on taxi operations. Black marketeers of all stripes and persuasions blanketed the area. One whose name popped up frequently was Odell Bridgers. Rumors abounded that if you wanted something badly enough, he could get it for you. A money lender, he was known for roughing up his debtors, and would enter the Atlantic Coast Line offices looking for them. Shipyard workers gave Manette Dixon rationing coupons for shoes, and she in turn bought black market gasoline for them. Louie Laytham worked there in the transportation department, John Mintz recalled, and "was able to get things for people, a wheeler-dealer, a good-time jolly—would do anything for you." But you paid a stiff price. Laytham would sell a 5-cent Coca-Cola to fellow workers for 50 cents.[38]

President Franklin D. Roosevelt asked Americans to "Hold the Line" against paying above-ceiling prices. OPA started a pledge campaign with housewives and businessmen: "I will buy no products which are listed above ceiling price; I will not buy products without surrendering the necessary ration points."[39] In a war fought Stateside by a multitude of slogans, "The Home Front Pledge" against inflation was only one more.

It wasn't long, March 1943, before the black marketeers entered the meat business when scarcity had peaked. "...Wilmington is one of a very few communities in the state in which the black market practice has been attempted on so heavy a scale...." No fixed plan for the rationing of meat existed, only a voluntary policy "designed to prevent purchase of more than two pounds...per person per week....The product is said to be difficult to obtain consistently in Wilmington."[40]

That such activities could exist in our nation during wartime raised both alarms and opportunities. "Black markets are a definite aid to the enemies of this country and all that it has gained in its troubled existence," the newspaper argued. "And if there are no customers, black markets will disappear. In dealing with black marketeers there is no reason to temper justice with mercy."[41]

Numerous area businessmen and citizens were investigated and hauled before OPA and ration board hearings, some even arrested for varying violations. Not all were considered to be operating illegally, just using improper judgment or feigning ignorance of the rules. Of course authorities did not find all violators. Almost everyone I spoke with knew a person who broke the rules one way or another, if not themselves. To the extent they could be uncovered and investigated, serious cases were prosecuted to the fullest. For example, two civilians received five years each in the Atlanta federal penitentiary for stealing gasoline "intended for military use and violation of the gasoline ration law." The judge said the April 1944 case was "far reaching" and the "worst one we had so far" as the most ramified "black market case...the low in patriotism." A court-martial sentenced a Camp Davis corporal to three and one-half years for his involvement. In another representative case, a shipyard worker got 90 days for reselling gas coupons above ceiling.[42] I can't imagine what it was like to forfeit the privilege of defending my country's freedom for jail time. How pitiful and worthless.

Wilmington: "The Worst OPA Violator in the State"[43]

The Raleigh District OPA office on May 27, 1943, called Wilmington "the worst OPA violator in the state...." A series of enforcement drives followed "with special emphasis on community price violations on 'cost-of-living' items.... The year ended with many noticeable shortages, but on the second anniversary of the rationing program, New Hanover officials were being lauded...."

The Second Anniversary, a Report—Wilmingtonians, who have been chiefly affected by the war through rationing, have on a "large percentage scale accepted rationing and price control as a program necessary to the...war effort," officials of the local board said on January 6, 1944, two years after its establishment. "The program has been very effective in bringing about a reasonable distribution of scarce commodities and in preventing a tremendous rise in prices," estimating that "food prices here would have been 50 percent higher...[and] rationing has prevented a breakdown of the transportation system."

The dates rationing of certain items started included:

New automobiles, January 1, 1942
Tires and tubes, January 1942
Typewriters, bicycles, sugar—War Ration Book No. 1, issued April 1942
Gasoline, May 1942
Rubber footwear, coffee, November 1942, and removed in 1943
Fuel oil, December 1942
Shoes, March 1943
Processed foods, March 1, 1943
Meats and fats, March 29, 1943
Stoves, September 1, 1943

The board established price ceilings on certain items in July 1942, and on all meat and food items served in restaurants on April 28, 1943. It issued three ration books per person in 1943. "The year brought much confusion because of rationing." The pleasure driving ban set on January 7, 1943, produced a 40 percent cut in gas sales, some drive-in establishments to close temporarily, and car sharing. Shortages of meats, cheese, butter, cooking fats and oils "apparently grew worse with the start of rationing on March 29, 1943." A meat black market was uncovered on March 5. "A rush to buy shoes before stamp No. 17 expired in June nearly resulted in a riot here. Wilmingtonians also caused confusion in stores by buying non-rationed shoes in April."

By 1944, the worst was about under control, but additional pitfalls lay ahead on Wilmington's share of the road to victory. Civilian supplies were yet to be curtailed. "The civilian is 'just beginning to feel the pinch' of wartime shortages and, despite government efforts to fill in the worst gaps in civilian supply, can expect no large-scale relief until the war ends.... 'Up to this point this country has suffered no serious privation,' said a War Production Board official. 'Now the war is coming home to civilians.'"

More of the Worst

The cigarette shortage—"If worse comes to worse and cigarettes actually disappear...there is no actual need for you to go fag-less—not, at least, as long as there is cornsilk. There must be something radically wrong with the kid who had not had a high old time behind the barn or down some alley with cornsilk cigarettes, even if the best wrapper he could get was newsprint and he inexpert at rolling his own. If it lacked the kick of nicotine it certainly contained an unexcelled kick by doing something that would bring a good hiding from a tobacco-saturated dad if discovered in the act." If not cornsilk, then what about dried clover, especially red clover, which "makes you dizzier than any other, and ready for mad adventure."[44]

My gang tried cornsilk probably no more than twice (the second time so you could say you were a "veteran"), and rabbit tobacco a few times, but never the clover stuff. We settled on Indian cigars from the trees in Oleander, but I relinquished after feigning masculinity and throwing up for real. *As for the writer of the foregoing statement, I believe (and hope) his tongue is still on fire.*

Chapter 9
The *Afrika Korps* at Home in Wilmington

El Alamein—Tobruk—Kasserine Pass—Casablanca—the Sahara—Patton—the Desert Fox—the Desert Rats. To a boy's fertile imagination, enhanced by adventurous spirit and a thirst for knowledge, each conjured up visions of an unusual war only an ocean away. A war fought in the sands of North Africa, the Dark Continent, mysterious and vast. How they fought there captivated me, but not nearly as much as what I was about to experience first-hand when the fighting stopped. Of the many fascinations of wartime within reach, perhaps the most stark reminder of what our nation was up against came in the form of living human beings dropped in our midst. The hundreds of German prisoners-of-war remnants from Rommel's Afrika Korps—*the erstwhile-dreaded super enemy—who made my hometown theirs for more than two years. With only a wire fence separating us, and within the range of smell, I had to wonder whether this one or that one had actually killed an American soldier.*

Austrian Leopold Dollfuss, a defeated German soldier, was 22 when the Allies captured him in Tunisia in the spring of 1943. By early 1944, he arrived in Wilmington's POW camp, and was sent home in 1946. In 1995 he returned "to remember the three years he spent in U.S. POW camps a half-century ago....'I didn't mind the time staying here. Because if I had to stay home, I would have had to fight, and I may have been killed.'" He visited the sites of the Carolina Beach Road and 8th and Ann Streets camps where he was interned. Of the latter, "I had a good feeling seeing it again."[1] Others, I'm told, revisited Wilmington over the years.

As another significant contribution to the war effort, Wilmington hosted three POW camps from February 1944 to April 1946. The first was at the intersection of Carolina Beach Road and Shipyard Boulevard two miles south of the city limits. The second was at the old Marine Hospital site in the four-square block area of 8th and Ann. When it opened, the first site closed. The third was a satellite camp at Bluethenthal Army Air Base.

The prisoners were a major attraction, to say the least, worth being included in those few "Sunday drives" for which area residents had saved gas. My parents drove me by the camps a number of times and slowed down to look. At the Ann Street stockade we got out. Even after the war ended, and until their departure, by reputation they remained fearsome, even if no longer my enemy. I still pictured them in khaki shorts in their dust-covered *Panzer* tanks with goggles and desert tan, as in the 1943 movie *Sahara*.*

* * *

Italians or Germans?

In Tunisia in May 1943, the Allies climaxed a two and one-half year battle in the North African desert by scoring their first major ground victory of the war in the European-Mediterranean Theater. The triumph included the surrender of approximately 250,000 German and Italian troops of Field Marshal Erwin Rommel's famed forces. Eventually hundreds were dispatched to Wilmington. Their interaction with our community and the mark they left is one of the area's most unusual wartime stories.

"What is to be done with them all?" the July 1943 headline asked, long before anyone had the foggiest idea of what was in store. "...All will have the necessities of life and be treated as humans, however misled, deserve." The country had room to intern them. "While we are obligated to take care of war prisoners with reasonable consideration, there would seem to be no good reason why they should not, under adequate safeguard harvest farm crops...and perform other labors for their board and keep. If this were done the farm labor problem would be practically solved."[2] The opinion was prophetic.

By November, the army had notified local authorities that 320 Italian POWs were being sent to Wilmington to work in fertilizer plants and in wood production. The intent was for the POWs not to take jobs from local persons. They were here for a "temporary emergency" only. All wages paid by fertilizer and pulp wood dealers for their work was to go to the federal government, with prisoners drawing the prescribed 80 cents per day, as approved by Geneva Convention agreement of 1929.† Once the emergency ended, they were to be removed from Wilmington.[3]

The more docile Italians, with reputation borne of their temperate fighting record, were deemed less potentially hostile than their more warrior German allies. "Certainly they are in a different category from Nazi

---

* Like many wartime movies, *Sahara* (Humphrey Bogart, Lloyd Bridges, J. Carroll Naish), about a U.S. tank crew stranded in the desert without water, helped shape my image of combat, albeit Hollywood-style—the next best thing.

† Firms utilizing POW services paid the U.S. Treasury the prevailing hourly wage rate paid to regular employees. For fertilizer plants, base pay of 42.5 cents per hour for each prisoner. The government then paid POWs 80 cents. Men began work in the plants on February 14, 1944.

or German prisoners, whom it would be difficult to view without alarm except behind barbed wire."[4] Once the site on Carolina Beach Road was agreed to, the newspaper conjectured. "...There would seem to be no reason for apprehension because of the presence so near the city. They will be behind barbed wire in camp and adequately guarded while en route to and from the places of employment chosen for them....There is no doubt that the existence of a war-prisoner camp at the edge of town will bring the war nearer than all the blackout rehearsals and bond campaigns and propaganda conducted to awaken the population...."[5] So true.

But someone was in for a rude awakening, and soon. I can only imagine the shock and apprehension when the government in February 1944 notified local officials it was sending exactly what was unexpected and feared. That the Germans came actually worked out positively. Bernard Rabunsky remembered that one of the American Jewish soldiers assigned as a POW camp guard came to his synagogue and said he would have been more afraid of the Italians "because the Germans represented discipline."[6]

* * *

Some German prisoners of war who worked daily on the Otto Leeuwenburg dairy farm east of town. The men had served with Rommel's famed *Afrika Korps* that surrendered in Tunisia in May 1943. The first POW camp opened in February 1944 at the corner of Shipyard Boulevard and Carolina Beach Road. In November the site moved to a four-square block area around 8th & Ann Streets across from Williston Industrial School.
Provided by son William C. "Bill" Leeuwenburg

The Carolina Beach Road Site

On the southeast corner of Carolina Beach Road and the new road to the shipyard, and across the street from Maffitt Village war housing, stood an abandoned camp formerly used by the National Youth Administration, an early-war federal social agency. After rejecting a proposal to quarter them in a Castle Hayne migrant laborer camp, the army decided in January 1944 to place the POWs there.* "A heavy wire fence will be stretched at a distance of 75 yards around the NYA buildings and the prisoners will be heavily guarded....They will work in squads of 20 with one guard assigned to every five men. This action is necessary because Wilmington is in a labor shortage area as certified by War Manpower Commission. 'POW labor is absolutely not competitive with local labor.'"[7]

The first prisoners, 250, arrived on February 7. The *Morning Star* reported their arrival:

> They "are making the camp habitable in preparation for their temporary stay...." When they would begin work in the area was unclear. "Apparently the Nazis were happy about their 'new surroundings' for they went about the job of erecting army cots and other duties of repairing the internment camp in an energetic manner. It was not all work to them, however, for one prisoner tossed one of this section's cockle burrs at another, who dodged and laughed. Another German chinned himself to an acting bar erected between two pine trees. An American officer predicted the Nazis would have the camp very 'homelike' soon by flowers being planted about the barracks, mess hall and dispensary.'"
>
> "Attired in black trousers, with undershirts, sweatshirts and other fatigue clothing worn at random, [they] worked energetically at their tasks...in the 25-acre rectangular enclosure....The Germans, all enlisted personnel, would for the first time as prisoners sleep on mattresses...a policy just announced by the War Department. They range in age from 17–42, most have served six years in the army, about 20 percent speak English, and others are learning the language at night classes. Sightseeing trips to the internment camp are apparently taboo....Spectators will not be allowed to loiter about the camp....Would be appreciated if the public would not visit there. Highway signs to direct traffic to 'move along' in that area are being erected...."[8]

The newspaper's concern extended its warning a few days later. "...It is difficult with Germans, who generally cling to the mistaken theory that they are supermen as Hitler taught them to believe....Consider that strong armed guards are to be in charge of the prisoners and that no violation of

---

* In February 2002, in a fitting ceremony noting the camp's wartime significance, the city and the World War II Wilmington Home Front Heritage Coalition installed a historic marker at the site, now a drug store.

discipline will be tolerated....Germans are better workers than Italians and can be expected to do a better job....At least it would be wise to withhold judgment for the present."⁹

Passing along the army's orders, and as if folks weren't apprehensive enough, the advice continued. "Curiosity might draw some to the camp and save for the discourtesy of looking at captives could do no harm. But it is possible that some persons might gather at the fence side for other purposes. There must be no communication with the prisoners. It will be advisable therefore for everybody to pass quickly by, for the guards will not be able to distinguish between conspirators and the merely curious, and must treat all alike."* The anticipation and arrival aroused the citizenry. Novelty, or witness to the starkness of war? And what about our boys in their places?

By the end of February, the camp contained 280. Five fertilizer plants employed 234, and one dairy nine. "The first indication that the Nazi POWs would be permanently stationed here was given....The men were doing 'excellent' work operating a machine that mixed, bagged, and weighed fertilizer. Employers were pleased. 'They seem to have a knack for machinery.'"¹⁰ Officials praised their attitude and performance, and allayed any suspicions. The men "'are rendering a great service to the community'" because "'we couldn't get local labor. They are not taking jobs away from Wilmington people....There have been no escapes, or attempted escapes....After they have caught on...there has not been one bit of trouble.'"¹¹

As would be expected, the public had to be convinced the POWs presented no threat. In mid-March, to counter the first wild rumblings, authorities issued "a blanket denial of the hundreds of rumors to the effect that German prisoners are escaping from the heavily fortified camp. The men wear uniforms bearing an unmistakable POW identification."¹² "Our main objective is to get work out of these men," stated Lieutenant R. H. Hazel, camp commanding officer, reminding Wilmingtonians that the Geneva Convention rules govern German as well as American POWs. "We have been severely criticized for being too lenient with the prisoners, but the men are 'strict in their courtesy toward American commissioned officers....And, after all, we want the best results.'"¹³

One month after the compound opened, a picture of routine had evolved. Copies of German-English dictionaries were plentiful. The men managed their own canteen and were allowed a bottle of beer daily which they paid

---

* Soldiers passing the stockade in truck convoys, not civilians, were involved in the first reported incident. Camp Davis commander Colonel Adam E. Potts "has severely rebuked troops of his command for jeering German POWs...," according to the *Camp Davis AA Barrage* newspaper. Potts stated such action violates the Geneva Convention. [*Wilmington Morning Star*, February 28, 1944] On the other hand, the prisoners had to be moved about to their jobs.

for out of earnings or allowances. They listened to news broadcasts (claiming they were all "propaganda") and read periodicals, but cared little for newspapers. Each radio was sealed and checked weekly for tampering. No one had attempted to escape. The barbed wire fence was covered by corner guard towers and illuminated at night. Civil authorities stood ready in case of fire. The men were allowed to write one letter and one postcard home each week on special government forms. Two men, one reputed the operator of one of Germany's largest nurseries, maintained the camp's gardens. They enjoyed movies in the mess hall, particularly Abbott and Costello because their pantomimes were easily understood. Men speaking English explained to those who didn't. Attendance on the job was 99 percent. One POW underwent minor surgery in the camp's three-bed hospital.[14] With warm weather a number of POWs assisted Castle Hayne and Wrightsboro farmers. In several cases, dairy and crop farms would have closed if POWs had not been employed.

* * *

The Old Marine Hospital Site

Culminating a 22-year effort, the city in August 1942 acquired for $20,000 the property of the old World War I-era Marine Hospital property and park area between 8th and 10th Streets, and Ann and Church. The federal government immediately leased it. By the year's end, 11 buildings had been constructed with federal funds as a camp for Wilmington-area members of the Women's Army Auxiliary Corps who had arrived to man the Information and Filter Center. In January 1944 the WAACs moved in from their temporary quarters, but within a few months they were transferred elsewhere, and the site became empty.

In September 1944 the Carolina Beach Road compound housed some 280 men and was considered "overtaxed" without adequate sanitation. Local fertilizer firms asked army and city officials to relocate the POW camp for quicker accessibility in transporting prisoners to their firms, some of which were located across the Cape Fear River. Mayor W. Ronald Lane and city manager A. C. Nichols "did not believe it is a good idea to place POWs in the center of the city." The city contended the site was "settled in the center of many residences and that citizens are already protesting the prospect of a POW camp in their midst...that disturbances precipitated by location of the camp there will necessitate the assignment of additional policemen to the territory." They suggested the abandoned army camp at Carolina Beach, about 12 miles from the present camp, which could accommodate 3,000. But the firms objected to the distance and extra fuel costs. The army didn't want to build more POW camps, and the city felt forced to accept the relocation.[15] On September 14 the Council withdrew its protest, their concerns ameliorated by an employment official's statement that the camp "'has had the best record in the state, both to man-days worked and the little trouble had with prisoners....'"[16]

Prisoners were relocated to the 8th and Ann compound in October after the construction of a stockade and additional facilities.* As their numbers soon increased to 500, the POWs played a key role in harvesting the fall crops in New Hanover and other counties. Their duties also included service in the city's mosquito control program, attending the officer's mess at Bluethenthal Field, and in sawmills, dairies, and fertilizer plants.† The January 1945 count was 530. Demands for their services far outstripped the ability to house them at the Marine Hospital. Rumors that four escaped from the camp in mid-month were "absolutely unfounded," Lieutenant Hazel stated.[17] One POW being transferred to Wilmington did leave his truck, where he was arrested loitering peaceably wearing his blue fatigue uniform with its yellow stenciled "PW" insignia.

Williston Industrial School students James Otis Sampson, Jr., and Cornelia Haggins looked out of school windows toward the POW camp across the street. They were so close yet so far removed. "We weren't allowed to go over there," James recalled.[18] Cornelia, who lived at 102 South 11th, and her friends were not allowed to go on the street "where the prisoners were. We never had to come in contact with them. We had no dealings with 10th Street at all."[19]

The camp was only about two blocks from Peggy Warren's 9th Street house.[20] She and her brothers Pat and Gene Warren and their friends had gone to the park almost every day to play ball. "The park was an important part of our lives. I was instructed not to get too close to the POW area where there were lookout towers and barbed wire fences. We were instructed never to smile, wave, or show any friendliness towards the prisoners. I remember seeing the young German soldiers exercising and playing what I know today is soccer."

"...She vividly recalls the fear that mysterious prisoners stirred in the heart of a six-year old," the newspaper reported about Margaret Sampson when she was a student at Williston Primary School across from the camp. They left a strong impression on her childhood. "That's when I learned to

---

* The site is now called Robert Strange Park and contains tennis courts, softball fields, recreation buildings, and a large playground. No camp remnants are standing, but the four-block square area can be visualized easily. During Wartime Wilmington Commemoration, 1999, the city erected a historical pole marker on the 10th Street perimeter facing Gregory Elementary.

† Shipyard worker Adrian Hurst hired POWs to remove nails from scrap lumber he brought from the yard to build his Masonboro Sound house. Building material was so scarce that lumber was reused. He picked them up in an activity bus. "They loved to be out of the building [camp]. He carried no guns. That's what happened when you had four children and you needed a house." [Interview with Ellen Gilliard Wychel, July 9, 1999]

climb trees," Margaret remembered. "If the prisoners were going to make a break they would wait until recess and run across where we were playing. They knew the guards would not shoot into a group of children. So the teachers taught us to climb trees. If we couldn't get back into the building, we'd climb a tree...." She saw "groups of prisoners as they walked with escorts from the train station downtown to the prison camp." She can picture the camp's "little white buildings, barbed wire fences and guard towers. [Escapes] If I was outside, I would run to the side of the house, climb on the garage and get down on top of the house and watch them chase them down Church and Glen Streets."[21]

The prisoners came to the fence when the children were outside. If teachers allowed them, "We'd dash across the street and give them candy and gum and talk to them....A lot of the times we couldn't understand them, but the gestures were friendly. School officials worried that the prisoners would escape and run straight for the school yard. The officials didn't want children to get shot, trampled or taken as hostages. Adults worried about it being so close to the school." But the children weren't afraid. Sometimes POWs escaped, Margaret recalled. She used to climb to the roof of her parents' house at 513 South 13th Street. From there, she witnessed two prison breaks."* "...People in authority have told me there weren't any prison breaks, but I knew there was."[22]

Prisoners with farm backgrounds were selected for dairy work, recalled John D. "Jack" McCarley III, whose family ran the Echo Farm Dairy.[23] His father, J. D. McCarley, Jr., was able to get some deferments for some of his regular workers. "The prisoners were a tremendous relief because almost every able bodied person had gone into the service." The McCarleys drove a truck to the camp to pick up the 10 POWs who usually worked for him. The guards knew who they were and had their prisoners waiting, accompanied by a guard with a carbine for protection. But he never followed them around, "just passed the time of day."

"Everybody realized they were just people like us. I can't recall a single incident. My father and grandfather [A. O. McEachern] reached out to help them. Max looked so young, he was only a few years older than me. I thought he was too young to go off to war. Max was definitely just a kid." He spoke some English. "They were all good workers. They were definitely not lazy. I heard Dad comment on that many times." One, a

---

* Fellow historian and friend Margaret Sampson Rogers is the only person I spoke with who either witnessed or claimed to know anything about POW escapes other than rumors. I found no record of any escapes. Years ago she researched some aspects of the POW camps which led to her writing a one-act play ("The Friendly Enemy") and a tome about her POW remembrances as a young girl. Wartime Wilmington Commemoration, 1999, presented her play. If there were escapes, security measures likely would have prohibited a public statement. While recognizing the possibility, I am skeptical.

mason, built a catch system for drainage from the plant where they processed and bottled milk. He built it much better than father had expected. Another tried to organize the POWs that they should do only one type of work. Dad didn't like that and reported it to the camp commander and it was soon stopped. One Christmas a POW asked his father for liquor. He went to the commander who okayed it. "He'd let that slide by. My dad's heart went out to them. He had compassion."

"I remember their faces as if it were yesterday," said Otto's son, William Charles "Bill" Leeuwenburg, when viewing photographs of those who worked on his north Market Street dairy.[24] "They were Germans but not Nazis." His father worked at least 50. One was George Ebert, a machinist in Germany, who repaired his farm machinery. He would give it to Bill to give to his father and tell him he found it repaired. Ebert didn't want the other POWs to know he'd done that, fearing they would deem him a potential collaborator. The POWs would not milk the cows by machine, but put Vasoline on their hands when they milked. One POW artist drew pictures for Bill's mother; another was a gardener. "Pretty soon the POWs began coming around [to farm] without guards." Before kids came to visit Bill on the farm, they had heard how awful the POWs were. When the men gave the kids candy bars, the boys were afraid to eat them because they thought the treats were poisoned. This soon changed.

The prisoners had one advantage. They were Caucasian, and interestingly enough, I heard of a couple of instances of local favoritism over Negro Americans. One in particular is illustrative. Fred McRee's father, Fred McRee, worked at the popular Big Ike's Shoe Repair at 114 Princess Street. One time an army lieutenant brought a few Germans into the shop to get their shoes repaired. The Germans acceded to a Negro woman customer who was there ahead of them. The owner, a white named Houston, overruled that courtesy and waited on the Germans as next in line for service.[25] By their submissiveness and perceived helplessness, the prisoners gradually defused hostility and inquisitiveness, perhaps even touching empathy and affections.

For a number of Wilmingtonians young and old who saw them, "they looked and acted like us." Forest Hills classmate Dudley Humphrey was typical. Meeting some prisoners at Echo Farm, he found they were just as nice as our soldiers, but happy to be out of the war.[26] Classmate Joseph H. "Joe" Johnson, Jr., played at Johnny Leeuwenburg's dairy in Devon Park. He remembered what they looked like, basically healthy and nice-looking young men. "They didn't look tough or as mean as one would have thought about the enemy."[27] Classmate Robert F. "Bobby" Cameron and friends rode their bikes and ponies past the POWs working on the Otto Leeuwenburg dairy. "They would leer at us."[28]

One year after the POW program began, individuals and companies using POW labor reported "they are finding their prisoner help much more satisfactory and things are running much more smoothly this year than last." The Taylor farm adjacent to Forest Hills became the area's fourth to use POWs.[29] Harold Laing and friends visited that farm at the north end of Mercer Avenue, climbed up into the barn and observed the POWs working below. Soon they were noticed. "What they were eating sure smelled good. They finally coaxed us down and fed us. It was a pleasant experience with the Germans."[30] Occasionally I saw them while playing around the Taylor farm, but not up close.

Cooperative and enthusiastic as they had been, many Germans tired of working in fertilizer plants. In late March 1945, between 150–200 who "displayed recalcitrance" over work details at the Swift & Company fertilizer plant, "changed their minds after [seven] hours segregation in a chilly corner of the stockade." Lieutenant Hazel "plans to have the group at fault [some 400] work Sunday to make up for the hours they missed...." All others worked their schedules without interruption. The night shift POWs employed there were accomplishing far less than the day shift. The army set phosphate tonnage goals. They failed to comply, and were thus penned in the camp's north end without food or additional clothing for 24 hours or until they agreed to perform their tasks. Hazel said the Wilmington POW camp rates "second to none" in productivity in his command area. About half the fertilizer processed locally had been done by his men.[31] Camp neighbor George Norman remembered when the POWs refused to work at the plant. "They said it stunk. They didn't do nothing."[32]

The confrontation generated news interest several days before V-E Day: "Local POWs Well Fed But are Forced to Work," the "life-and-culture" piece read.

> They grow their own vegetables which make up most of dinner and supper menus on approximately 14 acres of land contributed by two truck farmers. This fresh produce will save the government some $1,800 monthly this summer. They get meat in limited quantities, but it's mostly fish, bologna, and salami. The only fresh meats are kidneys, liver, and beef hearts. "The Germans, whose favorite food comprises potatoes and bread, are being made to eat vegetables," Hazel stated. They receive a balanced diet. "We're not coddling these prisoners....Everyone working the Germans had told him their work was superior to that of any employees they had, or had ever had."[33]
>
> They either complete their assigned work or go to guardhouse. No one has been confined in more than two months. The 531 men are performing about 50 different types of work. Night details of 25 men at fertilizer factories must produce 200 tons in eight hours. On a "rush" lettuce order at Castle Hayne, a reporter saw eight POWs pack and tie baskets deftly, working quietly and steadily as always. Only non-critical items

are for sale at their PX: ginger ale, orange, grape, and strawberry drinks—no colas or any kind of beer. Only "roll-your-own" tobacco is sold.[34]

Lieutenant Hazel added, "'They are expecting Germany to fall. They have their own radio and the *New York Times*. They've been a little quieter this week since the false armistice announcement...but this is because they don't know what will happen to them.'" He expects no trouble when Europe's war ends. "'We've made arrangements if there should be any trouble.'"[35]

* * *

The Bluethenthal Satellite

Handfuls of prisoners were assigned and rotated to duty at Bluethenthal Field to work in the officers' mess, office buildings, and on groundskeeping. Their compound included two storage-type buildings still standing and visible (pale yellow) from the wide driveway currently used to enter the airport terminal area from 23rd Street. Peggy Moore remembered the Germans "had free run of the air base raking leaves and doing chores—pretty funny to see them ambling around, no one seemed to be supervising. Maybe they were just glad to be here instead of over there."[36] Janet Rabunsky worked at the field. To get to the bathroom she had to walk past them ("looked like they were 16 or 17 years old") who were working near her, "I could have reached out and touched them."[37] POWs started the office fires in the morning before work hours. Some would not eat corn because it was also fed to the pigs. One was an opera singer and sometimes soloed for them in the warehouse.[38]

A couple of nights a week, Aline Hufham Spencer (NHHS '39) was a volunteer Red Cross Nurse's Aide at James Walker Memorial Hospital.[39] Occasionally she aided air force men being treated at the field's hospital. Mostly she rubbed their backs and played games, but she remembered helping a German POW. "I felt funny, but if Bill were a POW over there I would appreciate someone doing the same thing for him.* I turned as white as the patients did—would gag—really appreciated nurses and what they did."

My Nurse's Aide mother, Viola M. Jones, often assisted in the Bluethenthal hospital.[40] She was present when Ernest Bautz, 25, died in 1944, the first POW death. "I worked in the hospital & did help this man all I could," she wrote by a clipping in the margin of one of the wartime scrapbooks she kept for American Legion Post 10. Bautz died of blood poisoning "contracted after the removal of a splinter in his arm in a fall at Heide Trask's farm, after he attempted to jump from a truck." He was from Trier,

---

* At the time the present Aline Hartis was married to Wilmingtonian and NHHS classmate air force Lieutenant William A. Spencer, a B-24 *Liberator* pilot who was first missing in action over Germany in September 1944 and later declared KIA.

William A. "Bill" and Aline Hufham Spencer (NHHS '39 classmates) shortly after their 1943 marriage. B-24 pilot Spencer was KIA over Germany during a raid in September 1944.

Provided by Aline Hufham Hartis

Germany, where his wife and child lived. His body was shipped to Camp Butner, North Carolina, for burial in the German POW cemetery there.

* * *

Post-War POWs

The Germans "received the VE-Day news 'mighty fine,' will enjoy no let-up in their industrial and agricultural work, but rather have additional 'tasks' to perform in some instances." They "went about their tasks as usual. They were expecting the end."

At this time the number of prisoners peaked at 552. Those working in sawmills were assigned to cut 2,000 feet of timber during an eight-hour shift instead of the previous 1,000. Others working on farms, packing houses and elsewhere were already doing 12–18 hour days.[41] On May 26, Hazel noted "'the efficiency of the German POWs in Wilmington has improved greatly since the defeat of Germany....They are doing better work, are much quieter and are performing all their duties more efficiently.'" The guards said they "are easier to manage." V-E Day was the same as any other days and they put in a full day's work.[42] And they began using their garden cabbage to make sauerkraut for consumption next winter. Five weeks after Germany surrendered, he noted an improvement in their "attitude" and efficiency. Most were working in the pulpwood business.*

William N. "Bill" Kingoff's father Benjamin Kingoff owned and operated a popular Front Street jewelry store (still going strong).[43] Before the war ended, an army officer spoke to him about selling merchandise to POWs, but he didn't want to do it. The officer said the men had U.S. scrip and the government wanted them to spend it on merchandise and not take it out of the country. The Kingoffs and Leo Baum of McGrath's Music Company went out to the camp. McGrath's offered for sale a harmonica with only one side and a guitar without strings. Kingoff's offered reconditioned old scrap

---

* By July 1, 1945, about 1,360 POWs worked in the Wilmington area, 549 at 8th and Ann and 811 at Camp Davis. Camp Butner had 3,136. Approximately 9,400 Germans were working in the state relieving the manpower shortage. [*Wilmington Morning Star*, June 30, 1945]

watches, because it was hard to get new ones. MPs lined up men to come into the sale. The first one in said "Heil Hitler!" and gave the Nazi salute. A guard whacked him on the back of the head. "Those guys weren't stupid. They knew they had to buy something and couldn't take home scrip to get cash for it. Interesting experience for not having seen the enemy. Expected to see the master race, but they looked like ordinary people."

The government vacillated on when the Germans would be sent home and the Wilmington camp closed. Conflicting orders resulted, causing some concern among local farmers and other industries they supported who had to look elsewhere for labor help. In November 75 men, the first, were sent to Camp Butner for shipment to Europe. President Harry S Truman signed an order in January 1946 that all POWs would be returned by the end of June. The 305 men still in camp were working for local farmers, contracted on a daily basis. Some POWs wished to remain in America. "They have put their roots in Wilmington soil, and they don't want to have them torn out." On March 14, 100 left for return to Germany. "We don't want to leave Wilmington. We want to stay here and become citizens and till the land for you," they told the farmers they worked for. "'We hated to see the prisoners leave....We have treated them like human beings and paid them the regular farm labor wages, and, in return, they proved themselves to be human beings like you and me,'" said Castle Hayne farmer Adam Sondey, echoed by Anthony Schlegel.[44]

Mid-April appeared the most likely release date, but not without being disconcerting. "There is but one more month to work them. If a fair number of those in this area were turned over for work in the dairy industry, their month's work would have a beneficial effect on the supply of milk. But they are 'frozen' in the pulpwood industry by special order, and as a consequence dairymen are not able to do their full part in overcoming the milk shortage. A similar situation exists in the produce industry...."[45] The 180 men here in late March were allowed to finish their farm duties.

* * *

Auf Wiedersehn

On April 12, 1946, they were gone. Wilmington's 149 POWs were en route to Germany. "Behind them they leave a spring crop of vegetables....The prisoners' departure strikes three sad blows—one to the farmers, one to the community, and one to the prisoners themselves. The farmers have found the prisoners almost indispensable in helping them plant and tend the spring crops....Officials fought to keep the prisoners in America, not only to grow the food to feed this country but to feed the whole world. But the prisoners are on their way home today."[46]

By the end of May, the federal government had returned the old Marine Hospital buildings and site to the city, and in September accepted the city's bid of $10,000. Buildings on the site were set for dismantling and salvaging. By November the structures were sold at public auction, the city realizing approximately $6,000. Earl Sneeden purchased four guard towers at $15 each. What he did with them no one knows. The site itself was supposed to become the new municipal memorial auditorium. Whatever happened to that plan no one knows either.

Keeping in Touch with Former POWs[47]

John D. "Jack" McCarley III's dairyman father maintained contact with a number of his POWs after the war. These are some of the letters.

Werner Ollmann (POW no. AA-52159), POW Camp 36, Hartwell Dog Track, Near Aylesbury (Bucks) Great Britain to Echo Farm, Mr. McCarley, Jr., Wilmington, N.C., USA, 30 June 1946 [in English]

"As you see my repatriation ended here in England. I am put to work on the land and do any farm work and also making again there that I get home as soon as possible. How are you? I would be very glad to get any news from you."

* * *

Ollmann to McCarley, 29 September 1946

"As you will know we are fully engaged in harvesting now....Food shortage will last a long time owing to this bad harvest. Nearly everything is scarce in this country especially for us. Even cigarettes. Would it be possible for you to send me some? By the way with me is another chap who worked for you. But I think you do not know him because he worked on the farm and did not milk. His name is Clemens.

"Now the government is going to issue the repatriation scheme for us. But our release may take a long time because only 15,000 get home every week. I am sure I am not one of the first to go home. My time may be in one year's time."

* * *

J. D. McCarley, Jr., to Bernhard Thiel, Hanover, Germany, May 1, 1948

"All of you boys that worked for me during the war are in my thoughts quite often. Quite a few of you have written to me and I am always to hear that you have gotten safely back to your native land and I only wish that condition were so that all of you could find happiness and contentment.

"The farm is being operated about the same as when you were here, except of course I have American boys working for me. The cows are milking well and the crops have been good. I remember you used to enjoy riding Dan (the horse), he is still here and I rode him several days ago. I tried to send you some Camel cigarettes, but the post office would not accept them for shipment to Germany. Maybe later on they will accept them and if so I will send them to you."

* * *

McCarley to Thiel, July 31, 1948
"...Unfortunately I have not heard from Anton Weiss, so I am unable to give you any information concerning him. I am having a CARE package of food sent to you and I am sending it to the same address as this letter so be on the lookout for it. Please accept this as a present from me."

* * *

Max Speth, Regensburg, Germany, to The Manager of the Echo Farm, Wilmington, N.C., 23 January 1948
"Dear Sir:
"This is you former POW Max! Do you remember? At that time in 1944 I had to leave you for Camp Shanks New York and from there we were shipped over to England. Over there I did reparation work for 1-1/2 yrs. From time to time we were also in England busy on farms. But I never had as good a time as I had on your farm. Sometimes I remembered quite sadly your excellent doughnuts and the very good milk of the Echo Farm.

"Arriving at home I found my family healthy. The house and everything was in the old order. That means the best luck in this days. Since my arrival I lost 25 pounds of weight. The picture you find herein has been made a few days after my discharge. You certainly cannot imagine how conditions of life are in Germany."

Note from Jack McCarley: "Max was only 19 years old—much younger than other prisoners. I was 15. He spoke English well and we could have conversations. His family owned a landscape business back in Germany."

Postwar Bernhard Thiel, former German prisoner of war who worked on the McEachern-McCarley Echo Farm, stayed in touch with the McCarleys after the war.
Provided by John D. "Jack" McCarley III

* * *

McCarley to Speth, June 7, 1948
"I often think of you boys that worked for me during the war and it makes me very happy when I hear from one of you and learn that you have arrived home safely. I only wish the conditions were much better for you. I sincerely hope that food supplies and everything will return to normal very soon.

"Quite a few of the boys that were at the farm when you were here have written to me. Some of them have been very unfortunate in what they found when they arrived home. It makes me very sad for them. My youngest son remembers you when I read your letter to him, he recalled how you played with him in the yard. My oldest son is away at college. My wife often talked to you and she asks that I send you her best regards. The farm is being operated about the same as when you were here except of course I have American boys working for me."

* * *

Albert Waterman, Sendenhorst, Germany, to J. D. McCarley, Jr., 24 April 1948
"I thank you very much for you kind letter, in which you have send me the photos from your BIG FARM, where nearly I spent two years. And I must tell you, that about all I enjoyed very much.

"[Going home] Hoping soon to get discharged we crossed the ocean to Europe and reached London. There again we were occupied in a big farm. But that was not a farm, like yours. This English farm was rather obsolete. There were only a few machines. All types were 'Made in USA' and never I have seen 'Made in England.' We were treated like slaves (bad treatment and little money). What was it a difference between your camp and this English one.

"In March last year after a captivity of four years I was discharged and April 24th...I happily arrived home....I was very disabused [*sic*], when I heard, that my father had died some weeks before I came home....For our future we have no much hope."

Chapter 10
"Thieves Are Holding High Carnival"

Crime or law-and-order problems in Wilmington reported in articles in the daily paper didn't necessarily grab my attention. I barely absorbed them if at all. I remember seeing remnants of street fights and automobile accidents, and heard about fires and killings. But all of this was way beyond what I cared to comprehend, and because none of it affected my life directly. I had school, friends, and fighting Japs to keep me busy. Only during my research into this story did I realize the enormous impact of crime and disorder on the local area: a limited war within the home-front's war.

Wilmington's crime and law-and-order problems emerged in articles in the daily paper: "Wilmington is not meeting its crime emergency. Because the city has outgrown the police force and additional officers are unobtainable, thieves are holding high carnival. Homes are being robbed, guests in lodging houses are losing their money and other valuables, at an alarming rate. Very little of the loot is recovered, few of the thieves caught and punished....Something drastic must be done, and done quickly."[1]

Christmas 1941 ushered in a tempestuous three-plus years of heavy crime until the huge exit of military personnel and war workers from the population slowed it down to more "manageable proportions." The era's "duke's mixture" consisted of murders, assaults and rapes, larceny and petty thefts, fatal accidents, fires, street and café fights—and thousands of jaywalking and over-parking violations which law enforcement found much easier to handle. An average of 35,000 servicemen visited the city each weekend. Police nevertheless were proud of their role in the war effort, stating the only difference was the soldier's uniform was khaki, and the policeman's blue. Law enforcement, woefully undermanned with inadequate resources, had its hands full.

Justice was usually swift, with decisions often rendered within days or weeks of arrests. But did the punishment always fit the crime? Court decisions appeared to lack consistency in their never-ending merry-go-round of cases. Hindsight evaluation, with facts limited primarily to newspaper accounts, found numerous instances of puzzling verdicts and sentences. For instance, in 1943 two Negro youths drew six- and eight-month jail sentences for stealing two bicycles and riding them to Goldsboro. A Negro was sentenced to two years on the county roads for stealing two automobile tires that same year.

Most of the crime reported in the white newspapers was either indiscriminate or white-on-white. To the perpetrator, race may have been a motive one way or another, but Negro crime appeared to be directed mostly on each other. When a Negro was involved, the newspaper headline usually told you so. For example, a "free-for-all fight" among Negro soldiers and civilians one block from the Negro USO at 9th and Nixon resulted in the shooting of civilian Kilby James by a Negro MP in a struggle to break up the fight.[2] If race was unmentioned, those in question were always white.* There appeared to be no overt attempt to spotlight race as a causative, as a stereotype, or to inflame. Rather it was the most logical identifier of that day in a community that was divided into only two racial groups, black or white.

The stories, the statistics, show a different side of the Wilmington area that residents seemed more comfortable in ignoring then and would rather just forget about even now. The truth is that no matter how you looked at it, Wilmington was its own form of "Sin City" during World War II.

* * *

Fights, Assaults, and Rapes

Fights and assaults found fertile grounds on downtown streets, outside bars and clubs, and in the housing projects. Much was attributable to animosity, even some hostility, between civilians and military personnel, excessive consumption of alcohol, and the attraction of unsavory characters to a wartime boomtown.

Civilians and soldiers often had it out. Shipyard worker J. E. Wheeler objected to soldiers getting priority service at the popular Peacock Alley Soda Shop on South 17th Street.[3] After Camp Davis Sergeant Swan E. Nelson "remonstrated" with him, the two "buried their disagreements," shook hands, and headed for their cars. But Wheeler struck Nelson with a beer bottle, knocking him to the ground and partially paralyzing him. The army gave him a disability discharge. The case was settled 17 months later when Wheeler was sentenced to two years in the state penitentiary and to pay Nelson $1,250.

---

* The way you read it here is the way it was announced. Rape victims' names were made public. Negro MPs patrolled areas frequented by Negro soldiers, bringing them in contact also with Negro civilians. Segregation worked both ways. Except to do business, whites did not enter Negro establishments and at night stayed out of Negro neighborhoods. The same the other way around.

One soldier died and another was arrested following a street fight near Front and Grace in November 1943.[4] The pair argued in a news dealer's shop and after one of them struck the other with a bottle, both were ejected from the store. The fight erupted and "one soldier threw the other into a plate glass window in the Singer Sewing Machine Company office."

"Patrons and employees of the Southern Kitchen restaurant in the center of the business district gaped as a slashed and bleeding Negro raced through the restaurant to collapse on the sidewalk....An 18-inch butcher knife came winging through the air after him to slice through the screen door...."[5] Military police passing by arrested the knife thrower, Negro Henry Shavers, 16, while city police picked up Willie Crump, 21, off the sidewalk. The fight started over a two-cent loss in a card game at the nearby Dixie Café where both worked as dishwashers.

H. H. Waters "attempted to shoot his wife on a crowded section of Front Street...." First attacking her with his hands, when bystander Ralph Woods grabbed him he pulled out a pistol and threatened to shoot Woods, who then disarmed Waters. He was fined $100 and costs.[6]

When arrested, Raymond Russell went berserk, slugged two highway patrolmen including J. L. "Smokey Joe" Flowers, attacked two deputies at the hospital, bit the hand of the night nurse, "until he was put to sleep with a drug."[7] He got 18 months on the county farm.

Camp Davis soldier Jack Montgomery met a 13-year old girl on Front Street and asked her to accompany him to a movie. After the show, he took her to the bus station so she could go home, but she missed her bus and had to wait for the next one. "Reluctantly, she said, she agreed to walk around with the man....They entered a church yard at 4th and Grace where the attack subsequently occurred." She "struggled to resist the man's advances." When an MP found her she was bruised about the body and crying. Although the "maximum penalty for a case of this type...was death," a court-martial sentenced Montgomery to 30 days in military prison and a $30 fine.[8]

Five boys, including two juveniles, raped a middle-aged woman whose husband was serving in the South Pacific. At first she did not press charges, but eventually the oldest, Charlie T. Sutton, drew a sentence of 8–15 years in the state penitentiary. The district solicitor reminded the jury that "it took 'nerve and a strong heart' to fight the battle in the home front, referring to their position as citizens whose duty it is to protect those who were fighting on foreign soil for their country." One of the boys, Charlie Franks, already with a court record, later was sentenced to nine months on the state roads for breaking and entering.[9]

Negro laborer Arie Quick, 38, was indicted for raping nine-year old Negress Willie Baldwin. The attack took place in his apartment after her grandmother ordered her to deliver matches to him. The Negro Community Hospital treated the child for venereal disease.

The cleanup of taverns and "piccolo (juke-box) joints"—places where riffraff would gather for entertainment and no good, was an ongoing task.[10] The campaign began in July 1942. Of special note was the notorious Green Lantern Tavern on Campbell Street, where Negro MPs had fatally wounded a Negro Camp Davis sergeant. Police chief Charles H. Casteen said the tavern is "no worse than any other place of its sort. A lot of Negro soldiers congregate there and it's gotten a bad name. If we close it, they (the soldiers) will only go to some other Negro establishment which now has a good reputation and you'll have the same thing." "Bad name" means it "had a reputation for disputes" for its conflicts among Negro soldiers and civilians. A January 1944 fire of unknown origin gutted the establishment.

* * *

Thefts

Thefts of automobiles, new and retread tires, tubes, and other automotive supplies surged after rationing began. So did heists of alcoholic beverages and gasoline coupons. The police and OPA did their best to crack down on the larcenies and black-market resale. For every person arrested for stealing, usually one or more were arrested for receiving his stolen goods. Frequent cases were reported of breaking and entering shops, homes, clubs, grocery stores, filling stations, car dealerships, cafés, and schools.

You had to be on the lookout for pickpockets and petty thieves who could be anywhere, stealing wallets, railroad tickets, government checks, cash, watches, and other valuables. Hard hit were soldiers while sleeping in bus and train stations, spending nights in hotel rooms, or hitchhiking. Women and domestics were among those entering rooming houses to lift money from defense workers' rooms. One man carelessly left his wallet containing $525 on a store counter while making a purchase, and on realizing his mistake found it gone on his return. Thieves stole the army shoes of two GIs sleeping at the 2nd and Orange USO. "Barefoot and panting from their rush through the rain from a USO worker's automobile into the rationing office," their plea prompted the rationing board to issue them special shoe purchase certificates under an "extreme emergency" condition.[11]

Greedy thieves went after the government and charitable organizations. Negro Willie Smith stole two army barracks bags of loot rifled from United States mail bags at the ACL station that were awaiting Camp Davis pickup. "Telephone bandit" Negro John Greer in 1942 received 15 months in jail for taking cash from a war bond stamp cash box. In September 1944

Greer, 18, was sentenced to one year and a day in the Atlanta federal prison for robbing the American Red Cross headquarters of $80.

In 1943 Wilmington and Brunswick and Columbus Counties were hard-hit by an organized gang stealing them all, including cars, gasoline, tires, and liquor. The Federal Bureau of Investigation broke up the gang with the arrest of William C. "Rabbit" Hare and five others. Hare was "reported to be one of the 'big time' members" of the "largest group of its kind to be rounded up in this section in many years."[12] In May 1944 police arrested four 10- to 12-year old boys, "members of an organized gang with a clever 10-year old leader," who admitted to petty larcenies including school break-ins. They described their interest in crime thriller movies and reading crime books.[13]

A girl who said her name was "Mary" relieved a Camp Davis private of $375, a pen, and cigarette lighter at Cape Fear Hotel.[14] He "had been drinking in his room with that he had fallen asleep and awakened to find his possessions gone. He said he had met the woman just before he checked out of the hotel earlier in the evening" and that she went to his room.

Rosie Lee Burks, 23, who kept "books" on her two years of shoplifting activity, was charged with larceny and receiving merchandise valued at $5,000.[15] Items included shoes, candy, clothing, groceries, etc. She recorded the name of each store robbed, article taken, and the listed price.

Thievery, intertwined with the black market, became a thriving business. But by 1943, judges had begun lowering the boom. Youth Lonnie "Buster" C. Murphy, already serving a suspended sentence for automobile theft, in December 1942 received a 5- to 7-year sentence for automobile larceny. "This is the first time I have imposed such a sentence

Cape Fear Hotel, wartime. Wilmington's largest and finest, but also the scene of illegal and immoral activities including black marketeering and prostitution. Its reputation, however, was surpassed by that of the Wilmington Hotel several blocks away. The Cape Fear is now a senior retirement home. The Wilmington is no longer.

Provided by Aaron May

as this on a boy so young."[16] Negro Stanish Polite received 80–100 years imprisonment, the "longest term sentence for burglary recorded here in many years."[17]

* * *

Murders

Many Wilmington-area murders and other major crimes went unsolved, or the final disposition often went unnoted in the newspaper. Today's type of investigative reporting was unheard of, and Wilmington reporters lacked either manpower, time, experience, or access to records for full (or adequate) reporting on controversial subjects. Negroes figured prominently in *Star-News* accounts of murders.

This case illustrates the point. In July 1942 Negro Camp Davis soldier John E. Toliver drowned at Seabreeze, the Negro beach north of Carolina Beach.[18] Another Negro soldier, Sammy Jones, apparently pushed him into the Inland Waterway, and was charged. The body was later recovered in the Cape Fear River around the curve from the waterway. This case appeared in the papers several times, but we never knew what happened to Jones. Apparently the military took jurisdiction.

Otto Platt Maxwell discovered shipyard worker Johnnie A. Moore seated with Maxwell's wife in a parked car on South 6th near Castle at midnight.[19] He went up to the car. "Oh yes, I caught you with my wife and I should kill you both." Standing on the right side, Maxwell leaned across the woman and attempted to assault Moore. She pulled Maxwell's hat down over his eyes. Moore leaped from the car and the men scuffled briefly, and Maxwell stabbed him to death. A Superior Court jury found him not guilty to second degree murder and the judge set him free.

By December 9, 1941, "another Negress, the second in two days, was slain...at her home, 1009½ Hutaffs Alley."[20] Lela Mae Jenkins died when hit in the side with a shotgun blast from her brother Sam Jenkins. The other was Estelle Walker, 25, found dead at 8th and Green from bullet wounds. Police arrested James Brown and LeRoy Scott, "both colored," without bond.[21] For the second-degree pistol murder of Negress Eliza Corbett at a Brooklyn café, the court sentenced proprietor Johnnie McKoy to 20 years in the state prison. "I just got so mad that I shot her." The woman "hung around his place and cursed him. Witnesses testified that McKoy went to the door of the café and emptied his pistol at the woman as she stood outside after he had ordered her out of the café. He declared that she had slapped him."[22]

An argument over an alleged 10-cent taxi fare overcharge resulted in the shotgun death of the 19-year-old driver, Milton Buster Jackson, Jr., Wilmington native of the Coastal and Victory Cab Company.[23] Jackson "died almost instantly when a 12-gauge shotgun blast ripped into his chest" at shipyard worker Joseph Dewey Hinson's home in Lake Village. Hinson, who said Jackson threatened him with a large jack, went inside and returned with a gun and ordered Jackson to leave. He hit Hinson with the jack "and continued advancing until he was shot down at very close range. Even after being shot, Jackson grabbed the gun and took it from Hinson but died a few seconds later and fell on the gun." A cab passenger witness' testimony differed from self-defense: Hinson pointed the shotgun at Jackson and asked, "You believe I'll shoot you?" Jackson said yes. A few seconds later the gun went off.

"After an ice pick had failed to stop him, Joe Hall, alias Pompi, Negro, of 1312 Brooklyn Alley, was killed...at his home."[24] His wife, Virginia Hall, was arrested and admitted the killing. She and her husband had quarreled all day and she knifed him when he pulled a gun on her. Already a "two-time killer...she had served time before for murder of another man." Pleading not guilty, the court discharged her following her attorney's "non-suit" motion.

Strange justice.

* * *

Some Unusual Cases

Acting Wrightsville Beach chief J. B. Brooks, 25, "was given a fair chance of recovery" at the hospital after being shot by an army guard on the boardwalk at 1:30 a.m. on February 13, 1943.[25] The soldier, stationed with an infantry company at the beach, challenged and shot him, dressed in civilian clothes, "in front of Lumina pavilion, piercing stomach and kidneys. Sheriff C. David Jones said "the boardwalk is a public thoroughfare and outside the army's jurisdiction." Military authorities held the guard. "Slightly conflicting stories were told by witnesses." Brooks returned to duty.

"A case that began with an alleged 'hex'...[brought a] reprimand and warning for a 70-year old self-styled Negro preacher."[26] James Henderson alleged to have thrown an egg from which the white had been removed and which had been surrounded by bits of paper and string, on the roof of the porch of a Negro house. Negress Evangeline Bell, the accuser, told him, "You go home and quit bothering your neighbors." She found "goofer roots" and "goofer nuts," magical charms for exerting influences on their victims, around her home and believed he had put them there. Recorder Alton Lennon told him, "Don't let me catch you up here again." "The Negroes were afraid to even touch the egg," a policeman stated.

An unidentified sailor "decided to while away a dull Sunday afternoon by escaping from the military police cell block in the county courthouse building."[27] He tore the screen from a ceiling vent and crawled into the narrow space. "Despite radiators, pipes and other obstacles, he had progressed some 15 foot from his original point of entry and was nearly unconscious, apparently from heat exhaustion, when located." Firemen rescued him.

"Fashionably clad in the latest edition of the zoot suit, James Albert Willis, 23-year old Wilmington Negro, argued eloquently in his own behalf...before a Superior Court jury...but neither the jury nor Judge Luther Hamilton saw quite eye to eye with him."[28] The verdict was guilty of assault and aiding and abetting larceny, with 15 months on the county roads. Known as "Bootee," he wore the high-shouldered, long-cut zoot suit adorned with a purple carnation in lapel, matched by purple handkerchief in pocket, black pants tapered elegantly to stuffed cuffs a couple of inches above his brown shoes. "Out of 15 head of boys shooting crap on that corner they had to pick me. 'Course I admits being on the road gang and I was in the navy and got a undishonorable discharge. That's all it was. I made my mind to do the right thing afterwards. 'Course a fellow gets in a scrape every once in a while and gets in a argument over his girl." "That was a good speech, James," Hamilton said.

John B. Howard, 26, of Sunset Park, received a year's probation in U.S. District Court for admitting he sold the drug adrenaline, which would raise blood pressure, to prospective draftees.[29] Once facing "possible charges of sedition," Howard was suspected of assisting local draftees in failing army physical examinations. A "rather high percentage" of local men had been rejected for service because of high blood pressure.

Two women cited the same man as "being poor husband material." His first wife "dragged him into court on a charge of failing to support his 3 children adequately."[30] Judge H. Winfield Smith ordered him to pay her $20 a week and demanded a bond of $300. "No sooner had Smith disposed of this case than wife No. 2 appeared before him. "What do you want?" he asked. "I want to know how I can get rid of him. I had a good husband the first time. Then I got this one. He has been no account. I guess the third one will be worse," she volunteered philosophically. "Do you mean you want a third one after you divorce this fellow?" "Absolutely. I'm not going to hang around here by myself." Both "forgiving wives" and children brought "food and comfort" to him in jail.

It was easier for law enforcement and public sentiment to come down on lesser infractions. In the war's jittery early days, the newspaper urged residents to "Stop the Fireworks." "Although fireworks have been prohibited it is impossible for the police to catch all offenders....To nervous ears a giant firecracker all too easily could sound like a bomb....One scream could transform itself into a panic (December 1941)."[31] John King became the first Wilmingtonian to be arrested for violating the city's bicycle ordinance when he was apprehended for riding without lights and without a city bike permit (August 1942). Wilmington police made the first arrest of a motorist failing to purchase a city license tag. "City drivers have been given enough warning," police chief Charles H. Casteen said (March 1943).[32] The city council approved a law prohibiting soliciting or begging for alms within the city limits except in certain cases [undefined]. It will be "rigorously enforced (May 1943)."[33]

* * *

Morals and Vice

Wilmington had an untold number of "designated" whore houses (illegal, of course), and untold other edifices where illicit, commercial, or unmarried sex was a by-product. Sex for money was available, but what the authorities did to deter or clean it up is uncertain. If not on the corner, walk up one flight. Some downtown residences have been identified, and others rumored. Prostitutes worked the streets and the two large hotels, the Cape Fear and Wilmington. The latter especially had a shady reputation. Also unknown is whether organized rings pushed the trade or purveyors worked in small caches or alone. Assuredly I know only what I later learned from people who claimed they knew, and read about in the papers. Not only that, but the assumption that casual sex was also exchanged for instant gratification such as a restaurant supper is realistic. After all, Wilmington was at war and full of those who would fight it one way or another. The mantra "tomorrow we may die" certainly existed if not sublimely.

The south end of downtown was notorious. A whorehouse over a barber shop operated across from Louis Hanson's Spiritine Chemical Company office at 117 South Front.[34] Other downtown whorehouses were in the Lily Arms Apartments at the corner of Front and Nun, and northwest corner of 3rd and Castle where women hung out over the porches. New Hanover High ROTC student Heyward C. Bellamy was an air raid warden in the area: "A busy spot, never felt any danger, but didn't go to the red light houses."[35] Next door to 312 South 3rd a derelict house converted into an apartment building became a whorehouse for shipyard workers. Margaret Parks lived at 312 with her bedroom on back looking out into the one next door. A bedroom (pink and blue) window of the other house was open often. A bed was by the window. Margaret and other girls looked out and giggled a lot until her mother nailed the window shut.[36]

The three-story Berry house at 2nd and Nun, once a Confederate hospital, was a big whorehouse. W. Eugene "Gene" Edwards remembered plenty of prostitutes worked that area, rented rooms, and went after shipyard workers and GIs. Another was east of Roudabush's seed store at Front and Dock a

Chapter Ten

Wilmington's Front Street, the "main drag," looking north from the corner of Orange Street, 1943. This block included numerous "trouble spots."

Provided by Ronald G. "Ronnie" Phelps

couple of houses and sold bootleg whiskey. Gene watched the frequent police raids from his nearby business, but it was like the police only went through the motions periodically, just to show they were active, but never closed it down. The house's owner once told them, "you can't get me for selling liquor. I make a good living selling pussy." The price wasn't high—$5.00.[37]

The FBI in July 1942 reported on the area's "prostitution and its inevitable scourge of social diseases...," at no surprise to local law enforcement. Indeed, the problem extended to the doorstep of the very building in which they sat, the 2nd and Orange USO. A veteran revisiting the USO in 1997 recalled seeing during the war at least a dozen women, accompanied by willing soldiers, working the adjacent alley on weekend evenings. "And they weren't Junior Hostesses, either."[38] And the head of the state brewing industry warned dealers of the prostitutes' operating from "'"beer joints"'....It is your duty to rid the community of them and other undesirable characters, and VD.'"[39]

Arrests often cited false registrations at hotels. Somehow the police seemed to know who was staked out in what hotel and room. For instance, in June 1943, three teenage males and three young girls were given their choice of a $100 fine and the costs of leaving the county for two years under threat of a six-month sentence under charges of false registration at the Brunswick Hotel. The vice squad detective "testified that his attention was first attracted by a crowd staring at a window of the hotel....Two of the three...are infected with venereal diseases."

At the time only one city detective was on the shorthanded vice squad, but Camp Davis and the sheriff promised to assign additional personnel.[40] Still, vice squads frequently raided tourist cabins and small hotels. A 1942 raid on the Negro Russell Hotel in Seabreeze produced a couple that had been going together for three years. They were given time to marry, and the hotel operator was not charged. In receiving the case of Kathleen Head, charged with "false registration for immoral purposes," Judge John J. Burney noted, "'these women who go from camp to camp are doing our boys more harm than the bullets of the enemy.'"[41]

Branching out into multiple relationships seemed to have been generated by wartime. Three Negro male bigamists, "entangled in one of the most involved cases to appear in Recorder's Court* for some time....The tangle found that James E. Hill married Bessie Lee Bryant, and had two children by her." Then they separated without divorce. James married Evelyn Fullwood; Bessie married Leroy Tate (who had never received a divorce from Irene Clark). All defendants received probations or suspended sentences.[42]

Gambling

Oversight of neo-gambling operations was inconsistent. Some were allowed to slide regardless of the magnitude, and enough busts were made to make it appear enforcement was on the alert. R. D. Matthews, "'self-styled "custodian" of the Quarterman Club to furnish "social intercourse" for shipyard workers,'" in 1942 was fined for operating a gambling establishment. "'...Shipyard workers go there on payday, lose their entire paycheck, and leave the place without a cent.'"[43] Lewis Bray was fined for conducting dice and card games at Tom's News and Stuff on North Front. The court turned over to charity half the $140 confiscated there (splitting the rest with arresting officers) and destroyed the gambling paraphernalia.

"Wilmington said free from vice," the headline read in November 1943. An "undercover investigation of rumored vice and corruption in Wilmington has disclosed that moral conditions are excellent and the work and character of law enforcement officers of superior quality," city manager A. C. Nichols reported.

---

* The WWII-era Recorder's Court is now equivalent to the District Court.

It "found no evidence of connection with underworld characters....no prostitution as it is generally known, practically no street walking and pickup girls, and no house of prostitution....Gambling is confined to certain pool rooms between pool players and to a game called 'Amos and Andy' which game has the sanction of the courts. No numbers slips or horse race tickets could be found....The football racket at one place which the police closed out at once. Whiskey is sold illegally at some places, but this is on a small scale."

Puzzling was the reference to no "prostitution as it is generally known."[44] Nichols' statement at best represented wishful thinking. Most likely it was based on inadequate research or doctored numbers, showed total naivete, or was a wartime deception. Appearances were that the conclusion was unreal, regardless.

* * *

Juvenile Delinquency

Attacking the gnawing problem of juvenile delinquency, the act of youngsters getting into trouble, was a steady aim of local authorities. It had profound social as well as law enforcement implications. By September 1942, a report of the county's superintendent of public welfare disclosed delinquency had not increased in proportion to the rise in population since the war began. Petty thievery was the major complaint, and placement of children in foster homes a major concern. By January 1943, only a slight increase in delinquency was seen. Seven months later, however, "in a vigorous move to curb juvenile delinquency," county commissioners acted on recommendations from the Council of Social Agencies, which predicted a "terrible" rise in delinquency.[45] "With a great influx of new population and consequent inadequate housing, along with employment of mothers in war industry, Wilmington's juvenile problems have multiplied rapidly without constructive efforts to solve them....The council's recommendations...provide for consolidation of city and county juvenile courts under a single judge...." and more.[46]

The *Star-News* championed efforts to improve conditions. In November 1943 it wrote, "The fundamental obligation to save children from delinquency rests with parents or guardians....but it has had little practical application, as is so often the case with good theories. This is why the sentencing of those offending parents is important."[47] In January 1944, efforts were paying off, and cases showed a substantial decline over the previous 18 months. And the number of juveniles requiring attention also dropped. One year later, the courts still were not merged, but the suggestions for it continued. "...Youths unfortunate enough to be hailed into juvenile court find themselves shifted from one court to another, which is certainly not in the best interests of the children" and also means more work for officials.[48]

A December 1945 report found that Wilmington's delinquency had not followed the sharp rise of many U.S. cities, although incidents involving teenage boys had risen. The largest number of offenders was in the 16–21 age range.[49] But from 1943 to 1945, statewide delinquency increased 18.6 percent. Wilmington's was 41.4 percent, perhaps based on the 1940 population figure. Contradictorily, a May 1946 editorial said, "Juvenile delinquency did increase rapidly and alarmingly....The war period is past, but its effect upon the children and the youth of this community lingers. The war was as unsettling upon juveniles as upon adults. Wilmington has had some distressing examples of this....Chief among the needed means is proper home influence." I knew some tough and rowdy kids who infrequently horned in on our activities, but none I would remember as "juvenile delinquents."

Where did all these delinquents live? Certainly not within my line of sight, but mainly in "the projects."

* * *

Accidents

Neither civilians nor military personnel were as safety-conscious as we are today, whether behind the wheel or at home. Children were especially vulnerable to accidents, carelessness, inferior conditions, and stupidity. Two-year old Negro Vivian Holmes was fatally scalded when she and her brother James fell into a tub of boiling water while playing. A rat invaded the home of Negro Henry Thompson, five weeks, and his 10-year old brother Willie and bit them numerous times about the head and face. They were treated at James Walker Memorial Hospital and released. Charles Spencer, six, lost his eye when an alley cat scratched him while he was playing in his backyard on South 6th.

Fatal automobile accidents occurred all the time involving trains, buses, trucks, military vehicles, and other automobiles. Superior Court Clerk Thomas A. Henderson died after his auto left the Wrightsville Beach highway at night and crashed into a tree. British seaman M. B. Rorie, whom Henderson had picked up downtown for a trip to the beach, was driving. A coroner's jury held the death was an "unavoidable accident," a term frequently cited because either the laws were insufficient, road conditions and signage might be inadequate, automobiles were ill-equipped, drivers were improperly tested and prepared, or the judge couldn't figure it out.*

With all the military vehicles moving through the area, no wonder so many were involved in accidents. In 1943 an army tank sideswiped and damaged a civilian car. Jeeps, more stable at handling speeds in the field than city streets, were the most culpable. Corporal Wayne Jensen, 25, died

---

* These were the days long before today's safety features such as seat belts, air bags, interlocking brakes, and head restraints, all inconceivable in wartime.

of injuries received when a car driven by Aaron Goldberg struck his jeep on June 30, 1942. Jensen was driving west on Dock, and Goldberg, a prominent defense attorney, south on 13th. The jeep overturned and rolled about 74 feet on Dock. Goldberg was not convicted. A car driven by C. A. Millinor struck and overturned a Coast Guard ambulance at 2nd and Orange, killing an occupant and injuring his passenger wife. Military police cited Camp Davis Captain Jack E. Dudley for driving 70 mph on Highway 17. "Patrolmen said the officer told them he was late to a dance." The limit was 35.[51]

Seaman Second Class William Ivon Hocutt, home on navy rehabilitation leave after serving overseas, was killed on September 26, 1944, when the rear wheels of his 1941 car dropped off, causing it to spin around several times and hit a tree.[52] A fireman witness said it was traveling at a very high speed and turned over many times while plunging down the incline. One passenger was thrown 30 feet and another injured. Seven people—five soldiers and two civilians—died in one of the county's "worst automobile accidents in recent years" on December 21, 1942.[53] A 1937 Ford occupied by six Camp Davis men collided head-on with a 1941 Chevrolet containing three civilians. The "impact practically demolished both machines, forcing the engines of the cars back against the drivers' seats, and hurling several of the occupants out on the pavement." The Ford driver was removed from beneath the wheel. Four were due to be commissioned as lieutenants.

The sharp curve where South Front and 3rd came together at Greenfield Lake to form Carolina Beach Road at the city limits was extremely dangerous. Drivers, confused by the automobile headlights on Front, frequently ran off the road, causing deaths, property damage, and injuries. It came to be called "dead man's curve." The debate was joined. Whose jurisdiction was it? Should the state install a stop light? The curve "reflects upon Wilmington. No accident happens there that is not generally blamed upon Wilmington, not the county...."[54] The most horrific wreck at the curve occurred on November 12, 1944, when three Camp Lejeune Marines died. All had just returned from action on Tarawa, Saipan, and Tinian. One also fought on Guadalcanal. A coroner's jury found the automobile driver to be at fault in the collision with a McLean's company truck. The only Marine survivor was unable to identify who was driving.[55]

Late 1944 was extremely accident-prone and deadly. The weekend of December 15–17 claimed five more lives.[56] An accidental gunshot by Thomas Kimball, 18, while hunting at Greenville Sound killed Wilbur Smith, 17, both of Seagate. A Negro couple, Dan and Florence Williams, burned to death when their frame dwelling in McRae's Alley was destroyed by fire. Negro Edward Lovette died instantly when he stepped in front of a moving train at the Coast Line's 8th Street crossing early Saturday. The "curve" killed Sanford Randall of Maffitt Village when his car left the highway.

Bathers, swimmers, and boaters died in lakes and at beaches from heart attacks or drownings. Mysterious and freak accidents happened. In July 1943, the body of an elderly Oklahoma City man wrapped in cords of seine weights was found floating in the river. Defense worker Joe Gailliard, 50, employed at the Naco Fertilizer Company at the foot of Hanover Street, was "warned with other workers to 'stand back' when an overhead conveyor dropped a load of powdered phosphate into a curing bin. Gailliard obeyed so vigorously that he struck his head on a iron stanchion behind him. Staggering forward, he fell face down on the phosphate pile. Fellow workers lifted him out, became alarmed at his limpness, and called an ambulance."[57] A collision between a car driven by W. T. R. Godfrey and a bus shortly after midnight on dimmed-out Wrightsville Beach during the 1942 civilian defense restrictions resulted in his being charged with reckless operation. This type of accident happened more than once.

In March 1944 two shipyard workers, C. E. Rodgers and Thelma B. Hammel, living together on South 5th, died from drinking bootleg whiskey (methyl alcohol) thinking it was liquor.[58] In two Coca-Cola bottles, it probably came from the yard's paint shop where she worked. They invited J. M. Simpkins to join them, but he was "suspicious of the substance and consumed only a small portion." Both became intoxicated. Rodgers died at home. Hammel received emergency stomach treatment at the hospital and was released. She told a friend, "I don't want to die. If I do, I want you to take care of the letters in my room. And I want to tell you that Rodgers and I are not married." She died the next day in the hospital. (Methyl alcohol was used in blowtorches employed to detect leaks in refrigeration equipment on C-2 vessels.)

By mid-1943, it was apparent the city's four most dangerous downtown intersections were along Market Street at Front, 2nd, and 3rd, and at 3rd and Castle.[59] But the busy, crowded main cross-street at Front and Market proved deadliest. After a March 1944 pedestrian death there (the driver getting only 60 days on the county farm), an editorial pleaded, "It is hoped that the incident had been widely publicized for the benefit of other drivers widely predisposed to disregard the rights of pedestrians." The traffic code gave rights to pedestrians crossing on a green light over vehicles. "Many drivers persist in seizing the right of way over persons afoot."

The most careless intersection accident there killed city street sweeper Ezra Allen Hudson, 62, struck by a car in September 1944 at work. Driver David Galloway, 51, a Negro shipyard employee held on manslaughter charges, drove a canvas-covered 1936 Ford pickup loaded with yard workers. The truck knocked Hudson down with its right fender. Galloway got out of truck, asked if he was hurt, and Hudson said "he was 'all right.'" But later a passing policeman saw blood running from Hudson's face, and took him to hospital where it was determined he had head injuries. He developed blood clots on the brain and spine which subsequently caused death.[60]

* * *

The Crime Wave by Statistics

By spring of 1942, Wilmington's police were being "kept busy" as crime numbers fluctuated on an upward curve. Arrests totaled 1,415 in March and 1,302 in May, of whom 987 were whites and 315 Negroes. Approximately two-thirds had to do with automobile and traffic violations, and 53 for sexual offenses.[61] Arrests set a new record in November with 1,451. For the year, 22 violent deaths were recorded—19 homicides and two manslaughter deaths—with 20 solved. Wilmingtonians lost $120,151 in stolen property, with police recovering $79,159. The largest single classification was stolen automobiles (123).[62]

During the first nine months of 1943, 15 persons were murdered among the 29 violent deaths, and five committed suicide.[63] By October 1943, Camp Davis officials attributed their crime rate, which was lower than that of a civilian center of equal size, to the efficiency of the MPs in cooperation with Wilmington area law enforcement and Camp Lejeune MPs. Davis stationed MPs in Wilmington, the white and Negro beach communities, Holly Ridge, and Fort Fisher.

Murders, manslaughters, and burglaries peaked in 1942, but the total offenses continued to rise. Figures for 1943 included 16,497 warrants (with 16,815 arrests), 18 murders and non-negligent manslaughters, 17 rapes, 114 robberies, and 1,050 aggravated assaults among the 3,455 reported offenses (3,091 in 1942).[64] Additionally, the 935 automobile accidents and 9,017 traffic violations saw five fatalities.[65] Costs of maintaining the county jail—the area's designated lockup—rose from 1942 even though slightly fewer federal, county, and city "trusties" (15,879) were "lodged there."[66]

The Wilmington police department's monthly arrest average by May 1944 had increased five times "under the wartime stirrings of the city," from 300 in 1941 to 1,500. The rationale appeared to be based on a multiplied law enforcement effort, increased citizen alertness, and full cooperation with military authorities. The police force of 48 men was short by 5 to 15.[67] In the early summer city authorities were noting a significant downward arrest trend, from 1,456 in May 1943 to 1,068 a year later, including traffic citations. There were substantial decreases in drunkenness, larceny and receiving stolen goods, gambling, prostitution, and speeding.[68] But arrests by the county sheriff's department hit their highest in July, with traffic violations, forgeries, assaults with intent to kill, and fornication-adulteries leading the list.[69]

The girls are coming! Plus a few comedians (of secondary value, no less). Wartime traveling variety show under the tent tops, popular until rationing restrictions curtailed mobility.

Wilmington Sunday Star-News, May 2, 1942

With the exit of thousands of soldiers and war workers by spring 1945, arrests were way down, 744 compared to 1,068 in May 1944.[70]

For fiscal year 1944–45, total Wilmington arrests for other than parking citations dropped from 8,543 to 5,587. Whites totaled 2,845 and Negroes 2,742, by far the closest the two races had come statistically during the war when the usual ratio was approximately 2:1 or more.[71] Police records for 1945 revealed that Negroes committed 73 percent of the major crimes.

The war's end reduced crime, but one final surge of the hangover occurred in March 1946. "Crime Wave Increases" the headline read. City arrests were up 100 percent over the same time in 1945 "due to unemployment, general unrest and uncertain economic conditions." Most offenders were between 18 and 21, a nationwide trend. Petty crime rose. "Wilmington has more crime today...than was manifest during the boom years when the population was nearly doubled," a police official stated.[72]

Even with that news, an April 1946 FBI report covering two thousand cities shocked the community. "More crimes were committed in Wilmington during the past year, in proportion to population, than in most of the nation's cities. Wilmington police handled 1,861 cases, representing a rate of 5,310 offenses per 100,000 population." (The national rate for cities over 25,000 was 1,610 per 100,000.)[73] Local officials scurried to respond. Chief Charles H. Casteen "debunked the FBI survey," saying figures were based on the 1940 census, and citizens had been encouraged to report crimes. The population increase "would place Wilmington low on the per capita rating. Stating that he had never attempted to disguise the city's crime record, he added 'I...have always presented a full and detailed report of every violation including parking violations.'"[74]

The *Morning Star* weighed in: "...Wilmington is not different from the average American city. The FBI report...is obviously incorrect....At the same time, there is room for improvement....Long before the war cut off the supply of wire and globes and poles, Wilmington was inadequately lighted save for the distribution served by white ways."[75]

If lighting was to blame, you had the answer. Conflicting statistics, monthly increases and decreases, uneven trends, all could be argued forever. But both by facts and perception, the Wilmington area certainly was "Sin City" during WWII and its immediate aftermath. Crime and disorder created an ugly blot on its massive contribution to the war effort and its wartime legacy of self-sufficiency against the odds. By mid-1946, however, fire had become "Wilmington's most devastating criminal," showing "a slight advance in its depredations."[76] Attention was diverted, and life inched onward.

The Other Side

As if attempting to balance the other side of the ledger, Wilmingtonians—residents, service personnel, and defense workers alike—flocked to area churches. Attendance and participation in religious activities were two certain methods of blocking out (ignoring?) the crime and disorder around them, as well as providing spiritual uplift. Leading the way before packed houses were downtown old-line places of worship such as St. Mary Catholic, First Presbyterian, Temple of Israel, B'nai Israel, St. Stephen's AME, St. James Episcopal, Fifth Avenue Methodist, and St. Paul's Lutheran—all convenient to transients and weekend visitors. Worshipers attended not only regular Sunday and other weekend services, but used their edifices as bases for a dedicated involvement in the war effort and civic life. Many pastors and rabbis immersed themselves to the benefit of all in the community.

Chapter 11
"The Man of My Dreams"

My sister, Lib, spent her Agnes Scott College summer 1941 working in Montreat, North Carolina, and was home only part of the summer of 1942. Mother had an operation then to remove a large tumor from her abdomen, waiting a whole year after its diagnosis so that Lib, unaware of the problem, could take care of me. While Mother was hospitalized, Lib dated a young doctor. He served overseas in the army and returned to Wilmington in 1944, called Mother and got Lib's shipyard office phone number. He asked her out again, but by then she was engaged. Not long after, she rode past a local church and saw a wedding party coming out. There he was on the arm of the bride. "He was ready to get married. I managed to avoid him and married the man of my dreams."[1]

How the dreams evolved for this cautious girl comes later.

So many local men and women were not that discerning. And so many love relationships originated or consummated here during the war I conjecture that we "spread the seed of Wilmington" throughout all the 48 states. By October 1942, the war's impact on local long-term romance was reflected in the 16 marriage licenses issued in New Hanover County the week before, mostly to soldiers from nearby posts.* Corresponding turmoil was seen in the 34 divorce cases settled by October 21 for the previous two weeks. The pattern was set.

As a historian, to me the romantic side of wartime Wilmington is one of its most indelible and living legacies, and one for readers to enjoy. Scores of marriages have reached the 55-plus year mark for longevity, a startling condition I found in my research with countless hundreds of veterans and their wives throughout the country.

---

* Not all weddings involved military personnel. On July 1, 1944, "around the altar where Madame Chiang Kai-Shek's father was baptized," Maura Mei-lan Kwan of Vancouver, British Columbia, married Edward Yee Wing of Canton, China, in the Fifth Avenue Methodist Church. [*Wilmington Sunday Star-News,* July 2, 1944]

The *Wilmington Star-News* syndicated columnist on social issues, Ruth Millett, in 1943 was looking for an "up-side" to the matter of hasty or ill-conceived wartime marriages. She would caution a girl about to rush into a wedding.[2]

> "They're the kids who are starting the marriages in one room of somebody else's house who often don't get to see each other but once a week and who are neither afraid of the future nor unwilling to plan for it....They are supremely happy just being together whenever the war permits. Though they haven't much in the way of family possessions, they think they are plenty lucky to have each other. If they can find life as good as they are living it today, chances are their marriages will turn out all right.
>
> "...She might discover to her grief that she let panic push her into a marriage she wasn't ready for. There is the chance she'll look around when her husband has gone and see that there is still plenty of good husband material left, and that she wouldn't have been left out in the cold if she had taken a little more time about making a marriage. It's too bad so many girls are listening to the voice of super salesmanship and getting married because they think they may end up as old maids if they don't marry now."[3]

Was this and other similar advice coming from the caring mouths of concerned parents heeded? You could say apparently not in Wilmington.

* * *

The Camp Davis Connection

The regular weekend deluge of servicemen, mainly from Camp Davis, on the Wilmington area was bound to generate sparks. If matchups were destined, they were with military men. (I didn't hear about local belles marrying shipyard or defense workers—not "social enough." Naturally, the best pickings, the targets, were officers first.)

Frances Coughenour was one of the hundreds of local girls serving as a USO Victory Belle volunteer hostess. One night on "duty" at 2nd and Orange as usual she wore her name badge. Charles E. "Chuck" Dinsmore, a Camp Davis officer candidate from Pennsylvania, spotted her, glanced at her name, and impressed her by pronouncing it correctly ("Coin-our"). She was impressed. Immediately they began seeing each other and sometimes went to the Plantation Club to dance. In New Orleans on February 13, 1943, five days before he shipped out to Panama, they were married. Eventually he served in the Philippines Campaign. She still has the badge.[4]

Lottie "Clara" Marshburn met Dwight V. "Duke" Jacobs at a girlfriend's birthday party at the 2nd and Orange USO on February 28, 1945. He worked at the Camp Davis post office and had flown "the Hump" in China-Burma-India. One day he called on her at home. Without a car, he got off the bus at

A Selectee's Diary

Private Bob Voorhees, Battery E, 95th Coast Artillery/Anti-Aircraft Artillery Battalion, lightly portrayed Camp Davis life in 1941–42 through cartoons in the *Wilmington Star-News*. The "Soldiers Hut" referred to was the Woodrow Wilson Hut club on the City Hall grounds.

Newspaper Files of Bill Reaves, New Hanover County Public Library

the wrong stop, thumbed a ride to her house, and arrived late. Her daddy was angry at her for falling for him, and all of a sudden Duke showed up at her door. "Daddy didn't like him to call him 'Pop,' was furious when he called mother 'Mom,' but soon got over it. I was a daddy's girl. Later on my daddy really loved him." By April 7, they were engaged, and by June 9, married. They took the train to Florida on their honeymoon to see his family. They both rode for free, he as a soldier and she because of her job with the Coast Line.* It lasted 40 years until he died. They had four children.[5]

---

* The man Lottie later married, Carl Welker (NHHS '39), was engaged to Martha Williamson of Wilmington, whom he had known a long time. "It was a spur of the moment thing." He got a dear John. "She was good looking, younger, but found somebody else at the USO" while Carl was overseas. She returned his ring. [Interview with Carl Welker, October 2, 1998]

The biggest Forest Hills neighborhood military wedding of the war united my sister's dear high school classmate and lifelong friend Harriett Glasque Harrington to army Lieutenant Donald Hilary Connolly, Jr., on June 26, 1943.[6] Harriett had just graduated from Mary Baldwin College, he from West Point a year before and then was serving at Camp Davis. Her parents were Mr. and Mrs. Charles M. Harrington, and his army Major General and Mrs. Donald H. Connolly. The wedding was at St. Andrews Presbyterian Church, the reception at her family home. A couple of us boys hung around outside the house hoping for food and treats.

Chicagoan Don A. Dibble, 23, was a Camp Davis soldier.[7] In October 1941 he met Dorothy Bunn (NHHS '39) at Wilmington's Woodrow Wilson Hut, and asked for her phone number. "But he didn't call me" until November. On their first date they went to Lumina. He had no car. Before the end of November he asked her to marry him. "I waited a few days," but accepted at a Camp Davis dance. "I don't even buy a dress that fast. I am not an impulsive person. It's the one time in my life that I did something that stupid. I knew absolutely nothing about him except that he might have to go off to war. Here was a guy charming me off my feet."

Their December 7, 1941, date was to the movie *Sergeant York* at the Bailey Theater. A few days later his unit departed for Newport News, Virginia, for exercises. She joined him. The day after Christmas, three engaged couples who needed blood tests took the ferry to Norfolk, waited for the test results, returned to Newport News, and visited a minister. That night all were married in his house. "The love bug bit and that's all I know." She stayed there with him two days: "Money was at a premium." Neither had any, and she returned to Wilmington. In the spring of 1942 he sailed for Australia, eventually making 13 amphibious landings in New Guinea in a total of 38 months overseas. "Your life was at a standstill, waiting to hear from him. You heard all about the war, but you never heard about where he was or what he was doing. Life was going to work, coming home, trying to hear news, writing a letter." In April 1945 she received his telegram to go to Chicago and wait—he was coming home on rotation leave. Leaving her job, she waited in his family's home. They saw a newsreel announcing the government's eligibility for discharge. "We sat in the theater and added up the points and realized Don could be released." They moved to Cleveland, Ohio.

The October 1946 issue of *The Ladies Home Journal* featured an article about a 1942 romance between a Wilmington girl, Dorothy Glenn, and a Wilmington P-47 test pilot, Captain Carroll "Shortie" Olsen.[8] She waited tables in the Cape Fear Hotel coffee shop. "Dorothy watched hundreds come and go. Many a date was made in the coffee shop, and many a romance began....Dorothy maintained an admirable calm. She had plenty of fun without the help of the military....She was frankly suspicious of these strange young men wearing brand-new wings and feeling mighty big. Their jokes and their kidding, their cocky brash ways failed to impress her...." However, she "saw more than his noticeable good looks. She thought to herself that he was different. More quiet, more reserved and considerate." He noticed her blond hair. "He thought she was the prettiest girl he'd ever seen in his life....Each was too shy to make advances."

Shortie came in daily for breakfast, and Dorothy took his order. "That was the sum total of their conversation." Eventually they were presented to each other formally, "but it looked as though the first date might be their last." He was ordered to Myrtle Beach, South Carolina, for immediate shipment overseas. Their goodbye was punctuated when he "dropped out of a formation going south and rousingly buzzed the Cape Fear Hotel." Before departing he returned to Wilmington for their second date with three hours to spend. Dorothy quit her job, and they were married at midnight in a candlelight ceremony in Spartanburg, South Carolina.

* * *

Wilmingtonian army officer Henry Von Oesen met Randolph-Macon College student Alice Applewhite in 1942 in Macon, Georgia, on a blind date.[9] They married there on April 2, 1943, with his parents present. "I guess we had a long courtship—unusual for the war years," he said. "I didn't think it was a very good idea for an infantry officer to get married. They told us at Fort Benning we were expendable. I know we went to a lot of weddings." Henry's only leave during the war was the honeymoon. They went to Wilmington. "I just wanted her to see where I was born and the dances at Lumina. You had to go to the beach even though it was April."

Lucilla White knew Glendy "Glenn" Willard at the Presbyterian School of Religious Education.[10] So when Lucilla moved to Wilmington as director of religious education for the Church of the Covenant, naturally she got to know the Willard family. (Lucilla was a prominent figure in my religious life as a kid in that church.) One member was Joseph W. "Joe" Whitted whom she met at their Masonboro Sound home. They went together for six years, mostly apart. She rented a room in the family's house downtown. While Joe was away on duty, "one of the big moments was, I'd been writing her every other day asking her to marry me. She finally wrote back saying yes" in early 1944. On July 12, 1944, he was able to get home on leave. "I told him it was too hot in July and I didn't want to get married then. He said you take your leave when you can get it." The pastor at First Presbyterian Church asked her, "Are you sure you want to marry this man?" She said yes, and he responded, "Your children will be half-witted." Oh yes, she replied, "and half-White too." They were married in Richmond, Virginia, on July 15, 1944, but lack of gasoline kept many Willard family members from attending.

Army airman Robert Pershing Edwards from Kentucky was on temporary duty at Bluethenthal Field as a mechanic on B-24 *Liberator* bomber flying anti-submarine warfare patrols in early 1942.[11] One day returning from a patrol the crew dropped papers out of a window with notes and a telephone number: they wanted to meet local girls. An employee of Southern Bell Telephone Company had one fall in his yard and gave it to a girl at work. She dialed the number, and three girls including Burnette Owens made a date with three GIs.

Burnette later told Estelle Augusta Owens (no relation), another phone company worker, that the guy she was dating—Robert—was too young for her, but nice. She wanted Estelle to meet him, and had both over for dinner. Estelle and Robert began going out about several times per week. The first date was a walk in the sand at Wrightsville Beach, where they ruined their shoes from fuel oil from sunken ships that had washed ashore. Previously, the religious Estelle's social life centered around the 6th Street Advent Christian Church, which sponsored night activities and dancing but frowned on drinking and kissing. She had dated no one regularly.

Because of his pre-dawn bus-company job, Estelle's father went to bed early. He never missed a day of work, and he never met Robert. "He [father] didn't like him, would never talk to him. He was a foreigner, might as well have been from anywhere because he wasn't from Wilmington." She and Robert "made more telephone calls and wrote more letters. I got my phone calls for free." By the time his unit departed Bluethenthal "I knew he was the one for me." Robert phoned her parents to seek their permission before asking Estelle. They wed at the Greenville, South Carolina, air base on January 20, 1943: no music, just sister Selisece Owens Williams as maid of honor and her mother and niece, but not her dad. "He wanted no part of it," preferring she get married in Wilmington. "Dear Mother & Dad," an assuming Robert, "your son-in-law," wrote the Owenses on January 29.

> ...Estelle and I are really happy, she is a swell wife. The Lord meant for us to be one. I am going to make her the happiest girl in the world....Estelle can hardly wait to get to Ky. To meet my people. I wish that it was possible for us to be in both places but I guess we will go to good old Kentucky [on their honeymoon]. Dad I am sorry that I didn't get a chance to meet you yet. I almost feel that I have met you, for Estelle tells me how swell her parents are....I was planning so big on us being married in Wilmington until my furlough was canceled so I was so broken hearted that I asked Estelle if she would come up here.[12]

William "Bill" Schwartz (NHHS '39) and his future wife Bernice dated while students at UNC.[13] After graduating in 1943, they broke up when he became a naval officer. His first duty assignment—by a coincidence—was on a patrol craft out of Key West, Florida. While in Miami at the Versailles

Hotel she ran into Bill's fraternity brother, who told her Bill was coming there that night. They made up then and there and have stayed together ever since. Bill asked her to marry him before they had broken up—then asked her again in late 1945 when he came home from the Pacific. They married on March 31, 1946, in Savannah, Georgia.

"I had a sweetheart [Tom Obermeir]. He sent me a dozen yellow roses every week," remembered Sally Josey.[14] "Oh what a sad day when he was sent overseas." They became engaged and corresponded. "I was engaged to two men at one time." Late in the war friend Beth Slocum said, "Camp Davis is about to fold up. Why don't we go up to New York?" They got apartments and jobs ("of sorts"), Sally as a Monday night hostess at the Delmonico Hotel officers club. Boys escorted them home, and on the way stopped off for dinner and drinks. Then she met naval Lieutenant Henry "Hank" Crawford. He saw her from across the room and told someone, "You see that tall blonde over there? I'm going to marry her." He had fought in the South Pacific, his father had died, and in the fall of 1944 he had come home to Flushing, New York, to tend to family affairs. "When you went to those officers dances you didn't turn anybody down. You danced with them all. I met him at the officers club. He proposed in a night club, gave me a diamond ring in Central Station, all within six weeks."

Her mother went to New York. Sally asked her, "Did you come up here to talk me out of getting married or help me buy my trousseau?" Mother said, "I came prepared to do either one." Hank had to go back to his ship, the cruiser USS *Biloxi* (CL-80). Later as a lieutenant commander he captained a tanker and came home in early 1946. In April they were wed in Wilmington.

When she was 16 in 1940, Libby Goldberg had a blind date with Edward Nelson O'Quinn, 19, of Rocky Mount, North Carolina, at Wrightsville Beach.[15] They dated for three years, mostly bowling and movies. "My deadline was 11 o'clock at night and my father [attorney Aaron Goldberg] didn't mean five minutes after. If the good-nights last too long father got across the message sarcastically. He wasn't about to let me get married without graduating from high school. Going to college had been my plan. I was just a teenager in high school in love." After Pearl Harbor, Nelson worked at the shipyard.

They married in 1943. Libby said her own children still "can't believe my father let me get married at 18, but it was war, people were marching off to die." They honeymooned on a train to Richmond, Virginia. Nelson got as far as pre-flight but never graduated because the war ended. "I'm not sure I worried about him going away and not coming back." She had never left home until she followed him to duty stations. She remembered her friend Ensign Clifford McIver being killed. "I was this flighty

Marine First Lieutenant Robert Aaron "Bobby" Goldberg, Jr., with his F4U Vought *Corsair*. A pilot with the VMF-511 squadron, he flew from the carrier USS *Block Island* (CVE-106). On May 27, 1945, while searching for his wingman, he was KIA over the Ryukyu Islands. His friends had predicted "the sky was the limit" for the talented and popular Goldberg, a Wake Forest law graduate and the son of a prominent attorney. The family never fully got over his loss.

Provided by sisters Libby Goldberg O'Quinn and Frances Goldberg Walker

airhead....I wasn't thinking deep thoughts about the war. It impacted me less than it would have older people. I was confident I could deal with whatever I was dealt." But then in 1945 the Goldberg family lost her brother Bobby, a Marine fighter pilot, around Okinawa, a deep tragedy that vividly lingers today.

Wilmingtonians Evelyn Volk and Clifford Cohen "Cliff" Morris, Jr., became engaged in late 1943 right before he went overseas.[16] Evelyn reminded him, "I remember you giving me the ring in the sunroom." She was seven years behind Cliff still at New Hanover High. She lived on the near-vacant Columbia Avenue in Forest Hills with her parents, Marc G. and Edna Cameron Volk. Before that the Volks had lived at 2002 Pender Avenue next door to my parents at the time I was born. Cliff piloted 15th Air Force B-17s on 50 missions out of Italy beginning in June 1944. Her brother Ralph (NHHS '39) flew B-24s from the same base. On May 26, 1945, Reverend Walter B. Freed married them in St. Paul's Lutheran.

Carrie Congleton and friend Gladys Padrick visited Greenfield Park in 1942.[17] So did Camp Davis pals Sylvester "Buddy" Adkins and Harry Vander Pool. "They sorta stood back and watched us," Carrie remembered, "then came over to talk with us. They were interested in somebody to talk to; they were lonely, had nothing to do. I thought they were cute." Soon she took the bus home, but would not allow Buddy to accompany her. Buddy wanted to take her home. "She said her daddy would kill me if I went home with her." The following weekend they went to the Bailey Theater. "Her mama thought as much of me as if I were her own," but her daddy aggravated him. While they courted on the front porch swing, he would set an alarm clock for 9:00 p.m. and put it in the window near Buddy. That meant it was time for him to head for the base.

They dated for about five weeks that summer until he left for Camp Stewart, Georgia. They wrote each other but were not serious. "In my mind I didn't want to go over there and not come back and leave her a widow. Discussed it with her and decided to leave it until I got back." He phoned her on his return to the States on December 14, 1945, "asked her if she still wanted to get married, and she said yes." After being discharged in Kentucky, he had no job but caught the bus to Wilmington to see her in January 1946. They were quickly married on the 16th in her home on Middle Sound.

Elizabeth "Betty" Henderson (NHHS '39) and Daniel D. "Dan" Cameron, class of '38, were on-and-off high school sweethearts, dated

Lieutenant Clifford C. "Cliff" Morris, Jr., *left*, with his B-17 *Flying Fortress* crewman, assigned to the 32nd Squadron, 301st Bomb Group, 15th Air Force in Italy, 1944.
Provided by Morris

in college, then went their separate ways.[18] "It gave us a chance to meet people," she reasoned. Once Dan was stationed at Camp Davis, it took on a new perspective. Before he deployed to Europe in the summer of 1943, she rode to Davis with his father, Mayor Bruce B. Cameron, to see him. On the way home, she and the mayor discussed numerous personal matters including the relations between Dan and her, "just a really wonderful experience."

Before Dan left (they were apart 27 months), they talked about getting married but were not engaged. Knowing he was headed for combat, he was hesitant. "I don't know that she would have married me anyway." She demurred. "I was waiting for him." Betty "was the belle of the town" while he was away, openly dating many soldiers as discussed with Dan and his father, including two of his Virginia Military Institute 1942 classmates. She helped entertain at St. John's Tavern, and with friend Louise Wells (who later married Dan's brother Bruce B. Cameron, Jr.) arranged dates for friends with Marines. Dan recalled, "When my father died [in July 1944] that was the big news for a while. She didn't tell me much about her boyfriends. She loved me, but was still seeing others as we had agreed." Dan returned in October 1945, and they married in May 1946.*

As a Camp Davis sergeant, Daniel R. Shinder trained Negro troops. Later he was a Signal Corps lieutenant.[19] In Wilmington looking for a young Jewish group to join, he ventured into Finkelstein's pawn shop. Clerk Leon Stein told him about a meeting that night at the Rabunsky house in Brooklyn, and how to get there. "Sister [Frances] answered the doorbell," Janet Rabunsky recalled. "He arrived early. She was surprised, had curlers in her hair." Daniel was very fond of Mrs. Rabunsky. "He said he married my sister because of mother's cooking." On December 14, 1941, he and Frances were married. The army gave him permission to wear a civilian suit for two hours before having to change into uniform.

Camp Davis Sergeant Daniel R. Shinder met Frances Rabunsky through a B'Nai Israel function at her house. The army gave him permission to marry her in civilian clothes seven days after Pearl Harbor.

Provided by brother Bernard Rabunsky

At the 2nd and Orange USO from January 1943 to January 1945, Glenn Willard, representing the sponsoring YWCA, was in charge of women's activities, hostesses, and picnics.[20] This job included supervising the "Victory Belles," the "dancing girls" who danced with servicemen and helped them make recordings to send home.† Officer candidates hung around there to stay out of trouble. MPs looked for violations such as unbuttoned sleeves, undone neckties, and men weaving down the street.

When the small navy minesweeper YMS-15 sailed up the Cape Fear River for repairs, crewman Miles C. Higgins phoned his mother from the USO. "I had been working there a week. I didn't know any better," Glenn recalled. "He looked innocent because he came to call his mother. Most of them were wolves." He walked her home that first night and said he would

---

* When asked what he had intended to do when released from active duty, Dan replied, "To go home and chase Betty Henderson until I catch her."

† For this seven-day a week effort, with part of one day off, she earned $150 a month. "The day was divided into three parts. The place had to be covered for each shift. You would be on two parts, you were off the third part. It was fun. The 'cattle cars' would dump off Marines and soldiers."

marry her when he got back from the war. She replied, "You may never come back." They began corresponding and saw each other at the USO whenever his ship was in port. When he returned from the Mediterranean in October 1944, they agreed to get married. In April 1945, 117 Victory Belles, president Mildred Huhn presiding, and 10 senior hostesses honored Glenn with a complete set of crystal. The wedding took place on May 5, 1945.

Wilmingtonian Aaron May met his wife-to-be Norma in 1943 at the Fort Smith, Arkansas, USO.[21] His father said they ought to get married before he shipped out. So, in February 1944 she went to Wilmington to meet his parents before the wedding. At the Johnny Mercer pier at Wrightsville Beach, wanting to "jump the waves," she went in over her head, and had no way to get back to shore. Unable to swim to the pier, she cried for help. A fisherman pulled her in on his line and "saved my life." He said he had just put on a new line today and "if I hadn't I wouldn't have been able to save you. It was so embarrassing."

A rabbi married them in his home, she without a gown and only an aunt and uncles as witnesses. He landed in France after D-Day, fought into Germany, and returned to Wilmington after V-E Day. Awaiting her arrival from Fort Smith by train, a trip of two-plus days and two nights, he thought she was taking the ACL as most people did, but she was on the Seaboard. Aaron mistakenly went to the ACL station. "I never thought to tell him I won't be coming on the correct line." Both trains were scheduled to arrive at the same time. He finally found her at the other depot.

"Dear Heyward, Well, here we are on your last night before your going back to Iowa," Mary Cameron Dixon wrote to her soldier returning to flight school.[22] "It has really been wonderful these last three days. I wish you could have been here all along. But no matter what fun we missed. We'll make it all up someday. Heyward, I know that the future will bring you the best because anyone as grand as you are deserves it. With your firm belief and determination, your mental alertness, and your belief in the right, you will always go forward on the right path. Luck and love always, Mary."

She wrote at "12:30 midnight (remember)," June 14, 1943, a few days after her graduation from New Hanover High School, to Heyward C. Bellamy. When he entered the service they were good friends. "There were a great many young men in town. There was a great deal to do, had chores and responsibilities at home, was free to go to USO dances. Met a lot of nice people there." The school mailed Heyward his '43 diploma because he and other seniors had left NHHS early. After the war they wed.

Katharine Harriss met George Burrell Byers on the train going to an out-of-town New Hanover High football game in 1942.[23] "I snapped him right up." When George (NNHS '43) left for the army in August 1943, "we were fairly serious, not committed, going steady through the mails. I was dating other people but I don't guess he was." During training he wrote her: "There is one train trip I will never forget. Do you remember it? It was to Rocky Mount to see a football game. That was the first time I had ever seen you. The very first minute I laid eyes on you I knew what was to follow. I guess you thought I was a dope for staring at you so much but I couldn't help it." In high school they made arrangements to bump into each other accidentally. He walked the round trip to Sunset Park after going to her home at 1903 Market to see her. That summer she dropped her pocketbook off the Wrightsville Beach pier and lost some of the army pictures he had sent her, plus bobby pins which were hard to get during the war.

Meanwhile, Katharine liked the Camp Davis dances with her cousin Bell Gaither and "met the best looking captain you ever saw." She also danced at the 2nd and Orange USO. "Real crowded, hot, fun to be able to dance with so many people." He understood. She was still so young. "I hope you are having a good time at the beach," he wrote shortly after becoming a soldier. "Sure wish I could be there with you....If they ship the British soldiers [training at Davis] away what are you girls going to do?* I guess you will have to entertain the soldiers from Camp Davis."24 He returned home on March 9, 1946. She was a senior. They had become pledged sweethearts.†

* * *

By December 1944, wartime wedding bells had slowed down. With millions of young bachelors overseas, marriages declined. The next year

---

* British anti-aircraft troops trained at Camp Davis in July 1943 and again in November-December.

† This relationship began while George was a senior and Katharine a freshman and continued through her graduation until they wed. Excerpts from his letters to her, all saved but probably unopened for 50 years, occupy nearly 30 single-spaced pages in my computer files. Having researched hundreds of these types of WWII romances, I am taken with the durability of these two very young people in sustaining interest—much less building love—through the war years. Absence truly did make the heart grow fonder.

I regret not having the space to include these rather sophomoric boy-girl letters from the immature, homespun soldier gone to war—but developing fast—and the typical teenage, flighty high school girl back home whom he was dying to see. She unconsciously played him off in her own uncertainty. His letters were full of thoughts and wishes of any 18–20-year-old boy, and a thirst for information about home—football games, the beach, hangouts, Friday night dances, who was dating who, the like, and what was happening to friends in uniform. They wrote of being in love, but how were they to know? They expressed frequent concern over unanswered questions or letters, or worried over long-distance slights or rebuffs, real or imagined.

Facing unusual adversity, perhaps Katharine grew up more quickly than most girls of her time. Her father, Meares Harriss, committed suicide in 1941 and left her mother, NHHS teacher Laura Weddell Harriss, with six children 14 and under. Two brothers served in the navy, and Thomas, 9, accidentally killed himself at home with an "unloaded" gun in 1943. Katharine had to assume many family responsibilities a bit beyond her years. It's absolutely amazing that they waited for each other—and an endearing compliment. They remained married until his death in 2001.

(Above) Katharine Meares Harriss, *right*, with Jane Sprunt in front of Woolworth's on North Front Street, 1943, and army Private George Burrell Byers (NHHS '43) *(below)*, 1943. Although Harriss was three school years behind him, they maintained their relationship during his service in training, France, and Germany ("going steady through the mails"), and married after the war. It lasted until his death in 2001.

Provided by the Byerses

was expected to be below normal until most troops returned home. From 1940 to 1943, nationwide there were 6,579,000 marriages, the Associated Press reported. The normal rate would have been 5,461,000. The "surplus" was caused by better economic conditions and wartime psychology. "There should be another boom after World War II but...we will have a smaller backlog of single people."[25] The divorce rate went the other way. Much of it was attributed to "'war fatigue,'" the "'sheer weariness of workers, thousands of whom are toiling harder and longer....'"[26]

What a turnaround by war's end! The military had nearly evaporated here, and social contacts had drastically subsided. Mostly the only servicemen left were Marines 90 minutes north. "Plans for promoting better relations between Wilmingtonians and Camp Lejeune Marines...are progressing smoothly, with arrangements nearing completion for the transporting of 500 local girls to the Marine base for a formal dance....If the local group is successful in supplying young ladies for dancing partners for the Marines, Camp Lejeune intends to call on Wilmington for hostesses frequently."[27] Thus a new wave of girls had to be broken in, girls who when the war began might not have been in high school. The difference was, of course, the nation had to adjust to peace, but Southeastern North Carolina's future was up in the air.

As might be expected, not everything continued to click. "It was a surprise to hear that Eloise and Dougan's romance hit a snag. I'm sorry," wrote Colonel Donald J. Bailey to Mary Eloise Bethell, whose Oleander family had hosted so many Davis officers. "The uncertainty of war and its great distance, however, will upset many supposedly stabilized emotions. Heaven knows when any of us can expect to get home."[28]

The departures had no bearing on what the locals of means always did best, marrying each other. One of the late war's most visible weddings united Louise Washburn, daughter of the Benjamin Mills Washburns, and air force Lieutenant Colonel George S. Boylan, son of the George S. Boylans, at the First Presbyterian Church on January 27, 1945. Attendants and those who entertained the bride included many leading socialites and old line families.

Leave the last word to Ruth Millett. "'Girls, Be Sure, Don't Rush Into Hasty Marriage,'" she admonished in another local column. "'...She might discover to her grief that she let panic push her into a marriage she wasn't ready for.'"[29] Most of this advice, I believe, went unheeded.

Hanging out at the Robert Calder cottage at Wrightsville Beach, a popular pastime for local girls and army officers, 1942. The girls are second from left, Louise Washburn, Eugie Walters, and Jane Emerson. The latter two married men they met in Wilmington during the war, Louise a local boy.

Provided by Peggy Moore Perdew

No Smokers or Drinkers Allowed, Only Cake Eaters[30]

This is how my sister Elizabeth's dreams played out. Our parents cooperated with the 2nd and Orange USO's requests for residents to provide weekend berthing for visiting soldiers. "One requirement of would-be guests in our home was that the servicemen be screened and no fellows who smoked or drank were to be sent to the Jones home," Lib recalled. The USO respected our parents' wishes and screened "prospects." "Although Mother and Dad had frequently done so during the time I was away at college," she recalled, "the first time this extension was made after I returned home was...when four khaki-clad fellows from Camp Davis appeared [August 14, 1943]....Yes, I remember that date well because...fate played a role in the selection that the lady made of the four servicemen that she sent....'No fellows who smoked or drank,' or at least said they didn't....'Fate' was the inclusion of a fellow who would become my dear husband [George Hubbard Garniss]."

They proceeded to drink lemonade and eat almost an entire chocolate cake that Saturday night....Remember cake was a real treat in those days of sugar rationing. All four were invited to attend church with us

My sister and only sibling, Elizabeth Jones, and her husband-to-be, army officer candidate George H. Garniss, stationed at Camp Davis, 1943. He was referred to our home for dinner by the 2nd & Orange USO. George, a Maine native, served in India. They were married in June 1946, and still are.

Provided by the Garnisses

the following day; one did so, and he also stayed with us to have Sunday dinner, after which he donned an apron and insisted on washing the dishes. Wow! (Not until years later did I learn that this lieutenant had a bet with those other three guys that he was going to marry me....the bet was in the amount of 50 cents each.) Sensing the possibilities 'down the road' of having that kind of guy in my kitchen, I agreed to see him the following weekend, and the following, oh, well, you get the idea.

He rented a Saturday night room at the McClammy's home, conveniently just a block away. This continued until he was transferred to the embarkation port of New York...[eventually] to be shipped overseas to India, where he fought the battle of the Delhi Belly and humidity and monsoon rains, but, thank God, did not have to engage in any fighting. (And you know what? That Guy Who Stayed for Dinner never has collected his $1.50.)

Trepidation set in. "George, alias Budd, was, 'oh dear,' a Yankee—actually the damnedest kind of Yankee." Lib continued.

He had grown up in Maine, and that was really up north. My dad as well as my brother had our first encounter with a Yankee. It was my dear dad, the very essence of patience and tolerance, who still had ambivalent feelings about "those guys up north"....He was concerned about his only daughter's meeting, becoming interested in one of those Yankees. As Dad was reticent about voicing antagonistic opinions, he would simply walk out of the back door when Budd came in the front. He did, however, protest the celebration of 'that guy's' birthday in October. Naturally, my observant brother whom I called "Squirt" at the time was having his curiosity peaked by the "Yankee-Southerner matter." Did that spark at an early age his interest in the Civil War?....In retrospect it becomes clear that growing up in Wilmington during World War II had a direct bearing in creating a combined history and military man....

George, the son of Mr. and Mrs. George W. Garniss of Bloomfield, New Jersey, fondly recalled:

Every candidate looked forward to the weekends when they could climb aboard those buses that transported them back and forth to Wilmington. But for me, I remained on base [from March 1943] until the month of August before going into "town." My first encounter...was the USO. Needing sleeping quarters while visiting Wilmington, the USO made arrangements for myself and three other servicemen to be sent to Mr. and Mrs. Jones' home...a beautiful home where their daughter Elizabeth...and their young son, Wilbur, Jr., age nine, resided. That weekend in August became the most memorable of my life! It was the time that love at first sight became a true and everlasting meaning. This love survived three years in the army and 53 years of marriage to Elizabeth.... [I remembered the] people and their tremendous efforts to support the armed forces by their personal involvement with their churches, civic organizations, government...[and the] pride that each resident took in presenting a fine appearance....

Wilmington became my "home port" following graduation at Camp Davis, and being assigned to the 447th Automatic Weapons Battalion located at Fort Fisher. Not long after...the commanding officer received orders to be transported to England. Since this battalion had an "overstrength" of officers, 30 [were] transferred to other branches of the army. I was transferred to the Transportation Corps and assigned to the Staten Island [New York] port of embarkation loading supplies on ships bound for Europe—many of these ships had been built right there in Wilmington at the shipyard where my "wife-to-be" was working. [Later he was sent to New Delhi, India, in 1944][31]

Our parents announced the engagement in October 1944. They were married in St. Andrews-Covenant Church in June 1946. I was a junior usher, and lifelong friend Anne Hewlett the flower girl. In 2002 the Issaquah, Washington, couple celebrated their 56th anniversary.

Chapter 12
"No, We Were Always Chaperoned"

In accumulating information on Wilmington's varied and vigorous social scene during the war, an obvious follow-on question of both historical and prurient concerns kept surfacing. With all those young men in town, surely social contact with young women was not limited just to USO dancing, church suppers, and daylight walks on the beaches. Wouldn't it have been quite normal—for those who preferred not to visit houses that catered—for there to have been drinking and...unmarried sex? After all, as we kept hearing, it was wartime, and many of the traditional rules were being ignored or rewritten.

"No, we were always chaperoned," emphatically stated Eleanor "Elkie" Burgwin, who helped with the war effort as a Wilmington and Camp Davis USO hostess after her boyfriend Jimmy Coughenour went overseas. "With those little old gray-haired women on that bus you just didn't in those days. We talked and danced, that's all. I guess we were dumb and naive."[1] There was "never any hanky-panky," Lottie "Clara" Marshburn said. "Soldiers were gentlemen." Also, she knew of no assaults, no crime around the USO buildings. "We were never afraid of them."[2]

Muriel Williamson's parents "were very puritanical. I didn't know anything about sex. I guess the boys could tell the ladies from the rest of them. I was in total ignorance. People didn't talk about that sort of thing in those days. If it went on, I didn't know about it." And she was a virgin when she married in 1947. Muriel never drank whiskey until she went to work at Bluethenthal Army Air Base. "When one of the captains invited me to go to the officers club I never knew what I was doing and drank it right down, couldn't see straight. I was at the officers club and wanted to be right, didn't want them to think it was my first drink."[3]

Elkie, Clara, and Muriel were among those who attested the same, as if to infer, "Oh no, we wouldn't do such things" (or, tell someone else or worse, get caught), including whether girls drank alcohol, slept around, or shamed the family name. Sure, one must be careful not to apply today's relaxed norms and stretched morality to the 1940s. But the truth is, although the Victorian Age was long dead, people were raised and imbued with a stricter code, and they tended to practice that code at least up to the maximum limit of their temptations. But the likelihood is that these wartime passages—alcohol and sex (but definitely not drugs)—*had to happen*. If yesterday's boys and girls wish to feel better in retrospect about themselves as individuals or en masse, so be it.*

"Some of the guys came back to camp bragging about the women they had had, especially those at Carolina Beach," Justin Raphael recalled. He didn't do any of that, he said. "I don't know how much of it was true."[4] That a serviceman would automatically have "something" in mind

A Selectee's Diary

The Friday afternoon horde about to descend upon Wilmington for the weekend from Camp Davis, 35 miles and an hour's bus ride north on Highway 17. (By cartoonist Private Bob Voorhees, 1941.)
Newspaper Files of Bill Reaves, New Hanover County Public Library

---

* I do not doubt or second-guess those who claimed "nothing happened." As a historian, I report what I found, and am entitled to reach conclusions.

was not necessarily accepted. One moral code raised all. "[We] felt we were doing our bit for the war effort by entertaining soldiers at the USO," Marie Burgwin stated. "They were all very nice young men and never did anything out of the way. In fact, such a thought never crossed anyone's mind, I don't believe. They were just the 'boys next door.'"[5] Wilmington native Caroline Newbold was teaching school in Laurinburg, North Carolina, and came home on the bus for a weekend. A young sailor asked her if she would be his wife for a moment so he could get a seat on the crowded bus. She agreed, and after the trip never saw him again.

* * *

Unstoppable Social Life

War notwithstanding, Wilmington social life rolled on. The folks did admit to partying, 1940s style, for both natives and transients, with or without the spirits and intimacy. Cookouts were popular if a soldier could bring some steaks from the base mess, and Coca-Cola reigned supreme. Churches and the splendid USOs might have been the initial contact points, but for those who could, the nearby beaches and Greenfield Lake Park nudged out downtown's nefarious evening establishments for finding and pursuing either casual or long-term acquaintances.

Private and public club life purred. The area's most prestigious social organizations—the Cape Fear Country Club, Cape Fear Club downtown, and the Carolina Yacht Club at Wrightsville Beach—barely missed a beat. Their swirling activities included the Christmas holidays, the summer, weekly bridge parties, and the annual Cape Fear Horse Show. Residents did not ignore the war, but as long as they were not destitute, and supported the war effort, or showed some semblance, they felt free to exist according to their standards, lifestyles, and upbringing.

The *Star-News* society pages bubbled with announcements of engagements, weddings, balls, and ladies club teas (mixed with a plea for the war effort so as to not feel too self-conscious). The North Carolina Junior Sorosis, young matrons organizations such as the Spinsters and *Inter Se* Cotillion shared space with news of military social events, particularly involving senior officers at Camp Davis.

Activities linked to national defense received special attention. Movements were reported of anybody who was anybody, especially college students going to-and-from, people traveling to visit friends or for business events, if only to Raleigh, and out-of-town guests. Interestingly enough, in hard times with little gasoline, buses and trains jam-packed with service personnel, and government calls for limiting travel, some area residents still found the need and wherewithal to visit kin in uniform and make social trips around the country.

Dancing to popular swing music was the king of entertainment, whether as an obligation to visiting servicemen or a recreation eagerly anticipated each weekend. Taken by itself it was a free or cheap diversion unrelated to rationing shortages. The USO clubs were immensely popular with servicemen, young female volunteers the main reason.* Night (supper) clubs such as the Plantation Club and Famous Club, and the Green Lantern and The Barn for Negroes, boomed when not having to conform with inconsistent regulations, as did Wrightsville Beach's renowned old Lumina pavilion.

As Hannah Block aptly stated, "'It [life] wasn't all strained. There was a lot of humor in those days. We deliberately tried to make it light because these boys would work like dogs becoming soldiers. It couldn't be all work and no play. They had to have a relief on weekends and at night.'"[6] What social activities actually slowed down is not quite so apparent, except those impacted by restrictions. Even then, people seeking stress relief found alternatives. Had Wilmington not been "The Defense Capital of the State," however, its social life hardly would have been of this magnitude.

Wrightsville's nationally known Lumina was the dominant center of the area's social life. Primarily a bathhouse and big-band dance hall that served snacks and soft drinks, it cut across social and economic strata and military ranks. Any and all were welcomed, and they enjoyed day and night activities. Every Wilmingtonian has a favorite wartime Lumina story. Joseph R. "Joe" Reaves remembered "they had a bouncer down there who didn't take any foolishness off of anybody."[7] John W. "Bill" Walton grew up in Seagate. He and a friend with an automobile danced at Lumina under partial blackouts (on the ocean side it had to be shuttered). Drivers burned parking lights only. "There was lot of drinking going on" from people who brought their own bottles in brown paper bags.[8] In addition to bouncers, the presence of MPs and county deputies maintained order.

Lumina drew name dance bands. The "rapidly rising, handsome young..." Bob Astor's Band, "whose danceable tunes typify the taste of young Americans throughout the country," featuring vocalist Mary Glover, played in June 1943.[9] Artie Shaw performed in 1943, Tony Pastor in 1943 and 1944, Royce Stoenmer in May 1942, to name a few. Admission was $1, tax included. ("Gentlemen will not be admitted without coat, tie or proper attire for presence among ladies. Thank you, The Management.")[10] Year round, Lumina life almost guaranteed pleasure.

The Plantation Club on the Carolina Beach Road south of the city was "the in-place where everybody wanted to go," especially Saturday nights. Patrons dressed up for a fine supper and dancing well into the late hours,

---

* Other than a few leading male citizens on organization boards of directors or lending name support, hosts and management at the USOs were overwhelmingly women.

moments still relished by a number of wartime residents. Peggy Moore, whose father, Lewis T. Moore, ran the Chamber of Commerce, met officers from the navy's submarine-chasers stationed nearby. Officers took girls dancing at the Plantation where Jimmy Jett played. "We were primarily dating officers. There were many nice young men who were not officers, though." The Plantation, like the downtown St. John's Tavern, was a bit pricey and a little "out of range" for enlisted men. Hannah Block remembered a nice man coming into the Plantation in an army uniform; "everyone made a big fuss over him." The next Saturday he came as a Marine officer, and "they made a big fuss over him." The next time he came in dressed as navy, then the next week as army with navy insignia.[11] The FBI then learned of him.

* * *

Organized Recreation

As well as pursuing a vigorous social life, modified but not curtailed by the war, Wilmingtonians enjoyed numerous and varied recreational activities. Historic Thalian Hall was the stage for an array of professional boxing and wrestling cards, military shows, jamborees, war bond drives, demonstrations, and musical events in addition to plays. Headliner groups included The Tennessee Ramblers and Sam Poplin and his Cape Fear Rangers ("These boys are destined for a great future in the entertainment world."[12]) Minnie Pearl and her radio Station WSM Grand Ole Opry Gang appeared in March 1944. Theater productions continued. "World War II has brought no final curtain for the Thalians [begun in 1788]...it has resulted in redoubled efforts to provide relaxation and inspiration to a people weary of the grim realism of the times."[13] By December 1944, Thalian Hall was worn out. After numerous complaints, the seven hundred seats were repaired.

"Dynamite dames" Mae Young and Rose Evans came to town in November 1943, as wrestling "promoter Bert Causey is doing it again—bringing a Madison Square Garden attraction to Wilmington. Boys will be boys, and girls will be bus drivers, WACs, shipyard workers or even wrestlers...brawn can go with beauty....Hair is as useful for pulling as it is for adding to one's charm."[14] Young won, but "Miss Evans displayed a brand of wrestling which would put some of the male mat huskies to shame and for sheer dirty fighting, she really dished it out."[15] They had rematches.

Legion Stadium, the only outdoor venue of size, also held boxing and wrestling matches and other events. On September 19, 1942, N.C. State and Davidson played there to a scoreless football tie before 10,000 spectators.[*] Popular athletic events centered around the NHHS Wildcats teams:

---

[*] I believe this article was the first by R. J. Powell of the *Star-News*, whose career covering area sports lasted for more than 55 years. He was my mentor when I worked at the paper as a student.

fun to follow, but never very successful in any sport, and usually bad in football. At least their games were an outlet from wartime frustrations, but as a frequent reminder, many night-time games were played in daylight because of dimout restrictions. A high moment was the 1942–43 basketball team's 30–25 win over Durham which broke their 56-straight game Eastern Conference win streak.* The semi-pro Cape Fear Baseball League, with state senator J. E. L. Wade as president, played over two summers until they ran out of players in 1944. "It's hard on the fans. But that's war, and the war must be won, and Wilmington had a major job to do...."[16]

Stage and musical shows attracted big crowds and kind reviews. The NHHS glee club's April 1945 operetta "Naughty Marietta" drew the "largest crowd ever to be turned away from NHHS." I remember enjoying both "Pinafore" and the Hi-Y minstrel. The R&S Carnival, "Wilmington's Home Town Amusement Company," boasting one of the world's fastest Ferris wheels and touting "we like the record of not having a single arrest for misconduct in all that time [35 years in business]," appeared at Bellamy Park. Of course, the circus came to town, and yes, the animal smells and offloading parade are never to be forgotten. Downtown movie theaters included the Bailey (upscale, main features and specials), Royal (good war movies), Carolina (stage shows), Bijou (serials, westerns), Manor (B movies), and the Village (everything). Negroes sat in the upper balconies.

If what you needed to know wasn't in the newspaper or magazines, it had to be on the radio or at the movies. The living room floor-model radio was our family's main touch with the news, usually on the only local station, WMFD-630 (which is still on the air). We enjoyed "The Hit Parade," the "Fred Waring Show," "Victory Parade of Spotlight Bands," "The Ink Spots," Bob Hope, and other swing band and pop music broadcasts. We followed war news on the Blue, Mutual, CBS, and NBC networks. "The Breakfast Club with Don McNeil" was my mother's favorite (in 1946 she was a guest on the show in Chicago). My crowd were regular listeners to the Monday-through-Friday afternoon lineup of serials and specials throughout the war—especially for rainy days—that included:

    4:30 "Johnny Doughboy Reporting"
    5:00 "The Sea Hound"
    5:15 "Hop Harrigan"
    5:30 "The Lone Ranger"
    6:00 "Terry and the Pirates"
    6:15 "Lum and Abner"
    9:00 at night "Gangbusters"

---

*That NHHS team featured Leonard "Legs" McKoy, who led the state in scoring, and three players who were later KIA: Claude Cliff Owensby, Jr. (army, in Luxembourg in March 1945), William D. Halyburton, Jr. (navy, Okinawa, May 1945), and Ernest "Red" Mayhan (navy, Okinawa, June 1945).

Oh how I remember hours with my ears glued to the nearest radio set, or for background as we boys played something momentarily more urgent. You didn't have to hear every word. Supplementing the usual fare were shows like "Life of Riley," "Philco Radio Hall of Fame," "Jack Armstrong," "Blondie and Dagwood," "Inner Sanctum," "Harry Wismer Sports," "Watch the World Go By," various military-sponsored shows, and boxing from Madison Square Garden.

* * *

Entertaining, and Being Entertained

Peggy Moore was representative of girls of her generation. She and her friends "took a drink but were not heavy drinkers." Her friends smoked. She went to Camp Lejeune and Camp Davis in "cattle trucks" in long evening dresses. "I went one time—it wasn't my cup of tea to be herded around like that." Some officers rented cottages at the beach and had her group over to cook steaks for them. She also enjoyed the Dutch marines who visited Wilmington in 1945. "There were a lots of things that were unhappy, too, about the wartime, like these young men you knew who didn't come home."[17]

Sally Josey was another socially active girl of means.[18] She reflected on the truck convoys of girls sitting on the hard wooden benches. "There would be 10 men to every girl—you couldn't dance five steps before there was a break-in. It was wonderful." Officers clubs always had live music. "My sister [Atha, older], who was sort of a catbird, had dates at the same time, and neither one knew about it." Girls returned officers' steak cook-outs by inviting them home or to the Yacht Club or Cape Fear Country Club, and enjoyed invitations to Davis OCS graduations. "We'd all go out to a fine lunch. Some we saw again, some we never saw again. You never went to so many weddings." She knew at least 25 girls who got married during the war. "Mainly we liked to go dancing. In those days we danced cheek to cheek. They were just happy to have someone to latch on to." In 1945 she went around with a Dutch marine named Hank who was married and had been in the Underground. "They were so happy to meet people. They spoke English. Oh how they could dance. Some Dutchmen fell in love with local girls and vice versa." They didn't have much money and liked to visit the girls' houses. Her friend Marie Conley married one and moved to Holland.

"My daddy [school board member J. C. Roe] didn't approve of movies," said Laura Roe. "I had to go on the sly." (Ironically all her children are now in the movie business.) "I thought I had committed a crime." She dated the kids of GI fathers in her class. "They were interesting and fun." But nothing surpassed Friday and Saturday night fun at the "Top Hop," a dance floor built over the garage at Catherine Russell's a half block away in Oleander.[19]

Members of the First Composite Anti-Aircraft Battery, Royal Artillery, which trained at Camp Davis twice in 1943. The "ruddy Tommies in khaki" were a tremendous hit and swept away the hearts, if momentarily, of many local girls. The British ambassador, Lord Halifax, visited Wilmington for the unit's farewell in December.

Provided by Catherine Russell Stribling

He lived at 605 South 3rd; she lived next door. He had little social life; "she was courting somebody else," stated John Mintz about Manette Allen Dixon (NHHS '39).[20] "I would sit on my front porch after getting off work on the swing watching her come in and out. You didn't do very much courting—we worked 10 hour days." Turned down for the draft in 1941 because of a broken eardrum, John went into shipyard work. During the war all the two did was speak to each other. Sometimes he gave her a ride home from work in his Hudson car (had a private parking place). "If I had the money and time we would drive down to Johnny Mercer's [Wrightsville] pier and park," just kissing. They couldn't drive far because of the gas shortage even though he had extra coupons.

* * *

Wrightsville Beach*

A favorite sport for kids and adults was wetting down a mattress cover in the surf, running down the beach to fill it with air, tying the open end, and use the air-filled cover for flotation while riding it on the waves. "It was

---

* For another look at wartime life, see Rupert L. Benson and Helen S. Benson, *Historical Narrative 1841–1972 of Wrightsville Beach, N.C.* (Wilmington: Carolina Printing and Stamp Co., 1972).

the best ride possible," recalled an army officer and wife. They also enjoyed the bowling alley at Birmingham Street and North Lumina Avenue. "We went to sleep every night to the crashing of the bowling pins being knocked down and the serenade of 'Pistol Packin' Mama.' That song was apparently so popular that it was played at least seven or eight times each night."[21]

Betty Bugg and Ann Penton enjoyed playing on Robert F. "Bobby" Cameron's boat "Betty Ann," named for them.[22] Bobby's father bought the boat at the 1939 New York World's Fair. During the war there was some sailing but not much motor boating. The Coast Guard Auxiliary took over his father's 30-foot Mathews boat. With his older sister Rachel Cameron, Betty cut pieces of Octagon soap in squares, dipped them in chocolate syrup, took the concoction out on the beach, and asked some kid if he wanted chocolate candy. The reluctant mother gave in and allowed the kid to take it. Then Betty and Rachel ran away. (Strange move what with the scarcity of chocolate.) "She was like the big sister that I didn't have," recalled Betty. The Camerons and the E. B. Buggs lived next door to each other on Stone Street. Soldiers without places to change clothes on the beach except Lumina fell prey to Bobby and Betty who rented out his pup tents, but the parents soon stopped it. The Camerons rented their beach house to Camp Lejeune senior officers. In 1944 it caught fire and burned down, damaging the Buggs' house. Military personnel were down there a few days after the fire raking the sand looking for valuables.

William F. "Bill" McIlwain eyed the Landis cottage where young girls stayed in the summer.[23] In 1944 there he met Carrie Maie Wade of Charlotte, daughter of Jake Wade, sports editor of the *Charlotte Observer*. Bill had gone with freshman Ann Milburn during much of his just-completed senior year. Maie was "the most

Wilmington Mayor Bruce B. Cameron's Stone Street house burns to the ground, Wrightsville Beach, 1944. Other houses also burned, including E. B. Bugg's next door. Sons Bruce B., Jr., and Daniel D. Cameron were serving in New Guinea and France.

Provided by Dan Cameron

sophisticated girl we'd ever seen, just beautiful." Men opened the doors for her. One night after a date, Ann left her purple lipstick in his car. Maie found it and used it. After entering the Marines, he and Maie exchanged letters. He learned a man had attacked her and cut her throat, but she fought him off. She was wearing that lipstick. "She got it on his white shirt, and that's part of the reason why they caught him." (After Bill and Maie started going out, he and Ann broke up.)

On August 1, "The army came down in big trucks to evacuate us, no warnings, came up very suddenly," John Debnam remembered about the "big storm" of August 1944. Martial law was temporarily declared, and all had to leave the beaches. The family spent that night at their in-town home on Country Club Road. The next morning it was clear and beautiful, and they were able to go back. He looked up and saw a P-38 *Lightning* fighter coming over. The storm, of near-hurricane force, destroyed the boardwalk that ran along ocean front from Raleigh to Columbia Streets at the water's edge.[24] Water covered over island roads. Virginia Harriss rode in a big truck with someone's big fat Negro nanny, scared of the water, holding a chocolate cake.* Pearl Winner saw the Carolina Beach pier and the Fergus cottages fall into the sea. Her father lost two boats at the same time. The "big storm" was the most serious local natural disaster of the war.

Haskell Rhett lived nearby on Bradley Creek. "Probably no more than two hundred people lived on the beach year around during war." The beach speed limit was 15 mph; cars had slits for headlights. In 1943 he and Henry Meyer got adept at jumping on car running boards for rides to the beach. He saw glows from two ships burning offshore. "Rumors [of rubber boats landing from submarines, etc.] were flying all over the place in those days—most untrue I'm sure."[25]

Hangouts at Station 1 (the first stop of the old Wilmington to Wrightsville trolley which ceased operation in 1940) were transitioning when the war began. Pop Gray's soda shop with its wire chairs was where "you had to go there to be seen, had to check in there," stated Henry Von Oesen. Across the trolley tracks was Newell's, in 1943 growing from an open stand to regular store.[26] Leonard Gleason Allen (NHHS '43) and friends hitchhiked to the Carolina Yacht Club. Bobby Taylor allowed him to change clothes at his nearby cottage. Their hangouts included the Ocean Terrace Hotel, the Anchor, and the Tradewinds, with its nickelodeon, rooftop, soft

---

* The town, seeking to dispel impressions the storm had knocked it out of business, a few days later ran this ad in a statewide magazine: "Wilmington, N.C., 1944 Aug 6," placed by the Board of Aldermen, by J. R. Wood, mayor: "Please insert this telegram as paid advertisement. Reported storm damage to Wrightsville Beach grossly exaggerated. Resort facilities in full operation subject of course to wartime restriction. No devastating damages done to hotels, residence, business or boarding houses." [*The State: A Weekly Survey of North Carolina*, Raleigh, August 12, 1944]

drinks and beer, and dancing. While sail boating with Sanford Doxey in Banks Channel he could hear their melodious sounds. To one girl, the Anchor and its upstairs dance hall was where "you couldn't recognize anybody until you got to within kissing distance. The men were gentlemen and didn't drink much around us."[27]

Newell's was the center of beach activities, and the island's only "general store" of note until sold in the mid-1990s and replaced with a beach-junk store.* For Christmas 1943 it offered pipes, dolls, perfumes, leather goods, novelties, greeting cards, blankets, and "Novel! Unique! Handmade Wood Purses, $6 and $10." Books just received in February 1944 included "*The Robe*, Douglas ...$2.75; *Good Night Sweet Prince*, Fowler...$3.50; *Hungry Hill*, Du Maurier...$2.75; *A Tree Grows in Brooklyn*, Smith...$2.75; *So Little Time*, Marquand...$2.75; *A Bell for Adano*, Hersey...$2.50; *The Birds of America*, Audubon...$4.95."[28]

One of the best all-around family spots was the Mira-Mar on South Lumina Avenue. "Drive Your Car to Our Door or Use Bus to Our Door," the advertisement read. "We Offer For Your Pleasure: Playground for children; Grade A Restaurant for family; Soft drinks only—sandwiches, candy, ice cream, popcorn, novelties; Bowling; Bathing; Boating; Special 'Moonlit' Terrace; Picnic Ground 'If You Desire'; Public Phone Booth; Center of all social activities—under Management and Ownership Mr. and Mrs. Floyd W. Cox Sr."[29] The popular Glenn Cottage, "A Home Away from Home," and the Carolina-Temple Apartments are two of the few cottages still being rented.

As Frances Thornton said best, college boys gathered at Station 1 to pass a bowl of spirits, and girls drank sodas at Newell's. That was wartime Wrightsville.

Carolina Beach

As a shipyard worker before joining the Marines, Ray Funderburk owned an old Chrysler. One of his drillers, a Whiteville Negro, polished the car and drove him around. "Had a great time spending my money at Carolina Beach. We had a pocket full of money." He and other workers rented a cottage during summers at the northern extension. The Green Lantern tavern on the main boardwalk was "where all the young people went. There was a lot of difference [between Wrightsville and Carolina]. Carolina was *that other beach*. Wrightsville did not welcome enlisted men like Carolina, and Carolina Beach was out to get what it could out of them." He saw numerous fights there between GIs and Marines.[30]

The Carolina Beach approach was entirely different than Wrightsville's. Carolina marketed its entertainment; Wrightsville basked

---

* The disappointing sale and conversion of the classic beach store Newell's to the Wings chain in the early 1990s destroyed the one structure so many of my generation associated with life in Wilmington and the beach, and of course wartime.

The boardwalk and amusement area at Carolina Beach, 1945. These lifeguards were trained by Mrs. Charles (Hannah) Block, who along with numerous contributions to the war effort served as the lifeguard when its full-time man, Lonnie Peck, joined the Royal Canadian Air Force. Carolina was more popular with, and suited for, area enlisted personnel than Wrightsville, more the officers' beach.

Provided by Block

in the very low-key quiet family traditions. The 1945 season, expected to be good despite the continuing war, "offers greater and greater opportunities for amusement as the weekend crowds increase in numbers. Moonlight cruises are offered for those wishing to cruise on the river, ocean, or canal." "The Seashore Amusement Company officially opened...and offers aside from the conventional merry-go-round and Ferris wheels many other fascinating and thrilling rides such as the 'Tilt-O-Whirl.'" The Wave Theater boasted a fresh coat of paint. Admission was by war bond only to coincide with the first D-Day anniversary.[31]

Year-round beach residents recalled the reputation, "messed up by Marines and soldiers, fights, prostitutes, and flourished to the point where beer joints stayed open all night." Jim Fountain watched as one night on the boardwalk Fort Bragg paratroopers and Camp Lejeune Marines broke beer bottles over heads in a big fight. It took beach and Wilmington police to break it up. "They decided to continue it the next week—they set a date and kept it. They trucked in truckloads of MPs—tore up the boardwalk." In the end, Pearl Winner stated, "the locals made a lot of money off them [servicemen]. It was like a carnival down there. The boardwalk was a hopping place" of rides and arcades. Her father, Carl Winner, owned the Cork & Sinker bar-restaurant on the ocean front and an offshore fishing service.[32]

Carolina Beach created its mark early in the war and got livelier as more servicemen visited. "Judging from the size of the crowd at Carolina Beach over the weekend [Sunday, May 3, 1942], the resort is in for another peak year." More than five thousand jammed the beach. "It is the feeling of the [boarding house] operators that patrons will come and stay their entire vacations rather than split it between the mountains and the seashore....The ocean-front businessmen have already started putting in fixtures for the dim-out. Blue and green lights of low wattage are being installed...will be difficult to make out the beach's midway from a distance of a mile out."[33]

When head lifeguard Lonnie Peck joined the Royal Canadian Air Force, Mrs. Charles (Hannah) Block took his place, the first woman to become head lifeguard there. She sent him packages while he was a POW of the Germans. In 1945 some Dutch marines dived into the water not realizing it was a sandbar at low tide. One, "I know he had broken his neck." She treated him and sent him to the hospital. Later he returned and gave her the emblem off his hat (she showed it to me). Carolina had no clinic or doctors during the war. She went to her father-in-law, William Block, and got him to buy the equipment for establishing a first-aid station in May 1945.[34] "'Hurrah for Hannah...she's done it again,'" gushed the *Wilmington Evening Post*. "'If Congress gave medals for "outstanding action beyond the line of duty" at home, Hannah...would have several of them....Everyone, not only at Carolina Beach, but in Wilmington, is justly proud of this young woman and the interest she has taken in the two towns, in the young people, and in the service men and women who are stationed [here].'"[35]

"Closing of Camps felt at Beaches," the story read in September 1944, describing the "factor responsible for the suspension for the winter of some business establishments and housing accommodations." The boom was dying out. "Most business places on the [Carolina] boardwalk have closed completely, with only a few open in the afternoons and nights." At Wrightsville, the effects of Camp Davis removals "has yet to be felt" but the town expected housing vacancies this winter that had not been apparent since Pearl Harbor.[36] The full impact was yet to come, but by late 1945 beach business was headed for 1941 proportions.

* * *

The USOs[*]

Jocelyn Peck went to the movies on weeknights with Davis men, and visited the camp's USO (United Service Organizations) on the army buses.

---

[*] A thorough and informative account of the Wilmington area's World War II USOs and related organizations was written by historian Everard H. Smith, Ph.D., a monograph titled *Victory*

The largest and most popular USO club in New Hanover County was this one at 2nd and Orange Streets downtown, 1943. Now the city-owned Community Arts Center, plans are to renovate and restore the building to its wartime lobby appearance as a "living museum" for patrons and tourists.

Provided by George J. Green

"When you went in there it would be packed with servicemen. We used fake names" so the men wouldn't call at home.[37] Kathleen Somersett "went to the USO on Saturday nights to see how many people I could meet, boys and girls, and to learn about the war." A self-professed talker, "I could do all that talking with those boys." One night she helped two Camp Davis soldiers pay for their open face hamburger sandwiches at dinner, telling them not to allow the waitress to know she was doing it. (Southern women *just didn't* pay for a man in the '40s.) On her dates with soldiers she would "bring them home and let the family entertain them."[38]

The 2nd and Orange USO appealed to Muriel Williamson because she loved to jitterbug. "It was a lot of fun to talk with the guys and dance with them. That was our recreation, going to the USOs. I dated some guys from Camp Davis where she worked. I wish I had the money I spent on postage writing to them." She met a captain. I "thought he was the cat's meow." One day he came into her office. "I got so excited I put the lit end of a cigarette

---

on the Home Front: The USO in New Hanover County, N.C., 1941–1946 (Self-published, 1998). Consequently, *A Sentimental Journey* makes no unnecessary attempt to rewrite the details already superbly covered by Smith. Instead I concentrate on other vignettes of USO life, which was immensely important to wartime Wilmington.

into my mouth. I was humiliated. We did not socialize much because we knew it was a temporary thing. They'd soon be going off to war." Dates included movies, the USO, picnics, the beach—riding the bus because none of the boys had transportation.[39]

Girls from the Carolina Beach area flocked to that town's USO. Frances Jordan Wagner (NHHS '43) wrote, "since my mother was a volunteer hostess some weekends, I was allowed to attend those evenings. I wore out a pair of sandals from dancing one summer. Only enlisted men went to that USO. My father thought I should limit my activities to the officers club at Fort Fisher. But since they served alcohol and just sat around and talked, I enjoyed the USO much more. I never dated any of the soldiers."[40]

Sergeant Jack F. Hart, *center*, with actress Jinx Falkenburg during her tour of the Burma front, 1944.

Provided by Hart

Within the strict USO rules, and giving moral credit where due, a number of local wives and girlfriends acted as hostesses, not only dancing but serving in the canteens or aiding in other ways. Joy Hart, the wife of Wilmington soldier Jack F. Hart fighting in North Africa and Burma, was one. Many mothers and wives of local businessmen and professionals volunteered. Age, experience, and looks were no factors. But USOs were much more than merry-making and socializing. A few offered classes in photography and drama, Ping-Pong and fishing contests, make-a-record, variety hours, jam sessions, bridge, community sings, and quiz programs. One of the most popular programs was the religious-based "USO-Java Club" at 2nd and Orange.

How popular were local dances? The Hut staged 101 from July 1943 to July 1944.* Keeping records of the countless number of little activities such as letter writing, mending, buying gifts for relatives, etc., was impossible.[41] How popular was the Hut? Letters from servicemen in Africa, Australia, England, and Sicily "attest to the degree to which the [Hut]...has fulfilled its function in the two years...." Membership in the Dance Defense Group was

---

* The Woodrow Wilson Hut, a community-sponsored recreation center on the City Hall grounds, was dedicated on May 30, 1941, six months before the 2nd and Orange USO opened. Not associated with the USO, it was extremely popular during the war's first two years until eclipsed by the other clubs because of its small size.

open to girls 18 or older. Girls could not leave the dance building escorted by a soldier.[42]

Hannah Block still speaks of the "60 different girls" she frequently rounded up for dances at Davis and Camp Lejeune.[*] Her friend Bea Black ran the Lejeune officers club. One day she called Hannah for advice: the boys were tired of regular dances. "You had a lot of boys in from the farms in the Marines. I said, let's put on something different. Why not have a hog calling? Why not give a piglet as a gift?" Well, the piglet got drunk, and the officer who won it went back to his barracks to sleep and took it with him, but his buddies kicked him out.[43] Her girls were from all over Southeastern North Carolina. "A lot of them married the boys and I would have to replenish over the years. The USO pushed me into it. They [girls] came in and wanted to join up—didn't have to recruit much." The girls usually had day jobs. Events were at night.[44]

As war fortunes turned and men began coming home, the clubs trained volunteers on the psychology of entertaining men who had seen combat. By 1945, although fewer women were required, the need arose to recruit new volunteers to replace the weary ones, and to give longtime ones a "refresher course." "Sooner or later, the USO will go out of business," warned the editorial, "with the demobilization of the armed forces and the abandonment of military training camps....They have done a good job, on the whole and deserve great credit....What is to be done with the buildings and equipment when this time comes presents a problem that should have a place in any postwar planning....The main USO center at 2nd and Orange is city property. Its usefulness will not end with the war. Today is none too soon to consider what shall be done...."[45]

On January 31, 1946, the 5th and Orange officers USO held its final social function and officially closed. The main club three blocks west bid farewell on June 14–16, 1946. A month later the city acquired that property and the Negro club at 9th and Nixon. The clubs had an enormous impact on the Wilmington area's social life and contribution to the war

---

[*] Hannah Block is easily the most identifiable and appreciated symbol of the USOs and their impact on wartime Wilmington. Now in her late-80s and lively, she still enjoys plinking out '40s hit songs on her piano, as she did for so many GIs, girls, and war workers. We were neighbors in Forest Hills. The stage at the Community Arts Center (2nd and Orange USO) is named for her. She has been active in helping save the building believed to be one of only a handful such from WWII still standing. What stories she tells! What a historical inspiration she is.

Among her valuables ia a USO lapel pin, a tiny donut being dipped into a cup of coffee, the hallmark of the WWII program. In November 1997, USO president General Carl E. Mundy, Jr., officially cited her efforts and service to the organization. Her boys never forgot her, either. "While I doubt seriously that you could ever remember me, you can be sure that my thoughts traveled back to the fall and winter of 1941 and all those lovely and friendly people who helped make life so much more like home away from home. My thoughts went back to the Hut...." {Martin R. Buccieri to Hannah Block, September 25, 1961]

effort. Their very existence was a constant reminder of the job to be done. With the closings came the end of a turbulent four-year era, and the beginning of a long new one.

Postscript: Today

After the war the city turned the USO building into a community center for young people and other organizational activities. I attended numerous events there in grammar and high school, especially post-football game sock hops. Over the years the expanding arts community—dance, theater, painting, crafts, and others—under the umbrella Community Arts Center Accord, and the Cape Fear Community College have enjoyed its facilities administered for the city by The Thalian (theater) Association.

Now where are we? Believe it or not, hardly anything structurally inside or out except a handicap entrance is changed from WWII.* Wood floors, fixtures, and faded paint have hung around. The city in 1999 repainted the exterior a sand color, the roof a cardinal red, matching wartime schemes. In August 2000, following years of indecisiveness and some wrangling, the city council agreed to preserve the building forever and fund its badly needed physical renovations. With the Accord providing the impetus, and Tony-Award winning actress Linda Lavin (a Wilmington resident) the endorsement, private funds are being raised to help with the overall renovation and restoration of the lobby into a living museum representing what it looked like in 1943. Historian Dr. Everard H. "Ev" Smith and I are involved with the project as part of the effort by the World War II Wilmington Home Front Heritage Coalition to establish a separate wartime museum here. "The USO," as Hannah and a few of us old-timers will always call it, is the hub of our cultural-heritage trail brochure and map of WWII sites in Southeastern North Carolina due for release in 2002. The future for the building, our museum, and the preservation of our area's wonderful WWII history look exceedingly bright.

---

* To Ev Smith's knowledge, only a handful of federal government-built wartime structures for use as USOs still exist. Ours is by far the most "pristine," and is on the National Register of Historic Places. The club in Jacksonville, North Carolina, still serves Camp Lejeune Marines.

On December 1, 2001, the Coalition and Accord staged a highly successful 60th anniversary open house marking the 2nd and Orange and Negro 9th and Nixon clubs openings. More than five hundred visitors attended this wonderful WWII Wilmington afternoon and boosted our restoration efforts. Only a short time before I had learned my father had been on the committee that dedicated 2nd and Orange in April 1942. Then I realized I had another reason for working so hard to preserve the building.

Chapter 13

"Needed in So Many Occupations"

Aside from being employed for wages, supporting the war effort with more than pocketbooks, lip service, and renting rooms was primarily performed by men. Volunteering as Red Cross Nurse's Aides or directly servicing the troops—USOs, canteens, letter writing, etc., the more traditional roles—were exceptions. Men served in virtually all visible leadership positions except those more normally associated with women, wartime or not. Women were welcome to the team behind the scenes, or when not enough men were available.

Yet, in spite of the seriousness of volunteering for the national emergency, Wilmington-area women as a whole required coaxing to the point of humiliation. In January 1944, the *Star-News* chastised the unresponsiveness of area women, insinuating that those high on the social lists or who had no need to be employed were primarily to blame.

> Never in the history of this country have women been needed in so many occupations, and to their lasting credit be it said many are responding nobly to calls for volunteers, despite the fact that other thousands who could be doing something for their nation maintain their accustomed social schedules and give neither time nor work in an enterprise affiliated with the conflict or home defense....It is impossible to condemn too sternly other women who recognize no obligation for service in the war emergency. This is predicated upon the reluctance of many Wilmington women to take part in the present war bond campaign....The sad fact remains that there are enough capable women in Wilmington to discharge every duty urged upon them, who flatly refuse to lend a hand at any way or defense task or help in any campaign, claiming the war effort does not touch them or their lives.[1]

Of course not knowing how long the emergency would last, a tendency of both women and men was an inability to sustain interest or steady physical involvement. Some women, without kin in uniform and snugly free from harm, were willing to do without under wartime restrictions and shortages, but hesitated to step forward. Some of my friends' mothers were in the war effort like mine, a regular long-term Nurse's Aide and Legion post historian. Others did nothing, or tried volunteering for a short while and stopped, information disclosed or confirmed in numerous interviews for this book. The newspaper obviously noted this situation and frequently spoke out against a general unwillingness of women to spend serious volunteer time or open their homes to renters and the like, imploring their participation either by gentle persuasion or needle.

This is not to impugn the thousands of area women who regularly volunteered, without whose pitching-in the community would not have shouldered its responsibilities. An example is my neighbor Annie Worth Mitchell, who worked several times a week at the filter center and Union Station canteen. Her preserved ribbon citation cited her more than five hundred hours in civilian defense. Daughter Emma Worth Mitchell volunteered there also. Some gave an effort when they could work with others of their standing. For instance, the Gray Ladies, associated with the Red Cross, attracted the more genteel set. Letter writing, games, conversation, and reading for those in military hospitals was a safe and handy way to help, and they got to wear uniforms. The group headed by Florence Avery included Mary Belle Ormond, also a Motor Corps driver who often ferried expectant mothers to the hospital, and then home with their babies. "We were used in any capacity, unrestricted duty."[2] They felt useful, and undoubtedly made a difference.*

Recruitment of women began immediately after the war started. In June 1942 the city and women's organizations honored Mrs. Eddie

Mrs. Robert (Hattie) Hardwick, *left*, and Mrs. Lewis (Mary Belle) Ormond, volunteer members of the Wilmington American Red Cross Motor Corps, mid-war.
Provided by Ormond

---

* Asking me till near the end when this book was coming out, Mary Belle died in 2002 at 99, the age my mother would have been had she lived.

Rickenbacker, wife of the hero army aviator of World War I, at a luncheon at the Governor Dudley house. Mother attended. Mrs. Rickenbacker was here as a liaison officer of the Aircraft Warning Service (filter center). "'It is the duty and privilege of women to engage in this war,'" Mrs. Rickenbacker stated. "'Through the AWS you are protecting not only your lives and homes, but the stores of supplies which the men at the front must have....Some of the work may seem tedious and dull in the [filter] center, but months of preparation are needed, so that the women may work effectively and without panic when the test comes.'" She toured the center. "'I wouldn't mind working here myself. I'm glad to see the matrons taking their place here.'"[3]

* * *

The Filter Center

"Women, here's your chance to do your bit," the offer read, soliciting volunteers for the army Signal Corps' Information and Filter Center in the war's early hours.* "This is a vital defense nerve center. It requires devoted, quick-thinking, alert workers." Operating around the clock daily, the filter center was for a while the area's most popular civilian defense unit for attracting volunteers, particularly women. "There will be no time for diversion or relaxation—only faithful and continuous attention...and men of Wilmington will be engaged in more strenuous, if no more important, tasks."[4] The Wilmington center, located in the basement of the Front Street post office, was one of five major information and filter centers along the Southeastern Atlantic seaboard for the detection, tracking, and interception of enemy aircraft.

Before radar was installed the center was the only means of surveying our region's airspace. It contained a giant map of the North Carolina coast on a large table surrounded by telephone jacks connecting operators with volunteer spotters posted in lifeguard-type stands in the field from South Carolina to Virginia. Spotters telephoned the center with information on anything flying in their area, e.g., "One bi-motor, 15,000 feet, heading north-northwest." A plotter recorded the information on the map and the location of said aircraft was carefully monitored until it was out of reach of our command. The area south of Brunswick County's Long Beach was in the "Charleston overlap," and northward around Elizabeth City was in the "Norfolk overlap." Cora Preston headed the volunteers who assisted army troops in manning the center around the clock.

Kathleen Somersett moved from Brunswick County to work there when it opened before the war. Her jobs included operating the teletype connected

---

* The Information and Filter Center was part of the Wilmington Air Region, and overall under the Army Air Forces Aircraft Warning Service (Corps). The Corps included local Ground Observer Volunteers. Organized prior to Pearl Harbor, the WAR's primary mission was coastal protection.

to other East Coast sites, and placing tiny aircraft on the big map. With no one in her life to tell her what to do, she was free to spend time. She received a break every hour for 15 minutes and was permitted to work four hours per day. The army didn't feed the volunteers, but "everybody was super nice to you. If you needed information you felt free to ask for it." Somersett later joined the Women's Army Auxiliary Corps.[5] Wilmington high school student Catherine Russell's mother, Catherine Harper Russell, was one of the first volunteers. The daughter followed. "I had to be fingerprinted and cleared by the FBI, and issued a pass....Naturally I felt very important, and we took our work seriously."[6]

In September 1942, WAAC members began taking over volunteers' duties.[7] Lieutenant Mary E. Stanton arrived "smartly outfitted in the government-issued suit...in a straight khaki skirt, shirt, tie, jacket, cap, brown shoes and rayon hose," with gold bars on the jacket on either shoulder. She was to be addressed as "Lieutenant Stanton." By February 1943, the army ordered the WAACs elsewhere "to jobs that release military personnel for field duty in combat zones. This was the original plan for them."

The newspaper loudly questioned the army's judgment in sending the women here for only three months and disrupting the routine, asking the populace to "rally around the filter center and see that a sufficient staff is provided to perform the exacting duties....There must be many more persons enlisted if the burden is to be equitably shared." And in a theme becoming all too familiar regarding the enthusiasm for self-defense, "there are very many people in Wilmington who are not doing their duty in the war and defense effort.* This is their chance to make good."

From baby clinic to filter center, "just an incident in Miss Wood's life," read the article about Eleanor V. Woods.[8] "Here's someone who works as hard at soldiering, in her sphere, as a major general....She taught school at Wrightsville Beach until she went all out for defense." She works every Wednesday morning at the Sorosis Baby Clinic on 3rd Street, "and without lunch dashes to the [center] to do her daily afternoon shift," spending six afternoons a week and Sundays when necessary. Woods was one of more than three hundred women who each week devoted several hours at plotting or supervisory jobs. "Neither she nor the other women feel they are

---

* Too bad the paper didn't name names. That would have rebuked the norm, however. "Investigative reporting" and negative name identification were not often practiced by Wilmington's papers during the war. A rare exception was the *Morning Star*'s efforts to raise awareness of the plight of the county home mental health and detention facilities.

   From my unscientific random sampling during interviews, I encountered enough situations where natives or pre-war residents never volunteered for the war effort. From this I can postulate a large percentage did none. Sixty years later, there is nothing to be gained by my naming any. Many women who volunteered early in the war for filter center work obviously became bored or tired of it quickly, or were too inconvenienced. They didn't last long for one reason or another, including imposition on social or family life.

making a tremendous sacrifice...." She began working there when it opened in October 1941. Now she is operations room supervisor. She and her mother, Mrs. J. Russell Wood, also manned the beach observation post. One of them was there at all times. The two operated a tourist home, "and are compelled to do their own housework." "Does this work cause a hardship on the Woods women?" Miss Woods said, "We lived on the beach during the last war and saw the boats sunk just before our eyes, We've seen them sunk again this war. We're just making every effort to protect our home and those of our neighbors."

While soldier Robert B. Conway studied at the Camp Davis anti-aircraft artillery officer candidate school, his wife plotted at the filter center.[9] For the Wilmington residents, their jobs were somewhat the same—the defense of Wilmington and other American cities against enemy air raids. "It is not beyond possibility that she may one day plot the position of an enemy plane which her husband's guns will knock out of the skies. This husband and wife team illustrate the cooperative system among civilians and all branches of the armed forces developed for the defense of the United States...."

Worker availability fluctuated. Demands often exceeded the willingness of the volunteers. Community leaders implored citizens to work there, even suggesting a possible "draft" of workers, citing the imminent danger to enemy attack. But in October 1943 the civilian portion of the nation's AWS was virtually eliminated except as a reserve for emergency use. The War Department ordered most of it placed on alert status. Here, the order affected about three thousand civilian volunteers in Wilmington's aircraft warning system region. Regional commander Lieutenant Colonel Oscar Tigner asked volunteers to continue to staff the local operations room on a 24-hour basis, but placed the filter center on instant alert to operate periodically. Shortly thereafter Tigner presented AWS wings and awards of merit to 45 volunteers, and for all intents and purposes thanked and bade most goodbye. The number of volunteers on the filter center rolls, however, was never higher. The editors could feel pleased; their inspirational indictment had worked. The army took final action in June 1944, releasing all members of the Ground Observer Corps and other volunteers to emergency service recall, and deactivated the control room. It was time for the editors to say thanks.

On September 7, 1944, the army officially closed the center. So ended the wartime usefulness of one of the area's least colorful and most demanding, and, because it never spotted, tracked, and intercepted an enemy aircraft except in practice, one of the least productive civilian defense activities. Given the nature of national security in late 1941, its establishment and operation were mandatory. It rightfully deserved praise for having done its job simply by being on the job.

* * *

In the Armed Forces

Mrs. Dell J. Hintze and Kathleen Somersett left for Women's Army Auxiliary Corps training on August 9, 1942. Somersett claimed to be the first Wilmington woman to join.* In California, she kept the records for the general who assigned air crews overseas. "I was from the deep country, younger than most of the other women, and was supposed to be dumber. I was always taking orders from someone else. All the training I got was from men." Her commanding officer was glad he had no more "problem women" like her, although she never got into trouble. She declined a promotion. "I didn't want to outrank none of these men. I have to work with them till the end of the war. I would rather have these friends than a little more money in my pocket."[10]

By March 1945, 23 graduates of James Walker Memorial Hospital nursing school were on active duty in the army or navy, six were awaiting call, and two more were in government service. My great-aunt Lillian M. George, who maintained the local Nurses Registry,† said, "'The nurses here and elsewhere have not fallen down in response to military needs....We are making every effort we can to supply the civilian demands. We have a very acute shortage of nurses....We plead with the public not

Kathleen Somersett, who believes she was the first local woman to join the Women's Army Auxiliary Corps (later the WAC) in 1942. Before serving she worked at the army's Information and Filter Center in the post office basement.

Provided by Somersett

---

* The *Morning Star* stated on June 10 that Patricia Williams was the first, and on October 20, 1943, that Kathleen was among the second group to enter the WAACs, created in May 1942. The name was changed to Women's Army Corps (WAC) in July 1943.

† My mother's aunt Lillian ("Bill," a former nurse) and sisters Katie George and Jean Archer, with her husband, Mervin Archer, lived at 5th and Red Cross. Mother and Daddy frequently deposited me there while going about their activities. The others had outside jobs, but Bill minded the Registry, assigning available registered nurses with one phone from their living room. Many is the hour I played happily, but alone, along 5th Street across from St. Stephens AME Church, tended to their backyard chicken coop, sat on the solid railings of their porch eating Bill's specialty snack: hunks of white bread thickly spread with gooey margarine and sprinkled with sugar, watching for passing cars and walkers, and listening through an open window to my afternoon radio shows.

The aunts have been gone for more than 35 years, and the abandoned two-story wood house badly needs fixing if it is to survive. Yet every time I drive slowly by it, usually only for old-time's sake, sizeable pieces of my childhood pass.

to expect to have nurses as before...."[11] Three sisters joined the WAC in 1945: Virginia Ward and Mabel G. Lee of Wilmington, and Bessie G. Lawson. Navy WAVES Storekeeper 2nd Class Gladys Sheets had duty in Hawaii. She and her husband, merchant marine Chief Yeoman Francois Sheets, were former Wilmingtonians. Army Nurse Corps First Lieutenant Elizabeth L. Barry was stationed on a hospital ship.

Technician/5 Hattie E. "Kitty" Bass (NHHS '36) "saw history made in the little red schoolhouse at Rheims, France, on May 6 [1945], when she went there with General Eisenhower's staff to witness the signing [Germany's surrender]....'Although there was much work to be done, no one was in a working mood, and spent most of the day watching the Russians and Germans coming in and out of the building....I even saw the people who signed the surrender and was right there when it happened.'" She joined the WAC in October 1942 and had duty in London, Paris, Supreme Headquarters Allied Expeditionary Force, and in Germany.[12] When the A-bomb dropped on Hiroshima, Japan, WAC Technician/5 Mary Helen Moore, stationed at Los Alamos, New Mexico, was home on leave. "Even then she did not disclose she had been devoting her time, since her enlistment in the WAC, to that 'most secret of secret projects ["Manhattan" A-bomb.]'"[13]

* * *

Nurse's Aides

The Red Cross began recruiting heavily in mid-1942, appealing to women's "pride and gratification" in replacing "gaps in the ranks due to calls from the Armed Forces." "The work is hard. The course involves actual sacrifice. Only women willing to give up their social obligations and consecrate their lives to the service of suffering humanity...should sign up."[14] So went my mother and handfuls of others for mostly unpaid work. All trained at James Walker Memorial Hospital under nurse Augusta Futch. Mother's classmates included family friends Caroline Newbold and Evelyn Volk (NHHS '43). The first day Futch pointed out, "Girls, these are urinals, not flower pots."[15] By May 1943, only 33 women had taken the required 80 hours of training) out of the 600 needed. In April 1945 Mother received a 500-hour Volunteer service bar. She would do more in the post-war period. The nursing school dedicated its 1946 yearbook, *The Epitome,* to her.

Mary Cameron Dixon (NHHS '43) went right to work after graduation as a secretary for the Maffitt Village postmistress ("I could type 35 words a minute").[16] She earned her Nurse's Aide certification the summer of 1945 and was paid $60 a month for six days a week. The hospital was short-handed at night; sometimes only one or two licensed nurses staffed upper hall A, a floor with nearly 60 patients. She couldn't give medicine or shots

For the war effort, Mrs. Wilbur D. (Viola M.) Jones was heavily involved as a volunteer Red Cross Nurse's Aide at James Walker Memorial Hospital. The 1946 nursing school yearbook was dedicated to my mother for giving more than 600 hours.

The Epitome (JWMH), 1946

but could run errands, do bedpans, deliver mail, irrigate catheters (kept flow of water going through catheter to keep blood clots from forming), all the service chores, baths, change beds, generally assigned to men's wards. Often she handled nurses' duties as much as she could if the doctor needed a nurse somewhere else. One of her men patients jumped out of bed yelling help. She shouted to try to stop him, "catch him, somebody!" chased him down the hall and caught him. Once transferred to maternity, she asked to be sent back to the men's ward. "That's when I decided I didn't want to be a nurse."

Until Camp Davis closed in mid-1945, the Legion Post 10 Auxiliary entertained convalescents monthly at bingo. The unit's wartime presidents were Mrs. H. M. Roland, 1941–43, and Mrs. J. Carl Seymour, 1943–45. Mother was membership and memorial chairman. Often I went with her to veterans' funerals to place American flags at grave sites, and to sell poppies in front of the post office.* In work rooms at St. James Episcopal, Church of the Covenant, and the Sprunt Building, the local Red Cross volunteer unit made 74,309 surgical dressings, 2,180 garments and miscellaneous articles (November–December 1942); 843 women worked 5,479 hours, many sewing garments for the British and U.S. armies.

County rural women substantially contributed to the war effort, reflecting population increases mainly in county areas. Through 12 clubhouses, they became civilian defense volunteers, collected scrap, bought and sold war bonds, tended Victory gardens, and educated neighbors on

---

* Mother "kept a record and compiled a list of all the veterans of both wars who have died, been killed, missing, wounded, POWs, also those who have been liberated....The Gold Star mothers were remembered with flowers on Mother's Day and with cards at Christmas." As the Post's unofficial war historian, her clippings and notes became the Post 10 Wartime Scrapbooks. [Mrs. Jones in "Wilmington Unit, American Legion Auxiliary to Wilmington Post 10, Department of North Carolina, Year Book 1945–46"]

nutrition. More than 300 4-H youth clubs participated in food and clothing conservation programs, promoting health and safety, scrap collection, and farm work. Mrs. Addison Hewlett organized a group of 25 Negroes, which was later led by a Negro agent. The Red Cross Union (train) Station canteen served 25,209 servicemen. Chairman Mrs. Albert Perry said, "'their gratitude for the hot coffee, doughnuts, and crackers—and sometimes a cigarette—is sincere, the volunteer workers unanimously believe (after opening in the summer, 1942).'"[17]

Wilmington housewives turned in 1,395 pounds of cooking fats (grease) during January 1943 as collection of that item increased. Grease made munitions, and local merchants bought it and re-sold it to the government.* Tin can collection also accelerated that year—items easier for youngsters to forage for, collect, and sell for change or movie admissions for special showings. Yet, scrap salvage had its fits and starts. "What is the good of housewives rendering and hoarding the fats that pass through their kitchen...if there is no systematic collection after they reach the authorized depositories [butchers]?....This is similar to the situation that prevailed when households were urged to save tin cans."[18]

The paper's February 1944 admonishment preceded a March call for reorganizing the salvage operation, stating that the only successful drive had been the metals campaign sponsored by the paper itself. The specifics of the complaints appeared valid. Salvage Committee chairman W. H. Stewart disagreed. The city's fat collection was the state's second best, and housewives were to blame "who sabotage the campaign by putting sand and water at the bottom of their cans" or donate paper soiled by garbage.[19]

Men remained out front in war bond drives. But on one occasion, during November 1942's Women at War Week ("TNT: Today, not Tomorrow"), ladies groups manned war bond booths at the Bailey Theater, Belk-Williams department store, the filter center, and other spots. An editorial cited their work, if condescendingly: "The women will be in complete charge and...do the work. It becomes incumbent upon the men...to back the effort with their dollars as well as moral support....It will afford homemakers to re-budget the family income, to practice economies not previously necessary, to see to it that non-essentials in clothing, in entertainment, for the table, are eliminated in the interest of larger bond investments."[20]

The papers were full of tips "for the housewife" on how to conserve, save, and stretch. "Glorify Yourself" and "War Kitchen" were two columns frequently appearing in the newspaper's women's pages. April 1943 advice was to use more deodorant, which saves clothes, which aids the war effort.

---

* Wilmington housewives and restaurant owners contributed 461,370 pounds of fat during 1944. "Since the Allied setback in Belgium [Battle of the Bulge]," donations increased. [*Wilmington Morning Star*, January 5, 1945]

"Turn It Down, Lady!" read a 1943 Tidewater Power Company advertisement in providing "8 Ways You Can Help Save Gas...for the War Effort."[21] What were men asked to do without or reduce? Gasoline and tires, and going home for lunch.

* * *

For Pay

Of course local women took paid war jobs. Camp Davis was an early bonanza, and the shipyard eventually opened up to women in other than clerical positions. As men went away to war, women filled their places at home as best and willingly as they could. Peggy Moore worked full time for the American Red Cross, beginning at Bluethenthal Field. "I was full of patriotic fervor and chose the Red Cross over military service." To get to work at the field she rode a bike from Wrightsville Beach where she lived to Station 1, left it with a friend, rode the bus to Front and Grace, then caught a bus to Bluethenthal—an hour's trip.[22] In the first two weeks of November 1942, more than two thousand Wilmington women applied for jobs. "'The response...has been most gratifying....As girls and women have stepped into the usual "white-collar" positions as clerks, stenographers, grocery salesladies and meat market clerks, they are also taking on manual jobs...at filling stations, meat packing houses, veneer mills, bag plants, and are doing spot welding.'"[23] The U.S. Employment Service gave working women a big boost in July 1943 by lifting a two-year ban on going barelegged. The man who lifted the ban said "'he thought it was better for the women to put their money into war bonds than into stockings to wear to work.'"[24] Silk and nylon hose were nearly impossible to get, anyway, and women applied makeup to cover up.

On graduating from the all-girl Agnes Scott College in June 1943, my sister, Elizabeth, came home to live and immediately went to work in a job unrelated to her degree.[25] She took a six-week typing and clerical course for women taught by Mary Elizabeth Hood at the high school and landed a position at the shipyard. She typed orders for steel, making 16 copies "on those old manual typewriters. How presumptuous of me to think I was qualified to type those complex orders....What a lesson in humility that was for me. My boss, a Mr. Mayfield, had to be the very essence of patience! But I felt in some small way that I was helping Wilmington's war effort."

Lib's college and NHHS '39 classmate Elizabeth "Betty" Henderson also rushed down to the yard looking for work.[26] She had been promised a job there while home on spring break. Mabel Grimes, who hired her and other women, became her coworker. Betty stayed there until around V-J Day. "By that time we didn't have any jobs open, and I sat around twiddling my thumbs. Went to New York for a while."

She first classified as a clerk, then employment interviewer of women only in the employment office at 3rd and Marstellar. The yard eventually hired about five thousand women, some in the yard trades. She worked 7:30 a.m. to 5:30 p.m., and earned $25.90 for a 40-hour week, and time and half for overtime. "We had all sorts of women come through there." Another Agnes Scott grad came looking for job as a spot welder because there was more money for women in those types of jobs than in offices. She got it. "Not many of the people who came there had anything more than a high school education." One seamstress had been told jokingly she could get a job sewing up portholes. "I don't think we hired her. I seldom saw anyone with a college degree." There were more male interviewers.

Henderson "did not type, but tried. If I made a mistake I just backspaced and went over it again." Once general manager P. F. Halsey needed someone in his office as a temporary secretary, and she served there a while. He offered her a raise. "I wanted the pay raise but I really wanted to be rated as interviewer." Halsey changed her rating accordingly from clerk, a "lucky break of being in the right place at the right time."

Some men who thought women got jobs easier filed claims of discrimination against the yard. She was called to the witness stand in a labor relations discrimination trial. A man had asked her where to get hired for men's jobs, and she testified against his claim. At the time she had on her desk a radio and could remember exactly what time the man came by and approached her, and the contention of his case collapsed. Later the personnel director told her he was surprised one of his employees was listening to the radio at work.

By 1943, women bus drivers already furnished to employers were noted as having proved satisfactory, and the employment office sought more. A 1944 *Camp Davis AA Barrage* column featured "sandy-haired Mary Elizabeth Taylor, office secretary of the Red Cross at Fort Fisher."[27] The 20-year-old Taylor, an NHHS graduate, "is one of the most popular girls at this busy firing point, and boasts her one hundred percent attendance at post dances and USO shindigs. Employed at Fisher for one year and a former employee at the Carolina Beach post office, Mary's really on 'the know' when it comes to getting around the Carolina resort."

In late 1945 women who had worked away from Wilmington began returning. "Back home to what? Certainly not to idleness or routine housekeeping and bridge....They have training in special skills...[and] experience....Wilmington can use women like this."[28] Well spoken, but Southern traditions died hard. Like the rest of the country, women had to await their turn, or another national emergency.

Chapter 14
"What Are We Fighting For?"

Within the overall civilian defense program, authorities held separate courses for Negro citizens. Expected to volunteer just as whites, they worked only in their own neighborhoods or in Negro-only establishments such as the Community Hospital. Not all volunteer jobs were open to Negroes, including plotters and operators at the Information and Filter Center. Negroes held their own war bond, scrap, and used clothing drives, and registered for their own war ration books, all within the framework of the overall county drives administered by whites—with their own Negro community chairmen.

Race, never far from any issue, could divide how the public expressed its patriotism. In 1942 local Negroes celebrated Armistice Day* with their own parade of 800 Camp Davis Negro soldiers from the 9th and Nixon USO club to Williston Industrial School. Participants included the Williston band and local Negro veterans and civilian defense organizations. One wonders what was the impact on the Negro community of an admonishment by Governor J. Melville Broughton three months before. "Negroes are ill-advised if they take the position they are for victory in this war if something is to be done for them," he said "in addressing the opening session of the diamond jubilee meeting of the State Negro Baptist convention" of more than 1,500 attendees. "Negroes should put their full energy into the war effort, for failure means 'slavery of the worst sort' for white and Negro alike. The man or woman who uses this emergency as a means of stirring up strife between the white and Negro races is not a friend to either race and is not a good American."[1]

North Carolina Central president Dr. James Shepherd spoke at the Negro Chestnut Street Presbyterian Church, whose pastor, Reverend Joseph D. Taylor, had volunteered for duty as an army chaplain. "What are

---

* Armistice Day, November 11, later became Veterans Day.

we fighting for?" he asked. Bertha Todd answered years later. The Negro troops at Camp Davis "had to reconcile the question, what am I fighting for? I think many of the boys showed it. They were fighting for country. It was most difficult of times for [them]."² I probably never went near the 9th and Nixon USO, and over by Williston only a couple of times to peer at the German prisoners of war across the street. Except for bits and pieces heard from whites and any Negro women who came to help Mother clean house, I generally had no idea of what was going on in the Negroes' world.

* * *

In the Armed Forces

Negroes became eligible for voluntary enlistment in 1942. "Not only because this is the first time in the history of the navy that the colored man has been eligible for such enlistment, but because it is a step the navy has been considering for many years. Many Wilmington Negroes have asked for information." Three were sent to Raleigh in June as the first to enlist in North Carolina. "Formerly, Negroes were enlisted as mess attendants, a post which requires very little actual combat duty.'"³ The navy in July sent a Negro chief petty officer "to discuss enlistment...with members of his race" as apprentice seamen and mess attendants.⁴

The army placed infantry company clerk Derick G. S. Davis in officer candidate school and the Tuskegee (Airmen) pilot training program. But he washed out. "I had a classmate from [North Carolina] A&T who was a pilot who kept ribbing me. I lasted a little while but not too long. I had concerns with some of the planes Tuskegee was given to fly"—old P-40 *Warhawks* from the Flying Tigers. "I expressed my concerns and they were not well received." Discharged in 1944 after one year of service, Derick worked in the local shipyard until the war ended.⁵ Shipyard worker W. T. "Bill" Childs eventually received his draft notice in January 1943. After stating he had experienced dizzy and fainting spells, a psychologist rejected him for service. He missed being part of the 80 Negroes inducted then, the largest such contingent ever sent from Wilmington at that time.* "I was not unhappy because it would give me the opportunity to do something else." He moved to Chester, Pennsylvania, to work at Sun Shipyard.⁶

James Otis Sampson, Jr., became an army cook with the 24th Infantry Regiment. "It seemed so natural I don't know how I did it. I was so vibrant. When you're young you look for challenges." He stayed on base and didn't socialize. On Saipan in early 1945, a general inspected his kitchen and praised him. "I was just trembling." He worked his way up to mess sergeant "with a PFC stripe" and was promoted every other month to staff sergeant.

---

* The most Negroes assembled here for induction were 411 in March 1944. Determining, even guessing, how many area Negroes served in uniform is impossible.

The all-Negro 24th, with white officers, landed on Okinawa after the invasion began. He saw no combat but "I was around people who were dead and dying," including Marine Iwo Jima casualties. "You don't think things were bothering you because you were young. It was later on you realized what you had been through. I saw drugs when I was overseas. I was around a boy who smoked reefers. I was naive." They put that boy in a cage. On race relations: "You were jumping into the foxholes together, you were doing everything together." They later experienced segregation when they were separated on board ship going home from there.[7]

"Many Williston graduates and former students are now connected with the armed forces," the *Cape Fear Journal* reported in November 1942. "It is interesting to note than many of these young men have made steady advancements since they entered. Many letters have been received from these young men stating how the skill and knowledge received at Williston had helped them to advance."[8] On Navy Day 11 months later, Williston paid tribute to all their men serving in the navy.

Army cook Private James Otis Sampson, Jr., late war, a 1944 Williston Industrial School graduate and veteran of the Okinawa Campaign, 1945. His 24th Infantry Regiment was all Negro with white officers. His father, James O. Sampson, worked with my father at the Carolina Building (Savings) & Loan Association for 38 years. The younger man also worked there after school before entering the army.

Provided by Sampson, Jr.

Four local Negroes are known to have died in uniform.* Army chaplain Taylor died in New Guinea in March 1944 after a brief illness. Two navy seamen were killed on July 17, 1944, in the explosion of two ships being loaded at the naval ammunition depot at Port Chicago, California. They were James Jackson, son of Francis Asken Jackson of 508 Clay Street, and James Henry Nixon, son of Zilphia Nixon of Taylor Homes. The blast shook 14 communities and was felt 80 miles away, killing 323 sailors and

---

* My efforts to find additional information on this subject, including advertising in the African American *Wilmington Journal* and pursuing numerous local contacts, were inconclusive. Perhaps it was because there were no more dead.

civilians. These two sailors probably were stevedores. The *Wilmington News* added a postscript two and a half months later: the two were Negroes. A note in the American Legion Post 10 Wartime Scrapbooks stated a David W. Howard, "colored," died September 10, 1945. Taylor's name is on the Hugh MacRae Park memorial to WWII dead, but not the others.*

* * *

The Shipyard

An estimated 20 percent of shipyard employees probably were Negroes, the lone minority group represented on the payrolls. Overwhelmingly they had to be Wilmington residents when they signed on, because outsiders coming to the area for shipyard work required housing either in projects or local homes. Except for the limited Hillcrest, part of Maffitt Village, and Taylor Homes public projects, housing was sorely lacking.

Negro employees were subjected to segregation's similar abuses and ridicule as they were outside the gates. Management hired them to do only the physically hard, dirty, or menial tasks requiring little skill, training, or authority. Observers cannot imagine what the yard would have done without their willingness to clean ship bottoms, drill holes, haul steel, place rivets, or perform manual labor—and the impact on the ultimate production record. Negro men, too, were drafted and sent to war, and Negro labor, too, eventually was in short supply.†

The yard's *North Carolina Shipbuilder* paper published photographs of Negro employees, which the Wilmington dailies would not, to accompany favorable articles about them. Its April 1945 issue, for example, cited the sterling attendance records of Andrew Hill, material porter for the warehouse receiving depot, and riveter Wilson Wright, Jr. as being "among the best in the yard." Hill, 39, a Wilmington native, joined the yard in October 1941. "He has never been absent except when excused and has been excused only a few times. He is buying bonds through the payroll allotment plan and his foreman...reported that he contributes regularly to the Red Cross, Community Chest and other drives." Raleigh native Wright began in July 1941. "So outstanding was his work that he was sent to chipping school when it was started. He later went to the South side and has worked

---

* Williston student Leroy McFadden, 16, worked part-time as a messenger for Western Union, located next to the Bijou Theater. In July 1944 he delivered the telegram to Nixon's apartment at the Taylor Homes. He did not read it, but gave it to a family member at the door and got a signed receipt. It bore two stars which to him indicated someone had been killed. Jim Nixon was no more than 19 but had not graduated from WIS. [Interview with Leroy McFadden, July 27, 2000]

† Everyone I spoke with—African American or white—concerning shipyard worker attitude and performance had only praise and appreciation for the many contributions of patriotic local Negroes not only at the shipyard, but in all aspects of the local war effort.

on every hull launched there. No unexcused absences. Also has payroll deduction for bonds."[9]

James Whitted began working there in 1941.[10] Every morning Negro men gathered at employment manager Richard L. "Dick" Burnett's office like a daily labor pool. "That's how we were hired. The white folks probably had applications." Burnett would look over the group and holler, "You, you, you!" In the crowd he spotted Whitted and picked him the first day he went there. Being hired full-time was a strenuous physical process after that. "I supposed they trained the white folks. We didn't get no training." To Whitted, outside the main gate area was for whites only, the same as most areas inside from restrooms to dispensaries. On leaving work he did not delay heading for home.*

Whitted received no benefits. "That was a sorry operation down there. You'd think there would have been some." His job was to clean up residue from welders and other workers in the inner bottoms, and he came out "just as rusty as I could be." He worked his way into a "lead man" position and did the work right along with the men he led, receiving no extra pay for that role. Eventually his white superior took him out of inner bottoms into erectors where Negroes supervised other Negroes. The erectors gang took all the steel to the ships. "We lead men, instead of making us foremen or giving recognition for what we did, they would bring in some white guy from the farms. He would work along with us, didn't know anything until we trained him, then he would become the boss." Whitted started at 44 cents per hour and brought home $29 and a few cents each week.

"Big un' and little un'"—Elias T. Gore, largest employee at the North Carolina Shipbuilding Company, seven feet and 300 pounds, with a shoe size of 16. Ezekiel Williams, five feet, four inches and 163, is alongside. "These boys are good workers and are doing a good job for the shipyard."
The North Carolina Shipbuilder, May 1, 1943

---

* By 1943 all shipyard employment came under the U.S. Employment Service, whose main office was at 111 Grace. The Negro office, staffed by Wilmington native George N. Norman, was at 519 Red Cross.

The yard hired white women to weld before they would allow Negro men to weld.* "For a government program, the South was strictly segregated—drinking fountains, bathrooms, areas to sit when we got something to eat. The only blacks that made good money were chippers, riveters, and drillers—on piece work, where you made pretty good money. All the checkers were white. You didn't find a black man checking nothing. Black folks just didn't have a chance." Both Whitted and his brother continued to work there anyway and with it were deferred from the draft. Two weeks before the war ended his deferment expired, and he went to Raleigh to be examined. "I was a good worker. I went every day. My supervisor deferred me as long as he could. Sometimes I wish I could have gone in at end of war to get the benefits," but he didn't.

Burnett hired Bill Childs as a messenger, "a dignified word for janitor."[11] Childs had graduated from Williston and North Carolina A&T, had intended to teach. But "the money they were paying there was more attractive than the money they were paying in the school system. Every other black person who did not get hired as a driller or chipper was hired as a messenger. Our job was to clean up offices used by engineers and office folks. It was a clean job. We could go dressed up without work clothes."

The day Childs started work in the main administration building he noticed the sign hanging there expounding the merits of Executive Order 8802, signed by President Franklin D. Roosevelt: there would be no discrimination in the yard employment practices. "At least that's what it meant to me. Was some sort of mockery." One day a group of young engineers whose office Childs was cleaning wondered why a college graduate was doing that kind of work and recommended him for assignment to a water-testing laboratory. Officials refused to let him take a basic test on knowledge of chemistry and would not transfer him. Childs' friend and fellow A&T graduate Derick Davis also became a messenger.[12] Supervisor Frank Kanaly questioned why Davis was not allowed to his use his degree and made him a guide at the administration building. From there he escorted salesmen, delivery men, and other visitors around the yard, and had limited supervision over other Negro janitors in that building.

Had Edward "Ed" or "Pat" George not settled into a more traditional lifestyle, the 1940s man in the decade of the 1960s might have marched at the side of either Dr. Martin Luther King, Jr., or H. "Rap" Brown.[13] Slightly ahead of his time, he labored against the forces of normalcy while

---

* James B. "Jim" Stokley (NHHS '39) of the welders school never actually did any welding, but thought the hiring of females for that task was very unusual. "We thought at the time that some of the girls had help qualifying as welders, particularly the nice-looking women." [Interview with Stokley, February 16, 1999]

simultaneously feeding his family working for those forces. As a would-be union and NAACP organizer, he was an activist of minor stature, upstart to some, rabble-rouser to others. He simply sought to take advantage of wartime conditions to further those social and labor causes whose time he believed was coming. He was honorable, stalwart, and principled, and a good shipyard worker.*

A native Wilmingtonian, Ed had helped construct Camp Davis before joining the shipyard in 1942. All his bosses were white. He worked with the crew on Crane #4 and as a signalman on the shipways, with the Erectors Group cleanup gang on the turtle backs (where bulkheads and pieces of frame were assembled right on the shipways) and inner bottoms. "I would come out of there just as rusty as I could be." His wife Parthenia George helped him bathe and clean his clothes every night. Sometimes she took him a dinner of fried chicken, iced tea, and potato salad. Her only job was as a white children's nurse, including for my classmate L. W. "Billy" Humphrey, Jr. "She had an instinct for children."

Accident insurance was available for some. "We were trying to organize, and had skeleton benefits." Ed had joined the International Longshoremens Union, charter member #1426, when it cost 50 cents, but during the war organized on behalf of the Congress of Industrial Organizations (CIO). "The races got along fine, but there was total segregation." Workers for and against union activity often clashed. In organizing the NAACP in Wilmington, his advisor was Thurgood Marshall of national headquarters. "Wasn't a week gone by that he didn't advise me on the telephone." Marshall came to Wilmington in 1942 at George's invitation for a meeting at the Boys Club where both union and NAACP discussions took place. "Thurgood walked in and told them they could not interfere with me. I had a right to continue organizing." Dr. F. J. Rogers, Williston Industrial School principal, "was one of those against me." The group "was being paid by some whites to stop me. I was the first organizer for the NAACP in town. For some reason, I was pretty smart for being able to organize these things."

---

* Ed George "broke the color line" in Wilmington radio when he hosted a disk jockey show on station WMFD for several years in the 1940s–50s, for which he still thanks the late owner, Dick Dunlea. Old-timers remember him as "The Old Conductor" spinning his theme song "Stomping at the Savoy." I was on his show once as a student. He worked with my father at Carolina Savings & Loan Association for a number of years around the same time, into the 60s, and became a dear family friend. He frequently helped us around the house, particularly after I entered college and then joined the navy in 1956.

Ed ruffled feathers with his wartime activities, including among his fellow Negroes who still sought to harm him when he returned to Wilmington in 1947, and boycotted his show. But he never let it hold him back. He became a preacher, the "Reverend George," and floated among congregations in Southeastern North Carolina until retirement. He also retired from General Electric in Wilmington. His wife Parthenia died in 2001, and Ed now lives in New York with a daughter. He remains a true friend.

He traveled to Washington often, and in Detroit during the race riots dined with Eleanor Roosevelt several times, and with poet Langston Hughes, all in his spare time at union expense.

In 1942 while Ed was directing the picking up of deck houses and steel to place them on the ships, the crane operator dropped a No. 2 hook (the largest), hitting his leg. He showed me the scar. In another instance he was set up inside the ship in a gas-filled compartment but got out in time. "They tried to get me. I had a lot of close shades with death." Negro Thomas Jervay, who worked in the central yard office, later came to his side. "I seen some moments, heard some dreadful comments."

In October 1942, the NCSC fired two of George's Negro colleagues, James Scott and Solomon Harrell, for sleeping in the cab of a crane. The CIO said they it was because of their CIO affiliation. George drove both men to Philadelphia looking for work and got them jobs at Sun Shipyard in Chester. "Scott was a Ph.D. It was a trumped-up charge." Whites with rubber hoses and chains chased the three of them and others one night in Wilmington, smashed their car windows and slashed tires. George called the sheriff "to get them off of us. One boy went 'walking on the water'" at Greenfield Lake to escape, but could not swim. George's attempts to unionize the NCSC lost in a September 1943 election. He moved north to work in Sun Shipyard and Cramp Shipyard in Camden, New Jersey, where he also organized.

The NCSC named a Liberty ship for a Negro, the SS *John Merrick*, christened by his daughter, Martha Merrick Donnell. He founded the North Carolina Mutual Life Insurance Company in Durham, the "largest business enterprise in the world operated by and for Negroes." The naming "provides opportunity to give recognition to the yard's colored employees who have done their full share in its good production record."[14] (In February 1945, the insurance company's president, Dr. C. C. Spaulding, kicked off Negro History Week with a speech at the 9th and Nixon USO.)

At the launching, Governor J. Melville Broughton stated, "We are striving in North Carolina to give the Negro equal protection under the law, equal educational advantages, the full benefits of public health, agricultural advancement, decent housing conditions, and full and free economic opportunity....This is the assured path toward racial harmony and progress."[15] A progressive statement for that time; in retrospect it sounded more like a politically inspired morale booster.

Wilmington men were among the first to apply for work building Camp Davis. Whitted worked in the lumberyard. "Five or six of us would drive up, had to go there to be hired, they needed men. No special skills or experience needed." They carpooled to work in a Model A Ford.[16] First a plumber's helper, George then got a civil service job as a second cook and commuted in someone else's car. He could stay on post overnight or go home, and sometimes slept over in barracks #1 near Gate 4 until he got married. He cooked for officers and nurses at the camp hospital. "We had nothing but the best." The early coast artillery units—54th, 55th, and 99th—"began to spread out. Most of the fellows I knew at Camp Davis got killed, were shipped out right after Pearl Harbor."[17]

* * *

The Green Lantern, "The Barn," and Other Entertainment

Negro clubs thrived on Dawson Street, especially popular night clubs between 14th and 15th across from the Hillcrest war housing complex for the Negro middle class, defense workers, and military noncommissioned officers. Teachers also lived there. The rough-and-ready Green Lantern Tavern at 608 Campbell, the most popular hangout for Negro servicemen, was in and out of the news. For instance, in August 1942, owner Ben Harley, cooperating with churches, announced the establishment would close on Sundays. Three months later, the proprietor received a sentence of court costs or 30 days for operating a restaurant without a state license and failing to raise its standards. Beer was available for 35 cents a bottle. "It was a rough place. There was no telling what would happen to you if you went in there," remembered a deliveryman who serviced the establishment. "We handed out a lot of beer, but it was a weaker alcohol....It had to be weaker....They drank it by the pitcher."[18]

"The Barn" at 11th and Meares was a Negro jazz hot spot. Cover charge was high at $2.00. A shot of bourbon cost 50 cents. But it had headliners. "Military personnel and civilian war workers crowded the streets looking for entertainment....Black servicemen would attend social activities at the USO on [9th and] Nixon Street," historian Margaret Sampson Rogers wrote. Entertainers appearing at The Barn included an all-star lineup of Count Basie, Lionel Hampton, Ella Fitzgerald, Cab Calloway, Duke Ellington, Billy Eckstine, Buddy Johnson, and The Five Royals.* It was "a jazz mecca." As many as two thousand people would crowd The Barn on a weekend. Many performers including the famous Harlem Globetrotters stayed at Corbett's Hotel at 13th and Orange in "the Bottoms." Corbett's was the only full-service Negro hotel in town.[19] Charlie Whitted ran The Barn. Without a restaurant, it served only sandwiches, and sold no beer, only whiskey. The managers bought liquor from an ABC store and resold it to patrons they knew.

---

* Negro clubs were for Negroes only. The white clubs never came close to matching the Negro clubs for top-flight entertainers. That they came to Wilmington was a tribute to the reception they received from local patrons.

Wilmington native George N. Norman remembered the Negro VFW Club on Castle Street between 9th and 10th, and dancing at the Negro-owned Monarch Club on South 7th. The Del Morocco on Dawson Street was another club of note. Negro servicemen hung out prominently on Castle and Nixon Streets, the 9th and Nixon USO club, and Ruth's Hall. Marines particularly liked Castle with its streetwalkers.[20] At 7th and Nun, Ruth Hall ran a pool room on the first floor and dance hall upstairs. Big bands like Erskine Hawkins and Smiling Billy Stewart and His Florida Serenaders played there, and Cab Calloway's sister Blanche brought a band there. Local bands performing included the Joe Hunter (saxophone) Orchestra; John Telfair (a piano player, he lived in Kinston and brought his band here); and a local group who lived in Mrs. Jeannette Wheeler's boarding house at 9th and Red Cross that included "Hooks" the drummer, Joe Williams on banjo, and Freddy Townsend on piano.[21] (Mrs. Wheeler's son and WIS graduate William Wheeler served as an army doctor and later practiced here.)

Bill Childs and other Negro college graduate contemporaries gathered usually in homes. The popular Norcarn Grill was located on the other side of town on Red Cross Street. Original owners George Norman and Dr. George Carner sold it during the war to prominent barber Beecker Williams. Peggy Pridgen's father, a shipyard welder, started a band called Melody Barons, with Jesse Shaw on piano and Bo Anderson on vocal. "My daddy would have a gig every weekend at the USO. The soldiers had the time of their lives."[22] The Negro Wilmington Clowns semi-pro ball team played at the 11th and Ann diamond, and attracted white spectators to their games by reserving a section for them. Negro shipyard employees put on the snappy two-act "Step Lively" in June 1943 at Williston to benefit the "Colored Baseball Team."

Seabreeze

During the war the Seabreeze section along the Inland Waterway in southern New Hanover County "was really the only place in eastern North Carolina where blacks could visit the water." As with many other places for social contact, Negroes went there and whites stayed away. In its day Seabreeze was unsurpassed for its purpose.

> By the mid-40s, the most of the area was fully developed. There was a big pier out on the water where people could fish and crab; hotels, one of which was three stories high; and cafés which gained a reputation for their delicious clam fritters (which cost only a nickel), fried shrimp and all kinds of seafood. There was also a dance pavilion. People used to come to the waterfront community in farm trucks from all over the State for a few hours or days of relaxation. There was a row of vine-covered cottages which were used for overnight stays for people unable to drive and even an unofficial community jail. Photographers'

shops, where visitors could have their pictures taken as mementos of their summer visits...were scattered throughout the area...[and] "Barbecue Sam's Restaurant"...[with] a pigpen in the back yard...[and] rides—Ferris wheels, hobby horses, and chair-planes. In its heyday, it was a place known for its fishing, seafood, and all around good times.[23]

Bathers took boats across the Waterway to reach a designated oceanfront area called Bop City on Carolina Beach's northern extension. "We had to go through the whites' part to get to our part," said Cornelia Haggins. She remembered cabins, and fresh-cooked crabcakes, shrimp, oysters, and clams. Bruce Freeman (the Freemans made moonshine, "the best in town") ran The Boardwalk. Negroes were also allowed on the northern end of Wrightsville Beach but could not mingle with whites.[24]

* * *

Williston Industrial (High) School

Williston's class of 1943 also graduated on a patriotic theme but with much different overtones. It featured "a choric program, built around the theme of 'The Four Freedoms—Ours to Fight For'....'Freedom from Fear' was the valedictory address delivered by Alfred Mitchell and Ethel Mapson" before Superintendent H. M. Roland and Principal F. J. Rogers awarded diplomas.[25] A "fifth freedom" for racial equality might have been added. Those who were drafted into the armed forces went from a segregated home front into a segregated military. They were inducted, trained, and organized separately, often under white officers. Their chances of becoming casualties were significantly less than Wilmington whites' because there were far fewer combat units to which Negroes were allowed to be assigned.*

The next year's graduation theme changed to a history lesson, "The Negro in the Wars for Freedom," from the Revolutionary to the present. Reverend Clarence Thomas of the Seventh Day Adventist Church delivered the commencement sermon.[26] Levi Biggs was awarded a full-tuition National Collegiate Scholarship of $150 through competitive examinations. It was his second, the first one received from Talladega College in Alabama. Valedictorian Lee R. Shelton also received the Talladega award.[27]

As a student growing up in the war, James Otis Sampson, Jr., (WIS '44) recalled "pressures weren't too bad on me. War didn't have too much of an impact on me."[28] He didn't follow the war news and "got turned off by the war." He "had to be" a good student because of parental influence. Afternoons after school and during summers he operated the elevator and cleaned

---

* With the exception of certain infantry and armored units in Europe, and the famed Tuskegee Airmen, the role of most Negroes in uniform was that of service support: cooks, laborers, and other rear-echelon types.

at Carolina Building & Loan Association, his father's employer. "Mama sent me down there to keep me off the streets."

The army drafted many men from the 1945 class of Cornelia "Nealie" Haggins before graduating. They received diplomas in the mail. This was the first class to go through 12 grades. Her cheerleader sister Auldrie Haggins sang in the glee club. During the snowstorm of December 1943, Nealie didn't hear on the radio that classes were canceled and walked to school anyway. Hezekiah Marsh, who ran a corner store, asked her why she was going to school and told her about the radio message. She sat on the school steps waiting. When she graduated the principal ("we called him Professor Rogers") noted she had shown up that day. Nealie remembered the religious-based June commencement when Reverend S. A. Fennell gave the scripture and sermon, Reverend L. C. Dade the invocation, and the graduates sang *Onward Christian Soldiers*.

Nealie spoke warmly of WIS friend Private First Class Charles James, Jr., from Love Grove. "He probably had a crush on me. We were just friends." James served in an engineering aviation unit in New Guinea. Her 1944 boyfriend was soldier Willie Anthony Owens, nicknamed "Playboy," "Loverman," and "Pal." "Oh Lord yeah," she answered when I asked her the obvious, "did you write during the war?" On his photograph he sent her he wrote, "To Nealie, with all my love, Pal, U.S. Army." The Williston girls were favorably impressed with their schoolmates in the service, and mingled freely with Negro soldiers visiting Wilmington.

The first radio program presented from New Hanover High was by the Williston Glee Club on February 16, 1943, broadcast for 15 minutes by station WMFD and directed by John Thompson.[29] A June 1945 headline announced that two Williston girls had set records. Seniors Haggins and Ruth Thomas were neither absent nor tardy during the last 10 years. Teacher William Blount of the little three-room Acorn Branch Negro county school went 34 straight years without a day's

Army Private Willie Anthony Owens, to Williston Industrial School student Cornelia "Nealie" Haggins AKA "Playboy," "Loverman," and "Pal," her 1944 boyfriend.

Provided by Cornelia Haggins Campbell

absence or tardiness. Superintendent H. M. Roland said he was the school's "sole principal, teacher and spiritual mentor," annually taking summer school courses to "keep abreast of the times educationally...has always been outstanding in every way and he enjoys excellent health [and] has a very sunny disposition and leads a clean life." His motivation "is to serve his fellow man to the best of his ability."[30] In Wilmington "blacks with degrees were either teachers or preachers," remembered Childs.[31]

The Community Hospital on South 11th served area Negroes with Charles M. Walker as superintendent and W. D. McCaig as chairman of the board of managers. Doctors L. W. Upperman, Daniel C. Roane, Hubert Eaton, and Foster F. Burnett were among the more prominent physicians who practiced there.* Most babies were delivered at James Walker Memorial Hospital, but new mothers were not allowed to stay in the Marion Sprunt Annex. After delivery they were shuffled back to the Negro annex, regardless of the weather.† Community Hospital operated on a shoestring. By April 1945, the value of outstanding accounts and accounts receivable far outnumbered cash on hand. The county finally appropriated money to help treat indigents.

Two Negro candidates, George W. Allen, with one write-in vote, and Ben McGhee, ran unsuccessfully for city council in 1945. Wilmington Negroes, expected to shoulder their share of the load for national defense, as always were relegated last in line.

---

* The community has honored the long service of Blount and Eaton by naming elementary schools after them. The Upperman African-American Cultural Center at the University of North Carolina at Wilmington bears his name.

† JWMH and Community in 1967 merged to form the New Hanover Memorial Hospital on South 17th. Nothing is left of Community, and the only JWMH structure standing, the nurses building on Red Cross, is now public housing apartments.

The 9th and Nixon USO

The Negro (or colored, as it was called) USO was first located in the St. Thomas auditorium on South 2nd in October 1941, and moved permanently on February 1, 1942. "Through the untiring efforts of the many community organizations and especially the church groups consisting of both men and women volunteers, the servicemen's wives club, [et al.]...this club has enjoyed through the past year a varied program for the entertainment of the colored servicemen." Thomas C. Wheatley was the staff director.[32] Carrie Hargroves was the senior hostess. It included a colored guest house. "On Saturday nights the club takes care of 50 men in its dormitory and one of its biggest jobs is locating rooms for soldier wives."[33] The army's only Negro general, Benjamin O. Davis, once inspected troops at 9th and Nixon.

At the club's open house on March 28, 1943, Wilmington residents attended to "acquaint themselves with the facilities and activities provided for the Negro servicemen," who greeted visitors. Speakers included Camp Davis post commander Colonel E. A. Potts and State Senator J. E. L. Wade, both whites. F. J. Rogers and H. Carl Moultrie headed the program.[34] Groups as well as individuals used the facility. "The fighting 235's Battery B gathered at the decorative 9th and Nixon USO...where they stomped to the music of Davis' jazz combo, The Sledgehammersit."[35] Cornelia "Nealie" Haggins' "Mamma" was a hostess and chaperone there. One time she took her high school daughters to the Davis club. A GI asked her mother to dance, and she told him he would rather dance with her daughters and described them. He rounded them up and took them to her and said, "from now on consider them to be your sisters."[36]

The building was demolished years ago and is now the site of the Community Boys and Girls Club. The visible reminders are several 8-1/2x11" photographs of the USO shellacked to a bulletin board in the main hallway, but without description. At the Wilmington USOs' 60th anniversary program, "Nealie" spoke eloquently for those with memories of the club.

Chapter 15
Four "Breathless Years"

"1942 was a breathless year—for Wilmington," the newspaper's year-end roundup read. "Marked by firsts, by out-of-the-routine, by growth, by change, probably no year in the history of the city could boast 1942's scope...[and] reflects war in almost every phase of the city's life." The shipyard employed 19,000, built 53 Libertys, and received the Maritime Commission's "M" pennant with stars; war workers and families had occupied the Wilmington Housing Authority's 2,595 new housing units; the area recorded firsts in scrap metal collections, war bond sales, post-office Christmas mailing records, etc. Rationing affected numerous commodities. And dim-out regulations "dictated restricted activities on the beaches and driving-without-lights through some areas."[1]

An amazing year, all right. But all four were "breathless years" in the local war effort. By 1943, they had only just begun.

The newspaper outlined a litany of accomplishments or attempts. The Women's Auxiliary Army Corps "invaded Wilmington, and took over operation of the local filter center; Camp Davis added the coast artillery's officer candidate school....USO built and occupied seven new recreational clubs....Civilian defense tightened the city's home front preparing Wilmingtonians...how to conduct themselves in the face of air raids and attacks." February saw the worst snowstorm in 30 years, and low temperatures in December "accentuated the lack of fuel.* Early in the year ships were sunk off the North Carolina coast. (As a result the city developed plans for emergency evacuations of its entire civil population.) On December 20 five soldiers and three civilians died in an auto accident on

---

* Wartime's only significant snowstorm occurred a week before Christmas in 1943 when about four inches "blanketed" the area. Old-timers, unused to much sticking snow then and today, still talk about it. Naturally kids were more prone to remember our hasty efforts to employ rusted old sleds (but no skis) from the garage and construct snow forts (without plans) for inevitable snowball fights before the white stuff disappeared on unaccustomed warm ground.

Chapter Fifteen

My house at 102 Colonial Drive and Guilford Avenue, Forest Hills, following the snowstorm of December 1943. The Glenn Stanley family has lived there for years.

Author's collection

the Camp Davis highway. And, the city council planned to extend the city limits into the suburbs.[2]

Another report summarized a hectic and productive 1942: 450 persons enlisted in the armed forces; the two selective service boards sent 607 draftees; home builders constructed 1,413 new homes outside of wartime housing; 15 new businesses opened, most restaurants and dress shops; total bank clearances were $331 million as compared to $199 million in 1941; the city's population was estimated at between 80,000 to 100,000; "the school system has advanced with the rapid growth" with three new schools in operation; and the city's income had almost doubled. "'The influx of government agencies and new federal defense offices has brought...a cross-section of the entire nation. There is hardly a person in New Hanover County who is not indirectly connected with the national war effort....'"[3]

The "war effort." As a fixed home-front shibboleth it influenced thoughts, stirred emotions, and drove actions. In the life of a city in a vastly altered world, it was an elusive but constant measuring stick of patriotism, conscientiousness, and productivity. We could not let our boys down on the fighting fronts. Were we as a community or individuals doing enough? No matter how glorious in concept, maximum attention and participation was virtually impossible to sustain. Until, that is, someone would seriously or casually remind another, "Don't you know there's a war on?"

The year 1942 was for getting organized and adjusted, 1943 for ironing out the kinks and reacting to numerous regulations and lifestyle changes,* 1944 for settling into an accepted regimen, and 1945 for enduring whatever was needed with victory at hand, in spite of the government's admonishments and continued restrictions. The war effort was both cause and effect of the emergency's impact on local living.

In December 1941 area authorities, agencies, and civic organizations had been a bit prepared for the changes war might bring. A number of anticipated or evolutionary actions were already underway or soon thereafter set in motion. Concerned citizens (who was not?) individually and collectively started fund-raisers to volunteer for civilian defense service, open their homes to renters, or work on community committees. As a starter, on Christmas Day neighbor Charlotte Jones' father, Charles F. Jones, launched a campaign to purchase one or more bombers, making the first $100 donation himself.

* * *

War Bonds

Of the myriad methods of aiding the war effort, the most visible and long term was the sale of war bonds and stamps. Over a period of three-plus years, New Hanover County participated in seven national bond campaigns called War Loan Drives. The slogan "Buy More Bonds" rang out, with a hundred reasons why. One source urged that buying bonds would restore the fundamentals of independence, such as, "the privilege of buying what one craved to eat either at a restaurant or store. Another would be freedom from directives from this or that bureau. It would be fine to buy shaving cream without surrendering an empty tube, or find pins and needles and bobby pins and flat goods displayed in profusion, and buy tires as needed or have the old bus painted and repaired and travel where and when one pleased. Think of the luxury of driving to a service station and telling the attendant to 'fill her up.'"[4] Good to keep the people motivated.

Six days after Pearl Harbor, my father's Carolina Building & Loan Association still advertised "defense" bonds before their name was changed to "war" bonds shortly thereafter. "Do your part by buying your defense bonds today....We have them in amounts to suit your needs." Commercial marketing of this type continued into 1945.[5] Local financial institutions competed for bond sales, perhaps as goodwill gestures, although offering nothing different. Early efforts worked. "Hundreds of Wilmingtonians last week put their individual resources behind the nation's war effort...to an

---

* "As committee after committee springs into existence, serious folk who want to see this war progress more rapidly toward a successful conclusion are convinced we are over-committeeing [sic] our efforts....We have so many committees that however noble and helpful their objectives they get in each other's way and only a modicum of the work they attempt is done. Also, many of them do nothing....A coordinated program might be drafted...." [*Wilmington Morning Star*, April 24, 1943]

unprecedented height during the first week of the war." *Star-News* carrier boys alone sold nearly $1,500 worth of stamps along their routes, and five businesses employing five thousand pledged to support the first drive.[6] It was much easier then.

Film actress Jane Wyman appeared in the New Hanover High auditorium in September 1942 for a "monster bond rally." Lucretia Thornton got her autograph on a bond. "I was scared to death walking across the auditorium to get it. I was very shy then, and I was wishing it was someone else, not me." The day's climax was a $500 a-plate dinner for Wyman at the Cape Fear Country Club.[7] "A parade, radio talk by the mayor and a 15-minute nothing-but-bonds sale in the city stores...launched Wilmington merchants' month-long 'Retailers for Victory' war bond and stamp campaign" in July 1942.[8] Ships sliding down the ways at launchings wore the slogan "Buy More Bonds" painted on their sides. Johnny Mack Brown, "one of Hollywood's most popular cowboy stars," spoke at a shipyard rally on June 2, 1945. The crowd was one of the largest attending a bond rally since the war started.[9]

The entertainment drawing card worked. "Wilmingtonians cheered" the July 1943 all-army Camp Davis musical comedy "Strictly GI," held at the Thalian Hall, "with rounds of rich applause and war bond purchases in the amount of $62,000." A Davis spokesman called it the "most successful sale yet held in connection with an army show, even larger than the one that followed the New York triumph of Irving Berlin's "This is the Army."[10] Following a "gala parade" on June 12, 1944, officials sold more than half a million dollars in bonds. The mammoth parade included three companies of the Women's Army Corps and other army and Marine Corps units, followed by army equipment that later was exhibited downtown. "Enthusiastic citizens thronged the sidewalks."[11]

War-theme movies played a huge role in selling bonds, and offered an immediate escapism from hard work and social stresses. A New River (Camp Lejeune) Marine contingent was on hand for the September 1942 showing of the movie *Wake Island* at the Bailey. Admission was with a $25 bond, or in a special section for those purchasing a $100 bond or higher. The sold-out *Heaven Can Wait* raised $75,000 to kick off the Third War Loan Drive in September 1943. It helped buy a P-47 fighter "'that will carry the name of "Wilmington, N.C." to the enemy. It is to go with the next unit of men leaving Bluethenthal Field for the war zone*....We will take it over on the other side and get 10 to one for it.'"[12]

The Bailey showed *Destination Tokyo* to kick off the Fourth Drive in January 1944, while outside on Front Street Camp Davis displayed equipment and

---

* The plane turned out to be a P-51 *Mustang* fighter with its nose painted "City of Wilmington." Photographs appeared throughout the city and in the newspaper. In 1944 the name "North Carolina Shipbuilder" went on a B-29 *Superfortress* in honor of the yard's stellar bond record.

the 141st Army Band played.* "The picture pricked the sympathy strings...and stimulated the [auction] sale...to $300,368." Among the items auctioned was a German army helmet.[13] The final rally attraction, the "Army's Biggest Traveling War Bond Show," called "ASF ATTACK," landed at Legion Stadium in June 1945 before five thousand spectators. It was "a spectacular dramatization of the story of supply, depicting the close relationship between bond-buying and supplying the army and navy."[14]

Employers offered and urged participation in monthly payroll deductions. "Will you have a part in this great campaign to make the world safe for our children and our Democracy?" asked a Camp Davis pamphlet for civilians. "BONDS FOR VICTORY ARE CASH FOR TOMORROW."[15] For the April 1943 bond drive, chairmen James G. Thornton and Allen Ewing produced the slogan "They Give Their Lives, We Lend Our Money."[16] The county drive went "over the top" by 12 percent with $2.9 million in sales making it fifth in the state. This could be directly attributed to news the Japanese had executed several American aviators captured following the Doolittle raid on Tokyo a year before. School students sold $23,174 worth. Chestnut Street sold $11,150.60, but my Forest Hills only $329.20. Failing to meet the November 1943 goal, officials attributed it to Christmas shopping. "...Our spending for pleasure is interfering with our support of our fighting men."[17] Well, the war news also was having its ups and downs.

Throughout the war local officials and the newspaper condemned bond buyers who redeemed them before maturity, in effect taking their money back from government war use. "'Why were these bonds bought in the first place? Probably the chief reason is that the purchasers wanted to make a showing as "doing their part" in the emergency. They would have to face the stares of their associates if they refused to buy. They might be called slackers....It's a contemptible thing to do unless there is actual need for the money....'"[18] In spite of urgings, people cashed them.

As the war wore on, bond drive sales lagged until the shipyard and other companies or benevolent individuals came forth with last-minute pledges. After a discouraging campaign, the county's participation in the national Fourth War Loan Drive accelerated in the final days and "whizzed over the top," exceeding the $4,859,000 quota by $117,893.[19] Uniformed personnel visited to stimulate bond sales. In June 1944 alone, two merchant

---

* The equipment at the Front Street main post office included "a battle-scarred German tank destroyer mounted with a 76mm rifle...a German mobile field kitchen...[and] a complete searchlight outfit and an AA half-track."[*Wilmington Morning Star*, January 22, 1944] This was one of several such wartime displays I remember being awestruck to see. The post office was our town's gathering place for all people. On the steps folks shared the war news, casualty names, and community goings-on, and boosted one another. To this day when entering the building I can sense the spirit, the chatter, the activity that revolved in the lobby and front steps. It still has the same polished marble, WPA mural, restrooms—the same "feel."

marine crewmen who had seen action, a B-24 waist gunner veteran of 30 missions, and famous fighter pilot Captain Roland Wooten spoke to shipyard and Ethyl-Dow Company employees, and other organizations plugging support of the Fifth Drive.

The county's grand total of bonds and stamps sold is unknown, but the drives probably raised close to $45 million. Individual sales ran continually and likely generated about another $10 million. A grand total of anywhere near $55 million would be astounding considering the area's size. Bonds made great gifts (I received several and cashed them in during the post-war years), college funds, and hope-chest stuffers. Kids of course were more prone to accept the challenge of collecting war stamps and filling couponlike booklets. Oh what fun to paste the 10-cent stamps over the dreaded likenesses of Tojo, Hitler, Mussolini, and their henchmen. As soon as you filled the booklet, you traded it in for an $18.75 bond redeemable in a few years for $25. At school we had some spirited competitions to see who could sell/buy the most. Parents were prime customers. I still have one of my unused stamp books, the comical likenesses of the enemy Axis still scowling at me.

* * *

Scrap Drives

The war's first three drives to collect scrap metal, rubber, cooking fats, paper, and other recyclables for making war material gave citizens the opportunity to dive into the war effort without having to fork over cash. It was visible stuff your neighbor could see, not like privately writing checks for war bonds. The major emphasis came in 1942–43 (for instance, the requirement for rubber, steel, and aluminum petered out), but one commodity or another continued until V-E Day.

Scrap drives took off by the spring of 1942, headed by the first New Hanover County Salvage Committee chairman Alexander Sprunt. Organizations such as the Wilmington Rotary Club asked the city to dispose of anything that could be used by the war industries. Among the items placed in the scrap metal piles were rails from the defunct streetcar tracks, 28 cannons from the Wilmington Light Infantry, the landmark World War I "Y" depth-charge gun at the courthouse, two old locomotives, and two old fire trucks. A quick call for rubber in July 1942 netted more than 467,216 pounds, mostly old tires and tubes. Every conceivable item from tiny dime toys to boots and hot water bottles were solicited.

For some, a salvage drive was a counter-opportunity. "The meanest person in the world made his appearance in Wilmington yesterday," an observer noted. "A contributor to the scrap metal drive placed a large pile...in front of her home for pickup....Among the heap were two large brass urns, each weighing about 25 pounds." But someone stole the urns overnight.[20] In a statewide drive in October–November 1942, the county's 8.1 million pounds of metal placed it third in the state at 170 pounds per person. The Atlantic Coast Line turned in 1.03 million from its shops. The Boys Brigade Club, a "commando force" behind every scrap drive and directed by William A. Stewart, turned in 293,645 pounds through individual efforts. Camp Davis sent several army trucks each time to aid in street-to-street pickup and hauling the materials, a gesture the salvage committee much appreciated. It would appear the subject needed no pumping. But unfortunately universal enthusiasm eluded planners.

The need for waste paper fluctuated from dire necessity to surpluses. But as the war wound down, so did the national paper supply, by then the top priority material shortage. Publisher R. B. Page's newspaper again took aim at its convenient target, "the government," for consuming "precious paper" in publishing tons of publications that "crowd the mails daily and which have little or no practical value to the recipient."[21] Good people responded.*

The continuous scrap drives just had to succeed. A December 1945 story stated, "Aluminum Coming Home. The newspaper drive for scrap was tremendously successful. And we were so determined that aluminum should not be lacking that we collected more than could be utilized. No Wilmingtonian can forget the great bin placed by the Junior Chamber of Commerce in front of the post office and how slowly it filled at first, but as time went on many a housewife stripped her cupboard to add to the pile. These collections of scarce but needed metals were part of the home front's war effort....Now some of the metal is coming back."[22]

* * *

Employment

Felix A. Scroggs, head of the U.S. Employment Service office, which by late 1942 had taken over all defense hiring here, was one of the busiest men in town. In the peak hiring month (April 1943), the USES placed 2,454 persons, mostly in manufacturing and construction. Manpower rules frequently changed like all other government edicts, but with employment needs, the pool was tweaked to fit the requirements rather than letting "the market" prevail. "Essential" workers could not move or change jobs. By August 1943 the area's demands for labor had passed the peak. Some war plants had completed contracts without renewals, and others curtailed employment except in common labor. By late that year, returning servicemen began entering the labor pool in numbers, enhancing morale of other

---

* Whether national scrap drives ultimately enhanced the production of military items, or were intended primarily to mobilize the populace into "doing something" for the war effort, is debatable. Whatever its motives, the overall effect in Wilmington was beneficial.

The government's employment service Negro branch, headed by George N. Norman, *center*, assisted citizens in obtaining jobs and registering for the draft. He was also chairman of the Red Cross' Colored Division. He accepts a donation from A. E. Brown, Ideal Pharmacy owner, with secretary Mrs. Andrew Myers at the typewriter. Late war.
Provided by Norman

workers. A local bus company hired as an inspector a Marine who had lost his hand in the Pacific.

Local war production fell substantially by January 1945, but the labor pool availability fluctuated with job turnover and worker departures from Wilmington, now declared a "labor surplus area." Employers continued to hire. In the six previous months USES placed 16,000-plus of the 38,000-plus it interviewed. From then on, the job decline increased except for spring when the temporary Camp Davis reactivation gave it a brief upward surge.* Civilian employment in county nonagricultural establishments totaled 29,600 in September 1944, or approximately 17,700 more than in April 1940. The total included 18,100 in manufacturing. Expansion occurred chiefly in shipbuilding during the four-year period. The November 1943 figure (the peak) was 31,600. With the war's end, defense jobs disappeared, and discharged veterans swamped the manpower office with servicemen's adjustment claims. Layoffs increased. Estimating the total numbers unemployed

---

* A July 1945 USES survey of more than 400 workers being separated indicated the majority would remain in the area looking for work. "The predominant reason for wishing to change jobs was a desire for postwar security." [R. S. McKeithan quoted in *Wilmington Sunday Star-News*, July 22, 1945]

during the war was difficult, but by November 1945, unemployment compensation benefits reached a new high.

* * *

Semi-Ersatz (but good anyway) Christmas Toys

We kids had no choice but to give up some traditional toys for our ages as wood and fragile composites replaced metal. For Christmas 1943 Belk-Williams department store pushed its "sturdy wagon."* "He will love one of the new 'Victory Jeep' [plywood] models. The wheels have even been kept under water 48 hours so they will not warp."[23] Bicycles were the only rationed toy, as I recall. Anticipating a shutdown from manufacturers, buyers soon purchased most available ones by early 1942 (the same was true for new automobiles, also discontinued). The last Christmas where bikes and traditional toys galore were advertised was 1941. By the next holiday season, war production priorities, supply, and children's fancies, had all changed radically. So had I.

News reports told us kids something we were realizing fast:

> The Kiddie Car has become an All-American jeep and youngsters are all out for war games, but they'll play with non-priority equipment. Santa Claus's pack may be bulkier with armament miniatures. But it will weigh less this year. Wood and cardboard have replaced metals, rubber and other materials used by grownups at war. The little toy soldier won't collect rust. About all that could attack him would be fire or termites. Tanks, planes, battleships, jeeps and the complete list of war equipment are armored in heavy paint. Some even come already camouflaged. Many are of a size for the junior warrior to man himself....Games of strategy are popular with young boys." Map and flag puzzles and parlor games ("because they're staying at home more") were big items. "Setups of army encampments may be had complete from barracks to sandbags," and balsa wood models to be shaped for construction as weapons. "Even dolls fall in with war styles."[24]

---

* I guess my parents took no chances with that brand; so my 1941 "Flyer" model lasted the duration. There was something unforgettable about Christmas of 1943. Why I'm not sure, but Daddy placed the decorated tree in the short hallway between the front door area and the back door. Getting up before the crack of dawn while the other three slept, I leaned over the rail from upstairs and saw below what Santa had brought. In those days we didn't wrap kids' gifts like today (and wrapping paper was in short supply), and larger items such as plywood jeeps stood out anyway. The lead tinsel we had reused for years glistened among soft shadows.

That morning I was tempted to rush on down, but agonizingly waited on the others to arise (with some prodding). I got mostly "army stuff" and clothes—having reached that age when clothes were replacing toys. A neighborhood kid or two would always get a "Victory Jeep" or something of the sort and usually invite those without (like me) to have some turns. I was envious, especially when a father intervened and retired the machine to reduce wear and tear, which cut down our driving time.

Belk-Williams department store advertisement, *Wilmington Sunday Star-News*, March 21, 1943. They were talking about boys my age.

By Christmas 1944, toys in local stores were "a 'little better quality but the quantity is not much greater' than last year." Christmas merchandise went on sale in October because supplies were limited. Materials and finish were improved but wood, cardboard and paper items again dominated what was available. No steel or tin for toys existed.[25]

Most of my wartime collectibles are paper, wood or wood composite. On my ninth birthday in July 1943, besides his World War I revolver my father gave me, another special gift was a miniature plywood homemade submachine gun stained brown with liquid shoe polish. The neighborhood father of playmate Tommy Shannon, J. E. Shannon, Jr., also made one for Billy Humphrey. I still have what's left of mine.

Families in the War Effort

Supporting the war effort also included families' writing and sending items to service personnel overseas. To neighbor William G. "Billy" Broadfoot, Jr.'s fighter squadron in India in January 1945, "Our mail usually arrives in spurts....Holy smoke, 7 more packages just came. [He received more books, a roulette wheel, a checker-backgammon game, a Kostelanetz record (unbroken), gum, and Hershey bars]...."[26]

My classmate Evelyn Bergen's father, Charlie Bergen, served as an air raid warden.

Captain William G. "Billy" Broadfoot, Jr., a P-38 *Lightning* and P-40 *Warhawk* pilot with the 495th Fighter Squadron, relaxes with tea and smokes at his India base in 1944, dressed in his combination U.S. and British uniform. A Forest Hills neighbor and 1941 University of North Carolina graduate, he flew 125 missions in India-Burma, many over "The Hump," and recorded six aircraft kills.

Provided by Broadfoot

The Camp Davis telephone switchboard included operator Addie Lee Gaylord, seated on the right, 1941.

Provided by Gaylord

"Even though he had no talent for gardening, my father like everyone else we knew built a Victory garden in our back yard, planting a few vegetables....We never had much of a crop, however. My mother, Christine, helped out at the Red Cross canteen down at the railroad station....The greatest inconvenience to me was offering two of our three bedrooms for rent....My sister, Mimi, and I, at about ages 9 and 7, slept on cots in our parents' large bedroom." Their tenants: two USO managers occasionally brought them a whole box of very rare Hershey chocolate bars; "a shipyard worker whose wife kept her hair in curlers covered with a bandana all day (and all night, for all we knew!)...[and] quite a number of young married couples in the service, staying three to four months at a time. My mother kept up with several of them for many years afterward."[27]

J. V. "Pat" Warren (NHHS '43) remembered, "Our mother had defense workers in our house night and day. She cooked, cleaned, looked after everyone and just about worked herself to death....This was the first chance for some money and prosperity for our family. We were able to buy a 1941 Ford sedan....and [kept] it throughout the war. Our parents were offered four or five times what they had paid for the car....I bought it from [them] when I got out of the navy."[28] Mary Fisher's parents, Jimmy and Laura Fisher, hosted soldiers for Sunday dinner, even though "they were not financially able to do much. I don't remember many Sundays that we did not have one or two servicemen in our home. I can still see their faces, believe it or not! So young and handsome...even brought us gifts."[29]

Teenager John D. "Jack" McCarley III was a volunteer aircraft spotter at the Monkey Junction tower the locals built and manned around the clock. He also aided his air-raid warden father. When a telephone alert came, Jack jumped on his bike and rode to his distant Carolina Beach Road neighbors to tell them what was happening. When it was over he went back with the word. Relative Duncan McEachern was the port's physician. One night the sky glowed after a tanker had been torpedoed. The Coast Guard asked the doctor to go out that night in a boat to help administer to survivors. "Duncan was nervous. 'What happens if we hit a mine?' he asked a sailor, who said, 'you won't have to worry about it.' Duncan said it [the ship] was just burning to hell."[30] The seven Swart kids of Castle Hayne bought war stamps with money earned from working on the family farms. They had one camera in the family but couldn't afford another or film to take pictures. Thus they have no wartime memento photos.[31]

* * *

Governing

Local governments seemed to work all right. How were we to know any different? No constant policy, order, procedure, and certainly no mind-set emerged, except the goal of winning "the emergency." Governing above the routine consisted of seat-of-the-pants trial, error, and trying to fix. We pulled together and managed nevertheless, even if some folks responded more than others, and a minority not at all. The equalizers dictated that each family had to pay taxes, was governed by changing regulatory reactions, and endured common inconveniences. Noise, for example, impacted everyone within a distance, and could be silenced by neither wealth nor influence. Looking back, amazingly the Wilmington area not only prospered but soon stabilized after war broke out—then in spite of diversions and missteps maintained its victory focus. Old leaders kept leading, and new leaders arose.

The year 1943 saw all kinds of public health and communicable disease scares, especially during warm months. Much was due to the huge influx of people from all over and what they carried on them. School children were among those who readily received inoculations on the advice of county health officer Dr. A. H. Elliott. Except for meningitis (15 cases), chickenpox (293), whooping cough (317), scarlet fever (37), and diphtheria (11), the county disease rate by October was low.* From December through early January 1944, an influenza epidemic affected some 10,000 people. Schools had only about 30 percent of enrollment on returning from Christmas holidays. Our small number of overworked physicians failed to keep up with the necessary treatments. The flu strain was considered mild compared to 1918. In 1945 scarlet fever had increased slightly, whooping cough was way up, and chicken pox way down. Dr. Elliott pronounced the county free from epidemics in 1945 with no unusual outbreaks of diseases.

Warnings went out concerning community health and its potential to handicap the war effort, "in addition to the suffering it would bring and the deaths it might cause....The crowding of population in inadequate quarters" caused deterioration of "too much private property...."[32] From January to March 1944 the area experienced a mild measles epidemic (636 cases reported) and 343 cases of chickenpox. In the first eight months of 1944, the county had only 124 fewer births (1,737) than those reported in the same 1943 period, its record birth year. The birth rate was approximately three times the death rate, contrasting previous years when the two were about even. The county's new population was comprised largely of young women of child-bearing age married to war workers and soldiers.

By early 1945, the birth rate decreased along with the population. The 875 deaths in 1944 were 18 over 1943 and caused chiefly by heart disease. Sixty-eight died from accidents, 24 from tuberculosis, and 94 from pneumonia. (New cases of venereal disease totaled 2,001, including 348 of

---

* These communicable diseases of wartime, plus polio and typhoid fever, virtually faded as public health problems in the years shortly thereafter.

the 3,388 jail inmates found infected; 257 "were sent to rapid treatment centers.")[33] Treatment of VD cases in 1945 declined 50 percent from 1944's 20,706. Syphilis caused 637 and gonorrhea 686.

Polio (infantile paralysis) struck the most fear of any disease of my childhood. My pediatrician, Dr. J. Buren Sidbury, one of two in town, practiced at James Walker Memorial Hospital, the county's largest, and Babies Hospital. Somehow he managed to treat those in need, and relegated me into quarantine for measles and whooping cough. The yellow paper sign with the large "Q" attached to the front door signaled to all: stay away from here; family only. Into Mother's bed I went with drawn shades, pajamas only (washed daily), no stirring, a radio, and taking my medicine.

The unthinkable happened in August 1944. With the diagnosis of four cases, the Board of Health prohibited all gatherings of children under 15 in the county "because of the spread of infantile paralysis." It hit hard.

> Forbidden are picnics, street games, church gatherings, swimming pool parties, theater-going, operation of any day nurseries, home and playground parties....During outbreaks of infantile paralysis children should be kept from indulging in exercise that will produce exhaustion or an undue amount of fatigue, since this has been shown in many instances to be a contributing factor....Medical care early in the course of the disease is

James Walker Memorial Hospital nurses classmates Daphne Jeffords, Emma Dunley, Blanche Stanley (NHHS '39), and Ruby Raynor, May 1943. My neighbor Stanley's several acres had about 60 pecan trees around which we played games and soldiers (and purloined a few nuts, of course).

Provided by Blanche Stanley Sneeden

important in assuring a maximum degree of recovery....Since there is no vaccine or serum that will prevent infantile paralysis, full cooperation in carrying out these recommendations offers the best protection for everyone....The simple rule of keeping their children at home should be enforced by every father and mother.[34]

Officials delayed school opening for two weeks and included Sunday schools, beaches, and downtown in the ban. Apparently mothers cooperated, and few people filed complaints. President Franklin D. Roosevelt's earlier battles to overcome polio were common knowledge. What a dead neighborhood we had for that month. There went summer. Not only were we literally restricted to our immediate blocks (postponing any re-enactment of the Marianas Campaign), but we had to come inside so often, and much of the time lie down and rest (at a time when a kid thought himself way past the nap stage).*

An "iron lung" came to Wilmington in February 1945 for exhibition at Front and Market. "Now! While shopping or on your way to the movies. Everybody welcome to visit the emergency Iron Lung mobile unit," sponsored by the Jaycees. Visitors heard, "A diaphragm at the base of a 7-foot cylinder is operated by an electric motor, which reduces the inside pressure and ultimately returns the pressure so as to move the patient's diaphragm to induce breathing." Donations for the March of Dimes were accepted.[35] Looking inside gave me an awful feeling. Movies of people trying to live in these lungs caused me more apprehension than the disease. By July 1945, the county had no cases, although the national number had doubled.

Population

To a historian or two, and the generally curious, the open question of determining how many people lived in New Hanover County and Wilmington during the war remains unanswered. The numbers naturally fascinated and perplexed officials. But as regulations regarding rationing, manpower, and allocations, and requirements for housing, schools, and transportation descended upon the boomtown, local governments believed themselves shortchanged by Washington's apparent incredulous assumption the 1940 census figures were stable. No one will ever know for sure how many people—permanent and transient—lived within the county borders at any one time, or altogether. There is no way to tell. It makes a difference only in randomly stating that the population doubled/tripled/rose by 50 percent, etc., as if to bolster its claim to wartime uniqueness, and partially justify the problems it endured while contributing.

---

* Thirteen people died from polio in North Carolina in 1944 out of 618 treated cases, the lowest death rate on record. The grim reminder: "It plays no favorites—rich and poor, careful and careless are picked apparently at random." [*Wilmington Morning Star*, January 13, 1945]

Sheer population numbers, however, only slightly affected the uniqueness label.

The official census cycle fell outside the war years. The only definable measure available was the number of ration book registrations: one to a person, and probably more accurate than other means. Otherwise, local and Washington officials just estimated, and usually no two sets of numbers jibed. Complicating the calculations was the occasional mixing of and inability to distinguish between city-county numbers. When does "Wilmington" also mean "New Hanover County" or "area"? To begin with what we know, the city's 1940 census was 33,407, and the county's was 47,935 (including the city). By February 1943, the Chamber of Commerce estimated the city's population had tripled to 90,000 and the county's was 120,000, more than 200 percent in less than three years.[36] Adding to the uncertainty was the "floating population" of thousands of weekend visitors of the military and war workers and their families.*

A February 1944 figure from Washington of 81,285 was based on Ration Book No. 4. The July 1944 Census Bureau estimate indicated the 1943 "metropolitan area" had been 78,793. The percentage of males 15–19 dropped from 10.6 to 6.7, although their number actually increased slightly to 2,444. The age group of men and women 25–29 was the largest with 10,071 (12.8 percent) of the civilian population. County growth ranked the highest in North Carolina, which showed a loss of 6.1 percent of population since April 1940. The peak had passed. The county estimates ranged from 79,070 to 115,000, a huge disparity. I have heard some people say the high was around 130,000, a guess without foundation. Safely, but hardly surely, I have settled on a compromise of between 95,000 to 100,000, with whites approximately 70 percent.

* * *

The Peak

The boom peaked in mid-1943 and by year's end had leveled off. That year the yard launched 79 vessels and shifted to C-2 hulls. "Machine-gun mounted trucks escorted enormous payrolls from Wilmington banks. Military personnel continued pouring into town and "spent their coin on Front Street, on buses, trains—everywhere a dollar was eligible. Wilmington's war money enabled it to build...[and] furnished the community this year financial basis for dreams of a lively future in forthcoming days of peace."[37]

---

* National Bureau of the Census statistics, however, question this estimate. Mobile County, Alabama, with a 64.7 percent increase between 1940-44 was identified as the most heavily impacted urban area, followed by Hampton Roads, Virginia (44.7), and Charleston, South Carolina (38.1). Confusion by using ration book registrations was compounded by "inadequate sampling techniques, a lack of trained canvassers, and the difficulty in identifying different kinds of military, civilian, permanent, and transient residents." [Everard H. Smith, *Victory on the Home Front: The USO in New Hanover County, North Carolina, 1941-46* [Self-published monograph, 1998]

Wartime prosperity was so visible it became a matter of simply quantifying rather than just acknowledging its benevolence. By 1944, the city government had "lowered the tax rate; boosted its highest income; put aside a $100,000 capital reserve; built a new water plant; started a pipeline toward King's Bluff and a never-failing supply of fresh water...built a new fire station...initiated a broad recreation program...began a retirement system...[and] named a planning board to be ready with post-war projects. (Much federal money aided the city with its work.)" The county government "lowered its tax rate 20 percent; received its largest income; established a reserve fund; promised a new Red Cross TB sanitarium; and patched up its juvenile detention home...." Both jurisdictions joined in a new health center and a planning committee. The Wilmington Housing Authority completed its three-year, 5,500 war-unit project, and converted 228 old homes into war-worker residences.[38]

For all of this, the Chamber forecast a continued leveling of business, but with these profound words: "'As these casualty lists begin to reach greater proportions, there will be few persons unaffected. This will probably bring home to all of us, with a terrific jolt, the grim realities of war and should most certainly take us way from the monetary values which we have all placed ahead of our responsibilities to the men and women in armed services, to our country, and to our community. Our big job, and only job, is to win the war...[and create] as decent a place as possible....'"[39]

Local economic signs caused the jitters as 1945 began. Camp Davis had closed, ship construction contracts wound down, and war workers and military personnel were leaving. Officials and ordinary citizens searched for and tried to create turns of events. "Undaunted" became the efforts of the stout-hearted. Wishful thinking and good fortunes ebbed and flowed, such as the on-again, off-again Davis reactivation by the air force, and 15 additional C-2 ship awards (which had to expire someday).

"Swamped by wartime conditions—worse than all but a few other American cities—Wilmington has always graced well to wartime burden," the Camp Davis paper stated in recognizing the *Star-News'* support in fostering good relations. "To those who have not paused to mentally picture the tremendous demands made on that city since 1941 it may have seemed at times that the town's efforts were lukewarm. That is not so....Wilmington's heart has been repeatedly shown to be in the right place—which is four-square for the thousands of soldiers....Reflected judgement will leave a warm and grateful feeling for Wilmington in the hearts and minds of all of us, come another 10 years."[40]

Heart in the right place all right. But how my community actually rose to the top in supporting the war effort was purely a combination of teamwork, dedication, and outright good fortune.

Chapter 16
"Heroisms Won by Wilmington's Men in Khaki"

When war came, male members of the New Hanover and Williston High School classes of 1939 were either in college or working, some in defense jobs. Hundreds of whites had been activated with the National Guard in 1940 or had volunteered for the armed forces. Many graduates were treading water without any idea what they would do, waiting to see what evolved. It didn't take long. Thousands of area boys and girls went off to fight World War II. Tallying even approximate numbers is impossible because of the many residents and transients called to duty.

Three Wilmington native pilots received their Service's highest decorations for valor at the Battle of Midway. Unfortunately, few here even know what they accomplished much less who they were, or why they must be remembered. What you believe people know is that Midway, on June 4–7, 1942, was the most decisive battle of the Pacific War. The American victory stopped Japan's eastward expansion toward Hawaii and the continental United States. Thereafter Japan was on the defensive. Two of these local boys were bonafide heroes, the other not. Their stories follow. Judge for yourself if any missing parts make a difference. But it is likely all we will ever know.

"It will be a long time after the battle guns are quiet before the full sort of the hell experienced by and the heroisms won by Wilmington's men in khaki in this war be unraveled," the *Sunday Star-News* stated in October 1944, citing the sterling battle record of men of this city's former 252nd Coast Artillery Regiment. "But piecemeal, the tales come back to town folk of what the Wilmington fellows from one end of the world to the other are suffering and accomplishing. The news pieces that filter in do not fail to point to the military exploits" of the 265 men of the old National Guard who left here on September 16, 1940. Eighty were from Company I of the 120th Infantry; 75 from Battery A of the 252nd; 40 from the 252nd's headquarters detail; 40 from Company A, 105th Medical Detachment; and 30 from the 252nd's Band Section.[1]

Of the Wilmington area residents who served in the armed forces and merchant marine, another unknown number faced the enemy in the air, on land, and on and under the sea. Their encounters began with the attack on Pearl Harbor and continued until V-E Day and V-J Day in the Atlantic, Pacific, Asian, North African, Mediterranean, and European theaters. Their varied experiences are but a microcosm of combat anywhere, any time, by Americans during WWII.

Going away into the unknown to face possible death was itself a frightening and traumatic experience. Coming home as a much different person after living through hell was quite another. Who wouldn't have shared this reaction after V-E Day of George Burrell Byers (NHHS '43), 847th Ordnance Depot Company, who had fought deep into Germany. "I am fully counting on going to the Pacific but I am praying for the Good Lord to please let me go home first. If I get 30 days at home," he wrote sweetheart Katharine Harriss, "young lady you had better watch out because I may even ask you to marry me....Sometimes I get to thinking about going home and it worries me some. I have changed some since I have been here. I often wonder if everything will still be the same. I doubt if you would even recognize me now. I look quite a bit older in fact I am older. Did you know that I am 20 years old now—one more birthday and I will legally be a man."[2]

Several months earlier from France, before he became immersed in combat, he had written her with such bravado: "When I get home I'm gonna be hard to handle because the first week or so I'm really going to raise 'hell.' I'm going to head straight for Foy & Roe and buy some of the sportiest clothes you have ever seen. I think I'll just be a permanent beach comber, well for a while anyway."[3] The war ended before he was transferred to the Pacific, but it was mid-1946 before he got home.

* * *

Volunteers and Draftees

The day after Pearl Harbor, men began answering the call. The navy placed the recruiting station on a seven-day, 24-hour basis. Recruiter R. L. DeLoach signed up local worker Larry D. Moye, 21, waiting since before the doors opened, as the first wartime enlistment. Eleven joined that day, the busiest in months, and 65 during the week following the attack. Mental examinations were waived and physical requirements lowered, allowing men with minor ailments and disabilities to enlist in the reserves. On the 12th the army opened its recruiting office, also in the downtown post office, with Staff Sergeant Wilson Welch in charge.* He spoke of "unlimited vacancies" in Panama and Stateside, you can postpone being called until after Christmas, and "'married men can...be accepted if they have their wife's written consent.'"4

Army and navy recruiters drummed up volunteers. A 1942 *Morning Star* column written by navy recruiter Specialist First Class Jesse Helms stressed 60 trade schools in a drive to sign up 100 men, a drive assisted by 50 volunteer Wilmington women. From Pearl Harbor through August, local recruiters had processed more than 2,500 navy volunteers.† The local station led the state in June 1943 in the percentage of 17 year olds enlisted with 112. Sixteen were NHHS '43 graduates. Men working in essential war industries such as shipyards, or in school or on farms, were deferred indefinitely. No conscientious objectors were believed registered with either local draft board.

Sadly, as if representing the Depression in which they were raised, by March 1943, 54 percent of city draftees had been rejected for service because of physical disability. This included 73 percent of Negroes and 36 percent of whites reporting to Fort Bragg for examination. Rejection "invites a question as to what is wrong with the physical training courses at our schools," the *Morning Star* rightly opined. "The rejections are largely among the 18-year olds whom it would be natural to expect to be in top form....The fault would seem to stem from failure sufficiently to encourage health-promoting habits, with athletics a principal agency."5

A December 1945 study ranked New Hanover 50th of the one hundred counties with a total rejection rate of 45 percent. At 36.3 percent of white men examined, the county ranked 27th highest, and with 61.1 percent of Negroes rejected, was 62nd. "The lack of and need for a more efficient health program and broader health education in New Hanover County is proved," and citizens were urged to insist on modernized public health regarding a tuberculosis sanitarium and prophylactic prevention of "so-called social diseases."6

* * *

Dickinson, Peiffer, and Allen at Midway

The two deserved local heroes at Midway were pilots of SBD-3 *Dauntless* dive bombers of Scouting (Squadron) Six from the carrier USS *Enterprise* (CV-6), Lieutenant Junior Grade Clarence Earl Dickinson, Jr., and

---

* The local army recruiting station recruited men for both the U.S. Army and the U.S. Army Air Forces. Men seeking enlistment in the Marine Corps, Coast Guard, or Merchant Marine had to travel to Raleigh. Wilmington was the army and navy recruiting center for Southeastern North Carolina.

† Helms, a five-term U.S. senator from North Carolina, has spoken warmly of his service here during the war.

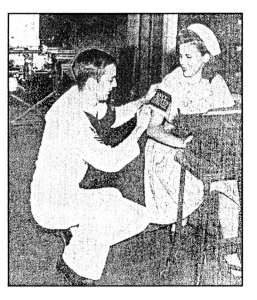

Navy Specialist First Class Jesse Helms "enlists" Mary Elizabeth Meaders to help in a 1942 recruiting drive. Helms, a future U.S. senator from North Carolina, spent two years in Wilmington as a recruiter.
Wilmington Morning Star, August 6, 1942

Corporal Thurston Eugene "Gene" Edwards (NHHS '43) in Germany, 1945. A member of the 251st Field Artillery Battalion, he defended the Rhine's Remagen bridge against the new German Me-262 jet aircraft.
Provided by Edwards

Ensign Carl David Peiffer. Each is believed to have helped sink the heavy carrier IJN *Kaga*, one of four Japanese carriers sunk there. Each received the Navy Cross for his actions, Peiffer posthumously. Dickinson, earlier credited with sinking an enemy submarine on the surface on December 10, 1941, the first Japanese vessel to be sunk after Pearl Harbor, ditched his plane returning to *Enterprise* and was rescued. Peiffer suffered fuel exhaustion and also ditched on the June 4 return. Last seen getting into a rubber life raft but never recovered, he was declared KIA after first considered to be missing.

The third hero, Lieutenant Colonel Brooke E. "Buzz" Allen, a B-17E *Flying Fortress* pilot, helped lead the B-17 attack from Midway on June 4. As second in command of the bomber flight, he led it back safely after the flight leader had to return early. Allen received the Distinguished Service Cross, the army's equivalent to the Navy Cross, but on the basis of results did not deserve it. None of his bombing group's bombs hit any Japanese target, although they did scatter the formations to aid the dive bombers. At the time when America desperately needed heroes, he came along. Allen later saw combat and in his career was promoted to major general. His nomination for the Midway decoration likely was based on several factors: erroneous after-action reports of damage inflicted by the B-17s, the navy's reticence to divulge the extent of its involvement after breaking the Japanese code, by default allowing the army air forces to claim undeserved public credit for the victory, and the country's thirst for heroes in a war it had been losing.

Dickinson

An NHHS ('32) and Naval Academy graduate, Dickinson was the son of Mr. and Mrs. C. E. Dickinson of Wrightsville Beach. Five weeks after Midway, he visited at home and spoke to local organizations. "A young navy flier described here this week the sensations of going through six months of modern warfare on the Pacific front...."

At Midway he led his flight section and "dove his Douglas dive bomber on one of the carriers with the other planes of his wing following him down through the hail of AA fire from the carrier. At the height of 600 feet above the carrier's deck, he released his bombs and pulled his plane out of the dive. At least seven hits were scored on the Japanese craft in the attack, he said. 'A minute later, there was an explosion and a tremendous ball of fire shot up from the carrier to the level of the clouds. You could see her decks rolling back under the force of the explosion'....A moment later there was another explosion and another ball of fire....The Japanese carriers have a tremendous red circle, surrounded by a ring, painted on their decks which makes them good targets. 'Sea warfare has boiled down to finding the enemy and knocking the hell out of him before he finds you and does the same.'" He escaped unscathed but crash-landed his plane when it ran out of fuel. A destroyer picked him up.[7]

That Peiffer dived on *Kaga* immediately ahead of or behind Dickinson is highly possible, and as interesting a coincidence as two Wilmington men serving together in the same squadron. "By the grace of God," Dickinson wrote,

> as I put my nose down I picked up our carrier target below in front of me. I was making the best dive I had ever made....We were coming from all directions on the port side of the carrier, beautifully spaced. Going down I watched over the nose of my plane to see the first bombs land on that yellow deck. At last her fighters were taking off and that was when I felt sure I recognized her as the *Kaga*; and she was enormous....The carrier was racing along at 30 knots, right into the wind. She made no attempt to change course....By the time I was at 12,000 feet I could see all the planes ahead of me in the dive. We were close together but no one plane was coming down in back of another as may easily happen....This was the absolute....After dropping I kicked my rudder to get my tail out of the way and put my plane in a stall. So I was simply standing there to watch it. I saw the 500-pound bomb hit right abreast of the island. The two 100-pound bombs struck in the forward area of the parked planes on that yellow flight deck. Then I began thinking it was time to get myself away from there and try to get back alive.[8]

About sinking the submarine Dickinson stated, "'I reported its location to the ship [*Enterprise*] and climbed up to get into position to make my attack....As I went into my dive my tail gunner was excitedly chattering into the inter-plane phone: "Lieutenant, have you armed the bomb? Mr. Dickinson, is the bomb armed?" I pulled out of my dive just over the sub. The bomb hit beside the sub and exploded. It went under rapidly in a great welter of fuel oil and debris and bubbles....'"[9] Naval historian Samuel Eliot Morrison wrote that Dickinson found the *I-170* surfaced (after sustaining a bomb hit it was unable to submerge), with men and debris in water alongside, dive-bombed and sank it at latitude 23–45 North, longitude 155–25 West.[10]

Dickinson received his first Navy Cross for action at Pearl Harbor and the sub sinking. On a December 7 scouting mission, he "was attacked by a superior number of enemy aircraft. Although his gunner was killed, his plane on fire and out of control, he continued to engage the enemy [he shot one down] until forced by fire to abandon the plane" and returned to the naval air station. Immediately manning another plane, he searched a 175-mile area.[11] Famous news commentator and author Lowell Thomas in 1943 wrote that Dickinson "acquitted himself heroically at Pearl Harbor, the Gilbert and Marshall Islands, and Midway" and was "the lone pilot in the sky when the Japs started their first attack [at Pearl]....The fearlessness with which he handled his little observer plane in the midst of the unceasing barrage by the enemy is bared in Thomas' most colorful language....His record will be taken as presenting a full range of flying heroes in the Pacific War."[12] Perhaps a bit premature, such pronouncements were the material for the posters, slogans, and adulation America needed.

Dickinson received his third Navy Cross for "leadership and the forceful manner in which he executed his mission" for the February 1, 1942, carrier raid on the Marshalls where his bomb hit a *Yawata*-class liner in Kwajalein harbor. In 1943 local librarian Emma Woodward announced the arrival of his 1942 wartime accounts,* earlier condensed in *The Saturday Evening Post*. The original copy is still on the county's main library shelf.† Go read it.

Peiffer

Carl David Peiffer, NHHS senior class president in 1934, graduated from the University of North Carolina in 1940 where he played varsity football for four years. He entered the navy that December. His Navy Cross citation reads: "...With fortitude and resolute devotion to duty, pressed home his attack in the face of a formidable barrage of anti-aircraft fire and fierce fighter opposition. His gallant perseverance and utter disregard for his own personal safety were important contributing factors to the success achieved by our forces...."[13]

The navy in January 1944 named a new destroyer escort for him, the USS *Peiffer* (DE-588).‡ At home, G. H. Rogers and operators of a small commercial and private grass airfield at Seagate named the field for Peiffer in June 1945. Open for only a few years, its traces now are a long clearing in the woods at the end of the one-quarter mile-long paved Peiffer Road.

In another mid-war "morale-builder" book, Clark Lee wrote that "Peiffer was tall and good-looking with deep-set eyes and deep lines on his face from smiling a lot. His chin was square and he wore his flier's cap at a

---

* Clarence Earle Dickinson, Jr., and Borden Sparks, *The Flying Guns: Cockpit Record of a Naval Pilot from Pearl Harbor through Midway* (New York: Charles Scribner's Sons, 1942). My op-ed piece in the *Morning Star* of June 3, 2002, "Wilmington Heroes at Midway," brought a phone call from Betty Sparks Eagles, a local resident. She identified herself as Dickinson's first cousin. Her father, Borden Sparks, had coauthored *Flying Guns*. "He was mad at the war. He was the big hero. He was in every parade and war bond rally." A postwar school teacher, Dickinson died in Coronado, California. [Interview with Eagles, June 3, 2002]

† Retired Captain Albert K. Earnest knew of Dickinson and his book, and said Dickinson probably received the Navy Cross for Midway because all the navy pilots who participated in the battle did, including himself, a member of Torpedo Squadron 8 who flew out from the island of Midway. [Interview with Earnest, July 27, 2000]

‡ Attending the launching were his mother and sponsor Adelaide J. Peiffer and his uncle, county Sheriff C. David Jones. The *Peiffer*'s combat action was in and around the Philippines. Decommissioned in June 1946, she was sunk as a target ship in May 1947.

jaunty angle." His flier buddy Ensign John Quincy Roberts boasted, "'When we get our first crack at them, I'm going to dive down and lay my egg right on the middle of the deck of their biggest carrier. And if I miss I'm going to keep right on diving down into the funnel and set that ship on fire.' And Peiffer would say, 'I'll be right behind you, JQ.'"[14] (This account may be true, but Lee's further descriptions of Peiffer's action are questionable, e.g., placement on the wrong carrier, crash dived into *Kaga*, etc.)

Peiffer's NHHS classmates including Harry Stovall, Henry Von Oesen, Margaret Banck, and Bruce Cameron remembered him as being voted Best Natured Boy and nicknamed "Baggy." Boys in those days wore knickers, and his were oversized. "Baggy was a very likeable chap, very easy to get along with," said Von Oesen. "He wasn't particularly social, nor was I. He was serious, sort of quiet, happy, always listening to a funny story. I liked him a whole lot."[15] His musician father, Frank W. Peiffer, led the orchestra at the local Royal Theater.[16] Banck remembered, "He was a fine young man, clean living. An outstanding member of our class and well thought of."[17] He "attained many superlatives, had a good voice, was very popular," Cameron recalled. Peiffer's parents lived next door to Bruce's Albert F. Fales grandparents on South 5th Street.[18]

Peiffer was the second Wilmingtonian to have a ship named after him during the war. The first was Lieutenant (Junior Grade) Douglas Wiley Gillette of the carrier USS *Hornet* (CV-8), KIA at Santa Cruz, Solomon Islands, in October 1942. His father was Colonel George Gillette, former army district engineer in Wilmington. His mother, Pearl M. Gillette, christened the destroyer escort USS *Gillette* (DE-681) at Quincy, Massachusetts, in September 1943. Wilmington hero navy Pharmacist's Mate 2nd Class William David "Billy" Halyburton, Jr. (NHHS '43), recipient of the Medal of Honor posthumously, was honored in 1984 with the frigate USS *Halyburton* (FFG-40). The launching of the destroyer USS *Edwards* (DD-619) in October 1943 in Boston had a Wilmington connection. It was named for Lieutenant Commander Heywood Lane Edwards, commanding officer of the destroyer USS *Reuben James* (DD-245) sunk by a German submarine on October 31, 1941, before the United States entered the war. His widow, Wilmingtonian Almeda Stewart Edwards, in 1943 served in the Pacific with the Red Cross. She died here in 2001.

Allen

Allen, 31, NHHS ('29) and Davidson College ('33), had survived the December 7, 1941, attack on Hickam Field. He took off from Hickam about 11:40 a.m., circled around Diamond Head, and was airborne for about seven hours searching for the departed Japanese fleet. "Allen reported being sent out with information that there were two Japanese carriers to the south, but he found very shortly after takeoff one American carrier to the south. Then, following his personal feeling that the Japanese would have come from the north, he put his compass on 'N' and headed straight north. How close he ever came to the carrier task force he never knew but 'returned with minimum fuel and a heart full of disgust that I had been unable to locate them.'" His was one of 48 sorties going out to search that day.[19]

He recounted his part of the Midway battle: "'From where we were flying it was quite a picture. Jap carriers were squirming around pretty fast, in a violent maneuver attempting to hide under clouds and avoid our bombs....I picked out one carrier, and we got direct hits on it. My trailing plane picked up his target—another carrier—and planted hits on it too.'" The article said Allen's *Flying Fortress* "'scored hits on a Japanese carrier, a battleship and a cruiser....'"[20] Neither this claim nor Allen's assertion were correct in any form. Later assignments included command of a bomber group on Guadalcanal in 1942–43.

Allen received a substantial amount of publicity and appeared not to avoid it, perhaps even believing his Midway claims. In September 1943 he spoke on the New York-based "March of Time" radio show before visiting his Wilmington parents, Mr. and Mrs. W. R. Allen of 304 South 2nd, the first time in four years. Called "one of Wilmington's foremost heroes in the present war....He will, if he chooses, dangle those medals before the eyes of his 18-month-old daughter whom he has never seen." Also awarded the Legion of Merit and Air Medal, he "has shown the city 'the stuff that heroes are made of.'"[21] By that time it was too late to deny or disclaim anything.*

* * *

"A Sergeant York of Its Own"

After reading that army infantry Captain Charles P. "Chuck" Murray, Jr., U.S. Army (NHHS '38) had been awarded the Medal of Honor, a member of the *Star-News* staff remarked, "Wilmington has a Sergeant [Alvin C.] York of its own." The June 12, 1945, statement referred to the previous war's Tennessee hero, and coincidentally the conditions were much the same.[22] Less than four weeks earlier, William David "Billy" Halyburton, Jr. (NHHS '43), a navy hospital corpsman assigned to the infantry 2nd Battalion, 5th Marines, was KIA on May 15, 1945, in the bloody battle at Okinawa's Wana Draw. He saved the life of a wounded Marine, for which he would be awarded the Medal of Honor posthumously in 1946.

I believe our school is the only high school in the country with more than one Medal of Honor recipient for World War II, a distinct honor and

---

* W. Eugene "Gene" Edwards (NHHS '28) is the only person I know who knew all three Midway heroes. While speaking fondly of Dickinson and Peiffer, he allowed that Allen's claims and acceptance of the decoration are understandable given his tendency to draw attention to himself and overstate his standing. [Interview with Edwards, July 6, 2001]

Wilmington Welcomes Congressional Medal Of Honor Winner

The city turned out to honor Medal of Honor recipient Captain Charles P. Murray, Jr., U.S. Army (NHHS '38), when he returned home in 1945. Seated with him are wife Anniemae King Murray and Mayor W. Ronald Lane.

Wilmington Morning Star, September 25, 1945

recognition not only for their actions, but for the type of men our community produced and sent to fight for our country.

Murray

Wilmington officially welcomed home Murray on September 26, 1945, with a parade down 3rd Street. Soon after his November discharge he resumed studies at the University of North Carolina. "Back of him are a mere 23 years, less than three years in the army but 150 days of grueling combat from the Vosges to the Alpine redoubt," his commanding officer wrote. Murray "guessed he 'would do the same thing again [the heroism]. It was the best plan.'"[23]

"News of the award was a complete surprise to his father, who lives in Castle Hayne," the newspaper reported, "and the officer's pretty brunette wife, Mrs. Anniemae [Anne] King Murray....It took 10 minutes for [the Associated Press wire story] to come through and when it was completed, a *Star-News* man ripped it off...and called Mr. [Charles Patrick] Murray at the Cape Fear barber shop which he manages. 'Mr. Murray, I've some good news about your son. He's been awarded the Congressional Medal of Honor. I suppose you know that's the highest they come,' he said. 'Well, well, that's a mighty big surprise. That's the first I've heard of it'....Mr. Murray called his daughter-in-law and told her the wonderful news....He'd written that he was getting a medal but he thought it was another Silver Star. We had no idea it was this,' she said."[24] (His mother, Florence Brown Murray, had died in 1941.)

The front-page story continued:

> Later in the afternoon a copy of the story was taken to the barber shop, where Mrs. Murray was waiting. She started reading it standing up but it was too much. She sat down in one of the chairs and, too excited to hold the paper, a friend held it while she finished learning the details of how her young husband became one of the country's top-flight heroes. She paused once or twice to correct a fact such as "he's not 24, he's only 23 years old" and he "isn't a native of Baltimore. He's always lived here." (The AP said he was a Baltimorian, perhaps because that was where he was born.) "I think it's wonderful. This is the happiest day of my life. I just can't say anything more," she beamed. "Everything seems to be happening at once. At noon today I received a letter from him. He didn't say a word about being promoted to captain but up in the corner, there it was 'Captain Charles P. Murray, Jr.' And now, THIS medal. This is almost too much." His father added, "We're mighty, mighty proud of him."[25]

"Thousands Accord Enthusiastic Welcome Home" to Wilmington's "No. 1 War Hero," "the modest holder of the Congressional Medal of Honor," lining the downtown streets with "one of the biggest spontaneous receptions in the city's history." Murray, who spoke briefly "and quickly sat down," told the crowd: "I guess you all know I'm scared to death....It's good to be home and it's good to have a place like Wilmington to come to." Mayor Ronald Lane said, "We not only honor Captain Murray as an individual, but through him, all American heroes." He is one of "Uncle Sam's boys." He remained shaking hands and giving autographs. Present were his wife, father, grandparents Mr. and Mrs. Ausia Murray, brothers William and Don Murray, other relatives, and in-laws Mr. and Mrs. R. S. King. Twelve P-47s thundered overhead several times "in faultless formation." "The streets were certainly lined with folks and I recognized a great many of them." Murray's decorations went on display in the window at City Optical Company.

Murray's citation reads:

> The President of the United States of America,
> authorized by Act of Congress, March 3, 1863,
> has awarded in the name of Congress the MEDAL OF HONOR to
> FIRST LIEUTENANT CHARLES P. MURRAY, JR.
> UNITED STATES ARMY

Citation: First Lieutenant *Charles Murray*, U.S. Army, for commanding Company C, 1st Battalion, 30th Infantry, 3rd Infantry Division, displaying supreme courage and heroic initiative near Kaysersberg, France, on 16 December 1944, while leading a reinforced platoon into enemy territory. Descending into a valley beneath hilltop positions held by our troops, he observed a force of 200 Germans pouring deadly mortar, bazooka, machine-gun, and small-arms fire into an American battalion occupying the crest of the ridge. The enemy's position in a sunken road, though hidden from the ridge, was open to a flank attack by First Lieutenant *Murray's* patrol but he hesitated to commit so small a force to battle with the superior and strongly disposed enemy. Crawling out ahead of his troops to a vantage point, he called by radio for artillery fire. His shells bracketed the German force, but when he was about to correct the range his radio went dead. He returned to his patrol, secured grenades and a rifle to launch them and went back to his self-appointed outpost. His first shots disclosed his position; the enemy directed heavy fire against him as he methodically fired his missiles into the narrow defile. Again he returned to his patrol. With an automatic rifle and ammunition, he once more moved to his exposed position. Burst after burst he fired into the enemy, killing 20, wounding many others, and completely disorganizing its ranks, which began to withdraw. He prevented the removal of three German mortars by knocking out a truck. By that time a mortar had been brought to his support. First Lieutenant *Murray* directed fire of this weapon, causing further casualties and confusion in the German ranks. Calling on his patrol to follow, he then moved out toward his original objective, possession of a bridge and construction of a roadblock. He captured 10 Germans in foxholes. An eleventh, while pretending to surrender, threw a grenade which knocked him to the ground, inflicting eight wounds. Though suffering bleeding profusely, he refused to return to the rear until he had chosen the spot for the block and had seen his men correctly deployed. By his singlehanded attack on an overwhelming force and by his intrepid and heroic fighting, First Lieutenant *Murray* stopped a counterattack, established an advance position against formidable odds, and provided an inspiring example for the men of his command.

/s/ Harry S Truman

THE WHITE HOUSE
July 5, 1945[27]

Born in Baltimore, Maryland, in 1921, Murray moved to Castle Hayne before he was a year old. As a boy he delivered newspapers for four years, worked at grocery stores, and at 10 was selling magazines on downtown streets. "I was a roughneck growing up in grade school and was a good marble shooter." At NHHS he managed the football and boxing teams, made the National Honor Society, and advanced to Life Scout. The army drafted him in September 1942 on completion of three years at Carolina.[28]

Follow as his story expands.[29] His replacement unit landed in France in September 1944 where he was assigned to the 30th Infantry Regiment, already veterans of North Africa, Sicily, and Italy. Through attrition he became the company commander on December 8. On the 16th, in a snow-covered pine forest overlooking Kaysersberg in the Vosges Mountains about 12 miles from the Rhine, his regimental commander "decided let's not just defend, let's attack. It was hand-to-hand." His company crossed the Weiss River, and he reconnoitered the area ahead. The citation told the rest. To reach the aid station after being wounded he had to walk two miles through snow. Several days after treatment he was allowed to return to his unit, but had no helmet or weapon, and reached it on the 29th. On New Year's Day night, the 63rd Infantry Division unit of Wilmingtonian John J. Burney, Jr., (NHHS '43) replaced his in the line. John recalled, "I used to go by the same bunch of Germans every night he [Murray] had killed. I counted the bodies to make sure they were all still there." Before the war the two had lived across Orange Street from each other.[30]

In late February Chuck entered a hospital at Nancy with bronchitis, where he learned he had been recommended for the Medal of Honor. On being released March 12, he headed with his unit for Germany and the Siegfried Line. From there he "would go through the roughest time of my service. I was told it would be 2–3 weeks to learn whether I would be reassigned for home or stay. I was extra careful" in the assault among heavy U.S. casualties. He arrived in Salzburg, Austria, by V-E Day.[31]

Chuck and Anne King grew up and ran around together and began dating when he was at UNC. Her NHHS '42 *Hanoverian* class prophecy said she would marry Charles Murray, and she did on November 28, 1942.

While he was away she worked at the Coast Line and lived with her parents, the Renouard S. Kings. Chuck graduated from UNC in 1946 with a degree in commerce and returned to active duty that September. His brother Billy Murray served two years in the navy including a year in the South Pacific.

Local officials and historians have made certain he will be remembered in his old hometown. In October 1999, he attended two ceremonies during Wartime Wilmington Commemoration: the groundbreaking for a new middle school with his name at Veterans' Park, and presentation of a bronze plaque by the Board of Education to NHHS bearing the names of Murray and Halyburton as its two Medal of Honor recipients from WWII. Murray also spoke at the school's formal dedication on December 7, 2001. The plaque will be installed along the front sidewalk at the high school.*

His schoolmates liked and respected him. "I used to tell Dad," friend Mac Wilson said, that "'Charles is going to do something great someday,' and he did." Mac could judge by Murray's posture when he walked.[32]

* * *

Halyburton

Halyburton was born in Canton, North Carolina, on August 2, 1924, the son of Mr. and Mrs. William D. Halyburton. He moved to Wilmington in the late 1930s to live with his aunt and uncle Mr. and Mrs. E. M. Milton in Winter Park. He attended NHHS for four years and graduated in 1943. They attended Winter Park Presbyterian Church. "He had been received by the Presbyterian church as a candidate for the ministry, and had engaged in several religious activities during his military service."[33]

Billy acted in school plays and participated in student government and varsity basketball and baseball. He impressed friends with his low-key, deeply religious convictions. Numerous school mates shared with me their favorable recollections of him. "I remember him as being very smart, real tall. I can see him right now," said Laura Roe.[34] Emma Mitchell added, "Some of the best ones at the school were killed—but they weren't in the crowd I ran with." Billy "was a real leader. I had so much respect for him."[35] And the 1943

---

* Murray retired as a colonel in 1973 following a successful career and more combat in Korea and Vietnam. In addition to the Medal of Honor, his decorations include the Silver Star with three Oak Leaf Clusters, Legion of Merit with three OLCs, Bronze Star, Air Medal with six OLCs, Purple Heart, Army Commendation Medal, French Croix de Guerre with Silver Star, the Republic of Vietnam Cross of Gallantry with Palm and Gold Star. He later served as a senior planner for the South Carolina Department of Corrections until retiring in 1983. He and Anne live in Columbia, South Carolina, and occasionally visit Wilmington. An active member of the Congressional Medal of Honor Society and frequent speaker on patriotism around the country, he remains as modest as in 1945.

Chapter Sixteen

Pharmacist's Mate 2nd Class William David "Billy" Halyburton, Jr., U.S. Naval Reserve (NHHS '43), corpsman serving with the 2nd Battalion, 5th Marines, 1st Marine Division. KIA on Okinawa, May 19, 1945. Awarded the Medal of Honor posthumously.
U.S. Marine Corps files

yearbook's class prophecy, "Looking Back," announced: "They Dood It!"— "Wilmington's missionary to Hollywood, Billy Halyburton, told of many of his experiences in reforming the movie colony."

The award of Billy's Medal of Honor was the climactic event at Miami, Florida's first V-E Day commemoration on May 8, 1946, and was broadcast on nationwide radio. His mother, then living there, and brothers Joseph and Robert Halyburton received it. The May 14 *Morning Star* ran photos of the ceremony and him as a senior. The August issue of the navy's *All Hands* magazine featured his deed. At the time of his death, Seaman 1st Class Joseph was on a battleship in the Pacific and Motor Mechanic 3rd Class Robert on a patrol torpedo boat in the Mediterranean. Also surviving was his sister, Jean Halyburton Taylor, of Miami.

At commencement exercises for the NHHS class of 1946, "the entire audience stood at silent attention, men baring their heads and a sprinkling of servicemen standing at salute, as, to the muffled roll of a military drum, the names of the school's graduates who lost their lives in the war were intoned...." A highlight was instituting the first "Billy Halyburton Teacher Award" to recognize the teacher who had contributed the most to the Bible Department work the previous year. The award was in his name "because he planned to study for the ministry [at Davidson College] after his return from the service of his country from which he never returned."[36]

Halyburton's citation reads:

> The President of the United States in the name of Congress takes pride in presenting the MEDAL OF HONOR posthumously to
>
> PHARMACIST'S MATE SECOND CLASS
> WILLIAM D. HALYBURTON, JR.
> UNITED STATES NAVAL RESERVE
>
> for service as set forth in the following
> CITATION
>
> For conspicuous gallantry and intrepidity at the risk of his life above and beyond the call of duty while serving with a Marine Rifle Company in the 2nd Battalion, 5th Marines, 1st Marine Division, during action

against the enemy Japanese forces on Okinawa Shima in the Ryukyu Chain on 10 May 1945. Undaunted by the deadly accuracy of Japanese counterfire as his unit pushed the attack through a strategically important draw and up the hill into an open fireswept field where the Company advance squad was suddenly pinned down under a terrific concentration of mortar, machinegun, and sniper fire with resultant severe casualties. Moving steadily forward despite the enemy's merciless barrage, he reached the wounded Marine who lay farthest away and was rendering first aid when his patient was struck for the second time by a Japanese bullet. Instantly placing himself in the direct line of fire, he shielded the fallen fighter with his own body and staunchly continued his ministrations although constantly menaced by the slashing fury of shrapnel and bullets falling on all asides. Alert, determined, and completely unselfish in his concern for the helpless Marine, he persevered in his efforts until he himself sustained mortal wounds and collapsed, heroically sacrificing himself that his comrade might live. By his outstanding valor and unwavering devotion to duty in the face of tremendous odds, Petty Officer Halyburton sustained and enhanced the highest traditions of the United States Naval Service. He gallantly gave his life in the service of his country.

/s/ Harry S Truman[37]

I remember the Billy Halyburton Teacher Award being given when I went to New Hanover, as do others, but the plaque dropped from usage long ago and might be buried in a storage closet. Unfortunately Wilmington has never recognized his honor with a suitable memorial. The handsome granite memorial slab to the county's dead of 20th-century wars at Hugh MacRae Park, sponsored by American Legion Post 10, does not list him. The Post's three-portrait montage painting of local Medal of Honor recipients Murray, Eugene Ashley, Jr. (posthumously awarded for the Vietnam War, and former Wilmington resident), and Edwin A. Anderson (Vera Cruz, Mexico, 1914) graces the main library and City Hall lobbies, but excludes Billy. The rationale is he met neither of their qualifiers: he was not born here and did not enter the service from here. The claim is he entered the navy from Canton. What a shame to split hairs and deny this man the recognition and his rightful place in our local history!

But I know different. *Billy did so enter the service from Wilmington.* It takes a little explaining. An item in the *Morning Star* of August 3, 1943, "Draft Board Two Inducts 55 Men," lists each man, including "William David Halyburton, Jr., Rt. 2, Winter Park." The draft contingent had left the city on August 2 for Fort Bragg for induction into the armed forces.[38] Several of his classmates, including Thurston "Gene" Edwards and Nick Fokakis, were in that draft and believe they remember him being along. On the fourth, Billy was sworn into—but technically did not enlist—the navy in Raleigh, North Carolina.

(A note: After January 1, 1943, men no longer had the freedom of voluntarily enlisting directly into the armed forces as before, and all had to come through the involuntary Selective Service System [the draft]. Fort Bragg was the state's eastern draftee induction center. Once inducted, customarily some draftees were allowed to select which service they wished to enter. In some cases it was granted, depending on accession needs. The exception to this procedure allowed men 17 years of age, with parents' written permission, to enlist directly without going through the draft.) Billy obviously had that choice at time of induction, chose the navy, and was shipped to Raleigh, the state's central navy procurement office, to be sworn in there. A typewritten Medal of Honor biography sheet on Halyburton dated "3-23-46" I obtained indicated (wrongly) that he "enlisted" at Raleigh on the 4th. Technically, therefore, his place of entry into the service could have been either of the three places, but from a practical standpoint, he departed from Wilmington to enter.

Winter Park Presbyterian, however, has an appropriate framed display of Billy and his citation on the wall just inside the sanctuary's front door. The navy remembers him extensively. The new (1995) Naval Hospital at Marine Corps Air Station Cherry Point, North Carolina, bears his name and contains a wall display to the hero. The USS *Halyburton* is homeported in Mayport, Florida. His name is on a road at Bethesda (Maryland) Naval Hospital, a living quarters at the former (deactivated) Charleston (South Carolina) Naval Station, and a barracks at the Naval Aerospace Medical Center in Pensacola, Florida.

The plaque once installed on the NHHS grounds for easy public viewing will replace a smaller, blackened bronze 1946 plaque recognizing both men which has been stuck on the wall in a corner of the upstairs lobby and ignored. I am not alone in pushing for proper recognition for him in Wilmington. The New Hanover County Board of Education has indicated its intent to honor Billy by naming a facility for him in the future.

"I was 21 Years Old. I Could Do Anything. Let Me Try It."

At age 21 in January 1945, at Moton Field, Tuskegee, Alabama, 1940 Williston Industrial School graduate Percy L. Heath received his pilot's wings and second lieutenant's bars. Checked out in P-40 *Warhawk* fighters, after almost two years of training, he was among only 16 single-engine qualified flyers out of a beginning class of seven hundred candidates. What made this moment special for the former auto mechanic and railroad worker, without any college education, was that Heath proudly became Wilmington's only member of the famed Tuskegee Airmen.

Slated for duty in Europe, his group soon transitioned to P-47 *Thunderbolt* fighters. When that war ended on May 8, he was destined for the Pacific Theater. Before leaving, Japan surrendered—so he never saw overseas service. Nevertheless, vivid memories remain.

After his 1923 birth in Wilmington, Heath's family moved to Philadelphia, Pennsylvania, where his father became one of the city's finest auto mechanics. For many summers Heath and brothers Jimmy and Albert ("Tootie") visited with their Wilmington grandmother, Mattie Stewart Fisher, in a house still standing and occupied by family on McRae Street. Enticed by her gift of a Dixie Flyer bicycle, he finished his last two years of high school at Williston.

Drafted in 1943, he accepted the army's offer to enter aviation (his first flight had been in Wilmington). "They were drafting all the intelligentsia from the black race to enter them into this new school they were putting together [Tuskegee]. As a first-classman you were a real dummy. I later realized it was all brainwashing and conditioning and military training." After flying Stearmans and Piper *Cubs* in primary, he upgraded to the AT-6 *Texan* for advanced and solo, often flying visiting officials around the area. When a close friend was lost during turbulence in P-40 training—"that shook up everybody"—he was more determined than ever. "I was 21 years old. I could do anything. Let me try it."

Before getting out of the army he visited Mrs. Fisher to show off his uniform. In Philadelphia he wore it around town telling people he wanted to be a jazz musician. He bought a bass, began playing, and was discharged in January 1946. Since then he has done quite well, playing with the greats, founding the Modern Jazz Quartet, performing with both brothers, and being recognized as perhaps the finest bass player in jazz history. He still performs.

Army aviation cadet Percy L. Heath, Wilmington native and Williston Industrial School graduate, in early 1945 prior to commissioning as second lieutenant and receiving wings as a Tuskegee Airman. Moton Field, Tuskegee, Alabama.

Provided by Heath

Epilogue

The forecast of a rosy future slipped away almost as quickly as it had arrived. Wilmington was certain it could convert its wartime boom into postwar prosperity. It all seemed so logical and simple for a while. But in late 1944 the army closed their operations at Camp Davis and Fort Fisher, and in late 1945 Bluethenthal Field. The government terminated war industry contracts, and suddenly the military folks were barely seen. In 1946 all ship construction activities expired. The few new small firms that had opened (grocery stores, clothing manufacturers, Front Street retailers) were not enough to sustain the economic blessings the war had showered. By 1946, Wilmington was holding its breath on expectations and projections.

Some immediate holdover opportunities arose. The shipyard became the state port authority, and the airfield a small authority with limited commercial activity. But without adequate highways, Wilmington essentially receded into its prewar hibernation. Not until the late 1960s and 1970s did the community at last make a determined effort to modernize, capitalize on its natural recreational facilities, and attract business, tourism, industry, and new residents—mainly triggered by the Atlantic Coast Line Railroad's abrupt departure in 1961.

"We hear men returning from military duty say: 'It's so good to be home,'" the *Morning Star* stated on July 30, 1945.

> And always all of them insist that Wilmington is the best place in the world to live. Then we hear men in the armed forces departing say that Wilmington is the worst town of all. And on inquiry the dissatisfied ones tell you it hasn't got this and hasn't got that, and it doesn't compare with the place they call home. Having heard both kinds of testimony for years, and from people transplanted not only in a war emergency but by new business or professional connections, we have concluded that the place we call home...is the best place in the world chiefly because they have put something into it....
>
> Soldiers coming back to Wilmington with comforted hearts probably gave the city the years of their schooling and the early years of their commercial careers. They put their childhood, their adolescence, their

young manhood, into Wilmington....Naturally they are happy to be home. These other soldiers, having given nothing, complain of Wilmington's deficiencies without realizing they are giving it nothing except a bad name....It is in giving that truest satisfaction lies.[1]

At that point a larger question loomed: What would Wilmington give the returning soldier? In spite of best intentions, efforts managed to fall short or linger unattended. The establishment still reigned, having weathered the boom's cycle intact. To some prominent families, leaders, and ordinary citizens, that wartime Wilmington was gone was a relief, an all-clear signal for prewar normalcy sprinkled with a periodic jolt of progressiveness to try staying even with the rest of North Carolina. That was the way

Most of our boys came home, but by my count 191 did not. Welcomed royally for the job they had done, they would experience a mixed local scene which while reverting to prewar institutions still sought to capitalize on its wartime bounty. It took decades for Wilmington to find itself. But for the moment, 1945–46 was for The Homecoming.

Wilmington Morning Star, May 1, 1945
Out Our Way reprinted by permission of
Newspaper Enterprise Association, Inc.

they liked it. Never mind money having been made by being in place at the most propitious of times in a totally seller's market. That the whole world now knew of their "Port City of Progress and Pleasure" was an awareness to be approached cautiously, maybe suspiciously. One small step at a time, and not to have to rush again.

As an example, civic-minded brothers Bruce and Dan Cameron, recently discharged army officers with combat duty from a distinguished business family, in November 1945 proposed something radical: a neighborhood shopping center on the eastern edge of town on Oleander Drive where Independence Boulevard is today. It "is one of the surest signs that Wilmington is really growing up....simply as a notice of intention....It should be a great convenience to residents in that vicinity....There should be no more shacks, such as sprung up beyond the city limits in such great number when the industrial expansion of Wilmington came with the war."[2] Here efforts matched intentions, but the downtown merchants roared. The planning board denied the request.

Change (ergo, each person's definition of "progress") would have to happen slowly, and under control. Having just experienced the turmoil of expediency-driven decisions and actions, Wilmington wanted to cool down. (Eventually the shopping center plan became Hanover Center, the first in town and still thriving.)

In spite of planning, the entire area was confused over its postwar role.[3] A 1945 year-end evaluation determined "all indications are that Wilmington and Southeastern North Carolina has settled down from the 'mining camp' hustle and bustle of the war days and survived the boom period without the deflation predicted by many persons. Real estate trading has been active, and development of new suburban home sites in several locations is announced by local firms. Scarcities in some items such as electrical supplies, automotive equipment and clothing have kept trading below normal demand. Purchasers are anxious to get new cars and refrigerators." And, "fall crops suffered seriously from heavy rains." The postwar area would again rely heavily on agriculture.

"When we came back here after the war it certainly was different from the sleepy little town we had left," engineer and ex-army infantry officer Henry Von Oesen remembered.[4] "Some of the population changed, but the old-timers had never changed. Their thinking was really archaic and not the world as it was today [1945]. A lot of these folks really and truly were not aware that the country around them had changed." But some differences were quite noticeable. "There was very little to offer them [veterans] here in the way of employment."

New Guinea and Philippines veteran Bill Walton returned home to high unemployment because "things had phased down." He like many other former GIs were unofficial members of the so-called "52–20 club"—52 weeks, at $20 per from the government. Men checked in at the employment office, found no jobs, and the office then recertified their eligibility. Walton eventually got a temporary job with his uncle as a carpenter's helper at $25 a week.[5]

The October 1946 Census Bureau report of 47,709 Wilmington residents showed the average one was female, about 25, and probably married, with a husband around 26.[6]

> Chances are that he works and she keeps house, although more than a third of the city's white adult female population either has a job or would like one. The husband would most likely be a craftsman or a clerical worker; his income would be a shade under $40 a week. His wife...would be engaged in a clerical occupation, with salary closer to $30 a week. There's a fair chance that he's a World War II veteran like one-third of Wilmington's white male citizens between the ages of 20 and 44....

"This hypothetical...family" was from a partial abstract of the recent census: 25,204 of residents were females, and well over 60 percent between 20 and 30 are married. Wilmington had a labor force of 20,736 versus 14,875 available in 1940. Workforce males were 19,115, females 6,575. Thirty-five percent of local Negro men were laborers, 22 percent operators with a degree of skill, and 13 percent were skilled craftsmen. In 1940 over half the Negro labor force was considered unskilled common laborers. "Ten months after V-J Day the city was still able to provide jobs for the bulk of its workforce." Unemployed then were 1,260; in 1940, 1,885.

At the end of 1945, the newspaper, citing the county's reluctance to "spend money to make money," stated we were "still backward when it might be leading the state in improvements." The commissioners rejected an idea for a junior college, to float a bond issue for a new tuberculosis sanitarium, and to renovate Legion Stadium ("in a deplorable condition"), and neglected the county home.[7]

Somebody here had money, either "old" or "new," generated or supplemented by wartime. In November 1946 a New York periodical reported that 62 Wilmington residents were worth $100,000 or more—a huge sum for that time—and 311 were worth $50–100,000. "Many changes were wrought by the war in the financial status of individuals throughout the country, some growing richer and some poorer, but Wilmington is still shown to contain a large number of wealthy people," and compared well with other North Carolina cities.[8] But who and when would anyone take the lead in spending it to invest and grow the area they called home?

A new family from out of town moved in across the street from us within a year or so after the war. I remember Mother talking about some unwritten rule that natives didn't "impose themselves" on newcomers until they had been here at least two years—meaning, first let them get used to the way things are done here before saying hello (and getting to know them would take even longer). It may have mattered to adults, even though Mother was normally the friendly type (she was *also Southern*). But for me the new family was an opportunity to expand my budding first business, at age 12 a serious lawn-mowing, weeding, and raking enterprise. At least I did my part to invigorate the business base.

Political change here has been significant. During the war the Democratic Party completely dominated local governments, spurred by overwhelming numbers of registered voters. Many offices were unopposed by Republicans, whose party was virtually nonexistent. This was also the nature of the state and the South for generations. Now, the local Republican Party not only competes but in recent years has held solid majorities on the Board of Commissioners and Board of Education, holds its own on the City Council and mayor's office, and has legislators in the General Assembly in Raleigh. This trend bucks the still-general tendencies of voters to elect Democrats to statewide offices while alternating at the presidential level.

* * *

The accomplishments of the Wilmington area's role in WWII—of which the community obviously is proud—must be preserved, exhibited, and interpreted for future generations as well as those who lived through it. To a large degree this is the purpose of *A Sentimental Journey*. Furthermore, to that end, two recent steps have been taken. The first was the Wartime Wilmington Commemoration, 1999, mentioned in the preface, which honored local men and women who served in uniform and on the home front, and recognized the area's role in the war effort. It was a "last hurrah" for the century's most defining event, and perhaps for many of these folks as well.

The second is the World War II Wilmington Home Front Heritage Coalition Campaign to establish a WWII museum. This four-phased project, supported by privately raised funds, includes working with the city to renovate and restore the 2nd and Orange historic USO building (Community Arts Center) to its 1943 appearance as a living museum; establishment of a cultural heritage trail brochure of area WWII sites; a semi-permanent exhibit in the Cape Fear Museum; and ultimately, a separate museum building. The Community Arts Center Accord, our partner restoring the historic USO, has been at this much longer. At this writing the project is progressing. I am privileged to serve as Coalition chairman.

Notes

PROLOGUE
1. *Wilmington Morning Star*, December 13, 1941.

CHAPTER 1
1. Interview with Gurney J. "Jack" Hufham, July 27, 1999.
2. Interview with Norman E. Davis, May 20, 1999.
3. Clarence Earle Dickinson, Jr. quoted in *Wilmington Morning Star*, July 16, 1942. Hereafter cited as *Star*.
4. *Star*, July 17, 1942.
5. Interview with Victor G. Taylor, April 29, 1999.
6. Interview with Joseph H. "Joe" Johnson, Jr., and Ann Williams Johnson, June 30, 1999.
7. Interview with Mary Emma Gresham, September 30, 1998.
8. Interview with Peggy Moore Perdew, March 18, 1999.
9. Interview with William "Bill" Schwartz, September 25, 1998.
10. Interview with William Nathan "Bill" Kingoff, June 1, 1999.
11. Interview with Addie Lee Gaylord, June 1, 1999.
12. Interview with Laura Roe Fonvielle, August 19, 1999.
13. Interview with McCulloch B. "Mac" Wilson, Jr., March 1, 2000.
14. Interview with Cornelia Nelliemae Haggins Campbell, June 16, 1999.
15. *Star*, December 9, 1941.
16. Ruth Millett quoted in *Star*, January 1, 1943.
17. Millett quoted in *Star*, April 10, 1943.
18. Millett quoted in *Star*, October 27, 1943.
19. Harold D. Meyer quoted in *Star*, September 9, 1943.
20. Roddy Cameron Survey, November 6, 1998.
21. Interview with Evelyn Volk Morris, May 11, 1999.
22. *Star*, May 5, 1944.
23. Interview with Taylor, April 29, 1999.
24. *Star*, December 2, 1943.
25. *Star*, December 7, 1943.
26. *Star*, January 28, 1944.
27. James G. Thornton quoted in *Star*, January 29, 1944.
28. *Star*, March 11, 1944.

29. Interview with Virginia Harriss Holland, May 5, 1999.
30. *Star*, April 13, 1945.
31. *Wilmington Evening Post*, April 12, 1945. Hereafter cited as *Post*.
32. *Wilmington Sunday Star-News*, September 20, 1942. Hereafter cited as *Star-News*.
33. Interview with Joseph Roy "Joe" Reaves, March 10, 1999.
34. Interview with James Madison "Jim" Lee, June 21, 1999.
35. *Star*, January 3, 1942.
36. Interview with Bruce B. Cameron, April 28, 1999.
37. Interview with Richard C. "Dick" Andrews, July 14, 1999.
38. *Star*, August 24, 1944.
39. *Star*, March 30, 1945.
40. *Star-News*, April 29, 1945.
41. *Star*, May 2, 1945.
42. Ibid., May 8, 1945.
43. Ibid., May 8, 1945.
44. Associated Press item in *Star*, May 9, 1945.
45. *Star*, May 9, 1945.
46. *Post*, April 12, 1945.
47. *Star*, August 7, 1945.
48. *Star*, August 15, 1945.
49. Interview with Sally Josey Crawford, April 22, 1999.
50. Interview with Glendy "Glenn" Willard Higgins, June 18, 1999.
51. Interview with Manette Allen Dixon Mintz, April 7, 1999.
52. Interview with Patty Southerland Seitter, April 27, 2000.
53. Interview with Claude Daughtry and Mary Daughtry, October 8, 1998.
54. Interview with Lucretia Thornton McDaniel, February 15, 1999.
55. Evelyn Bergen Loftin e-mail to author, June 6, 1999.
56. Interview with R. E. Corbett, Jr., October 6, 1998.
57. Interview with John H. Debnam, July 13, 1999.
58. Interview with Tabitha Hutaff McEachern, March 8 2000.
59. Interview with George Hutaff McEachern, March 8, 2000.
60. Interview with William F. "Bill" McIlwain, July 6, 1999.
61. Interview with Suwanna Elizabeth "Betty" Henderson Cameron, July 29, 1999.
62. Interview with Bertha Buck and Betty Buck Page, May 12, 1999.
63. Interview with Gibbs Holmes Willard, May 19, 1999.
64. Interview with Jocelyn Peck Strange, June 17, 1999.
65. Interview with Laura Roe Fonvielle, August 19, 1999.
66. Interview with Willie Stanford Leiner, January 28, 1999.
67. Interview with Johnson and Johnson.
68. Interview with Raymond H. Holland, Jr., May 5, 1999.
69. World War II Memoir of Elizabeth Jones Garniss, February 2, 1999.
70. World War II Memoir of Elizabeth Jones Garniss, April 5, 2000.
71. Interview with Mary Cameron Dixon Bellamy, March 31, 1999.
72. Interviews with Hannah (Mrs. Charles C.) Block, July 22 and October 11, 1998.
73. Item of January 20, 1942, in American Legion Post 10 (Wilmington, N.C.) Wartime Scrapbooks. MS Accession #70, William Madison Randall Library, University of North Carolina at Wilmington. Hereafter cited as Post 10 Scrapbooks.

74. Item of December 28, 1941, in Post 10 Scrapbooks.
75. *Star*, May 5, 1942; Items of December 28, 1941, and August 27, 1949, in Post 10 Scrapbooks.

CHAPTER 2

1. Interview with Cecelia Black Corbett, October 6, 1998.
2. Interview with Victor G. Taylor, April 29, 1999.
3. Interview with Louie E. Woodbury III, April 19, 1999. The hill and cliffs still stand undeveloped, although not as imposing as they were in the 1940s.
4. Interview with Ronald G. "Ronnie" Phelps, February 3, 1999.
5. Author's Personal Collection.

CHAPTER 3

1. *Wilmington Morning Star*, July 20, 1942. Hereafter cited as *Star*.
2. *Star*, July 20, 1942.
3. Star, December 19, 1941.
4. *Star* and *Wilmington News*, December 8, 1941.
5. *Star*, December 18, 1941.
6. *Star*, December 11, 1941.
7. *Star*, December 20, 1941.
8. *Star*, January 1, 1942.
9. *Star*, December 13, 1941.
10. *Star*, January 2, 1942.
11. Louise Young quoted in *Star*, December 7, 1942.
12. *Star*, December 16 and 17, 1941.
13. *Star*, January 1, 1942.
14. M'Kean Maffitt quoted in *Star*, December 31, 1941. F. P. O'Crowley eventually replaced Maffitt as city warden, and E. L. White filled that role for the county.
15. *Star*, December 12, 1941.
16. *Star*, December 23, 1941.
17. *Star*, July 25, 1942.
18. *Star*, June 4, 1942.
19. *Star*, July 2, 1943.
20. *Star*, September 10, 1943.
21. *Star*, February 2 and 9, 1944.
22. *Wilmington Sunday Star-News*, December 31, 1944. Hereafter cited as *Star-News*.
23. *Star*, January 1, 1945.
24. Sarah McCulloch Lemmon, *North Carolina's Role in World War II* (Raleigh: State Department of Archives and History, 1964), 50.
25. *Star*, December 18, 1941.
26. Associated Press item quoted in *Star*, July 9, 1942.
27. *Star*, December 1, 1942.
28. *Star*, December 11, 1942.
29. *Star*, May 22, 1943.
30. *Star*, February 2, 1943.
31. *Star*, August 12, 1942.
32. Interview with James Millard "Jim" Fountain, Jr., and Pearl Winner Fountain, March 2, 2000.
33. Lemmon, 51.

34. Interview with Hannah (Mrs. Charles C.) Block, October 22, 1998.
35. Interview with Carlton H. Sprague, April 7, 2002.
36. Interview with Billy Sutton, August 8, 2000.
37. Associated Press item quoted in *Star*, October 26, 1942.
38. *Star*, April 29, 1943.
39. *Star*, November 2, 1943.
40. "The Sinking of the SS *John D. Gill*," Chris Suiter, Southport (N.C.) Historical Society, undated. On March 12, 1994, the Society unveiled a monument to crew members of the tanker *Gill*, torpedoed and sunk off the Cape Fear River near Southport on that day 52 years earlier. This sidebar is from remarks made at the ceremony.

    For additional information on *Gill*'s sinking and the *U-158*, see Homer H. Hickam, Jr., *Torpedo Junction: U-Boat War off America's East Coast, 1942* (Annapolis, Md.: Naval Institute Press, 1989).
41. Interview with Ralph T. Horton, July 27, 1999.
42. *Star*, March 22, 1946.
43. William S. Pritchard quoted in *Star*, October 23, 1943.
44. Catherine Crowe Ragland to author, October 31, 2001.
45. Frances Jordan Wagner to author, April 18, 1999.
46. Interview with George Burrell Byers, May 10, 1999.
47. David W. Carnell in *Star*, July 31, 1998.
48. Carnell to author, May 29, 2000. Carnell, a World War II destroyer officer and retired chemical engineer, researched the plant's history which led to the installation of a state historic marker. He continued: "Next to the Wright brothers flight, the...plant at Kure Beach was...the most important engineering development that occurred in North Carolina. It was the first time in the history of mankind that an element, not a compound such as salt, was extracted from seawater....The Ethyl-Dow plant was unique until Dow duplicated it in Texas."
49. Ben Steelman in *Star-News*, February 4, 2001.

CHAPTER 4

1. *The State* Magazine, Raleigh, North Carolina, September 9, 1944.
2. Clayton Smith e-mail to author, May 23, 1999.
3. Interview with Richard C. "Dick" Andrews, July 14, 1999.
4. Ibid.
5. L. A. Sawyer and W. H. Mitchell, *The Liberty Ships: The History of the 'Emergency' Type Cargo Ships Constructed in the United States During the Second World War, Second Edition* (New York: Lloyds of London Press, 1985), 108-109.
6. *The North Carolina Shipbuilder*, May 1, 1943. Hereafter cited as *Shipbuilder*.
7. *Shipbuilder*, June 1944.
8. *Wilmington Morning Star*, April 27, 1944. Hereafter cited as *Star*.
9. *Star*, December 8, 1944.
10. *Star*, July 8, 1943.
11. Richard L. "Dick" Burnett quoted in *Star*, February 3, 1944.
12. *Star*, September 13, 1944.
13. E. S. Land quoted in *Shipbuilder*, May 1, 1943.
14. *Shipbuilder*, May 1, 1943. NCSC Libertys *Virginia Dare*, *William Moultrie*, and *Nathanial Greene* all received the Maritime Commission's "Gallant Ship Awards" for their heroism and service on the notorious dreaded runs in and out of Murmansk, Russia.
15. *Shipbuilder*, May 1, 1945.
16. *Star*, November 21, 1942.

17. *Star*, December 1 and 2, 1943.
18. W. H. Blakeman quoted in *The State*.
19. Philip "Phil" Dresser Memoir, April 1996.
20. Roger Williams in "Five Years of North Carolina Shipbuilding," North Carolina Shipbuilding Company (May 1, 1946).
21. *Wilmington Sunday Star-News*, November 11, 1945. Hereafter cited as *Star-News*.
22. Alan D. Watson, *Wilmington: Port of North Carolina* (Columbia: University of South Carolina Press, 1992), 156.
23. Industrial Survey of Wilmington and New Hanover County, N.C., Wilmington Industrial Commision, 1941, 15.
24. Interview with Mary Belle Ormond, August 25, 1999.
25. Glenn Hoffman, and Richard E. Bussard, eds., *Building a Great Railroad: A History of the Atlantic Coast Line Railroad Company* (CSX Corporation, 1998), 244-45.
26. Ibid.
27. *Star*, August 9, 1943.
28. George Elliott quoted in ACL advertisement in *Star*, November 3, 1943.
29. *Star*, January 24, 1945.
30. *Star-News*, January 2, 1944.
31. *Star*, April 7, 1943.
32. *Star*, April 9, 1943.
33. *Star*, January 13 and May 31, 1945.
34. *Star*, July 27, 1945.
35. *Star*, November 15, 1946.
36. *Star*, December 20, 1946.
37. John A. Parrish quoted in *Star*, May 23, 1944.
38. *Star-News*, December 7, 1941; *Star*, December 10, 1941.
39. *Shipbuilder*, November 1, 1945.

CHAPTER 5

1. Darrel Ottaway quoted in David A. Stallman, *A History of Camp Davis* (Hampstead, N.C.: Hampstead Services, 1990), 20.
2. Stallman, 3.
3. *The State: A Weekly Survey of North Carolina* magazine, May 31, 1941, quoted in, 4–5.
4. Loney Alberti quoted in Stallman, 20.
5. Charles Jones and Stanley E. Smith, Jr., quoted in Stallman, 21.
6. "Introducing Camp Davis" undated monograph, Fourth Service Command, Camp Davis, N.C. Hereafter cited as "Introducing Camp Davis."
7. Joe Cross Memoir, October 29, 1998.
8. Interview with Muriel Williamson, October 5, 1998.
9. "Introducing Camp Davis."
10. Interview with Justin Raphael, February 8, 1999.
11. *Wilmington Sunday Star-News*, February 17, 1946. Hereafter cited as *Star-News*.
12. Stallman, 20.
13. *Star*, September 17, 1942.
14. *Star*, October 2, 1942.
15. *Star*, October 3, 1942.
16. *Star*, September 29, 1944; *Star-News*, October 1, 1944.

17. Interview with William Nathan "Bill" Kingoff, June 1, 1999.
18. Interview with Helen Swart Simmons and Robert S. "Bob" Swart, August 23, 1999.
19. Interview with Emerson Willard, April 22, 1999.
20. *Star*, February 29 and March 3, 1944.
21. *Star*, March 20 and 28, 2000.
22. Interview with Raymond H. Holland, Jr., and Virginia Harriss Holland, May 5, 1999.
23. *Star-News*, May 14, 1944.
24. Interview with Richard C. "Dick" Andrews, March 14, 1999.
25. *Star*, December 21, 1941.
26. Interview with Robert Doetsch, October 2, 2000.
27. Adrian L. Lawson to author, July 27, 1998.
28. *Camp Davis AA Barrage*, July 22, 1944. Hereafter cited as *Barrage*.
29. Chrysler Corporation in *Star*, October 3, 1946.
30. *Star*, August 27 and 28, 1942.
31. *Star-News*, August 30, 1942.
32. Interview with Richard B. "Dick" Jones, May 27, 2000.
33. *Star-News*, September 26, 1943.
34. *Barrage*, January 22, 1944, quoted in Stallman, 15.

CHAPTER 6

1. Interview with Elizabeth Jones Garniss, May 19, 2000.
2. Interview with Gurney J. "Jack" Hufham, July 27, 1999.
3. Henry J. Emory quoted in *Wilmington Morning Star*, June 17, 1942. Hereafter cited as *Star*.
4. Interview with H. G. Bryant, August 19, 1999.
5. Interview with Mary Cameron Dixon Bellamy, March 31, 1999.
6. Louie E. Woodbury, Jr., quoted in *Star*, March 17, 1944.
7. *Star*, April 6, 1944.
8. *Wilmington Sunday Star-News*, May 3, 1942. Hereafter cited as *Star-News*.
9. *Star*, May 6, 1943.
10. Interview with Addie Lee Gaylord, June 1, 1999.
11. Interview with R. E. Corbett, Jr., October 6, 1998.
12. *Star*, April 14, 1944.
13. *Star*, October 31, 1942.
14. *Star*, February 1, 1943.
15. *Star-News*, January 3, 1943.
16. *Star-News*, June 21, 1942.
17. *Star-News*, February 7, 1943.
18. *Star*, October 13, 1943.
19. Wilbur D. Jones, "Report of the Defense Service Committee," Church of the Covenant Wilmington, N.C., May 22, 1943.
20. *Star*, September 10, 1942; Frederick H. Smith quoted in *Star*, September 12, 1942.
21. Everard H. Smith, *Victory on the Home Front: The USO in New Hanover County, NC, 1941-1946*. Self-published monograph, 1998.
22. *Star*, June 24, 1943.
23. *Star*, March 12, 1945.
24. Kenneth R. Murphy e-mail to author, May 30, 1999.

25. George J. Green to author, October 1, 1998.
26. Interview with Claude Daughtry and Mary Daughtry, October 8, 1998.
27. Interview with Dorothy Ames "Dotty" Harriss Weathersbee, July 22, 1999.
28. Interview with Elizabeth Bell Day, May 4, 1999.
29. Interview with Catherine Ann Solomon, April 6, 1999.
30. Interview with James Madison "Jim" Lee, June 21, 1999.
31. Interview with Caroline Newbold Swails, November 12, 1998.
32. Interview with Millard James "Jim" Fountain, Jr., and Pearl Winner Fountain, March 2, 2000.
33. Interview with W. Eugene "Gene" Edwards, December 9, 1998.
34. Henry R. Emory quoted in *Star*, December 10, 1941.
35. *Star-News*, December 21, 1941.
36. *Star*, June 12, 1945.
37. Jay Jenkins in *Star-News*, December 9, 1945.
38. Earl M. Page memoir.
39. *Star*, July 11 and August 26, 1942.
40. *Star*, January 11, 1945.
41. Jenkins in *Star-News*.
42. *Star*, August 10, 1946.
43. Interview with Perida (Mrs. H. M.) Roland, Dorothy Roland Norako, and Vincent Norako, January 15, 1999; Vincent Norako memoir, December 1980.
44. Interview with Roland, Norako, and Norako, January 15, 1999; interview with Vince Norako, November 6, 1999.

CHAPTER 7

1. *Wilmington Sunday Star-News*, June 10, 1945. Hereafter cited as *Star-News*.
2. Ruth Millett in *Wilmington Morning Star*, May 22, 1943. Hereafter cited as *Star*.
3. "Industrial Survey of Wilmington and New Hanover County, North Carolina," Wilmington Industrial Commission, 1941, 54–55.
4. *Star*, December 16, 1941.
5. *Star*, January 3, 1942.
6. *Star*, August 27, 1942.
7. *Star*, September 12, 1942.
8. H. M. Roland quoted in *Star*, April 17, 1943.
9. *Star*, July 27, 1943.
10. *Star*, September 16, 1943.
11. *Star*, March 16, 1944.
12. *Star-News*, April 29, 1945.
13. "History of Forest Hills School and the PTA," undated paper provided by Forest Hills School; *Star*, August 27, 1942.
14. Interview with Harold P. Laing, July 20, 1999.
15. Receipt from Russian War Relief, Inc., New York City, to Forest Hills School, Wilmington, N.C., June 9, 1944, in Forest Hills PTA records.
16. Interview with Ronald G. "Ronnie" Phelps, February 3, 1999.
17. Interview with Caroline Newbold Swails, November 12, 1998.
18. Interview with Robert F. "Bobby" Cameron, January 11, 1999.
19. Forest Hills School PTA Scrapbook, 1943–44.

20. Interview with Cecelia Black Corbett, October 6, 1998.
21. *Star-News*, March 25, 1945.
22. *Star*, May 22, 1943.
23. *The Hanoverian*, New Hanover High School, 1943.
24. Interview with John J. Burney, Jr., October 20, 1998.
25. *The Wildcat*, New Hanover High School, November 25, 1942. Hereafter cited as *Wildcat*.
26. Interview with Mitchell Saleeby, Jr., February 24, 1999.
27. Interview with Haskell S. Rhett, Jr., May 11, 1999.
28. Interview with Leonard Gleason Allen, April 2, 1999.
29. *Star*, April 29, 1943.
30. Interview with Haskell S. Rhett, Jr., May 11, 1999.
31. Interview with Emma Worth Mitchell Wilcox, February 25, 1999.
32. Interview with Mary Cameron Dixon Bellamy and Heyward C. Bellamy, March 31, 1999.
33. *Star*, May 7, 1943.
34. *Star*, June 5, 1943.
35. *Star*, August 21, 1945.
36. *Wildcat*, December 18, 1941.

CHAPTER 8

1. W. Eugene "Gene" Edwards quoted in *Wilmington Morning Star*, June 16, 1943. Hereafter cited as *Star*; Interview with Edwards, December 9, 1999.
2. *Star*, December 19, 1941.
3. *Star*, July 11, 1945.
4. Interview with Ann Williams Johnson, June 30, 1999.
5. *Star*, May 4, 1942.
6. Interview with Tabitha Hutaff McEachern, March 8, 2000.
7. Star, May 5, 1942.
8. NEA item quoted in *Wilmington News*, December 2, 1942.
9. Interview with Rae West, July 29, 1999.
10. *Wilmington Sunday Star-News*, September 19, 1943. Hereafter cited as *Star-News*.
11. *Star*, February 20, 1945.
12. *Star-News*, December 15, 1945.
13. *Star*, November 2, 1946.
14. *Star*, July 22, 1942.
15. *Star*, August 4, 1942.
16. *Star*, January 12, 1943.
17. *Star*, June 24, 1943.
18. O. H. Shoemaker quoted in *Star*, April 21, 1943.
19. Ruth Vick Everett quoted in *Star*, January 23, 1943.
20. *Star-News*, December 13, 1942.
21. *Star*, January 22, 1943.
22. *Star*, February 25, 1943.
23. *Star*, March 6, 1943.
24. *Star*, February 23, 1943.
25. *Star*, April 6, 1943.
26. *Star*, April 14, 1943.

27. R. W. Galphin quoted in *Star*, December 3, 1943.
28. Interview with Claude Daughtry and Mary Daughtry, October 8, 1998.
29. *Star*, July 4, 1945.
30. Agnes E. Meyer quoted in *Star*, May 12, 1943.
31. *Star*, April 6, 1943.
32. *Star*, April 8, 1943.
33. *Star*, April 9, 1943.
34. *Star*, June 15, 1943.
35. W. D. MacMillan quoted in *Star-News*, October 31, 1943.
36. *Star*, May 5, 1944.
37. Interview with Edwards.
38. Interview with Manette Allen Dixon Mintz and John Mintz, April 7, 1999.
39. Star, October 15, 1943.
40. *Star*, March 5, 1943.
41. *Star*, September 16, 1942.
42. *Star*, April 27, 1944.
43. *Star*, January 6, 1944; Associated Press item quoted in *Star*, June 29, 1944.
44. *Star*, December 16, 1944.

CHAPTER 9

1. *Wilmington Morning Star*, April 29, 1995. Hereafter cited as *Star*.
2. *Star*, July 26, 1943.
3. *Star*, November 4, 1943.
4. *Star*, November 25, 1943.
5. *Star*, January 15, 1944.
6. Interview with Bernard Rabunsky, July 8, 1999.
7. *Star*, January 15, 1944.
8. *Star*, February 9, 1944.
9. *Star*, February 10, 1944.
10. *Wilmington Sunday Star-News*, February 27, 1944. Hereafter cited as *Star-News*.
11. Felix A. Scroggs quoted in *Star*, March 3, 1944.
12. *Star*, March 14, 1944.
13. *Star-News*, April 9, 1944.
14. *Star-News*, April 9, 1944.
15. *Star*, September 13 and 14, 1944.
16. Scroggs quoted in *Star,* September 15, 1944.
17. *Star*, January 16, 1945.
18. Interview with James Otis Sampson, Jr., March 8, 1999.
19. Interview with Cornelia Nelliemae "Nealie" Haggins Campbell, June 16, 1999.
20. Peggy Warren Longmire Memoir of World War II.
21. *Star*, October 3, 1983.
22. *Star-News* Supplement, "Southeastern North Carolina in World War II," 1992.
23. Interview with John D. "Jack" McCarley III, August 25, 1999.
24. Interview with William Charles "Bill" Leeuwenburg, May 28, 1999.
25. Interview with Fred McRee, September 29, 1998.
26. George Dudley Humphrey Survey, November 5, 1998.

27. Interview with Joseph H. "Joe" Johnson, Jr., June 30, 1999.
28. Interview with Robert F. "Bobby" Cameron, January 11, 1999.
29. *Star*, February 16, 1945.
30. Interview with Harold P. Laing, July 20, 1999.
31. *Star*, March 16 and 24, 1945.
32. Interview with George N. Norman, November 18, 1998.
33. R. H. Hazel quoted in *Star-News*, May 6, 1945.
34. *Star-News*, May 6, 1945.
35. Hazel quoted in Ibid.
36. Interview with Peggy Moore Perdew, March 18, 1999.
37. Interview with Janet Rabunsky Everson, July 8, 1999.
38. Interview with Muriel Williamson, October 5, 1998.
39. Interview with Aline Hufham Hartis, February 22, 1999.
40. Undated 1944 article from newspaper (believed *Wilmington News*), in American Legion Post 10 (Wilmington, N.C.) Wartime Scrapbooks. MS Accession #70, William Madison Randall Library, University of North Carolina at Wilmington.
41. Hazel quoted in *Star*, May 10, 1945.
42. Hazel quoted in *Star*, May 26, 1945.
43. Interview with William Nathan "Bill" Kingoff, June 1, 1999.
44. *Star*, March 15, 1946.
45. *Star*, February 27, 1946.
46. *Star*, April 12, 1946.
47. John D. "Jack" McCarley III Collection of Prisoner of War Letters of World War II.

CHAPTER 10

1. *Wilmington Morning Star*, November 18, 1942. Hereafter cited as *Star*.
2. *Star*, April 18, 1944.
3. *Star*, August 30, 1944, January 7 and 18, 1945.
4. *Star*, November 4, 1943.
5. *Star*, June 11, 1943.
6. *Star*, February 3, 1945.
7. *Star*, September 23, 1944.
8. *Star*, May 2, 1944; *Wilmington Sunday Star-News*, May 28, 1944. Hereafter cited as *Star-News*.
9. *Star*, August 11 and 29, October 7, 1944; *Star-News*, May 2 and 20, 1945.
10. *Star*, July 23, 1942.
11. *Star*, August 2, 1944.
12. *Star*, January 12, 1943.
13. *Star*, March 18, 1944.
14. *Star*, August 8, 1944.
15. *Star*, December 27, 1944.
16. *Star*, January 12, 1943.
17. *Star*, January 14, 1943.
18. *Star*, July 8, 9, 10, 1942.
19. *Star-News*, September 27, 1942; *Star*, October 1 and November 13, 1942.
20. *Star*, July 31, 1942.
21. *Star*, December 9, 1941.

22. *Star*, July 31, 1942.
23. *Star-News*, July 25, 1943; *Star*, July 27, 1943.
24. *Star*, August 21 and October 4, 1944.
25. *Star-News*, February 14, 1943.
26. *Star*, July 19, 1942.
27. *Star*, August 30, 1943.
28. *Star*, March 17, 1943.
29. *Star*, January 28, 1944.
30. *Star*, August 8 and 12, 1944.
31. *Star*, December 13, 1941.
32. *Star*, March 24, 1943.
33. *Star*, May 4, 1943.
34. Interview with Richard V. "Dick" Hanson, April 1, 1999.
35. Interview with Heyward C. Bellamy, March 31, 1999.
36. Interview with Catherine Russell Stribling, October 28, 1998.
37. Interview with W. Eugene "Gene" Edwards, December 9, 1998.
38. *Star* July 1942 edition quoted in, and Smith research, in Everard H. Smith, *Victory on the Home Front: The USO in New Hanover County, N.C., 1941–1946*. Self-published monograph, 1998.
39. Edgar H. Bain quoted in *Star*, February 25, 1944.
40. *Star-News*, January 17, 1943.
41. John J. Burney quoted in *Star*, February 23, 1943.
42. *Star-News*, March 5, 1944; *Star*, March 24, 1944.
43. Alton A. Lennon quoted in *Star*, July 18, 1942.
44. *Star*, November 19, 1943.
45. *Star*, July 20, 1943.
46. *Star*, July 21, 1943.
47. *Star*, November 19, 1943.
48. *Star*, January 22, 1945.
49. *Star*, December 2, 1945.
50. *Star*, May 4, 1946.
51. *Star-News*, November 1, 1942.
52. *Star*, September 27, 1944.
53. *Star*, December 22, 1942.
54. *Star*, December 20, 1944.
55. *Star*, November 13 and 17, 1944.
56. *Star*, December 19, 1944.
57. *Star*, March 2, 1945.
58. *Star*, March 28 and 29, 1944.
59. *Star*, March 17, 1944.
60. *Star*, September 27, 1944.
61. *Star*, June 4, 1942.
62. *Star-News*, January 3, 1943.
63. *Star*, October 1, 1943.
64. *Star*, January 6, 1944.
65. *Star*, January 8, 1944.
66. *Star*, July 20, 1944.

67. *Star*, May 3, 1944.
68. *Star*, June 6, 1944.
69. *Star-News*, August 6, 1944.
70. *Star*, June 6, 1945.
71. *Star*, July 20, 1945.
72. *Star-News*, March 24, 1946.
73. *Star*, April 8, 1946.
74. *Star*, April 9, 1946.
75. *Star*, April 10, 1946.
76. *Star*, October 25, 1946.

CHAPTER 11

1. World War II Memoirs of Elizabeth Jones Garniss, February 2, 1999, and April 5, 2000; interview with Garniss, May 19, 2000.
2. Ruth Millett quoted in *Wilmington Morning Star*, September 17, 1943. Hereafter cited as *Star*.
3. Millett in *Star*, January 27, 1943.
4. Interview with Frances Coughenour Dinsmore, June 29, 2000.
5. Interview with Lottie "Clara" Marshburn Welker, October 2, 1998.
6. *Wilmington Sunday Star-News*, April 11 and June 27, 1943. Hereafter cited as *Star-News*.
7. Interview with Dorothy Bunn Dibble, April 6 and August 28, 1999.
8. *Star-News*, September 29, 1946.
9. Interview with Henry Von Oesen, January 19, 1999.
10. Interview with Joseph W. "Joe" Whitted and Lucilla White Whitted, June 18, 1999.
11. Interview with Estelle Owens Edwards, August 23, 1999; *Star-News*, January 3, 1943.
12. Robert P. Edwards to Mr. and Mrs. Robert E. Owens, January 29, 1943. Provided by daughter Beth Edwards Wooten.
13. Interview with William "Bill" Schwartz and Bernice Schwartz, September 25, 1998.
14. Interview with Sally Josey Crawford, April 22, 1999.
15. Interview with Libby Goldberg O'Quinn, April 21, 1999.
16. Interview with Evelyn Volk Morris and Clifford Cohen Morris, Jr., May 11, 1999; *Wilmington Evening Post*, May 23, 1945.
17. Interview with Sylvester "Buddy" Adkins and Carrie Congleton Adkins, October 28, 1998.
18. Interview with Suwanna Elizabeth "Betty" Henderson Cameron and Daniel D. "Dan" Cameron, July 28, 1999.
19. Interview with Janet Rabunsky Everson, July 8, 1999.
20. Interview with Miles C. Higgins and Glendy "Glenn" Willard Higgins, June 18, 1999.
21. Interview with Aaron May and Norma May, March 1, 2000.
22. Mary Cameron Dixon to Heyward C. Bellamy, June 14, 1943.
23. Interview with George Burrell Byers and Katherine Harriss Byers, May 10, 1999; Byers to Katherine Harriss, September 24, 1943. Wartime Letters of George Burrell Byers to Katherine Harriss. Hereafter cited as Byers Letters.
24. Byers to Harriss, August 29, 1943. Byers Letters.
25. Associated Press report in *Star-News*, November 12, 1944.
26. Millett in *Star*, March 29, 1944.
27. *Star*, August 22, 1945.
28. Donald J. Bailey to the Bethells, April 15, 1945. World War II Letters of Mary Eloise Bethel, Lower Cape Fear Historical Society.

29. Millett in *Star*, January 27, 1943.
30. Elizabeth Jones Garniss Memoirs; interview with Garniss, May 19, 2000.
31. George H. Garniss Memories of Wilmington During World War II, April 2, 2000.

CHAPTER 12

1. Interview with Eleanor "Elkie" Burgwin Fick, June 23, 2000.
2. Interview with Lottie "Clara" Marshburn Welker, October 2, 1998.
3. Interview with Muriel Williamson, October 5, 1998.
4. Interview with Justin Raphael, February 8, 1999.
5. Marie Burgwin Sanborn e-mail to author, October 28, 1998.
6. Hannah Block quoted in *Wilmington Morning Star*, December 6, 1991. Hereafter cited as *Star*.
7. Interview with Joseph Roy "Joe" Reaves, March 10, 1999.
8. Interview with John W. "Bill" Walton, Jr., August 19, 1998.
9. *Star*, June 12, 1943.
10. *Star*, May 2, 1942.
11. Interview with Hannah Block, July 22, 1998.
12. *Wilmington Sunday Star-News*, January 31, 1943. Hereafter cited as *Star-News*.
13. *Star-News*, November 21, 1943.
14. *Star*, November 1, 1943.
15. *Star*, November 6, 1943.
16. *Star*, April 17, 1944.
17. Interview with Peggy Moore Perdew, March 18, 1999.
18. Interview with Sally Josey Crawford, April 22, 1999.
19. Interview with Laura Roe Fonvielle, August 19, 1999.
20. Interview with Manette Allen Dixon Mintz and John Mintz, April 7, 1999.
21. Claude Daughtry and Mary Daughtry e-mail to author, October 9, 1998.
22. Interview with Betty Bugg Crouch, January 28, 1999.
23. Interview with William F. "Bill" McIlwain, August 2, 1999; McIlwain to parents, September 2, 1944. Wartime Letters of William F. McIlwain, Jr. Provided by McIlwain.
24. Interview with John H. Debnam, July 13, 1999.
25. Interview with Haskell S. Rhett, Jr., May 11, 1999.
26. Interview with Henry Von Oesen, January 19, 1999.
27. Interview with Crawford.
28. *Star-News*, December 5, 1943; *Star*, February 27, 1944.
29. *Star*, May 20, 1944.
30. Interview with Ray Funderburk, May 24, 1999.
31. April Henderson in *Wilmington Evening Post*, May 23, 1945. Hereafter cited as *Post*.
32. Interview with Millard James "Jim" Fountain, Jr., and Pearl Winner Fountain, March 2, 2000.
33. *Star*, May 4, 1942.
34. Interview with Block, July 22, 1998.
35. Henderson in *Post*.
36. *Star*, September 22, 1944.
37. Interview with Jocelyn Peck Strange, June 17, 1999.
38. Interview with Kathleen Somersett, April 30, 1999.

39. Interview with Williamson.
40. Frances Jordan Wagner to author, April 18, 1999.
41. *Star*, July 26, 1944.
42. *Star*, September 10, 1943.
43. Interview with Hannah Block, July 20, 1998.
44. Interview with Block, July 22, 1998.
45. *Star*, September 8, 1944.

CHAPTER 13

1. *Wilmington Sunday Star-News*, January 23, 1944. Hereafter cited as *Star-News*.
2. Interview with Mary Belle Ormond, August 25, 1999.
3. Mrs. Eddie Rickenbacker quoted in *Wilmington Morning Star*, June 19, 1942. Hereafter cited as *Star*.
4. *Star-News*, December 14, 1941.
5. Interview with Kathleen Somersett, April 30, 1999.
6. Catherine Russell Stribling memoir, October 28, 1998.
7. *Star*, September 16, 1942; *Star-News*, February 7 and 8, 1943.
8. *Star*, June 10, 1942.
9. *Star*, June 20, 1942.
10. Interview with Somersett.
11. Lillian M. George quoted in *Star-News*, March 18, 1945.
12. Hattie E. "Kitty" Bass quoted in *Star*, June 14, 1945.
13. *Star*, September 25, 1945.
14. *Star*, August 17, 1942, and January 31, 1943.
15. Interview with Caroline Newbold Swails, November 12, 1998.
16. Interview with Mary Cameron Dixon Bellamy, March 31, 1999.
17. Mrs. Albert Perry quoted in *Star*, January 20, 1943.
18. *Star*, February 25, 1944.
19. *Star*, April 4, 1944.
20. *Star*, October 30, 1942.
21. *Star*, April 21, 1943.
22. Interview with Peggy Moore Perdew, March 18, 1999.
23. Felix A. Scroggs quoted in *Star*, November 12, 1942.
24. Ruth Millett in *Star*, July 11, 1943.
25. World War II Wilmington Memoir of Elizabeth Jones Garniss, February 2, 1999.
26. Interview with Suwanna Elizabeth "Betty" Henderson Cameron, July 28, 1999.
27. *Camp Davis AA Barrage*, July 22, 1944.
28. *Star*, September 10, 1945.

CHAPTER 14

1. *Wilmington Morning Star*, August 4, 1942. Hereafter cited as *Star*.
2. Bertha Todd presentation at Chestnut Street Presbyterian Church, August 22, 1999.
3. Jesse Helms in *Star*, June 8, 1942.
4. *Star*, July 13, 1942.
5. Interview with Derick G. S. Davis, November 17, 1998.
6. Interview with William T. "Bill" Childs, October 28, 1998.

7. Interview with James Otis Sampson, Jr., March 8, 1999.
8. *Cape Fear Journal*, November 29, 1942.
9. *The North Carolina Shipbuilder*, North Carolina Shipbuilding Company, April 1, 1945.
10. Interview with James E. Whitted, October 8, 1998.
11. Interview with Childs.
12. Interview with Davis.
13. Interviews with Edward "Ed" "Pat" George, July 29, 1998; and January 3, 2000.
14. *Wilmington Sunday Star-News*, July 11, 1943.
15. *Star*, July 12, 1943.
16. Interview with Whitted.
17. Interview with George, July 29, 1998.
18. Robert Pierce quoted in Everard H. Smith, *Victory on the Home Front: The USO in New Hanover County, N.C., 1941–1946*. Self-published monograph, 1998.
19. Margaret Sampson Rogers memoir, "Local Blacks and the Local Scene." July 1998; interview with Rogers, July 30, 1998.
20. Interview with Cornelia Nelliemae "Nealie" Haggins Campbell, June 16, 1999.
21. Interview with George N. Norman, November 18, 1998.
22. Peggy Pridgen presentation, Chestnut Street Presbyterian Church, August 22, 1999.
23. "Seabreeze: A Heritage Renewed." Monograph, New Hanover County [N.C.] Planning Department, 1988.
24. Interview with Campbell.
25. *Star*, June 5, 1943.
26. *Star*, May 14, 1944.
27. *Star*, July 4, 1944.
28. Interview with Sampson.
29. *The Wildcat*, New Hanover High School, February 25, 1943.
30. *Star*, June 9, 1945.
31. Interview with Childs.
32. *Star*, February 3, 1944.
33. *Camp Davis AA Barrage*, June 24, 1944. Hereafter cited as *Barrage*.
34. *Star-News*, March 28, 1943.
35. *Barrage*, July 22, 1944.
36. Interview with Campbell.

CHAPTER 15

1. *Wilmington Morning Star*, January 1, 1943. Hereafter cited as *Star*.
2. *Star*, January 1, 1943.
3. Louise Young in *Wilmington Morning Star*, December 7, 1942.
4. *Star*, September 22, 1943.
5. *Star*, December 13, 1941.
6. *Wilmington Sunday Star-News*, December 14, 1941. Hereafter cited as *Star-News*.
7. Interview with Lucretia Thornton McDaniel, July 13, 2000; *Star-News*, September 20, 1942.
8. *Star*, July 2, 1942.
9. *Star-News*, June 3, 1945.
10. *Star*, July 2, 1943.
11. *Star*, June 13, 1944.
12. Colonel Dyke F. Meyer quoted in *Star*, September 8, 1943.

13. *Star-News*, January 16, 1944; *Star,* January 19, 1944.
14. *Star*, June 16, 1945.
15. "Civilian Employee Orientation Booklet," Army Service Forces, Camp Davis, N.C., 1944.
16. *Star*, April 9, 1943.
17. *Star*, December 11, 1943.
18. James G. Thornton quoted in *Star*, October 4, 1944.
19. *Star*, February 18, 1944.
20. *Star*, October 7, 1942.
21. *Star*, December 10, 1944.
22. *Star*, December 8, 1945.
23. *Star*, December 7, 1943.
24. Associated Press item quoted in *Star*, October 20, 1942.
25. *Star-News*, October 8, 1944.
26. William G. "Billy" Broadfoot, Jr., to his parents, January 27, 1945. Wartime Letters of William G. Broadfoot, Jr.
27. Evelyn Bergen Loftin e-mail to author, June 6, 1999.
28. Peggy Warren Longmire interview with J. V. "Pat" Warren, September 1998. Provided by Longmire.
29. Mary Fisher Eason to author, January 5, 2000.
30. Interview with John D. "Jack" McCarley III, August 25, 1999.
31. Interview with Bessie Burton Swart, Helen Swart Simmons, James Edward Swart, Bettye Rivenbark Swart, and Robert S. Swart, August 23, 1999.
32. *Star*, April 15, 1943.
33. *Star*, May 17, 1945.
34. *Star*, August 8, 1944.
35. *Star-News*, February 4, 1945; *Star*, February 7, 1945.
36. *Star*, February 7, 1943.
37. *Star*, January 1, 1944.
38. Ibid.
39. F. O. Fockler quoted in *Star*, January 1, 1944.
40. *Camp Davis AA Barrage*, July 22, 1944.

CHAPTER 16

1. *Wilmington Sunday Star-News*, October 8, 1944. Hereafter cited as *Star-News*.
2. George Burrell Byers to Katharine Harriss, June 5, 1945. Wartime Letters of George Burrell Byers to Katharine Harriss. Hereafter cited as Byers Letters.
3. Byers to Harriss, January 28, 1945. Byers Letters.
4. Wilson Welch quoted in *Wilmington Morning Star*, December 13, 1941. Hereafter cited as *Star*.
5. *Star*, April 23, 1943.
6. University of North Carolina newsletter cited in *Star*, December 8, 1945.
7. Clarence Earle Dickinson, Jr., quoted in *Star*, July 16, 1942.
8. Clarence Earle Dickinson, Jr. and Boyden Sparks, *The Flying Guns: Cockpit Record of a Naval Pilot from Pearl Harbor through Midway* (New York: Charles Scribner's Sons, 1942) 153-55.
9. Dickinson quoted in *Star*.
10. Samuel Eliot Morison, *History of United States Naval Operations in World War II (vol. 3, The Rising Sun in the Pacific, 1931–April 1942* (Boston: Little, Brown and Co., 1951), 217

11. Records of Decorations, World War II, Naval Historical Center.
12. Lowell Thomas, *These Men Shall Never Die* (Philadelphia: John C. Winston Co., 1943), quoted in *Wilmington Sunday Star-News*, November 21, 1943. Hereafter cited as *Star-News*.
13. *Star-News*, January 16, 1944.
14. Clark Lee, *They Call It Pacific: An Eyewitness Story of Our War against Japan from Bataan to the Solomons* (New York: Viking Press, 1943), 314–16.
15. Interview with Henry Von Oesen, June 27, 2000.
16. Interview with Harry Stovall, June 29, 2000.
17. Interview with Margaret Banck, June 28, 2000.
18. Interview with Bruce B. Cameron, July 6, 2000.
19. Leatrice R. Arakaki and John R. Kuborn, *7 December 1941: The Air Force Story* (Hickam Air Force Base, Hawaii: Pacific Air Forces, 1991), 137.
20. Brooke E. Allen quoted in *Star*, August 6, 1942.
21. *Star*, September 1, 16, and 19, 1943; and November 19, 1942.
22. *Star-News*, June 10, 1945.
23. *Star-News*, September 25, 1945.
24. Charles P. Murray, Jr., and Anniemae King Murray quoted in *Star*, June 9, 1945.
25. Ibid., June 9, 1945.
26. *Star*, September 25 and 26, 1945.
27. Murray, Jr., and various sources.
28. Interview with Murray, Jr., April 9, 1999.
29. Interview with Murray.
30. Interview with John J. Burney, Jr., February 3, 1999.
31. Interview with Murray.
32. Interview with McCulloch B. "Mac" Wilson, Jr., March 1, 2000.
33. *Star*, June 16, 1945.
34. Interview with Laura Roe Fonvielle, August 19, 1999.
35. Interview with Emma Worth Mitchell Wilcox, February 25, 1999.
36. *Star*, May 14 and 31, 1946.
37. Various sources.
38. *Star*, August 3, 1943.

EPILOGUE

1. *Wilmington Morning Star*, July 30, 1945. Hereafter cited as *Star*.
2. *Star*, November 23, 1945.
3. Meares Harriss in *Star*, December 31, 1945.
4. Interview with Henry Von Oesen, January 19, 1999.
5. Interview with John W. "Bill" Walton, Jr., August 19, 1998.
6. *Star*, October 26, 1946.
7. *Star*, December 12, 1945.
8. *Star*, November 22, 1946.

Glossary

A-bomb—Atomic bombs dropped on Hiroshima and Nagasaki, Japan, August 6 and 9, 1945

AA—Anti-aircraft

AAA—Anti-aircraft artillery

AAF (USAAF)—(U.S.) Army Air Forces

ABC—Alcoholic Beverage Control (state agency)

ACL—Atlantic Coast Line Railroad

AEF—American Expeditionary Force

AKA/aka—Attack cargo ship (C-2 hull); also known as

AME—African Methodist Episcopal church

AP—Associated Press

Armed Forces—The U.S. military and naval establishment, including army (and army air forces), navy, Marine Corps, Coast Guard

ASF—Army Service Forces

ASW—Anti-submarine warfare

A&T—North Carolina Agricultural and Technical College (Negro), Greensboro.

AWOL—Absent without leave (from military)

AWS—Aircraft Warning Service (Corps)

(the) bomb—See A-bomb

BAAB—Bluethenthal (Field) Army Air Base

BOQ—Bachelor officers quarters

CA—Coast artillery

CAP—Civil Air Patrol

CBS—Columbia Broadcasting System

CD—Civilian defense

CIO—Congress of Industrial Organizations
C.O.—Commanding officer
Coast Line—See ACL
colored—See Negro
Davis—Camp Davis
D-Day—Date of an amphibious landing; at Normandy, France, June 6, 1944
D+2—The second day after D-Day
dinner—Southern for noon meal (lunch)
DFC—Distinguished Flying Cross
DNB—Died from non-battle causes
DSC—Distinguished Service Cross (army)
duration—Until the war is over
EWT—Eastern war time
FBI—Federal Bureau of Investigation
FDR—President Franklin Delano Roosevelt
4-F—Rejected for military service for physical incapacity
GI—Nickname for army/army air forces soldiers; also generic name for armed forces personnel
GMC—General Motors Corporation (truck)
grammar school—(grades 1-8) Today's elementary school
gyrene—United States Marine nickname
IJN—Imperial Japanese Navy (ship)
HACOW—Housing Authority of the City of Wilmington
here—Wilmington and New Hanover County area
'hot-bunking (bedding)"—Use of the same bed in a rooming house by defense shift workers
HRO—Housing Registration Office
(the) Hut—Woodrow Wilson Hut Servicemen's club
jukebox—Commercial record-playing machine
JWMH (James Walker)—James Walker Memorial Hospital
KIA—Killed in action
KP—Kitchen police duty
liberty—Navy and Marine term for authorized free time away from duty station

Liberty ship—Cargo merchant ship (C-1 hull) built in Wilmington for the Maritime Commission
LST—Navy landing ship, tank
Lumina—The Lumina pavilion, Wrightsville Beach
MIA—Missing in action
military—Usually the army (soldiers), but sometimes means armed forces in general
MM—U.S. Merchant Marine
MP—Military police
(the) newspaper—*Wilmington Morning Star/News/Sunday Star-News* (same publisher, one a.m., one p.m., one Sunday)
NAACP—National Association for Advancement of Colored People
NBC—National Broadcasting Company
NCO—Noncommissioned officer (military)
NCSC—North Carolina Shipbuilding Company
Negro—African American/black, also colored
Negress—Female Negro
NHHS—New Hanover High School (also New Hanover)
NYA—National Youth Administration
OCD—Office of Civilian Defense (New Hanover County)
OCS—Officer candidate school
OLC—Oak Leaf Cluster (for multiple awards of same decoration)
OPA—U.S. Office of Price Administration
party line—Operator-dialed phone service serving multiple customers; you waited your turn, or listened in
PFC—Private first class
piccolo joint—Jukebox, beer, and snack hangout
POW(s)/PW—Prisoner(s) of war
PT boats—U.S. patrol torpedo boats
PX—Military post exchange (store)
(the) railroad—See ACL
ROTC—Reserve Officers Training Corps
R&R—Rest and relaxation
Seaboard—Seaboard Air Line Railroad
(the) shipyard—See NCSC

Star-News—See (the) newspaper
States/Stateside—Back in the continental United States
supper—Southern for evening meal
TB—Tuberculosis
TWPC—Tide Water Power Company
U-boat—German submarine
UNC—University of North Carolina (Chapel Hill)
USA—United States Army
USCGC—U.S. Coast Guard cutter
USMC—United States Marine Corps
USN—United States Navy
USO—United Service Organizations
(the) USO—Any USO club; specifically the one at 2nd and Orange Streets
USES—U.S. Employment Service
USS—United States Ship
VD—Venereal ("social") disease
V-E Day—Victory in Europe, May 8, 1945
V-J Day—Victory over Japan, August 14, 1945 (U.S. time) (some historians cite September 2, the day the peace treaty was signed)
VMF—Marine Corps fighter squadron
WAAF—Women's Auxiliary Air Force
WAAC—Women's Army Auxiliary Corps (forerunner to WAC)
WAC—Women's Army Corps
WAR—Wilmington Air Region
WASPs—Women's Airforce Service Pilots
WAVES—Women Accepted for Volunteer Service (navy)
WC—Women's College of the UNC, Greensboro
WFD—Wilmington Fire Department
WHC—War Housing Center (Wilmington)
Williston—See WIS
WIS—Williston Industrial (High) School
WLI—Wilmington Light Infantry
wolf whistles—sharp, short lip whistle blasts by a male on seeing an attractive female nearby
WPA—Works Progress Administration

WPB—U.S. War Production Board
WPD—Wilmington Police Department
YMCA—Young Men's Christian Association
YMS—Navy small minesweeper
YP—Navy patrol craft
YWCA—Young Women's Christian Association

Bibliography

Interviews

Adkins, Carrie Congleton—October 28, 1998
Adkins, Sylvester "Buddy"—October 28, 1998
Alberti, Herman G.—November 4, 1998
Allen, Leonard Gleason—April 2, 1999
Alexius, Harold D.—July 3, 2000
Allsbrook, Elizabeth—June 16, 1999
Andrews, Richard C. "Dick"—July 14, 1999
Banck, Margaret—June 28, 2000
Bellamy, Heyward C.—March 31, 1999
Bellamy, Mary Cameron Dixon March 31, 1999
Benton, Hulon—December 2, 1998
Black, Catherine—October 6, 1998
Black, D. J. "Jackie," II—October 6, 1998
Blake, Donald P. "Don"—May 5, 1999
Block, Hannah (Mrs. Charles C.)—July 20 and 22, 1998; October 11, 1998
Boylan, George S.—January 28, 1999
Boylan, Louise Washburn—January 28, 1999
Broadfoot, Mary Bason—February 24, 1999
Broadfoot, William G. "Billy," Jr.—February 24, 1999; January 26, 2000
Brown, Gladys—December 2, 1998; August 20, 2000
Bryant, H. G.—August 19, 1999
Buck, Bertha—May 12, 1999
Burnett, Gilbert—November 6, 1998
Burney, John J., Jr.—October 20, 1998; February 3, 1999
Burney, Louis A.—October 20, 1998
Byers, George Burrell—May 10, 1999
Byers, Katharine Harriss—May 10, 1999
Cameron, Bruce B., Jr.—April 28, 1999; July 6, 2000
Cameron, Daniel David "Dan"—February 1, 1999; July 28, 1999

Cameron, Robert F. "Bobby"—January 11, 1999
Cameron, Suwanna Elizabeth "Betty" Henderson—July 28, 1999
Campbell, Cornelia Nelliemae "Nealie" Haggins—June 16, 1999
Cantwell, Betty Garrabrant—July 30, 1998
Cantwell, Robert C. "Bob," III—July 30, 1998
Chavers, James D.—February 19, 1999
Childs, William T. "Bill"—October 28, 1998; July 11, 2000
Clayton, John E., Jr.—July 28, 1999
Clayton, Ruth Middleton—July 28, 1999
Copeland, Clara—May 28, 1999
Corbett, Cecelia Black—October 6, 1998
Corbett, R. E., Jr.—October 6, 1998
Crawford, Sally Josey—April 22, 1999
Creech, Judson Y.—June 16, 2000
Cross, Eva Sanders—June 11, 1999
Crouch, Betty Bugg—January 28, 1999
Daughtry, Claude—October 8, 1998
Daughtry, Mary—October 8, 1998
Davis, Derick G. S.—November 17, 1998
Davis, Lee Lewis—May 20, 1999
Davis, Norman E.—May 20, 1999
Day, Elizabeth Bell—May 4, 1999
Day, Fred N., III—May 4, 1999
Debnam, John H.—July 13, 1999
Dickinson, Sarah—July 5, 2000
Dibble, Dorothy Bunn—April 6, 1999
Doetsch, Robert "Bob"—October 2, 2000
Eagles, Betty Sparks—June 3, 2002
Eason, Frank Delane—January 22, 2000
Edwards, Estelle Owens—August 23, 1999
Edwards, Thurston Eugene "Gene"—June 19, 2000
Edwards, W. Eugene "Gene"—December 9, 1998; July 6, 2001
Everson, Janet Rabunsky—July 8, 1999
Fick, Eleanor "Elkie" Burgwin—June 22 and 23, 2000
Fokakis, George T.—June 12, 2000
Fokakis, Nichalos T.—June 12, 2000
Fonvielle, Laura Roe—August 19, 1999
Fountain, Millard James "Jim," Jr.—March 9, 2000
Fountain, Pearl Winner—March 2, 2000
Fox, Mary Daniel Carr—June 1, 1999
Funderburk, Ray—May 24, 1999

Fussell, Harold—June 22, 1999
Garniss, Elizabeth Jones—May 19, 2000
Garrabrant, Marjorie "Margie"—November 2, 2000
Gaylord, Addie Lee—June 1, 1999
George, Edward "Ed" "Pat"—July 29, 1998; January 3, 2000
George, Parthenia—July 29, 1998
Gideon, J. C.—May 10, 1999
Gigax, Vernon—August 20, 2000
Glover, Lucy Ann Carney—January 15, 1999
Gordon, Diane Snakenburg—February 4, 2001
Gordon, Frank—February 4, 2001
Gore, Isabell Russell—June 18, 1999
Graham, Jean McKoy—May 6, 1999
Grant, Oscar—May 26, 2000
Gresham, Mary Emma—September 30, 1998
Gresham, Sam T., Jr.—September 30, 1998
Hanson, Richard V. "Dick"—April 1, 1999
Hardy, Gladys—August 20, 2000
Hart, Jack F.—September 2, 1998
Hart, Joy—September 2, 1998
Hartis, Aline Hufham Spencer—February 22, 1999; April 1, 1999
Hartis, Herman—February 22, 1999
Headquist, Percy—July 28, 1999
Hewlett, Margaret Tiencken—September 14, 1998
Higgins, Glendy "Glenn" Willard—June 18, 1999
Higgins, Miles C. Higgins—June 18, 1999
Holland, Raymond H., Jr—May 5, 1999
Holland, Virginia Harriss—May 5, 1999
Hood, Mary Elizabeth—September 4, 1998
Horton, Ralph T.—July 27, 1999
Hufham, Gurney J. "Jack"—July 27, 1999
Humphrey, Eloise B.—September 7, 1998
Humphrey, L. W. "Billy," Jr.—September 7 and 30, 1998; May 17, 2000
Hutteman, Ann Hewlett—September 14, 1998
Johnson, Ann Williams—June 30, 1999
Johnson, Joseph H. "Joe," Jr.—June 30, 1999
Jones, Richard B. "Dick"—May 27, 2000
Kearney, Peggy Jones—June 12, 2000
Kingoff, William Nathan "Bill"—June 1, 1999
Knox, Joseph C. "Joe," Jr.—May 21, 1999; January 23, 2000
Laing, Harold P.—July 20, 1999

Lee, James Madison "Jim"—June 21, 1999
Leeuwenburg, Carol Bunch—May 28, 1999
Leeuwenburg, William Charles "Bill"—May 28, 1999; July 24, 2000
Leiner, Willie Stanford—January 28, 1999
Lynch, Thomas—July 22, 1999
McCarley, John D. "Jack," III—August 25, 1999
McDaniel, Lucretia Thornton—February 15, 1999; July 13, 2000
McEachern, George Hutaff—March 8, 2000
McEachern, Tabitha Hutaff—March 8, 2000
McFadden, Leroy—July 27, 2000
McIlwain, William F. "Bill"—July 6, 1999; August 2, 1999
McIver, Malcolm—July 25, 2000
McRee, Fred—September 29, 1998
Mann, Harry—March 8, 2000
May, Aaron—March 1, 2000
May, Norma—March 1, 2000
Meier, Tanky—June 24, 2000
Metts, John Van B.—April 12, 1999
Michaelis, John Frederick "Mike"—May 19, 1999
Mintz, John—April 7, 1999
Mintz, Manette Allen Dixon—April 7, 1999
Morris, Clifford Cohen "Cliff," Jr.—May 11, 1999
Morris, Evelyn Volk—May 11, 1999
Murray, Charles P. "Chuck," Jr.—April 9, 1999
Norako, Dorothy—January 15, 1999
Norako, Vincent—November 6, 1998; January 15, 1999
Norman, George N.—November 18, 1998
O'Quinn, Libby Goldberg—April 21, 1999
Ormand, Mary Belle—August 25, 1999
Page, Betty Buck—May 12, 1999
Pennington, Anna Feenstra—February 23, 1999
Pennington, James C. "Skinny"—February 23, 1999
Perdew, Peggy Moore—March 18, 1999
Phelps, Ronald G. "Ronnie"—January 27, 1999; February 3, 1999; May 17, 2000
Pollock, Robert S. "Rob"—October 29, 1998
Rabunsky, Bernard—July 8, 1999
Raphael, Justin—February 8, 1999
Raphael, Shirley Berger—February 8, 1999
Reaves, Joseph Roy "Joe"—March 10, 1999
Rehder, Stanley—October 29, 1998
Renstrom, Keith—February 20, 1999

Retchin, Daniel D. "Dan"—May 27, 1999
Reynolds, Frances Thornton—February 15, 1999
Rhett, Haskell S., Jr.—May 11, 1999
Rogers, Margaret Sampson—July 30, 1998
Roland, Perida (Mrs. H. M.)—January 15, 1999
Rountree, George, III—April 14, 1999
Saleeby, Mitchell "Mitch," Jr.—February 24, 1999
Sampson, James Otis, Jr.—March 8, 1999
Schwartz, Bernice—September 25, 1998
Schwartz, William "Bill"—September 25, 1998
Seitter, Patty Southerland—April 27, 2000
Simmons, Helen Swart—August 23, 1999
Sinclair, Myrtle Reynolds—August 10, 1999
Sinclair, R. T. "Tom," Jr.—August 10, 1999
Sistrunk, Simpson Fuller, Jr.—August 18, 1999
Smith, Clayton—May 21, 1999
Sneeden, Blanche Stanley—January 13, 1999
Solomon, Catherine Ann—April 6, 1999
Somersett, Kathleen—April 30, 1999
Stein, Leon—May 27, 1999
Sternberger, Frederick B.—May 25, 1999
Stokley, James B. "Jim"—February 16, 1999
Stovall, Harry—June 29, 2000
Strange, Allen Taylor—June 17, 1999
Strange, Jocelyn Peck—June 17, 1999
Stribling, Catherine Russell—October 28, 1998
Sutton, Billy—August 8, 2000
Swails, Caroline Newbold—November 12, 1998
Swart, Bessie Burton—August 23, 1999
Swart, Bettye Rivenbark—August 23, 1999
Swart, James Edward—August 23, 1999
Swart, Robert S. "Bob"—August 23, 1999
Taylor, Victor G.—April 29, 1999
Turner, Jim—June 18, 2000
Tyson, Norman E.—May 25, 2000; July 13, 2000
Venters, Mark D., Jr.—May 10, 1999
Von Oesen, Henry—January 19, 1999; June 27, 2000
Walker, Benjamin D., III—January 8, 1999
Walker, Frances Goldberg—April 21, 1999
Walton, John W. "Bill," Jr.—August 19, 1998
Weathersbee, Dorothy "Dotty" Ames Harriss—July 22, 1999
Welker, Carl—October 2, 1998

Welker, Lottie "Clara" Marshburn—October 2, 1998
West, Rae—July 29, 1998
Whitted, James E.—October 8 and 12, 1998
Whitted, Joseph W. "Joe"—June 18, 1999
Whitted, Lucilla White—June 18, 1999
Wilcox, Emma Worth Mitchell—February 25, 1999
Willard, Emerson—April 22, 1999
Willard, Gibbs Holmes—May 19, 1999
Willard, Martin S., Jr.—May 19, 1999
Williams, Christine W.—July 9, 1999
Williams, Evalina Campbell—August 24, 1999
Williamson, Muriel—October 5, 1998
Wilson, McCulloch B. "Mac," Jr.—March 1, 2000
Woodbury, Louie E., III—April 19, 1999
Wychel, Ellen Gilliard—July 9, 1999

Wartime Letters

William G. Broadfoot, Jr.
John J. Burney, Jr.
George Burrell Byers
Cornelia Nelliemae "Nealie" Haggins Campbell
Mary Daniel Carr Fox
Jack F. Hart
John D "Jack" McCarley Collection of German POW Letters
William F. McIlwain, Jr.
Malcolm C. McIver
James B. Stokley
Allan T. Strange
Martin S. Willard, Jr.

Memoirs

Thelma Kelly Canady World War II diary. Provided by Rae B. West.
R. C. Cantwell, III memoir, "History of the World."
Joe Cross memoir, October 29, 1998.
Fred N. Day, III World War II memoir.
Philip Dresser memoir, April 1996.
Elizabeth Jones Garniss World War II Wilmington memoir, February 2, 1999.
Elizabeth Jones Garniss World War II Wilmington memoir #2, April 5, 2000.
George H. Garniss, "Memories of Wilmington During World War II," April 2000.
Jack F. Hart handwritten notes.
Peggy Mae Warren Longmire Memoir of World War II.

Vincent Norako memoir, December 1980.
Earl M. Page memoir, June 1, 1999.
Robert S. Pollock memoir, October 20, 1998.
Margaret Sampson Rogers memoir, "Local Blacks and the Local Scene," July 1998.
James B. Stokley memoir.
Allan T. Strange World War II memoir.
Catherine Russell Stribling memoir, October 28, 1998.
Martin S. Willard, Jr. memoir, "Random Reminiscences of Two Wars," March 1999.
Doris Dickens Wilson World War II memoir, 1996. New Hanover County Public Library.
Jane Ellen Baldwin Yates memoir, "Story of a Wartime Marriage." Provided by Mary Daniel Carr Fox.

Books, Monographs, Pamphlets, Papers

Allegood, Jimmy. "Down Exchange Alley: The 50-Year History of Exchange Club of Wilmington, North Carolina, 1924–1974," 1974.

Benson, Rupert L., and Helen S. Benson. *Historical Narrative 1841–1972 of Wrightsville Beach, N.C.* Wilmington: Carolina Printing and Stamp Co., 1972.

Cashman, Diane Cobb. *Champions: The History of the Cornelia Nixon Davis Health Care Center at Porters Neck, Wilmington, N.C., 1966–1991.* Wilmington: Wilmington Printing Co., 1991.

Al Derecho Creations. "The Poetry of a Man: The Life and Poetry of Percy C. West." Mesa, Ariz: 1993. Provided by Rae B. West.

Dickinson, Lieutenant Clarence Earle, Jr., USN, and Boyden Sparks. *The Flying Guns: Cockpit Record of a Naval Pilot from Pearl Harbor through Midway.* New York: Charles Scribner's Sons, 1942.

Fielder, James M. *495th Fighter Squadron: The Twin Dragons, CBI, 1943–1945; A History*, 1993. Provided by William G. Broadfoot, Jr.

"Five Years of North Carolina Shipbuilding," North Carolina Shipbuilding Company, Wilmington, N.C., May 1, 1946.

The Hanoverian. Yearbooks of New Hanover High School, Wilmington, N.C., 1938–47.

Hickman, Homer H., Jr. *Torpedo Junction: U-Boat War off America's East Coast, 1942.* Annapolis, Md.: Naval Institute Press, 1989.

Hill's City Directory, Wilmington and New Hanover County, North Carolina, Vol. 25, 1943. Richmond, Va.: Hill Directory Co., 1943. New Hanover County Public Library.

Hill's City Directory, Wilmington and New Hanover County, North Carolina, Vol. 26, 1944–45. Richmond, Va.: Hill Directory Co., 1945. New Hanover County Public Library.

"History of Forest Hills School and PTA," undated paper provided by Forest Hills School.

Hoffman, Glenn, and Richard E. Bussard, eds. *Building a Great Railroad: A History of the Atlantic Coast Line Railroad Company.* CSX Corporation, 1998.

"Industrial Survey of Wilmington and New Hanover County, N.C.," Wilmington Industrial Commission, 1941.

"Introducing Camp Davis," undated monograph (believed 1944), by Fourth Service Command, Camp Davis, N.C. Provided by Mary Daniel Carr Fox.

Lee, Clark. *They Call It Pacific: An Eyewitness Story of Our War against Japan from Bataan to the Solomons.* New York: Viking Press, 1943.

Lemmon, Sarah McCulloh. *North Carolina's Role in World War II.* Raleigh: State Department of Archives and History, 1964.

"North Carolina Manual 1943." Raleigh: Secretary of State, 1943.

Reaves, William M., and Beverley Tetterton, eds. *Strength through Struggle: The Chronological and Historical Record of the African-American Community in Wilmington, North Carolina 1865–1950.* Wilmington: New Hanover County Public Library, 1998.

Sawyer, L. A., and W. H. Mitchell. *The Liberty Ships, Second Edition.* New York: Lloyds of London Press, 1985.

Scrapbooks of the Forest Hills School PTA, 1943–45, provided by Forest Hills School.

"Seabreeze: A Heritage Renewed." Wilmington: New Hanover County Planning Department, 1988.

"The Sinking of the SS *John D. Gill*," undated paper. Provided by Christopher A. Suiter, Southport (N.C.) Historical Society.

Smith, Everard H. *Victory on the Home Front: The USO in New Hanover County, N.C., 1941–1946.* (Self published monograph, 1998).

Stallman, David A. *A History of Camp Davis.* Hampstead, N.C.: Hampstead Services, 1990.

Tillman, Barrett. *SBD Dauntless Units of World War II.* Oxford, England: Osprey Publishing, 1998.

"1948 update to Sanborn Insurance Maps," "Insurance Maps of Wilmington." New York: Sanborn Map Co., 1915, updated. New Hanover County Public Library.

Watson, Alan D. *Wilmington: Port of North Carolina.* Columbia: University of South Carolina Press, 1992.

"We Ripened Fast: Unofficial History of the Seventy-Sixth Infantry Division," undated. Provided by Dan Retchin.

Willcox, George W., and Bruce Barclay Cameron. *The Camerons of Wilmington,* 1994. Provided by Daniel D. "Dan" Cameron.

"Wilmington Unit, American Legion Auxiliary to Wilmington Post No. 10, Department of North Carolina, Year Book 1945–46." Provided by John J. Burney, Jr.

Newspapers and Periodicals (Partial)

The AA Barrage newspaper. Camp Davis, N.C., 1943–45.

The American Jewish Times, "Jewish Communities in the South: Wilmington, N.C," undated (ca. 1944).

Cape Fear Journal. Wilmington, N.C., November 29, 1942.

David W. Carnell letter in *Wilmington Morning Star,* July 31, 1998.

Ex-CBI Roundup. "Birth of the Twin Dragons," January 1999.

Evening Post, Wilmington, N.C., various 1944–45.

Gab newspaper, 1942. Provided by Beth Wooten.

Globe, Camp Lejeune, N.C. newspaper, various 1944.

Lower Cape Fear Historical Society Bulletin. "A Picture of the Wilmington Homefront During World War II: Mary Eloise Bethell Tells the Story." May 1999.

Lower Cape Fear Historical Society Bulletin. "For Better of for Worse: The Odyssey of an Army Wife." Dorothy Ulrich Troubetzkoy, July 1999.

Lower Cape Fear Historical Society Bulletin. "Robert Ruark and World War II." Lucy Ann Glover. October 1999.

News & Courier. Charleston, S.C., 1943.

The North Carolina Shipbuilder. Newsletter of the North Carolina Shipbuilding Company. Wilmington, N.C., 1942–45.

The Park City Daily News. Bowling Green, Ky. March 22, 1942. Provided by Beth Wooten.

"Sixth District Soundings" newsletter. U.S. Coast Guard Auxiliary, Charleston, S.C., 1943–45. Provided by Richard V. Hanson.

"Southeastern North Carolina in World War II." *Wilmington Star-News* Supplement, 1992.

The State: A Weekly Survey of North Carolina magazine, 1942–44.

Ben Steelman in *Wilmington Sunday Star-News*, February 4, 2001.

Tidewater magazine, January 1985.

The Wildcat newspaper. New Hanover High School, Wilmington, N.C., 1941–45.

Morning Star. Wilmington, N.C., 1941–46, and later years.

News. Wilmington, N.C., various 1941–45.

Sunday Star-News. Wilmington, N.C., 1941–46, and later years.

Waves and Currents newsletter. Cape Fear Museum, Wilmington, N.C., May 1999.

Wilmington (N.C.) Telephone Directory, Southern Bell Telephone and Telegraph Co., March 1945. Provided by Vincent Lindenschmidt.

Woman's Home Companion. "Those Incredible Doctors," by Helena Huntington Smith, February 1945.

Surveys

Roddy Cameron, November 6, 1998.

Claude Daughtry, July 25, 1998.

Irving T. Glover, November 4, 1998.

Mary B. Walton Hawkinson, October 16, 1998.

Sandra Kinlaw Huddle, October 29, 1998.

George Dudley Humphrey, November 5, 1998.

Jeannine Stanley Jones, August 20, 1998.

Nancy West Jones, November 13, 1998.

Peggy Mae Warren Longmire, September 2, 1998.

Earl M. Page, June 1, 1999.

Robert S. Pollock, October 20, 1998.

Margaret Sampson Rogers, July 24, 1998.

Marie Burgwin Sanborn, October 21, 1998.
Blanche Stanley Sneeden, October 26, 1998.

Correspondence (Partial)

Captain Luciano Callini, Italian Navy, Italian Embassy, to Leonard Kiesel, January 1995. Provided by Kiesel.
David W. Carnell to author, May 29 and October 24, 2000.
Harriett Harrington Connolly to author, October 25, 1998.
Thelma Barclift Crowder e-mail to author, November 3, 1998.
Claude and Mary Daughtry e-mail to author, October 9, 1998.
Dorothy Bunn Dibble to author, August 28, 1999.
Mary Fisher Eason to author, January 5, 2000.
George J. Green to author, October 1, 1998.
John R. Hicks to author, September 9, 1998.
George F. Hunt, Jr., notes to author, 1999.
Viola M. Jones to George and Jo Chadwick, August 12, 1969. Provided by Jo Chadwick.
Adrian L. Lawson to author, July 27, 1999.
Evelyn Bergen Loftin e-mails to author, November 6, 1998 and June 6, 1999.
Kenneth R. Murphy e-mail to author, May 30, 1999.
Arvel Harrison Perryman e-mail to author, June 5, 1999.
Bernard Rabunsky e-mail to author, July 9, 1999.
Catherine Crowe Ragland to author, October 31, 2001.
Marie Burgwin Sanborn e-mails to author, October 28, 1998 and June 26, 2000.
Clayton Smith e-mail to author, May 23, 1999.
Frances J. Wagner to author, April 18, 1999.
Jane Baldwin Yates to author, December 11, 1999.

Miscellaneous (Partial)

American Legion Post 10 Wartime Scrapbooks, MS Accession #70. William Madison Randall Library, University of North Carolina at Wilmington.
"The Bridge" pamphlet [believed 1946]. Provided by Thurston "Gene" Edwards.
Bronze Star Citation, 5th Marine Division, FMF [1945]—Private First Class Mitchell N. Saleeby, Jr., USMCR. Provided by Saleeby.
Game program, "1st Infantry Division Organization Day Football," October 21, 1945 Nuremberg, Germany. Provided by Fred N. Day, III.
"Greetings from Camp Davis, N.C."—post card folder, Service News Co., Wilmington N.C. Provided by Richard Witherspoon.
Headquarters, Armed Forces Induction Station, Fort Bragg, N.C. August 3, 1943. Special Orders Number 184. Provided by Heyward C. Bellamy.
Margaret Tienken Hewlett, St Paul's Evangelical Lutheran Church funeral bulletin October 23, 1999.

Roger W. Hewlett, CBM, USCGR (T) Citation: for completing 600 hrs of active service as a temporary member of the U.S. Coast Guard Reserve. Provided by Anne Hewlett Hutteman.

Elizabeth Davis Kinlaw, song 1944, *The Victory Ship*. © Elizabeth Davis Kinlaw. With permission of Sandra Kinlaw Huddle.

Miscellaneous ship, aviation, and personnel records of the Naval Historical Center, Washington, D.C.

"New Hanover County Public Schools Teachers' Bulletin, 1943–44." Provided by Ronald G. Phelps.

Arthur J. Newman, Major, memorandum "To Whom It May Concern," re Muriel Williamson, 12 Nov 45. Provided by Williamson.

North Carolina Shipbuilding Company. *Wartime Plant Protection Bulletin No. 4*. "Air Raid Warnings and Blackouts," December 20, 1941.

Notes from presentations given during "An Afternoon of Sharing: World War II and African-Americans," August 22, 1999, at Chestnut St. Presbyterian Church: Cornelia Haggins Campbell, Peggy Pridgen, Bertha Todd, George E. Norman.

Lieutenant General G. S. Patton, Jr., commanding Third U.S. Army, April 16, 1945, to Commanding General, 95th Infantry Division. Provided by Allan T. Strange.

Program of "Shipyard Days, 1999," Wartime Wilmington Commemoration, 1999, North Carolina State Ports Authority.

Program for the unveiling of the Commemorative Marker to be placed Shipyard Boulevard and Carolina Beach Road for North Carolina Shipbuilding Company, 1941–1946, on October 1, 1992. Provided by Robert S. Pollock.

"Report: History of 51st Field Hospital, 10 September 1943 to April 1945." Provided by Tom and Myrtle Sinclair.

"Reunion Yearbook," New Hanover High School Class of 1942 (50th, June 5–6, 1992).

Lieutenant General W. H. Simpson, commanding Ninth U.S. Army, to Major General Harry L. Twaddle, 95th Infantry Division, May 6, 1945. Provided by Allen T. Strange.

Dr. Everard H. Smith, "The Wilmington USO Building and Community Arts Center" flyer, 1998.

"Souvenir Program of the First (and maybe last) Musical Revue, 366th Fighter Group, Monday November 15th [1945], Base Theater, Army Air Base, Bluethenthal Field, Wilmington, N.C." Provided by Hannah Block.

Temple of Israel Bulletin, Wilmington, N.C., April 5, 1944. New Hanover County Public Library.

J. V. "Pat" Warren interview by Peggy Mae Warren Longmire, September 1998.

Dr. Barbara Frey Waxman, ed., "1898–1998 B'Nai Israel: The First Hundred Years," 1998, B'Nai Israel Synagogue, Wilmington, N.C.

Index

Photographs noted in *italics*.
First names given where known.
See preface for explanation of female single/
married names listings.

A

Abbott and Costello, 132
Academy Award, 10
Acorn Branch School, 218
Adkins, Sylvester "Buddy," 169, 170
Africa, 49, 81, 193
　The Dark Continent, 127
Afrika Korps, xxi, 127, 129. *See also* Prisoners
　of War (German POWs) in Wilmington
　North Africa(n) Campaign. *See* North
　Africa(n), Campaign
Agnes Scott College, Decatur, Georgia, xxiii,
　19, 204–6
Air Corps. *See* United States (U.S.) Army Air
　Forces
Aircraft (U.S), Army and Navy
　"Aluminum Overcast" WWII B-17G bomber,
　　xvi, xvii
　AT-6 *Texan* trainer, 255
　B-17 *Flying Fortress* bomber, xxii, 23, 68,
　　80, 97, 113, 169, *170,* 242
　B-17 "Sentimental Journey," 23
　B-17(E), 242, 246
　B-24 *Liberator* bomber/anti-submarine
　　warfare bomber, 69, 80, 137, 138, 167,
　　169, 226
　B-26 *Marauder* bomber, 80
　B-29 *Superfortress* bomber "North Carolina
　　Shipbuilder," 83, 224
　F4U *Corsair* fighter, *169*
　OQ28A drone, 74
　P-38 *Lightning* fighter, 79, 188, 231
　P-40 *Warhawk* fighter, xxi, 80, 208, 255
　P-47 *Thunderbolt* fighter, xxi, 80–82, 93,
　　165, 224, 249, 255
　P-47 activities, xiii, 35, 78–80
　P-51 *Mustang* fighter "City of Wilmington,"
　　224
　Piper *Cub* trainer, 255
　SBD-3 Douglas *Dauntless* scout/dive
　　bomber, 2, 240, 242
　Stearman trainer, 255
Air Forces (U.S.). *See* United States (U.S.)
　Air Forces (air force)
Airlie Gardens, 106
Alabama, 217, 236
　Mobile County, 236
Alberti, Herman, xxviii, 72, 78, 86
Alberti, Loney, 73
Allen, Brooke E. "Buzz," 2, 246
　at Battle of Midway, xxii, 240, 242, 246
　at Pearl Harbor, 245, 246
Allen, Ernest and Vivian, 5
Allen, George W., 219
Allen, Leonard Gleason, 3, 106, 188
Allen, Mr. and Mrs. W. R., 246
Allies (Allied) (powers), 10, 44, 47, 49, 97,
　127, 128, 204
America(n)(s), xiv, 4, 8, 10, 12, 23, 25, 37, 38,
　49, 64, 67, 97, 109, 110, 113, 127, 129,
　131, 135, 139, 140, 142, 200, 207, 225,
　229, 237, 238, 242, 246, 249
American Legion, 203
　American Legion Auxiliary (Post 10), 89, 203
　American Legion Post 10, xiv, 10, 24, 137,
　　197, 203, 210, 253
　Department of North Carolina, 203
American Red Cross, 18, 29, 65, 147, 197,
　202–6, 232, 237, 245
　Colored Division, 228
　Red Cross Motor Corps, *197*
　Red Cross Nurse's Aide(s), xiv, 8, 79, 137,
　　196, 197, 202, *203*
Anderson, Bo, 216
Anderson, Edwin A., 253

294

Index

Andrews Mortuary, 82
Andrews, Richard C. "Dick," 14, 57, 82
Anguar, Battle of, 15
Applewhite, Alice (Von Oesen), 166
Archer, Jean, 201
Archer, Mervin, 201
Arkansas, 172
Armed Forces (U.S.). *See* U.S. Armed Forces (Military)
Army (U.S.). *See* United States (U.S.) Army (army)
Arnhem Bridge, Holland, Battle of, xxiii
Asheville, North Carolina, 32
Ashley, Eugene, Jr., 253
Asia(n), 16, 239
Associated Press, 5, 15, 175, 248
Astor, Bob band, 182
Atlanta, Georgia, Federal prison. *See* Georgia.
Atlantic, Battle of the, 48, 49, 54
Atlantic City, New Jersey, 84
Atlantic Coast Line Railroad (ACL, Coast Line), 123, 256
 as employer, 52, 64, 251
 infrastructure, 30, 156
 in war effort, xxi, 56, 64, 65, 227
Atlantic Ocean (Theater), xvii, xviii, 47, 80, 239
 Atlantic coast, 30, 54, 67
 South Atlantic, 64, 66
 Southeastern Atlantic, 198
 Trans-Atlantic, 49
 Western Atlantic, 49
Audubon, (John James), 189
Australia, 165, 193
Austria(n), 127, 250
 Salzburg, 250
Autry, George, 31
Avery, Florence, 197
Avery, Glenn, 31
Axis (powers), 10, 105, 226

B

Babies Hospital, 234
Bacon family, 92
Bailey, Donald J., 175
Bailey Theater. *See* Theaters (movie)
Baldwin, Willie, 145
Banck, Margaret, 245
Barden, Annie, 96
Barn, The, 182, 215
Barnes, Walter orchestra, 109
Barry, Elizabeth L., 202
Basie, Count, 215
Bass, Hattie E. "Kitty," 202
Bataan Death March. *See* Philippines, Campaigns in (1941–42, 1944–45)

Battery Island, 51
Battleship North Carolina Memorial, xiii
Baum, Leo, 138
Bautz, Ernest. *See* German prisoners of war (in Wilmington)
Beaufort, North Carolina, 108
Beaumont neighborhood, 28–30, 33
Belgium, 18, 204
 Belgian army, 18
 Campaign in, xxii, 204
Belk-Williams Department Store (Belks), 204, 229, 230
Bell, Elizabeth (Day), 93
Bell, Evangeline, 149
Bellamy, Hargrove, 39
Bellamy, Heyward C., 101, *108*, 109, 151, 172
Bellamy Park, 184
Bennett, Rex, 34
Benson, Helen S., 186
Benson, Rupert L., 186
Bergen family
 Charles "Charlie" Bergen, 18, 230
 Christine DeBusscher (Bergen), 18, 232
 Evelyn Bergen (Loftin), 18, 230, 232
 Jacques DeBusscher, 18
 Mimi Bergen, 232
Berger, Shirley (Raphael), 76
Berlin, Irving, 224
Bermuda, 51
Bernatti, Leo G., 81
Berry house, 151
Bethell, Mary Eloise, 175
Biggs, Levi, 217
Bijou Theater. *See* Theaters (movie)
Bischoff, (Regina), 105
Black, Bea, 194
Black, Cecelia (Corbett), 32, 103
Black, Jackie, 32, 103
Bladen County, North Carolina, 57
Block family
 Mrs. Charles (Hannah) Block, 20, 47, *48*, 83, 182, 183, 190, 191, 194, 195
 Joe Block, 34
 William Block, 191
Blount, William, 109, 218, 219
Bluethenthal Army Air Base (Field, BAAB), xxviii, 35, 50, 55, 70, 78–83, 167, 205, 224
 deaths, 80–82
 employment, 75, 179
 military activities, 54, 133
 B-24 anti-submarine warfare base and air intercept base, xxi, 78, 79, 167
 P-40 and P-47 fighters training base, xxi, 78, 79

296 Index

postwar, 256
as POW camp, 127, 137, 138
pre-war, 78, *79*
recreation, *83*
Wilmington Army Air Base/Airport, xvi, 78
Bluethenthal, Arthur, 78
B'nai Israel synagogue, 161
Bogart, Humphrey, 128
Boney, Charles H., *6*
Books
   Arming the Eagle: A History of U.S. Weapons Acquisition Since 1775, 49
   A Bell for Adano, 189
   The Birds of America, 189
   The Flying Guns: Cockpit Record of a Naval Pilot from Pearl Harbor Through Midway, 244
   Good Night Sweet Prince, 189
   Guadalcanal Diary, 26
   Gyrene: The World War II United States Marine, 23, 27, 30
   Hawaii Goes to War: The Aftermath of Pearl Harbor, 4, 5
   Historical Narrative 1841–1972 of Wrightsville Beach, N.C., 186
   Hungry Hill, 189
   The Robe, 189
   So Little Time, 189
   A Tree Grows in Brooklyn, 189
   Victory on the Home Front: The USO in New Hanover County, N.C., 1941–1946, 191, 236
The Bottoms neighborhood, 6, 215
Boylan, George S., Jr., 13, 68, *69*, 175
Boylan, Mr. and Mrs. George S., 175
Boys Brigade Club, 227
Bradley Creek neighborhood, 106, 188
Bradley Creek School, 106
Bradshaw, Evelyn, 77
Bray, Lewis, 153
Bridgeport, Connecticut, 81
Bridgers, Odell, 123
Bridges, Lloyd, 128
Britain (Great), 66, 67, 140
   Aylesbury (Bucks), 140
British forces, 53, 173, 203, 231
   First Composite Anti-Aircraft Battery, Royal Artillery, 186
   soldiers training at Camp Davis, 173, *186*
   submarine chasers, 53
   "WAAFs," xvii
British people, 155, 184
Broad Circle Food Store, 113
Broadfoot family
   Bryan Broadfoot, 34

William G. Broadfoot, Jr. "Billy," 34, 230, *231*
Winston Broadfoot, 34
Brooks, J. B., 149
Brooklyn neighborhood, 148, 171
Brookwood neighborhood, 24, 32, 34, 64, 92, 96
Broughton, J. Melville, 61, 66, 207, 214
Brown, A. E., *228*
Brown, H. "Rap," 212
Brown, James, 148
Brown, Johnny Mack, 224
Brown, Olive Jean (Anderson), 25
Brown, William Albert, Jr., 24, 25
Brunswick County, North Carolina, xxi, 41, 48, 52, 54, 57, 63, 80, 82, 147, 198
Brunswick River, 63
Bryant, Bessie Lee, 153
Bryant, H. G., 89
Buccieri, Martin, 194
Buck, Betty (Page), 19
Buck, Bob, 19
Bugg family, 187
   Betty Bugg (Crouch), 103, 187
   E. B. Bugg, 34, 103, 187
Bulge (Belgium), Battle of the, xxiii, 204
Bunn, Dorothy (Dibble), 165
Burgwin, Eleanor "Elkie" (Fick), 179
Burgwin, Marie (Sanborn), 181
Burkheimer, Graham, 31
Burks, Rosie Lee, 147
Burma, Campaign in. *See* China-Burma-India Theater
Burnett, Foster, 219
Burnett, Richard L. "Dick," 60, 211, 212
Burney family
   Effie Burney, 89
   John J. Burney, 89, 153
   John J. Burney, Jr., xxviii, 89, 105, 106, *107*, 250
   Louis Burney, 89
Burnt Mill Creek, 28, 34, 103
Butler, Robert H., 62
Byers, George Burrell, 54, 172, 173, *174*, 239

C

Calder, Robert cottage, *176*
California, xxiii, 24, 101, 106, 201, 209, 244
   Coronado, 244
   Hollywood, 55, 71, 85, 128, 252
   Long Beach, 21
   Los Angeles, xii
   Port Chicago. *See* Port Chicago, California, depot explosion
   San Diego, 106

Southern California, 36
Calloway, Blanche, 216
Calloway, Cab, 215, 216
Cameron family, 187
  Bruce B. Cameron (mayor), 13, 89, 170
  Bruce B. Cameron, Jr., 13, 170, 187, 245, 258
  Daniel D. "Dan" Cameron, 13, 77, 170, 171, 187, 258
  Rachel Cameron, 187
  Robert F. "Bobby" Cameron, 103, 135, 187
  Suwanna Elizabeth "Betty" Henderson (Cameron), 19, 52, 170, 171, 205, 206
Cameron, Roddy, 8
Camp Butner, North Carolina, 138, 139
Camp Davis, North Carolina (Davis), Holly Ridge, North Carolina, xx, xxvii, 27, *40*, 69–78, 82, *85*, 94, 123, 180, 205, 222
Camp Davis AA Barrage, 84, 86, 131, 206
  closing, 63, 72, 76, 92, 99, 168, 191, 203, 237, 256
  command, 131, 153, 158, 220
  establishment, 72, 78, 214
  Farnsworth Hall, 74, 77, 86
  impact on Southeastern North Carolina, 55, 72, 74, 76
  military activities, 119, 138, 224, 225
  nicknames
    "Camp Muddy," 72, 74, *77*
    "Camp Swampy," 72, 74, *77*
    "Swamp Davis," 72
    "Swamp Hollow," 74
  officer candidate school, xx, 74, 91, 185, 200
  present, 76
  reopening, 101, 120, 228
  Sears Landing, 74, 76
  social/recreational/community activities, 72, 86, 163, 164, 173, 175, 179, 185, 194
  training, 13, *73*, 80, 83–85
  units and personnel stationed there, 2, 3, 18, 71, 84, 87, 91, 108, 115, 120, 124, 144–48, 156, 165, 169, 170, 171, 176, 177, 192, 207, 208, 215, 221, *231*
  WASPs (Women's Airforce Service Pilots). See WASPs (Women's Airforce Service Pilots)
Camp Lejeune Marine Corps Base, Jacksonville, North Carolina. See United States (U.S.) Marine Corps (USMC Marine[s])
Camp Sequoyah (summer), 32
Camp Shanks, New York, 141
Camp Stewart, Georgia, 170
Canton, North Carolina, 251
Cantwell, Betty Garrabrant, 25

Cantwell, Robert (Ethyl-Dow), 53
Cantwell, Robert C. III, 73
Cape Fear, 51, 248
Cape Fear Baseball League, 184
Cape Fear Club, 181
Cape Fear Community College, 195
Cape Fear Country Club, 181, 185, 224
Cape Fear Hotel, 120, *147*, 151, 165, 166
Cape Fear Journal. See *Wilmington Journal*
Cape Fear Museum, 9, 37, 260
Cape Fear River, 51, 132
  activities on, xxi, xxv, 48, 53, 66, 148, 171
  relation to shipyard, xx, 52, 58, *59*
Cape Gloucester, New Britain, Campaign on, xxii
Cape Hatteras, 49
Caribbean, xxiii
Carnell, David W., 54
Carner, George, 216
Carney, Emily, 103
Carolina Beach, North Carolina, 20, 70, 80, 82, 188, 189, *190*, 193, 206
  civilian defense/war effort, 46, 47, *48*, 53, 93
  military activities, 54, 71, 83, 84, 132
  present, xvii
  social life, 84, 180, 189–91
  vacation/recreation beach, 84, 148, 217
Carolina Beach School, 100
Carolina Building (Savings) & Loan Association, xxiii, 209, 213, 218
Carolina Printing & Stamp Co., 186
Carolina-Temple Apartments, 189
Carolina Volunteer Training Corps, 106
Carolina Yacht Club, 181, 185, 188
Carson, Susy, 51
Casteen, Charles H., 146, 151, 160
Castle Hayne neighborhood, xxv, 21, 71, 78, 81, 130, 132, 136, 139, 232, 248, 250
Causey, Bert, 183
Central Pacific. *See* Pacific Ocean Theater
Central Station (New York), 168
Chamber of Commerce, 183, 236, 237
Chapel Hill, North Carolina, 3, 106
Charles Scribner's Sons, 244
Charleston, South Carolina. *See* South Carolina
Charlotte, North Carolina, 187
Charlotte Observer, 187
Cheney, Edward F., 51
Chestnut Street Presbyterian Church, 207
Chestnut Street School, 100, 225
Chiang Kai-Shek, Madame, 162
Chicago, Illinois, 165, 184
  Chicagoan, 165
Childs, William T. "Bill," xxvii, 208, 212, 216, 219

China, 121, 162
  Canton, 162
China-Burma-India Theater, 59, 163, 231
  Campaign in Burma, xxiii, 193
  "The Hump," 59, 163, 231
Chinese Americans, xvi, 35
Church of the Covenant Presbyterian. *See* St. Andrews-Covenant Presbyterian Church
The Citadel, 18
City Hall. *See* Wilmington municipality, wartime
Civil Air Patrol, 53
Civil War (U.S.), 28, 178
Civilian defense (war effort), xx, 43, 44, 79, 113, 221, 223
  Aircraft Warning Service (AWS), 41, 198, 200
  Citizen Service Corps, 41
  Civilian Defense Corps, 41
  Ground Observer Volunteers (Corps), 98, 200
  Information and Filter Center (filter center). *See* (Information and) Filter Center (filter center)
  New Hanover County Defense Council, 41
  Office of Civilian Defense, 41, 43, 50
  Wilmington Air Region, 198
Clark, Irene, 153
Clark, J. Bayard, 83
Clemens (German POW), 140
Cleveland, Ohio, 165
Coast Guard Auxiliary. *See* United States (U.S.) Coast Guard
Coast Line. *See* Atlantic Coastline Railroad
Coast Line Convention Center, 65
Codington, H. A., 109
Codington, John, 106
Cold War, the, 16
Colmar Pocket, Battle of, xxiii
Colonial Village neighborhood, 25, 34
Colorado, 42
Columbus County, North Carolina, 57, 147
Community Arts Center. *See* Second (2nd) and Orange Streets USO (United Service Organizations)
Community Arts Center Accord, 260
Community Boys and Girls Club, 220
Community Chest, 210
Community Hospital, 80, 146, 207, 219
Confederacy, the, 83
  Confederate forces, 95, 151
Congleton, Carrie (Adkins), 169
Congress (U.S.), 3, 191, 249, 252
Congress of Industrial Organizations (CIO), 213, 214

Congressional Medal of Honor Society, 251
Conley, Marie, 185
Connolly, Donald Hilary, Jr., 165
Connolly, Maj. Gen. and Mrs. Donald H., 165
Conway, Robert B., 200
Copeland, Bobby, 31
Coral Sea, Battle of the, xxiii
Corbett, Eliza, 148
Corbett, Gladys, 89
Corbett, R. E., 18, 89
Corbett's Hotel, 215
Cornwallis (Lord), 74
Coughenour, Frances (Dinsmore), 163
Coughenour, James Arthur "Jimmy," 105, 109, 179
Council of Social Agencies, 154
Country Club Pines neighborhood, 35
Cox, Mr. and Mrs. Floyd W., 189
Cramp Shipyard, 214
Crawford, Henry "Hank," 168
Cross, Joe, 74
Crowe family
  Catherine Crowe (Ragland), 53
  Margaret Crowe (Hatcher), 53
  William Crowe, Jr., 53
Crump, Willie, 145
Customs House (U.S.). *See* Federal Government (U.S., wartime)

D

Dachau. *See* Germany (the country of)
Dade, L. C., 218
Daughtry, Claude, 18, 93, 119
Daughtry, Mary, 18, 93, 119
Davidson College, Davidson, North Carolina, 183, 245, 252
Davis, Benjamin O., 220
Davis, Champion McDowell "Champ," 64
Davis, Derick G. S., 208, 212
Davis, Elmer, 10
Davis, Norman E., 1
D-Day (June 6, 1944). *See* Normandy, Campaign in
Debnam, John, 18, 188
DeBusscher, Christine, and Jacques. *See* Bergen family
December 7, 1941, 1, 21, 68, 245
Decorations (non-U.S.)
  Croix de Guerre (France), 251
  Republic of Vietnam Cross of Gallantry, 251
Decorations (U.S.)
  Air Medal, 81, 246, 251
  Army Commendation Medal, 251
  Bronze Star, 106, 251
  Distinguished Flying Cross, 81

Distinguished Service Cross, xxii, 25, 242
Legion of Merit, 246, 251
(Congressional) Medal of Honor, xxi, xxviii, 109, 245–54
Navy Cross, xxii, 2, 26, 242–44
Oak Leaf Cluster(s), 81, 251
Presidential Unit Citation, 81
Purple Heart, 107, 251
Silver Star, 248, 251
"Defense Capital of the State" (Wilmington). *See* Wilmington in war effort
Delgado-Spofford Mills neighborhood, 28, 34
DeLoach, R. L., 239
Democratic Party, 260
Department of Defense (U.S.), xii
Department of Defense Systems Management College, 49
Depression, the Great, xxv, 18, 57, 111, 240
Devon Park neighborhood, 135
Dibble, Don A., 165
Dick, Stedman, 1
Dickinson, Clarence Earle, Jr., 242–44, 246
  attack on Gilberts and Marshalls, 243, 244
  at Battle of Midway, xxii, 240, 242, 243
  at Pearl Harbor, 242, 243
  in Wilmington, 2, 242
Dickinson, Mr. and Mrs. C. E., 242
Dinsmore, Charles E. "Chuck," 163
Disney World, 93
District of Columbia, 91. (*See also* Washington, D.C., the government in)
District Court (New Hanover County), 153
Dixon, Manette Allen (Mintz), 16, 123, 186
Dixon, Mary Cameron (Bellamy), 20, 89, 172, 202
Doenitz, Karl, 15, 49
Doetsch, Robert, 84
Dollfuss, Leopold, 127
Donnell, Martha Merrick, 214
Doolittle (James) Raid (on Japan), 225
Dosher, Billy, 103
Douglas, Lloyd C., 189
Doxey, Sanford, 1, 106, 189
Dresser, Philip "Phil," 62, 63
Dry Pond neighborhood, 88
Dudley, Jack E., 156
Duke University, Durham, North Carolina, 86
Du Maurier, Daphne, 189
Dunlea, Dick, 213
Dunley, Emma, *234*
Duplin County, North Carolina, 57
Durham, North Carolina, 86, 184, 214
Dutch. *See* Holland

E

Eagles, Betty Sparks, 244
Earnest, Albert K., 244
East Coast (U.S.), xxi, 42, 49, 54, 199
Eastern Conference (high school), 184
Eaton, Hubert, 219
Ebert, George, 135
Echo Farm Dairy, 118, 134, 135, 140, 141
Eckstine, Billy, 215
Education, Board of. *See* New Hanover County Board of Education
Edwards, Almeda Stewart, 245
Edwards, Heywood Lane, 245
Edwards, Robert Pershing, 167
Edwards, Thurston Eugene "Gene," *241*, 253
Edwards, W. Eugene "Gene," 93, 112, 122, 123, 151, 152, 246
Eisenhower, (Dwight D.), 202
Elizabeth City, North Carolina, 198
Ellington, Duke, 215
Elliott, A. H., 233
Emerson, Jane, *176*
Emirau Islands, Campaign in, 33
Emory, Henry R., 88
England, xvi, xvii, 44, 49, 141, 178, 193
  English people, 142
  London, xx, 42, 142, 202
  Londoners, 42
English (language), 48, 130, 134, 185
English Channel, xviii
Ennett, Clarence, 35
Ennett, Marion, 35
Epitome, The, 202, 203
Ethyl-Dow Chemical Company, xxi, 51–54, 226
  firing on by German U-boat, xxi, 47, 51–54
Europe(an) Theater, xxi, 13–16, 30, 67, 79, 90, 102, 137, 139, 142, 170, 178, 217, 239, 255
European-Mediterranean, 128
Evans, Rose, 183
Everett, Julian, 105
Ewing, Allen, 225
Experimental Aircraft Association, xvi, xvii

F

Fales, Albert F., 245
Falkenburg, Jinx, *193*
Fayetteville, North Carolina, 106
Federal Bureau of Investigation (FBI), 147, 152, 160, 183, 199
Federal Government (U.S., postwar), xii
Federal Government (U.S., wartime), 88, 94, 101, 117, 139
  Customs House, 71

300 Index

National Bureau of the Census (Census Bureau), 236, 259
Federal Bureau of Investigation (FBI). *See* Federal Bureau of Investigation (FBI)
Federal Works Agency, 102
Immigration Service, 39
National Housing Authority, 89, 94
National Youth Administration, 130
Office of Price Administration. *See* Office of Price Administration (OPA)
(The) Pentagon, 96
Secretary of War, 77
U.S. Employment Service (USES), 205, 211, 227, *228*
U.S. Treasury Department, 128
War Department, 27, 68, 78, 130, 200
War Manpower Commission, 130
War Mobilization, office of, 113
War Production Board, 125
Federal Point, 52
Fennell, S. A., 218
Fergus cottage, 108
Ferguson, Robert, 6
Fifth Avenue Methodist Church, 161, 162
(Information and) Filter Center (filter center), 7, 8, 39, 43, 132, 197–201, 204, 207, 221
First Composite Anti-Aircraft Artillery Battery, Royal Artillery. *See* British forces
First Presbyterian Church, 53, 161, 175
Fishburne Academy, 14
Fisher family, 232
  Jimmy Fisher, 232
  Laura Fisher, 232
  Mary Fisher (Eason), 232
Fisher, Herbert, 57
Fisher, Mattie Stewart. *See* Heath family
Fitzgerald, Ella, 215
(The) Five Royals, 215
Florida, 48, 64, 66, 164, 252, 254
  Jacksonville, 64, 66
  Key West, 167
  Mayport, 254
  Miami, 167, 252
  Pensacola, 254
Flowers, J. L. "Smokey Joe," 145
Flying Tigers, 208
Fokakis, Nick, 253
Fonvielle, Chris E., xxviii, 28
Forest Hills neighborhood, xxiii, xxv, xxviii, 22–37, 64, 88, 136, 194, 231
  activities, 45, 165
  friends, playmates, schoolmates, 25, 32, 135
  scene of war games, 8, 22, 27–29
Forest Hills School (present), xii, xiii, *31*, 97

Forest Hills School (wartime), xiv, xxiii, 5, 34, 102, *104*
  activities, 22, 102–5, 225
  5th grade class, *104*
Fort Belvoir, Virginia, 49
Fort Benning, Georgia, 75, 166
Fort Bliss, Texas, 13
Fort Bragg, North Carolina, 2, 190, 240, 253, 254
Fort Caswell, North Carolina, xxi, 71
Fort Caswell Naval Station. *See* United States (U.S.) Navy (navy)
Fort Eustis, Virginia, 75
Fort Fisher, North Carolina, 70, 83–85, 95, 158, 206, 256
  as advanced anti-aircraft artillery training base, xxi, 40, 47, 48, 76, 80, 84, 178
  as Civil War bastion, 74, 83
  recreation/social life, 84, 193
Fort Johnston, North Carolina, 51
Fort Myer, Virginia, 96
Fort Smith, Arkansas, 172
Fountain, M. J., Sr., 93
Fountain, Millard James, Jr. "Jim," 47, 93, 190
Fowler, Gene, 189
France, xvii, 14, 18, 28
  Paris, 14, 202
  Rheims, 202
France, Campaign in, 6, 105, 107, 172, 174, 187, 239, 249, 250
  Alpine(s), 248
  Colmar Pocket. *See* Colmar Pocket, Battle of
  Kaysersberg. *See* Kaysersberg, Battle of
  Nancy, 250
  Normandy. *See* Normandy, Campaign in
  Rhine River, 250
  Vosges Mountains, 248, 250
  Weiss River, 250
Franco-Americans, 14
Franks, Charlie, 145
Freed, Walter B., 169,
Freeman, Bruce, 123, 217
Freeman family, 122, 217
French (country), 26
French (people), 14
Fullwood, Evelyn, 153
Funderburk, Ray, 189
Fussell, Harold, xxvii
Futch, Augusta, 202

G

Gaillard, Joe, 157
Gaither, Bell, 173
Galloway, David, 157
Garniss family, 177

Index

George Hubbard "Budd" Garniss,
   at Camp Davis, 91, 176
   sister's date/fiancé/husband, 16, 91, 176, *177*, 178
   Mr. and Mrs. George W. Garniss, 178
   Viola Elizabeth Jones Garniss. *See* Jones, Wilbur D. family
Garrabrant family
   Betty Garrabrant Cantwell. *See* Cantwell, Betty Garrabrant
   Bill Garrabrant, 25, 105
   John Richard "Dick" Garrabrant, *25*
   Margey Garrabrant, 25
Gaylord, Addie Lee, 3, 89, *231*
General Assembly (North Carolina), 260
General Electric Co., 213
Geneva Convention, 128, 131
George, Edward "Pat," "Ed," "Reverend," "Old Conductor," 212–14
George, Katie, 201
George, Lillian M. "Bill," 201
George, Parthenia, 213
Georgia, 75, 147, 166, 168, 170
   Atlanta, 20, 147
   federal prison, 147
   Macon, 166
   Savannah, 168
Gerdes, John, Jr., 25
Germans/Germany (as enemy)
   the Boche, 14
   German(s), 26, 30, 38, 49, 60, 61, 70, 225
   Germany, xiii, 3, 4, 15, 26, 30, 110, 137, 138, 202
German-English (languages), 131
German forces
   army, xii
   German(s), xxi, 15, 18, 25, 30, 44, 46–49, 51, 52, 54, 84, 127, 128, 131, 138, 191, 202, 241, 249, 250
   navy, 48
   spies and saboteurs, 47, 48
German prisoners of war (POWs) in Wilmington. *See* Prisoners of War (German POWs) in Wilmington
German U-boats
   firing on Ethyl-Dow Chemical Company plant, xxi, 47, 51–54
   operations/threat off North Carolina coast, xx, 30, 38, 45, 47–49, 52, 54, 80, 84, 88, 245
   U-158, 51
German weapons and equipment
   Focke-Wulf 190 fighter aircraft, 97
   Me-262 jet fighter, 241
   mobile field kitchen, 225
   Panzer tanks, 128
   tank destroyer with 76mm rifle, 225
   U-boats (submarines). *See* German U-boats
   V-2 rockets, 44
Germany (the country of), xvii, 18, 132, 135, 137, 139–42
   Dachau, 20
   Hanover, 140
   Regensburg, 141
   Rhine River, 30
   Sendenhorst, 142
   Trier, 137
Germany, Campaign in, xxii, 13, 18, 24, 105, 106, 138, 172, 174, 239, 241
   Remagen bridge, 241
Gestapo (Nazi), xiii
Gilbert Islands, attack on, 243
Gillette family
   Douglas Wiley Gillette, 245
   George Gillette, 245
   Pearl M. Gillette, 245
   USS *Gillette* (DE-681). *See* United States (U.S.) Navy (navy) ships, craft, and units
Glen Arden neighborhood, 35
(The) Glenn cottage, 189
Glenn, Dorothy, 165, 166
Glover, Mary, 182
Godfrey, W. T. R., 157
Goins, John J. "Johnny," 105, 109
Goldberg family
   Aaron Goldberg, 156, 168
   Frances Goldberg Walker, 169
   Libby Goldberg (O'Quinn), 168, 169
   Robert Aaron "Bobby" Goldberg, Jr., xxiii, *169*
Goldsboro, North Carolina, 144
Gore, Elias T., *211*
Governor Dudley house, 198
Grable, Betty, 77, *85*
Grace Line, 67
Graham, Charles, 34
Grand Ole Opry. *See* Station WSM Grand Ole Opry Gang
Gray Ladies, 197
Great War. *See* World War I (WWI, Great War)
Green (in North Carolina history), 74
Green, George J., 92, 192
Green Islands, Campaign in, 33
Green Lantern (Wilmington), 146, 182, 215
Green, Lehman, 110
Greensboro, North Carolina, 108
Green Swamp, 82
Greenfield Lake, xxv, 87, 113, 156, 214
   Greenfield Park, 13, 169, 181
Greenfield Terrace housing. *See* Public housing projects (the projects)

Greenville Sound neighborhood, 156
Greer, John, 146, 147
Gresham, Mary Emma, 3
Gresham, Sam, 3
Grimes, Mabel, 205
Grise, J. W., 109
Guadalcanal, Campaign on ("the Canal"), xxiii, 2, 26, 30, 156, 246
  Tenaru River, Battle of, 26

H

Hackler, Jim Frank, 34
Haggins family
  Auldrie Haggins, 218
  Cornelia "Nealie" Haggins (Campbell), 5, *6*, 98, 133, 217, 218, 220
  "Mamma" Haggins, 220
  Mary Haggins, *6*
Halifax, Lord, 186
Hall, Joe "Pompi," 149
Hall, Ruth, 216
Hall, Virginia, 149
Halsey, P. F., 206
Halyburton family
  Jean Halyburton Taylor, 252
  Joseph Halyburton, 252
  Robert Halyburton, 252
  Mr. and Mrs. William D. Halyburton, 251
  William David "Billy" Halyburton, Jr., xxii, xxviii, 105, 109, 184, 245, 246, *252*, 253
    Medal of Honor Citation, 252, 253
  Mr. and Mrs. E. M. Milton, 251
Hamilton, Luther, 150
Hamilton, Thomas Tristan "T-Square," 106, *107*, 109
Hamlet, North Carolina, 66
Hammel, Thelma B., 157
Hampton, Lionel, 215
The Hanoverian (New Hanover High School). See New Hanover High School (NHHS)
Hanson family
  Louis A. Hanson, *23*, 53, 151
  Louis A. Hanson, Jr., 33
  Richard "Dick" Hanson, 33
Harbor Island, 19
Hardwick, Mrs. Robert (Hattie), *197*
Hardwicks, A. R., 82
Hare, Bryant, 102, 103, 105
Hare, William C. "Rabbit," 147
Hargroves, Carrie, 220
Harlem Globetrotters, 215
Harley, Ben, 215
Harrell, Solomon, 214
Harrington, Mr. and Mrs. Charles M., 165
Harrington, Harriett Glasque (Connolly), 165

Harriss, Dorothy Ames "Dotty" (Weathersbee), 93
Harriss, Meares family, 173
  Katharine Meares Harriss (Byers), 172, 173, *174*, 239
  John Weddell Harriss, 98
  Laura Weddell Harriss, 173
  Meares Harriss, 173
  Thomas Harriss, 173
Harriss, Virginia (Holland), 12, 82, 188
Hart, Jack F., *193*
Hart, Joy, 193
Hawaii, xix, 1, 2, 202, 238
  Diamond Head, 245
  Hickam Field, 5, 245
  Oahu, 4, 5, 9
  Pearl Harbor, xix, 1, 3, 4, 21, 23, 243
  Schofield Barracks, 5
  Wheeler Field, 23
Hawkins, Erskine, 216
Hayes, Doris Iretta, 98
Hazel, R. H., 131, 133, 136–38
Head, Kathleen, 153
Heath family, 255
  Albert "Tootie" Heath, 255
  Percy L. Heath, *255*
  Jimmy Heath, 255
  Mattie Stewart Fisher, 255
Helms, Jesse, 240, *241*
Henderson, Betty (Cameron). See Cameron family
Henderson, James, 149
Henderson, Thomas A., 155
Hersey, John, 189
Hewlett, Mrs. Addison, 204
Hewlett, Ann (Hutteman), 178
High, Billy, 52
Higgins, Miles C. See Willard-Whitted family
High Point, North Carolina, 89
Hill, Andrew, 210
Hill, James E., 153
Hillcrest housing project. See Public housing projects (the projects)
Hilton Park neighborhood, xxv, 45
  Hilton bridge, 68
Hinson, Joseph Dewey, 149
Hintze, Mrs. Dell J., 201
Hitler, (Adolf), 15, 110, 130, 139, 226
Hobbs, Dewey, 105
Hobbs, Scooter, 34
Hocutt, Ivon, 156
Hoggard, John T., 99, 109
Hogue, Susanne, 3
Holland, xvii, 185
  Dutch marines, 185, 191

Dutchmen, 185
  Hank (Dutch marine), 185
Holland, Carolyn, 82
Holland cottage, 82
Holland, Raymond H., Jr., 82
Hollins College, Roanoke, Virginia, 19
Holly Ridge, North Carolina, postwar, xxviii, 71, 72
Holly Ridge, North Carolina, wartime, 72–75, 85, 158
  activities, 75, 84
  site of Camp Davis, xviii, 40, 71, 72, 75
Holly Shelter, 71
Hollywood. *See* California
Holmes, Gibbs (Willard). *See* Willard-Whitted family
Holmes, James, 155
Holmes, Vivian, 155
Hood, Mary Elizabeth, 204
"Hooks" (drummer), 216
Hope, Bob, 184
Horrell, Harvey Howard, 21
Horrell, Maggie, 21
Horton, Ralph T., 47, 52
Housing Authority of the City of Wilmington (HACOW, Wilmington Housing Authority), 88, 94, 95, 221, 237
  Defense Housing, 88
  Home Registration Office, 88
  projects/public housing. *See* Public housing projects (the projects)
  War Housing Center, 87, 90
Housing, defense/war. *See also* Public housing projects (the projects), 87–94
Houston (owner of Big Ike Shoe Repair), 135
Howard, David W., 210
Howard, John B., 150
Howes, Mrs. D. S., 14
Hudson, Ezra Allen, 157
Hufham, Gurney J. "Jack," 1
Hugh MacRae Park memorial, xxvii, 24, 210
Hughes, Jimmy, 105
Hughes, Langston, 214
Huhn, Mildred, 172
The "Hump." *See* China-Burma-India Theater
Humphrey, Dudley, 135
Humphrey, Liston W., family, 2, 17, 75
  Elise Humphrey (Coble), *17*
  Eloise Humphrey, 2
  Liston W. Humphrey, 2
  L. W. "Bill/Billy" Humphrey, Jr., 2, *17*, 30, 31, 32, 72, 75, *104*, 213, 230
"Viola Jones Humphrey," 16

Hundley, Harry L., 24, 34
Hunter, Joe, 216
Hurst, Adrian, 133

I

India. *See also* China-Burma-India Theater, xx, xxiii, 16, 121, 122, 177, 178, 230
  New Delhi, 178
Information and Filter Center. *See* (Information) and Filter Center (filter center)
Inland (Intracoastal) Waterway, xx, 48, 80, 216, 217
International Longshoremens Union, 213
Iowa, 172
Isaac Bear School, 100, 108
Issaquah, Washington, 91
Italy, 36
  Anzio, 12
  Rome, 12
  Campaign in (Italian Campaign), xxii, 8, 26, 169, 170, 250
Italian(s), 128, 131
  Italian *Afrika Korps* prisoners of war. *See* Prisoners of war (German POWs) in Wilmington
Iwo Jima, Battle of, xxiii, 15, 23, 26, 30, 106, 209

J

Jackson, Francis Asken, 209
Jackson, James, 209
Jackson, Milton Buster, Jr., 148, 149
Jacksonville, North Carolina, xxi, 72, 85
Jacobs, Dwight V. "Duke," 163, 164
James, Charles, Jr., 218
James, Kilby, 144
James Walker Memorial Hospital (JWMH), xxiii, 137, 155, 201–3, 219, 234
  Marion Sprunt Annex, 219
  nursing school, 203, *234*
Japan (country), 15, 16, 202
  Hiroshima, 15, 202
  Tokyo, 225
  Tokyo Bay, 15
Japan (as enemy), 3, 11, 30, 105, 110, 255
  government, 15
Japanese (Japs/Nipponese), general usage, 1, 2, 8, 15, 16, 39, 60, 244
Japanese (Japs), boyhood neighborhood "enemy," 22, 26, 27, 36, 97, 143
Japanese forces, xix, xxii, 1, 2, 11, 15, 30, 68, 225, 242, 253
  Imperial Japanese Navy (fleet), 245, 246
  carrier IJN *Kaga*, xxii, 2, 242, 243, 245
  midget submarine captured in Hawaii, *9*

304 Index

submarine *I-170*, 2, 242, 243
   Yawata-class liner, 244
Jeffords, Daphne, *234*
Jenkins, Lela Mae, 148
Jenkins, Sam, 148
Jenness, John Henry, 35
Jensen, Wayne, 155, 156
Jervay, Thomas, 214
Jett, Jimmy orchestra, 183
Jewell, Douglas, 106
(SS) *John D. Gill*, 51
Johnson, Buddy, 215
Johnson, George family
  Dr. George Johnson, 3
  George Johnson, Jr., 3
  Mrs. Johnson, 3
Johnson, Joseph H. "Joe," Jr., 3, 19, 34, 103, 135
Jones, Carroll Robbins, xxviii, xii, 4, 5, 121. *See also* Jones, Wilbur D. family
Jones, C. David, 15, 41, 149, 244
Jones, Charles, 73
Jones, Charles F., 223
Jones, Charlotte (Parker), 223
Jones County, North Carolina, xxiii
Jones, Richard B. "Dick," 86
Jones, Lonnie, 35
Jones, Oscar Rockwell, 109
Jones, Philip, xxviii
Jones, Pop, 73
Jones, Sammy, 148
Jones, Wilbur D. family, 16, 22, 23, 176, 178
  house at 102 Colonial Drive, *222*
  Mr. and Mrs. Wilbur D. Jones (parents), xii, xiii, 1, 7, 25, 55, 66, 87, 106, 111, 169, 178, 229
  Viola Elizabeth Jones (Garniss) (Lib, Sister), xx, xxiii, *xxiv*, 1, 20, 23, 87, 91, 162, 176
    at Agnes Scott College, 87, 162
    as date/fiancé/wife of George Hubbard Garniss 16, 91, 176, *177*, 178. *See also* Garniss family
    at shipyard, 55, 205
  Viola Murrell Jones (Mother, Mrs. Wilbur D. Jones), xxiii, 16, 17, 22, 36, 87, 91, 100, 113, 114, 118, 121, 162, 176–78, 201, 208, 259, 260
    with Post 10 American Legion Auxiliary, xiv, 10, 137
    as Red Cross Nurse's Aide, 115, 137, 197, 202, *203*
    in other war effort, xxiii, 198, 203
  Wilbur D. (David) Jones (Father, Daddy) (W. D. Jones), xxiii, *xxiv*, 7, 22, 34,

    37, 71, 75, 118, 176–78, 201, 213, 229
    in business and civic life/war effort, xiv, 39, 91, 103, 115, 121, 209
    with Carolina Building (Savings) & Loan Association, 213, 223
    in World War I naval service, xxiii
  Jones, Wilbur D., Jr. (author) in photographs, *cover*, xvi, xxvix, *31*, *104*
Jordan family
  Frances Jordan (Wagner), 53, 193
  Lula K. Jordan, 53
  Luther J., Jordan, 53
Josey, Atha, 185
Josey, Sally (Crawford), 16, 168, 185
Junior Chamber of Commerce (Jaycees), 227, 235

K

Kaiser, Henry J., 58
IJN *Kaga*. *See* Japanese forces
Kanaly, Frank, 212
Kaltenborn, H. V., 10
Kaysersberg, Battle of, 249, 250
Kellum, Ida B., 101
Kentucky, 64, 167, 170
Kimball, Thomas, 156
King, John, 150
King, Martin Luther, Jr., 212
King, Mr. and Mrs. Reynouard S. *See* Murray-King families
Kingoff family
  Alex Kingoff, 3
  Benjamin Kingoff, 138
  William Nathan "Bill" Kingoff, 3, 81, 138
  Nellie Kosch, 3
King's Bluff, 237
Kinston, North Carolina, 85, 216
Knox, Frank, 48, 49
Korean War, 13, 63, 105, 251
Kosch, Nellie. *See* Kingoff family
Kostelanetz (Andre orchestra), 230
Kure's (Kure) Beach, North Carolina, xxi, 51–54
Kwan, Maura Mei-lan, 162

L

Laing, Harold, 32, 47, 102
Lake Forest housing. *See* Public housing projects (the projects)
Lake Forest School, 100, 101
Landers, Ann, 7
Landis cottage, 187
Lane, W. Ronald, 12, 132, *247*
Lanham Act, 101

Laurinburg, North Carolina, 181
Lavin, Linda, 195
Lawson, Adrian, 84
Lawson, Bessie G., 202
Laycock, Eugene, 105
Laytham, Louis, 123
Lee, Clark, 244, 245
Lee, James Madison "Jim," 13, 69, 93
Lee, Mabel G., 202
Leeuwenburg, Johnny dairy, 135
Leeuwenburg, Otto, 135
  Otto Leeuwenburg dairy, 119, *129*, 135
Leeuwenburg, William Charles "Bill," 119, 129, 135
Legion Stadium, 5, 50, 98, 183, 225, 259
Leiner, Louis, xv
Lend-lease program, xxi, 66, 67
Lennon, Alton, 71, 149
  Alton Lennon Federal Building, 149
  Customs House, 71
Levine, Miss (Polly), 108, 109
Lewis, Gentry, 34
Liberty ships. *See* Ships constructed at North Carolina Shipbuilding Company
Lindenschmidt, Vince, xxvii
Little League baseball, 23
Long Beach, North Carolina, 198
Loughlin, John, 34
Louis, Joe, 77, 86
Lounsbury family
  Bobbie Lounsbury, 34
  James B. Lounsbury, 34
  Jean Lounsbury, 34
Love, A. B., Jr., 52, 53
Love Grove neighborhood, 80, 218
Low, Fowler, 32
Lovette, Edward, 156
Lower Cape Fear Historical Society, xiii, xxviii
Lumina Pavilion, xx, 149, 165, 182
Luxembourg, xxii, 184
Lynch, James B. "Jim," II, xxiii

M

MacMillan, Henry, Jr., 106
MacMillan, W. D., Jr., 106
Madison Square Garden, 183, 185
Maffitt, John Newland, 95
Maffitt, M'Kean, 43
Maffitt Village housing. *See* Public housing projects (the projects)
Maffitt Village School, 101
Magnolia Place neighborhood, 35
Maine, 177
"Manhattan" (A-bomb) Project, 202

Maple, Mary, 12
Mapson, Ethel, 217
Marianas Campaign, 235
Marine Distinguished Service Medal (Merchant Marine), 51
(Old) Marine Hospital. *See* Prisoners of War (German POWs) in Wilmington
Marine(s)(Marine Corps). *See* United States (U.S.) Marine Corps (Marine[s])
Maritime Commission, xx, 61–63, 67, 221
Marquand, John, 189
Marsh, Hezekiah, 218
Marshall, Thurgood, 213
Marshall Islands, attack on, 243, 244
  Kwajalein, 244
Marshburn, Lottie "Clara" (Welker), 163, 164, 179
"Mary" (hotel thief), 147
Mary Baldwin College, Staunton, Virginia, 165
Maryland, 250, 254
  Baltimore, 248, 250
    Baltimorian, 248
  Bethesda, 254
Masonboro Island, 81
Masonboro Sound neighborhood, 21, 133, 166
Massachusetts, 245
  Boston, 245
  Quincy, 245
Mathews, E. L., Jr., xxviii
Matthews, R. D., 153
Maxwell, Otto Platt, 148
May, Aaron, 147, 172
May, Norma, 172
Mayfield, Mr., 205
Mayhan, Ernest "Red," 184
McCaig, W. D., 219
McCarley, J. D., Jr., 134, 140–42
McCarley, John D. "Jack" III, 134, 140, 141, 232
McClammy family, 177
McClammy, Herbert, *xxiv*, 31
McCormick, Walter Lee, 19
McCumber, Bobby, 31, 33
McCumber, Colonel James, 33, 34
McDonald, Harriett, xiii, 101
McEachern, A. O., 134, 141
McEachern, Duncan, 232
McEachern, George Hutaff, 19
McEachern, Miriam, 101
McEachern, Tabitha Hutaff, 19, 113, 122
McFadden, Leroy, 210
McGee, William, *cover*, *xxix*, 87
McGhee, Ben, 219
McIlwain, William F. "Bill," 18, 187, 188
McIver, Clifford, 168

McKeithan, R. S., 228
McKoy, Johnnie, 148
McKoy, Leonard "Legs," 184
McRee, Fred (father), 135
McRee, Fred (son), 135
McWathy, Gene, 93
Meaders, Mary Elizabeth, *241*
(Congressional) Medal of Honor (U.S.). *See* Decorations (U.S.)
Mediterranean (Theater) Sea, 239, 252. *See also* Europe(an) Theater
Melody Barons, 216
Mellus, Johnny, 86
Melton, Herbert "Bert" Franklin, 21
Melton, Mr. and Mrs. George, 21
Mercer, Johnny pier, 172, 186
Mercer Avenue-East Wilmington neighborhood, 28
Merchant marine, xxii, 51, 239, 240
Merchant ships. *See* Ships constructed at North Carolina Shipbuilding Company
Metts, Jimmy, 3
Meyer, Agnes E., 120
Meyer, Henry, 188
Meyer, John, *xvi*
Michigan, 52, 82
  Detroit, 92, 214
  Ludington, 52
  Trenary, 82
Middle Sound neighborhood, 170
Midway, Battle of, xxii, 2, 23, 238, 240, 242–46
Milburn, Ann, 187, 188
Military (U.S.). *See* United States (U.S.) Armed Forces (Military)
Millett, Ruth, 7, 98, 163, 175
Millinor, C. A., 156
Mintz, John, 3, 123, 186
Missouri, 21
  St. Louis, 21
Mitchell, Alfred, 217
Mitchell, Mrs., 105
Mitchell family
  Annie Worth Mitchell, 197
  Charlie Mitchell, *17*, 33
  Emma Worth Mitchell (Wilcox), 108, 197, 251
  George L. Mitchell, Jr., 33
Modern Jazz Quartet, 255
Monkey Junction neighborhood, 232
Montgomery, Jack, 145
Montreat, North Carolina, 162
Moody, Mrs. (Dessie B.), 102
Moore-Fonvielle Realty Company, 28, 103
Moore, Haywood, 52
Moore, J. R. family
  Clyde Carson Moore, 2, 21

Mr. and Mrs. J. R. Moore, 21
Jack Moore, 21
Maie Waters Moore, 21
Ralph E. Moore, 21,
Robert H. Moore, 21
Moore, Johnnie A., 148
Moore, Lewis T., 183
Moore, Mary Helen, 202
Moore, Peggy (Perdew), 3, 137, 176, 183, 185, 205
Moore, W. Houston, 94
Morehead City, North Carolina, 85
Morris, Clifford Cohen "Cliff," Jr., 8, *170*
Morrison, Samuel Eliot, 243
Morse, Cornelius, 33
Morse, Neil, 33
Moultrie, H. Carl, 240
Movies
  Destination Tokyo, 224
  Fury in the Pacific, 15
  Guadalcanal Diary, 26
  Heaven Can Wait, 224
  Movietone News, 22
  Pearl Harbor, 23
  Sahara, 128
  Sergeant York, 165
  Wake Island, 224
Moye, Larry D., 239
Mundy, Carl E., Jr., 194
Murphy, Kenneth, 32, 92
Murphy, Lonnie C. "Buster," 147
Murphy, Marvin, 92
Murray-King families
  Anniemae King "Anne" Murray, 247, 248, 250
  Mr. and Mrs. Ausia Murray, 249
  Charles P. "Chuck" Murray, Jr., xxii, xxviii, 246, 247, 248–51, 253
    Medal of Honor Citation, 249, 250
  Charles Patrick Murray, 248
  Don Murray, 249
  Florence Brown Murray, 248
  Mr. and Mrs. Renouard S. King, 249, 251
  William "Billy" Murray, 249, 251
Murrell, Hattie, xxiii
Murrow, Edward R., 10
Muscovites, 42
Mussolini, (Benito), 226
Myerow, Cathy, xxviii
Myers, Mrs. Andrew, *228*

N

NAACP (National Association for the Advancement of Colored People), 213
Naish, J. Carroll, 128

National Cemetery, St. Louis, Missouri, 21
National Collegiate Scholarship, 217
National Register of Historic Places, 195
Naval Academy, Annapolis, Maryland, 2, 242
Nazi(s), 15, 30, 39, 45, 49, 52, 130, 131, 135, 139
Nelson, Swan E., 144
(Charles T.) Nesbitt Courts housing. *See* Public housing projects (the projects)
Neuer, Emma K., xiii, *xiv*, 101
Neuer, John, xii
New Bern, North Carolina, 64, 85
Newbold, Caroline (Swails), 93, 103, 181, 202
Newbold, Jessie, 93
New Brooklyn Homes housing. *See* Public housing projects (the projects)
Newell's (store), 188, 189
New Guinea, Campaign in, 13, 165, 187, 209, 218, 258
New Hanover County Memorial Hospital, 219
New Hanover County, North Carolina (postwar), 52, 260
New Hanover County, North Carolina (wartime), xiv, xviii, xxv, 35, 41, 109
  in civilian defense, 45
  economy, 119, 121, 133
  geographical/topographical area, xxi, 52, 83, 192, 216, 236
  government, 91, 125, 162
  growth, 113
New Hanover County Board of Education, xxv, 99, 101, 251, 254, 269
New Hanover County Board of Health, 237
New Hanover County Public Library, xxii, xxvii, 7, 164, 189
New Hanover County schools, 98, 108
  population, 117, 235, 236
  public health, 233–35, 237, 240
    iron lung, 235
  residents in uniform/deaths, xxii, xxviii, 21
  in war effort, 79, 222, 223, 226, 240
New Hanover High School (NHHS), xxi–xxiii, *xxiv*, 3, 4, 8, *17*, 36, 85, 98, 172, 246, 251, 253, 254
  activities, 98, 100, 105, 109, 110, 169, 183, 184, 218, 224, 250
  classes and members
    1928, 246
    1929, 245
    1932, 242
    1934, 244
    1938, xxii, 13, 246, 247
    1939, xvi, xxiv, xxvii, 8, 16, 79, 81, 93, 139, 164, 165, 169, 186, 205, 211, 234, 238, 241
    1942, 5, 250
    1943, xvi, xxii, xxvii, 3, 8, 53, 54, 105, 107, 108, 172, 174, 188, 193, 202, 232, 239, 240, 245, 246, 250
    1944, 13, 69
    1946, 252
    1951, xxiii, xvii
  faculty, 106, *107*, 108, 109, 173
  graduates, 2, 21, 106, 202
  The Hanoverian (yearbook), xxiv, 4, 107, 250
  ROTC (Junior Reserve Officers Training Corps), 5, 6, 13, 105, 106, 109, 151
  students, 5, *17*, 245
  The Wildcat (newspaper), 106
  Wildcats athletic teams, 106, 183, 184
New Jersey, 91, 178, 214
  Bloomfield, 178
  Camden, 214
New Mexico, 202
  Los Alamos, 202
New Orleans, Louisiana, 163
Newport News Shipbuilding & Drydock Company. *See* North Carolina Shipbuilding Co. (NCSC, the shipyard)
New River (North Carolina) Marine Barracks/Base. *See* United States (U.S.) Marine Corps (USMC, Marines)
Newspaper Enterprise Association, Inc., 27, 29, 122, 257
  "Out Our Way" cartoon, 27, 257
  "Side Glances" cartoon, 29, 122
New York, 26, 81, 96, 141, 168, 178, 205, 213, 224, 244, 246, 259
  Brooklyn, 81, 96
  Coney Island, 84
  Flushing, 168
  New York City, 168
  Staten Island, 178
New York Times, 25, 137
New York World's Fair (1939), 187
Nichols, A. C., 132, 153, 154
Ninth (9th) and Nixon Streets USO (United Service Organizations) (Negro/colored) club, 144, 194, 195, 207, 208, 214–16, 220
  60th anniversary, 195, 220
Nixon, James Henry "Jim," 209
Nixon, Zilphia, 209
Norako, Vince, 96
Norman, George N., xxvii, 136, 211, 216, *228*
Normandy, Campaign in, xxiii, 13, 25, 30, 52, 61
  D-Day (June 6, 1944), xxiii, 4, 25, 172, 190
  Montebourg, 25
  Omaha Beach, 4

308 Index

Utah Beach, 25
North, D.C., 32
North Africa(n), Campaign in, xxi, 30, 97, 127, 129, 193, 239, 250
  Afrika Korps. See *Afrika Korps*
  Casablanca, 127
  Desert Fox, 127
  Desert Rats, 127
  El Alamein, 127
  French Northwest Africa, 30
  Kasserine Pass, 127
  Rommel, Erwin. See Rommel, Erwin
  Sahara Desert, 30, 127
  Tobruk, 30, 127
  Tunisia(n), Campaign in, xxii, 30, 129
North Carolina (N.C.) (present), xii
North Carolina (N.C.) (state), xxi, 21, 32, 79, 98, 101, 106, 116, 140, 162, 181, 188, 203, 208, 240, 251, 254, 257, 259
  Carolina coast, 45, 74, 198, 221
  Eastern North Carolina, 91, 216
  Western North Carolina, 20
North Carolina (N.C.) (wartime), xviii, 42, 121, 214, 235, 236, 253
North Carolina A&T (Agricultural & Technological) College, 208, 211
North Carolina Central College, 207
North Carolina Mutual Life Insurance Company, 214
North Carolina Shipbuilding Co. (NCSC, the shipyard), xx, xxviii, 30, 41, 55–68, 87, 94, 115, 130, 210, *211*, 212–14, 224
  beginning, 56, 58, 78
  civilian defense, 53, 54
  closing, 72, 256
  employment/workers, xiii, 11, 20, 56, 60, 70, 89, 95, 99, 162, 178, 183, 205, 206, 210, *211*, 216
  launchings, 55, *59*, *62*
  management and organization, 55, 57, 58, 60, 63, 67
  Newport News Shipbuilding & Drydock Co., 57, 62, 63
  North Carolina Shipbuilder newspaper, 61, 210, 211
  production record, xx, 58–61
  ships constructed at NCSC. See Ships constructed at North Carolina Shipbuilding Co.
  in war effort, 224, 225
North Carolina (N.C.) State College, Raleigh, 106, 183
North Carolina State Port (postwar), xxviii, 58, 67, 256. See also Port of Wilmington (wartime)
Northeast (Cape Fear) River, 66, 68

Norway, 61
Norwegian, 61
Nurse's Aide(s). *See* American Red Cross

O

Oakdale Cemetery, xxiii
Obermeir, Tom, 168
Ocean Isle, North Carolina, 82
Odom, Dan, 52
Office of Price Administration (OPA), xix, 12, 91, 92, 111–16, 118, 120, 121, 123, 124, 146
  Raleigh, North Carolina district office, 112, 125
  Washington, D.C. office, 112
Okinawa (Shima), Battle of, xxii, 3, 15, 26, 96, 169, 184, 209, 246, 152, 253
  Ryukyu Islands (Chain), 169, 253
  Wana Draw, 246
Oklahoma City, Oklahoma, 157
Oleander neighborhood, xxv, 25, 34, 35, 126, 175, 185, 258
Ollmann, Werner, 140
Olmstead, Angus, 113
Olsen, Carroll "Shortie," 165, 166
Onslow County, North Carolina, xx, xxi, xxiii, 22, 71
"Operation Bumblebee," 76
O'Quinn, Edward Nelson, 168
Oregon, 58, 89
Ormond, Lewis F., 64
Ormond, Mrs. Lewis F. (Mary Belle), 64
Ottaway, Darrel, 71
Ottaway family, 77
Owens, Augusta Estelle (Edwards), 167
Owens, Burnette, 167
Owens, Willie Anthony "Playboy," "Loverman," "Pal," *218*
Owensby, Claude Cliff, Jr., 184

P

Pacific Ocean Theater, 10, 21, 61, 63, 68, 97, 123, 168, 228, 239, 242, 245, 255
  Central Pacific, 22, 26, 33
  South Pacific, 15, 23, 62, 145, 168, 251
  Southwest Pacific, 11, 33
Pacific War, xii, 4, 29, 30, 35, 238, 244
Padrick, Gladys, 169
Page, Earl, 95
Page, R. B., xix, 227
Panama, 163, 240
Parks, Margaret, *46*, 151
Parnell, Jerry, xxvii
Pastor, Tony orchestra, 182
Patti, Theodore F., 81
Patton, (George S., Jr.), 127

Index

Peabody School, 100
Pearce, Linda, xxvii
Pearl Harbor, Hawaii, Japanese attack on, xix, xxiii, 1–5, 21
Pearl Harbor (post-attack), xxii, 9, 10, 13, 39, 47, 68, 78, 84, 85, 94, 99, 101, 110, 115, 168, 191, 198, 215, 223, 239, 240, 242–44
Pearl, Minnie, 183
Pearsall, Horace, Jr., 3
Peck, Jocelyn (Strange), 191
Peck, Lonnie, 190, 191
Peiffer family
    Adelaide J. Peiffer, 244
    Carl David "Baggy" Peiffer, xxiii, 2, 245, 246
    at Battle of Midway, xxii, 240, 242, 243, 245
    Frank W. Peiffer, 245
    USS *Peiffer* (DE-588). *See* United States (U.S.) Navy (navy), ships, craft, and units
Peleliu, Battle of, xxiii, 15, 26
Pender County, North Carolina, xx, 57, 71
Pennington, Ann Feenstra, 79
Pennington, James C. "Skinny," 59
Pennington's Flying Service, 79
Pennsylvania, 163
    Chester, 208, 214
    Philadelphia ("Philly"), 51, 84, 214
    Shippensburg, 5, 30
(The) Pentagon. *See* Federal Government (U.S., wartime)
Penton family,
    Ann Penton, 103, 187
    Howard Penton, 105
    Margie Penton, 103
Periodicals
    All Hands, 252
    Collier's, 8
    Liberty, 69
    Life, 8, 22
    Ladies Home Journal, 165
    The State: A Weekly Survey of North Carolina, 72, 188
    Saturday Evening Post, 8, 244
    Time, 8
    War Comics, 26, *113*
Perry, Mrs. Albert, 204,
Perry, Artie, 103
Phelps, Kenneth, 104
Phelps, Ronald G. "Ronnie," xxviii, *31*, 32, 34, 102, 103, *104*, 152
Philippines (country), 51
Philippines, Campaigns in (1941–42, 1944–45), xxiii, 10, 76, 163, 244, 258
    Bataan Death March, 10, 16

Ipo Dam, Battle of, 76
Lingayen Gulf, 76
"Philly." *See* Pennsylvania
Plantation Club, 163, 182, 183
Polite, Stanish, 148
Pollock, Robert S. "Rob," *67*
Port Chicago, California, depot explosion, xxiii, 209
Postma, Herman, 32
Post office (main, downtown), 71, 198, 203, 225, 239
Port of Wilmington (wartime), xxi, 30, 56, 66, 67, 232
Potts, Adam E., 131, 220
POWs (German). *See* Prisoners of War (German POWs) in Wilmington
Powell, Dick, 77
Powell, R. J., 183
Presbyterian School of Religious Education, 166
President Franklin D. Roosevelt. *See* Roosevelt, Franklin D.
Preston, Cora, 198
Preston, Lester, 34
Pridgen, Peggy, 216
Prisoners of War (German POWs) in Wilmington, xxvii, 127–42. (*See also Afrika Korps* and North Africa[n], Campaign in)
camp sites
    Bluethenthal Army Air Base, 127, 137, 138
    Carolina Beach Road and Shipyard Boulevard, 127, 129–31
    8th and Ann Streets (Robert Strange Park), 127–29, 132, 133, 136, 138
    old Marine Hospital, 127, 132, 133, 139
closing/departure, 138–40
duties and work routine, 131, 133, 135, 136, 138, 139
establishment, 128–33
historical markers, 130, 133
possible Italian POWs, 128, 129
postwar letters to J. D. McCarley, Jr., 140–42
Public housing projects (the projects), 94, 95
    Greenfield Terrace, 94
    Hillcrest, 2, 94, 95, 210, 215
    Lake Forest, 94, 95
    Lake Village, 149
    Maffitt Village, 71, 80, 94, 95, 103, 130, 156, 202, 210
    Nesbitt (Charles T.) Courts, 94, 95
    New Brooklyn/Taylor Homes, 94, 209, 210
Purdy, Richard, 6

Q

Quick, Arie, 145

R

Rabunsky family, 171
 Bernard Rabunsky, 129, 171
 Frances Rabunsky (Shinder), *171. See also* Shinder, Daniel R.
 Janet Rabunsky (Evenson), 137, 171
Radio networks
 Blue, 184
 CBS, 184
 Mutual, 184
 NBC, 184
Radio shows
 "Blondie and Dagwood," 185
 "Bob Hope," 184
 "The Breakfast Club with Don McNeil," 184
 "Fred Waring Show," 184
 "Gangbusters," 184
 "Harry Wismer Sports," 185
 "The Hit Parade," 184
 "Hop Harrigan," 22, 184
 "The Ink Spots," 184
 "Inner Sanctum," 185
 "Jack Armstrong," 185
 "Johnny Doughboy Reporting," 184
 "Life of Riley," 185
 "The Lone Ranger," 22, 23, 184
 "Lum and Abner," 184
 "March of Time," 246
 "Philco Radio Hall of Fame," 185
 "The Sea Hound," 184
 "Terry and the Pirates," 22, 184
 "Victory Parade of Spotlight Bands," 184
 "Watch the World Go By," 185
Raleigh, North Carolina, xix, 112, 181, 188, 208, 210, 211, 240, 253, 254, 260
Raleigh News & Observer, 57
Randall, Sanford, 156
Randolph-Macon College, Lynchburg, Virginia, 166
Random House Publishers, 26
Raphael, Justin, 75, *76*, 180
Rationing. *See* War effort (specific)
Raynor, Ruby, *234*
Reaves, Bill, 164, 180
Reaves, Joseph Roy "Joe," 13, *14*, 182
Reaves, Joseph W., *14*
Recorder's Court, 149, 152, 153
Red Cross/Red Cross Nurse's Aide(s). *See* American Red Cross
Redskins, Washington, 1

Republican Party, 260
Revolutionary War, 217
Rhett, Haskell, 106, 188
Richmond, University of, Richmond, Virginia, 86
Rickenbacker, Eddie, 198
Rickenbacker, Mrs. Eddie, 198
R. J. Reynolds Tobacco Co., 58
Roane, Daniel C., 219
Robert Strange Park, 1, 133
Roberts, C. S., 119
Roberts, John Quincy, 245
Roberts, Linwood, 52
Robertson, LeRoy C., Jr., 24
Robinson, Gene, 35
Rocky Mount, North Carolina, 168, 173
Rodgers, C. E., 157
Roe family
 Elizabeth Roe, *46*
 J. C. Roe, 185
 Laura Roe (Fonvielle), 3, 19, *46*, 185, 251
Rogers, G. H., 244
Rogers, F. J., 99, 109, 213, 217, 218, 220
Rogers, Margaret Sampson. *See* Sampson, Margaret (Rogers)
Roland family, 96
 Dorothy Roland (Norako), 96. *See also* Norako, Vince
 H. M. Roland, 96, 98, 100, 101, 109, 217, 219
 Mrs. H. M. (Perida) Roland, xv, 96, 203
Rommel, Erwin, 30, 127–29
Roosevelt, Eleanor, 214
Roosevelt, Franklin D., 12, 235
 December 8, 1941 speech to Congress, 3, 5, 20, 105
 as president and commander-in-chief, 51, 105, 124, 212
Rorie, M. B., 155
ROTC (Junior Reserve Officers Training Corps). *See* New Hanover High School (NHHS)
Rountree, George III, 35
Royal Canadian Air Force, 181, 190
Ruffin, Peter Browne, 34
Russ (Bluethenthal pilot), 82
Russ, Rebecca, 108
Russell, Catherine (Stribling), *46*, 185, 186, 199
Russell, Catherine Harper, 199
Russell, Raymond, 145
Russia, 52, 61, 105
 Murmansk (run), 61
 Reds (Soviets), 15

Russian War Relief Drive (1944), 102
Russian(s), 102, 202
Soviet Union, 66
Ryukyu Islands. *See* Okinawa (Shima), Battle of

S

Saffo, George, *6*
St. Andrews-Covenant Presbyterian Church, 50, 91, 165, 166, 178, 203
    Defense Service Committee, 91
St. James Episcopal Church, 3, 12, 161, 203
St. John's Tavern, 170, 183
St. Mary Catholic Church, 161
St. Paul's Lutheran Church, 161, 169
St. Stephen's AME Church, 161, 201
St. Thomas auditorium, 220
Saipan, Battle of, xxiii, 15, 24, 33, 156, 208
Saleeby, Mitchell "Mitch," 106
Salem College, Winston-Salem, North Carolina, 108
Salvation Army, 96
Sam Poplin and His Cape Fear Rangers, 183
Sampson, James Otis, 209
Sampson, James Otis, Jr., 133, 208, *209*, 217
Sampson, Margaret (Rogers), xxvii, 133, 134, 215
Santa Cruz, Battle of. *See* Solomons (Islands), Campaigns in
Santiago, D. R. (West Indies), 37
Saunders, Leroy W., 82
Schlegal, Anthony, 139
Schmid, Al "Machine Gun Smitty," 26
Schwartz, Mr., 42
Schwartz, Bernice, 167, 168
Schwartz, William "Bill," 3, 167, 168
Scott, James, 214
Scott, LeRoy, 148
Scroggs, Felix A., 227
Seaboard Air Line Railroad, 66, 172
Seabreeze Beach, North Carolina, 148, 153, 216, 217
    Bop City beach, 217
Seagate neighborhood, 156, 182, 244
Sears Landing. *See* Camp Davis, North Carolina (Davis), Holly Ridge, North Carolina
Sears, Olga, 14
Second (2nd) and Orange Streets USO (United Service Organizations) club, *192*, 194. *See also* Ninth (9th) and Nixon Streets USO, and USO clubs
    activities, 20, 84, 146, 152, 163, 176, 177, 193
    dances, 171–73

postwar Historic USO/Community Arts Center, 192, 194, 195, 260
60th anniversary, 195, 220
Selective Service System, 254
Sepanen, Arthur E., 82
September 11, 2001 terrorist attacks, 97
Seventh Day Adventist Church, 217
Seymour, Mrs. J. Carl, 203
Shannon, J. E., Jr., 230
Shannon, Tommy, 230
Shavers, Henry, 145
Shaw, Artie, 182
Shaw, Jesse, 216
Shelton, Lee R., 217
Sheets, Francois, 202
Sheets, Gladys, 202
Shepherd, James, 207
Shigley, Monroe, 54
Shinder, Daniel R., 171. *See also* Rabunsky family
Ships constructed at North Carolina Shipbuilding Company, 55–68
    AKA attack cargo, xx
        USS *Torrance* (AKA-76). *See* United States (U.S) Navy (navy) ships, craft, and units
    C-1 Liberty(s), xx, 3, *58*, 59, 61, 67, 214, 221
    in action, 61
    Liberty(s) hulls
        SS *Henry Bacon*, 61
        SS *John Meany*, 68
        SS *John Merrick*, 214
        SS *Virginia Dare*, 61
        SS *William Moultrie*, 61
        SS *Zebulon B. Vance*, 3, 58, *59*, 68
    C-2 Victory(s), xx, 60, 61, *62*, 66, 157, 236, 237
    C-2 hulls
        SS *Santa Isabel*, 67
        SS *Sweepstakes*, *62*
Shipyard, the (NCSC). *See* North Carolina Shipbuilding Company (NCSC, shipyard)
Shoemaker, O. H., 114–16, 118
Sicily, Campaign in, xxiii, 193, 250
Sidbury, J. Buren, 234
Siegfried Line, Battle for the, xxiii
Simpkins, J. M., 157
Sixth Naval District. *See* United States (U.S.) Coast Guard
6th Street Advent Christian Church, 167
The Sledgehammersit jazz combo, 220
Sloan, Jack, 105
Slocum, Beth, 168

Smiling Billy Stewart and His Florida
    Serenaders, 216
Smith, Clayton, *56*
Smith, Everard H. "Ev," xxviii, 91, 191, 192,
    195, 236
Smith, Frederick H., 91
Smith, H. Winfield, 150
Smith, Phyllis, 189
Smith, Stanley E., Sr., 73
Smith, Wilbur, 156
Smith, Willie, 146
Snakenburg, Diane (Gordon), 42
Sneeden, Earl, 140
Snipes, Q. B., 31
Solomon, Catherine, 93
Solomon, Louise, 93
Solomons (Islands), Campaigns in, 22, 26,
    245
    Battle of Santa Cruz, 245
Somersett, Kathleen, 192, 198, *201*
Sondey, Adam, 139
Songs
    Coming in on a Wing and a Prayer, xvii
    Mairzy Doats, 103
    Onward Christian Soldiers, 218
    Pistol Packin' Mama, 187
    Star Spangled Banner, 105
    Stomping at the Savoy, 213
South (Deep), 89
South Carolina, 33, 63, 66, 67, 166, 167, 198,
    236, 251, 254
    Charleston, 33, 63, 66, 67, 198, 236, 254
    Columbia, 251
    Greenville, 167
    Myrtle Beach, 166
    Spartanburg, 166
South Carolina Department of Corrections,
    251
Southeastern North Carolina (SENC), xviii,
    175, 213
    geographical/topographical area, 78, 194,
        195, 240
    life and culture, 40, 60, 76, 258
    in war effort, 55, 57, 71
Southerland, Patty (Seitter), xxii, *17*, 18, 85
Southport, North Carolina, 3, 51, 82
    Dosher Hospital, 51
    Southport Historical Society, 51
Soverel, Ralph, 25
Soverel, Ralph Waldo, Jr., 24
Soviet Union (Soviets). *See* Russia
Spanish (language), 108
Spanish marauders, 74
Spanish-American War, 41
Sparks, Boyden, 244

Spaulding, C. C., 214
Spencer, Aline Hufham (Hartis), 137, *138*
Spencer, Charles, 155
Spencer, William A. "Bill," 137, *138*
Speth, Max, 134, 141
Sprague, Carlton H., 48
Sprunt, Alexander, 226
Sprunt, Jane, *174*
Stallman, David A., xxviii, 77
Stanford, Willie (Leiner), xv, 19,
Stanley, Blanche (Sneeden), *234*
Stanley, Glenn family, 222
Stanton, Mary E., 199
Station WSM Grand Ole Opry Gang, 183
Steelman, Ben, 54
Stein, Leon, 171
Stewart, W. H., 204
Stewart, William A., 227
Stimson, Henry, 77
Stokely, James B. "Jim," 212
Stoenmer, Royce orchestra, 182
Stovall, Harry, 245
Suiter, Chris, 51
Sun Shipyard, 208, 214
Sunset Park neighborhood, 54, 57, 150, 173
Sunset Park School, 100
Superior Court, 155
Supreme Headquarters Allied Expeditionary
    Force, 202
Surinam, 24
Sutherland, Dorothy, 109
Sutton, Billy, 48
Sutton, Charlie T., 145
Swails, Jimmy, 103
Swart family, 81, 232
    Bob Swart, 81
    Helen Swart (Simmons), 81
    Swart Dairy, 118
Symmes, Eliza, 3

T

Talladega College, Talladega, Alabama, 217
Tarawa, Battle of, 10, 26, 30, 156
Tate, Leroy, 153
Taylor, Bobby, 106, 188,
Taylor farm, 136
Taylor Homes housing. *See* Public housing
    projects (the projects)
Taylor, Joseph D., 207, 209, 210
Taylor, Mary Elizabeth, 206
Taylor, Robert R., 94
Taylor, Victor G., 2, 34
Taylor, Walker III, 34
Telfair, John, 216
Temple of Israel, 161

Index

Tennessee, 246
Tennessee Ramblers, 183
Tetterton, Beverly, xxvii
Texas, 13, 51, 54, 76
  Freeport, 51, 54
Thalian Association, the (Thalians), 195
Thalian Hall, 183, 224
Theaters (movie)
  Bailey, 15, 165, 169, 184, 204, 224
  Bijou, 15, 184, 210
  Carolina, 184
  Manor, 15, 184
  Royal, 15, 184, 245
  Village, 184
Theater productions
  "The Friendly Enemy," 134
  "(HMS) Pinafore," 184
  "Naughty Marietta," 184
  "Step Lively," 216
  "Strictly GI," 224
  "This is the Army," 224
Thiel, Bernard, 140, *141*
Thomas, Clarence, 217
Thomas, Heatwole, 109
Thomas, Lowell, 243, 244
Thomas, Ruth, 218
Thomason, Margaret family, 28, 29
Thompson, Henry, 155
Thompson, John, 218
Thompson, Tommy, 35
Thompson, Willie, 155
Thornton family
  Bill Thornton, 34
  Frances Thornton (Reynolds), 24, 189
  James G. Thornton, 11, *24*, 25
  James Goodlet Thornton, Jr. "Jim" "Jimmy," 18, *24*, 25, 34
  Lucretia Thornton (McDaniel), 18, 25, 224
Tide Water Power Company, 80, 205
Tienken, Doris, 89
Tigner, Oscar, 200
Tileston School, 100
Tingzon, Catalino, 51
Tinian, Battle of, 15, 33, 156
Tisdale, W. L., 53
Todd, Bertha, 208
Todd Shipbuilding Company, 63
Tojo, (Hideki), 226
Toliver, John E., 148
Tony Award, 195
Topsail (Island) Beach, North Carolina, 40, 74
  Historical Society of Topsail Island, 77
  Missiles and More Museum, 77
  "Torpedo Junction," 49

Townsend, Freddy, 216
Trask, Heide farm, 137
Travelers Aid, 65, 90
Tregaskis, Richard, 26
Trinity Methodist Church, 108
Truman, Harry S
  President, 15, 113, 139, 249, 250, 253
  Senator—Investigating Committee, 58
Tunisia. *See* North Africa(n), Campaign in
Tuskegee Airmen, 208, 217, *255*
Tuskegee Institute, Tuskegee, Alabama, 94, 255
  Moton Field, 255
Tyndall, Cliff, 76, 77
Tyson, Herman E., 25
Tyson, Norman E., 26, 103

U

U-boats, German. *See* German U-boats
Union army, 83
Union Station canteen, 197, 204
United National Clothing Collection for War Relief, 102
United States of America (United States, U.S., USA), xviii, 8, 38, 44, 50, 54, 105, 140, 142, 146, 200, 238, 245
United States (U.S.) Armed Forces/Military, xxii, xxiii, 1, 21, 60, 70, 105, 109, 201, 202, 208, 217, 222, 238, 239, 254
United States (U.S.) Army (army), xxii, 8, 10, 13, 21, 24, 25, 29, 40–42, 45–47, 52, 56, 71–84, 87, 93, 119, 120, 130, 132, 155, 162, 167, 172, 176, 178, 183, 184, 199, 200, 203, 208, 218, 225, 229, 239, 240, 242, 246, 247, 249
  aircraft. *See* Aircraft (U.S.), Army and Navy
  Air Service Command, 71
  anti-aircraft artillery (AA/AAA), xx, 71, 72, 75, 76, 78, 83, 86
  Army Chemical Warfare Service, 43
  Army Corps of Engineers, 79
  Army Nurse Corps, 202
  Camp Davis. *See* Camp Davis, North Carolina
  Coast Artillery (CA), xx, 71, 215, 221
  Fourth Corps Area Quartermaster Depot, 71
  infantry, 75
  Military Academy. *See* West Point (U.S. Military Academy), New York
  National Guard, 238
  Signal Corps, 171, 198
  Temporary Harbor Defense Office, 71
  Transportation Corps, 71, 178
  Women's Army Auxiliary Corps (WAAC)/ Women's Army Corps (WAC), 7, 132, 183, 199, *201*, 202, 221, 224

United States (U.S.) Army units
  Battery A, 252nd Coast Artillery Regiment, 238
  Battery B, 235th AAA Battalion, 220
  Battery C, 558th Anti-Aircraft Artillery Automatic Weapons Battalion, 48, 84
  Battery E, 95th Coast Artillery/Anti-Aircraft Artillery Battalion, 164
  Company A, 105th Medical Detachment, 239
  Company C, 1st Battalion, 30th Infantry, 3rd Infantry Division, 249
  Company I, 120th Infantry, 238
  8th Infantry Regiment, 25
  847th Ordnance Depot Company, 239
  4th Infantry Division, 25
  Fourth Service Command, 106
  55th Coast Artillery Battalion, 215
  54th Coast Artillery Battalion, 215
  Fort Fisher. See Fort Fisher, North Carolina
  576th Automatic Weapons unit, 75
  481st AAA Automatic Weapons Battalion, 84
  447th Automatic Weapons Battalion, 178
  99th Coast Artillery Battalion, 215
  156th Infantry, 84
  141st Army Band, 225
  104th Infantry, 83
  63rd Infantry Division, 105, 107, 250
  69th Infantry Division, 6
  30th Infantry, 250
  24th Infantry Regiment, 208, 209
  251st Field Artillery Battalion, 241
  254th Infantry Regiment, 63rd Infantry Division, 105, 107
  252nd Coast Artillery Battalion, 238
  252nd Band Section, 239
United States (U.S.) Army Air Forces (air force), xxi, 13, 21, 24, 68, 69, 78–82, *83*, 108, 240
  aircraft. See Aircraft (U.S.), Army and Navy
  anti-submarine warfare (ASW), See Bluethenthal Army Air Base (Field, BAAB)
  Army Air Corps, 83
  Army Air Forces Aircraft Warning Service (Corps) (AWS), 198
  Bluethenthal Army Air Base. See Bluethenthal Army Air Base (Field, BAAB)
  Bomber Command, 80
  8th Air Force, xvi, xvii
  15th Air Force, 169
  First Air Force Interceptor Command, 79
  495th Fighter Squadron, 231
  32nd Squadron, 301st Bomb Group, 15th Air Force, 170
  Tuskegee Airmen. See Tuskegee Airmen
  WASPs (Women's Airforce Service Pilots). See WASPs (Women's Airforce Service Pilots)
United States (U.S.) Coast Guard, xxi, 38, 39, 48, 51, 52, 54, 71, 156, 232, 240
  Captain of the Port, 71
  Coast Guard Auxiliary (CGA), xxi, 33, 48, 53, 187
  Coast Guard Reserve, 33
  Commissary Supply Depot, 71
  Marine Inspectors Office, 71
  Quarterboat "General Frederick Hodgson," 71
  Sixth Naval District CGA, 33
United States (U.S.) Marine Corps (USMC, Marine[s]), xxi, xxiii, 10, 15, 30, 71, 72, 76, 78, 96, 106, 175, 224, 240, 246, 252
  aircraft. See Aircraft (U.S.), Army and Navy
  Camp Lejeune Marine Corps Base (Lejeune) (wartime), Jacksonville, North Carolina, xxi, 14, 30, 34, 71, 72, 85, 92, 96, 109, 156, 158, 183, 185, 187, 190, 194
  Marine Corps Air Station Cherry Point, North Carolina, 85, 254
  Marine Corps Reserve Center (postwar), 58, 67
  New River Marine Barracks/Marine Corps Base, Jacksonville, North Carolina, xviii, 71, 224
  2nd Battalion, 5th Marines, 1st Marine Division, 246, 252
  6th Marines (World War I), 37
  VMF-511 fighter squadron, 169
United States (U.S) Navy (navy), xx, xxii, xxiii, 10, 14, 21, 23, 37, 62, 63, 71, 156, 171, 173, 183, 184, 202, 208, 225, 232, 239, 240, 244, 246, 251, 253
  aircraft. See Aircraft (U.S.), Army and Navy
  Assistant Industrial Manager, 71
  Bethesda (Maryland) Naval Hospital, 254
  Charleston Naval Station, South Carolina, 254
  Fort Caswell Naval Station, North Carolina, xxi, 48
  Naval Aerospace Medical Center, Pensacola, Florida, 254
  Naval Hospital, Marine Corps Air Station Cherry Point, North Carolina, 254
  Naval Intelligence, 71
  Navy Department, 71
  Port Chicago (California) Naval Ammunition Depot, xxiii, 209

Index

Port Director, 71
Secretary of the Navy, 48
Tenth Fleet, 49
U.S. Naval Reserve, 252
United States Naval Service, 253
V-7 Program, 3
WAVES (Women Accepted for Volunteer Emergency Service), 202
United States (U.S.) Navy (navy) ships, craft, and units (wartime)
  Scouting (Squadron) Six, 2, 240
  Torpedo Squadron 8, 244
  USS ARDC-1, 68
  USS *Arizona* (BB-39), xxiii, 21
  USS *Biloxi* (CL-80), 168
  USS *Block Island* (CVE-106), 169
  USS *Edwards* (DD-619), 245
  USS *Enterprise* (CV-6), xxii, 2, 240, 242, 243
  USS *Gillette* (DE-681), 245
  USS *Hornet* (CV-8), 245
  USS *Missouri* (BB-63), 15
  USS *Oklahoma* (BB-37), 21
  USS *Peiffer* (DE-588), 244
  USS *Reuben James* (DD-245), 245
  USS *Robalo*, 25
  USS *Shaw* (DD-393), 5, 21
  USS *Torrance* (AKA-56), 60
  USS *Wasp* (CV-7), 106
  YMS-15, 171
United States (U.S.) Navy, postwar, 245
  USS *Halyburton* (FFG-40), 245, 254
University of North Carolina (at Chapel Hill) (UNC, Carolina), xxiii, 3, 28, 36, 106, 167, 231, 244, 248, 250, 251
University of North Carolina at Wilmington (UNCW), xxvii, xxviii, 36
  Upperman African-American Cultural Center, 219
  William Madison Randall Library, xxvii, 36
Upperman, L. W., 219
U.S. (United States), 49, 54, 74, 128, 138, 155, 231, 240, 241, 250
U.S. District Court, 150
U.S. Employment Service (USES). *See* Federal Government (U.S. wartime)
USO(s) (United Service Organizations), xxviii, 70, 85, 90, 93, 146, 164, 172, 179, 181, 191, 193, 196, 206, 216, 221, 232
USO clubs, 181, 191, 195, 220
  Carolina Beach, 84
  Catholic USO Center, 90
  5th and Orange Streets, 194
  Jacksonville, North Carolina, 195
  9th and Nixon Streets (Negro, colored). *See* Ninth (9th) and Nixon Streets USO (Negro/colored) club

2nd and Orange Streets. *See* Second (2nd) and Orange Streets USO (United Service Organizations) club
Southport, North Carolina, 51
3rd and Grace Streets, 90

V

Vancouver, British Columbia, 161
Vander Pool, Harry, 169
V-E Day, 15, 16, 50, 136, 138, 172, 226, 239, 250, 252
Vera Cruz, Mexico, 253
Veterans Park, 251
(Negro) VFW (Veterans of Foreign Wars) Club, 216
Victory ships. *See* Ships constructed at North Carolina Shipbuilding Company
Vietnam War, 13, 63, 251, 253
Virginia, 21, 34, 49, 53, 57, 64, 66, 75, 96, 165, 198, 236
  Fort Myer, 96
  Hampton Roads, 236
  Newport News, 57, 62, 67, 165
  Norfolk, 21, 34, 66, 165
  Northern Virginia, xii, 36
  Richmond, 64, 168
  Virginia Beach, 53
Virginia Military Institute, Lexington, Virginia, 13, 170
Virginia Tech, Blacksburg, Virginia, 74
V-J Day, xiii, 15–17, 205, 239, 259
Volk family, 169
  Edna Cameron Volk, 169
  Evelyn Volk (Morris), 8, 105, 169, 202. *See also* Morris, Clifford Cohen, Jr. "Cliff"
  Marc G. Volk, 169
  Ralph Volk, 8, 169
Von Glahn, Katherine, xiii, *xiv*, 103, 105, 109
Von Oesen, Henry, 29, 30, 166, 188, 245, 258
Voorhees, Bob, 164, 180

W

Wade, Carrie Maie, 187, 188
Wade, Jake, 187
Wade, J. E. L., 220
Wake Forest College, Wake Forest, North Carolina, 86, 105, 169
Walbach, James, 34
Walker, Charles M., 219
Walker, Estelle, 148
Walker, Frances Goldberg. *See* Goldberg family
Walker, George H., Jr., 25
Walters, Eugie, *176*
Walton, John W. "Bill," 182, 258, 259

War bonds, 204, 207, 223–26
War (Bond) Loan Drive(s), 204, 207, 223–26
  Third War Loan Drive, 224
  Fourth Loan Drive, 224, 225
  Fifth War Loan Drive, 226
Ward, Virginia, 202
War Department. *See* Federal Government (U.S., wartime)
War effort (specific), xviii–xxiii, 221–37
  Civilian Defense. *See* Civilian Defense
  rationing, 111–25
  New Hanover County War Price & Rationing Board, 111, 115, 116
  New Hanover County Salvage Committee, 204, 226
  Salvage Committee, 204
  scrap drives, 204, 207, 226, 227
  Women at War Week, 204
Warren family
  Gene Warren, 133
  J. V. "Pat" Warren, 133, 232
  Peggy Warren (Longmire), 133
Wartime Wilmington Commemoration, 1999, xiii, xvi, xxviii, 36, 58, 66, 76, 133, 134, 251, 260
Washburn, Mr. and Mrs. Benjamin Mills, 175
Washburn, Louise Worth (Boylan), 175, *176*
Washington, Booker T., 94
Washington Catlett School, 34
Washington, D.C. (the government in), xix, xx, 1, 2, 44, 76, 94, 96, 100, 112, 120, 214, 235, 236
Washington Post, 120
Washington (state), xxiii, 178
  Issaquah, 178
  Seattle, xxiii
WASPs (Women's Airforce Service Pilots), 75, 77
Waterman, Albert, 142
Waters, H. H., 145
Watters, Charles W. "Uncle Charlie," *14*
Weapons (German). *See* German forces
Weapons and equipment (U.S.)
  AA gun, 85
  bazooka, 85
  50-cal. machine gun, 8, 75, 84
  40mm anti-aircraft gun, 84
  half-track vehicle, 75, 225
  jeep, xvii, 8, 35, *46*, 156
  M1 Garand rifle, 8
  1903 Springfield rifle, 106
  OQ28A drone, 74
  105mm howitzer, 8
  PT (patrol torpedo) boat(s), 52
  searchlight outfit, 226

Sherman tank, 97
Smith & Wesson revolver, 37
sub-chaser, 54
tank, 8, 155
37mm gun, 78
2-1/2 ton truck, 8, 77
Weiss, Anton, 141
Welch, Wilson, 240
Welker, Carl, 164
Wells, Louise, 170
West, Billy, 32
West, Rae, 113
West Point (U.S. Military Academy), New York, xiii, 3, 13
West Virginia, 42
Wheatley, Thomas C., 220
Wheeler, J. E., 144
Wheeler Mrs. Jeannette, 216
Wheeler, Raymond A., 13, 69
Wheeler, William, 216
White Cliffs of Dover, xvii
White, Ellis, 108
White, Lucilla (Whitted). *See* Willard-Whitted family
White, Olin Hughes, 109
White House, The, 2, 250
White Mane Publishing Company, 5, 30
Whiteville, North Carolina, 189
Whitted, Charlie, 215
Whitted, James, 211, 212, 214
Willard-Whitted family
  Emerson Willard, *81*
  Gibbs Holmes (Willard), 3, 19
  Glendy "Glenn" Willard (Higgins), 81, 166, 171, 172
  Joseph W. "Joe" Whitted, 166
  Lucilla White (Whitted), 166
  Martin Willard, *81*
  Miles C. Higgins, 81, 171
William, Loyd, *6*
Williams, Ann (Johnson), 3, 19, 112
Williams, Beecker, 216
Williams, Dan, 156
Williams, Florence, 156
Williams, Ezekiel, *211*
Williams, Joe, 216
Williams, Patricia, 201
Williams, Roger, 63
Williams, Selisece Owens, 167
Williamson, Martha, 164
Williamson, Muriel, 74, 179, 192
Willis, James Albert "Bootee," 150
Williston Industrial (High) School (Williston, WIS), xii, *99*, 129, 207, 209, 217–18
  activities, 207, 217–18

Index

faculty/students, 5, *6*, 133, 213, 217
graduates, xvi, *209*, 211, 216, 218, 238, *255*
Williston Middle School, 133
Williston Primary School, 100, 133
Wilmington as an address, 140, 141, 188
Wilmington area, xxi, xxvi, xxvii, 51, 71, 98, 132, 138, 144, 148, 160, 191, 194, 196, 233, 236, 239, 260
Wilmington (North Carolina) Army Air Base/Airport. *See* Bluethenthal Army Air Base (Field BAAB)
Wilmington Clowns baseball team, 216
Wilmington as destination/geographic location/downtown, xx–xxiii, 35, 38, 40, 42, 45, 63, 71, 80, 82, 84–86, 92, 96, 102, 122, 123, 128, 133, 136, 138, 139, 162, 163, 165–72, 176, 178, 186, 188, 206, 213, 215, 218, 228, 240, 241, 249, 251, 254
Wilmington economy/life and culture, xviii–xxiii, xxv, 68, 179–81, 183, 185, 189, 236, 237, 256–60
Wilmington Evening Post, 12, 191
Wilmington home front morale/impact, xii, xxv, xxvi, xxviii, 6, 7, 12, 13, 15, 16, 22, 28, 30, 34, 48, 57, 62, 70, 74, 76, 87, 88, 111, 120, 147, 192, 194
Wilmington as my hometown, xii, xxviii
Wilmington Hotel, 147, 151
Wilmington Housing Authority. *See* Housing Authority of the City of Wilmington (HACOW, Wilmington Housing Authority)
Wilmingtonian(s), xxvii, 2, 5, 10, 11, 13–15, 52, 55, 245
 in armed forces, xxii, 21, 25, 68, 137, 161, 166, 172, 245, 250
 on home front, 16, 38, 46, 63, 65, 75, 78, 82, 87, 118, 125, 131, 135, 151, 158, 161, 175, 182
 in war effort, 223, 224, 226
Wilmington International Airport, xxviii
 Airport Authority, 78
Wilmington Journal, xv, xvii, 209
Wilmington Light Infantry, 226
Wilmington Morning Star, xiv, xxvii, 27
 reporting, xix, 29, 35, 44, 50, 60, 72, 78, 83, 105, 106, 109, 113, 119, 122, 130, 131, 138, 201, 204, 221, 223, 225, 240, 241, 244, 247, 253, 256, 257
Wilmington municipality, wartime
 city government/City Council, 91, 132
 civilian defense program, 44, 49
 City Hall, 13, 71, 164, 193, 253
 crime wave (law and order), 143–60

Housing authority. *See* Housing Authority of the City of Wilmington (HACOW, Wilmington Housing Authority)
housing and other problems, 50, 93–96, 113
population, xvi, 235, 256, 259
South Wilmington, 94
Wilmington Police Department, 12, 65, 151, 158, 190
Wilmington News, 210
Wilmington personnel in armed forces, 27, 29, 48, 69, 202, 217, 238, 240, 243, 257
Wilmington, postwar, 8, 63, 83, 252, 260
Wilmington, present, xii, xiii, xvi, xvii, 36, 37, 260
Wilmington, prewar, 22, 59, 64, 83, 116
 as "New Town," 95
Wilmington Railroad Museum, 65, 66
Wilmington Real Estate Board, 92
Wilmington residents (pre-war and wartime), 2, 5, 14, 21, 53, 81, 101, 106, 112, 150, 164, 199–201, 205, 208, 211, 214, 216, 219, 220, 246, 255
Wilmington Rotary Club, 2, 97, 112, 226
Wilmington Star-News newspaper company, xiv, xv, 2, 19, 22, 148, 163, 164, 183, 197, 224, 237, 248, 253
 community "voice of conscience," xix, 237
 editorial activism, 46, 116, 119, 120, 124, 154, 157, 160, 194, 196, 199, 204, 225, 227, 238
 "the newspaper," 1, 90, 113, 259
Wilmington Star-News reporting, xvi, 7, 10, 54, 93, 104, 181, 246
Wilmington Sunday Star-News, xiv, 11, 229
 reporting, 39, 48, 68, 82, 85, 94, 101, 113, 116, 117, 159, 162, 228, 230, 238
Wilmington in war effort, 55, 57, 60, 66, 67, 90, 113, 124, 125, 127, 130, 175, 182, 184, 191, 198, 204, 224, 227, 237
 "Defense Capital of the State," 55
Wilsey, Julie, xxviii
Wilson, Doris Dickens, 7
Wilson, James Blanie, *6*
Wilson, McCulloch B. "Mac," Jr., 5, *6*, 251
Winchell, Walter, 10
Wing, Edward Yee, 162
Winner, Carl, 191
Winner, Pearl (Fountain), 47, 93, 188, 190
Winter Park neighborhood, 78, 80, 251, 253
Winter Park Presbyterian Church, 251, 254
Winter Park School, 100
WMFD-630 (radio station), 1, 3, 22, 184, 213, 218
Women's Army Auxiliary Corps/Women's Army Corps. *See* United States (U.S.) Army (army)

Wood, J. R., 188
Wood, Mrs. J. Russell, 200
Woodbury, Louie E., Jr., 34, 88, 89
Woodbury, Louie E. III, 34, 35
Woodrow Wilson Hut, 20, 164, 165, 193, 194
Woods, Eleanor V., 199, 200
Woods, Ralph, 145
Woodward, Emma, 244
Wooten, Roland, 226
World War I (WWI, Great War), xxiii, 5, 7, 14, 22, 28, 29, 37, 41, 58, 63, 78, 109, 132, 198, 226, 230
World War II (WWII), xii, xiii, xxii, xxviii, 7, 68, 77, 78, 82
  50th Anniversary, xiii
  the global war, xix, xxv, 54, 246
  home front, xiv, 121, 194
  impact on Wilmington area, xviii, xxvi, 16, 19, 51, 105, 144, 160, 173, 175, 178, 183, 191, 238, 239, 251
  postwar, 58, 63, 79, 195, 260
  remembered/veterans, xv, xvi, xxvii, 13, 23, 30, 36, 57, 69, 195, 210, 259
World War II Wilmington Home Front Heritage Coalition (Coalition), xiii, 130, 195, 260

Wright, Wilson, Jr., 210
Wrightsboro neighborhood, 78, 132
Wrightsville Beach, North Carolina, xxi, 12, 35, 38, 80, 82, 93, 186, 188, 199, 205, 243
  business and government, 119, 122, 188
  civilian defense activities, 45, 47, 48
  military activities, *46*, 53, 149
  social life, xx, 18, 84, 167, 168, 172, 173, *176*, 181, 182, 186, 190, 191, 217
  Station 1 neighborhood, 187–89, 205
Wychel, Ellen Gilliard, 133
Wyman, Jane, 224

Y

YMCA (Young Men's Christian Association), 23
York, Alvin C., 246
Young, Mae, 183
YWCA (Young Women's Christian Association), 171

Z

SS *Zebulon B. Vance*. *See* Ships constructed at North Carolina Shipbuilding Company

— The Author —

Wilbur D. Jones, Jr., is a nationally known Wilmington native author, military historian, battlefield tour leader, and lecturer. He was an assistant to President Gerald Ford, and is a retired Navy captain with 41 years of service to the Department of Defense, including 12 as a professor at the Defense Acquisition University.

The author of 16 books, his principal fields of study are World War II, the Civil War, and defense issues. *A Sentimental Journey* received the North Carolina Society of Historians' 2003 Willie Parker Peace Book Award.

His five statewide awards in 2005 included North Carolina Historian of the Year (East) and the NCSH book award for *The Journey Continues: The World War II Home Front,* the sequel to *A Sentimental Journey.* He founded and chairs the WWII Wilmington Home Front Heritage Coalition, devoted to identifying, preserving, and interpreting Southeastern North Carolina's rich WWII history, and the 2005 recipient of two statewide history awards.

In 2006 he received a national Award of Merit from the American Association for State and Local History for his WWII books and preservation accomplishments, and the Lower Cape Fear Historical Society's Clarendon Award for best regional book, *The Journey Continues.*

Visit his website: *www.wilburjones.com*

— Cover Illustrations —

The author with Lieutenant William McGee, Camp Davis officer, who rented a room in our house during 1942–43, *Author's collection;* Cape Fear Hotel, wartime, *Provided by Aaron May;* USO club in New Hanover County, 1943, *Provided by George J. Green;* Wartime New Hanover High School in Wilmington, *Provided by Patty Southerland Seitter;* Wilmington's Front Street, 1943, *Provided by Ronald G. "Ronnie" Phelps*

White Mane Publishing Co., Inc.

To Request a Catalog Please Write to:
WHITE MANE PUBLISHING COMPANY, INC.
P.O. Box 708 • Shippensburg, PA 17257
e-mail: marketing@whitemane.com
Cover Designed by Angela M. Guyer

Printed in the United States
68343LVS00003B/1-84

9 781572 493186